CASCADING STYLE SHEETS

Designing for the Web

Second Edition

Håkon Wium Lie

Bert Bos

Addison-
Wesley

An imprint of Pearson Education

Harlow, England • Reading Massachusetts • Menlo Park, California
New York • Don Mills, Ontario • Amsterdam • Bonn • Sydney • Singapore
Tokyo • Madrid • San Juan • Milan • Mexico City • Seoul • Taipei

PEARSON EDUCATION LIMITED

Head Office:
Edinburgh Gate
Harlow CM20 2JE
Tel: +44 (0)1279 623623
Fax: +44 (0)1279 431059

London Office:
128 Long Acre
London WC2E 9AN
Tel: +44 (0)20 7447 2000
Fax: +44 (0)20 7240 5771

Website: *www.awl.com/cseng*

Second edition first published in Great Britain 1999

© Pearson Education Limited 1999

The rights of Håkon Wium Lie and Bert Bos to be identified as authors of this work have been asserted by them in accordance with the Copyright, Designs and Patents Act 1988.

ISBN 0-201-59625-3

British Library Cataloguing-in-Publication Data
A catalogue record for this book is available from the British Library

Library of Congress Cataloging-in-Publication Data
Applied for.

The programs in this book have been included for their instructional value. The publisher does not offer any warranties or representations in respect of their fitness for a particular purpose, nor does the publisher accept any liability for any loss or damage arising from their use.

Many of the designations used by manufacturers and sellers to distinguish their products are claimed as trademarks. Addison-Wesley has made every attempt to supply trademark information about manufacturers and their products mentioned in this book. A list of trademark designations and their owners appears on page viii.

10 9 8 7 6 5 4 3 2

Typeset by Pantek Arts, Maidstone, Kent.
Printed and bound in the United States of America.

The publishers' policy is to use paper manufactured from sustainable forests.

Foreword

When the Web was in its infancy, seven years ago or so, I felt greatly relieved at the final removal of all the totally unsolvable problems of fixed format presentation. In the young Web, there were no more pagination faults, no more footnotes, no silly word breaks, no fidgeting the text to gain that extra line that you sorely needed to fit everything on one page. In the window of a Web page on the NeXTStep system, the text was always clean. Better than that: I decided what font it came out in, how big I wanted the letters, what styles I chose for definition lists and where tabs went.

Then we descended into the Dark Ages for several years, because the Web exploded into a community that had no idea that such freedom was possible, but worried about putting on the remote screen exactly what they thought their information should look like. I've read recommendations against using structured markup because you have no control over what comes out the other side. Sad.

You have by now understood that I'm firmly in the camp of those who think that quality of content comes first, and presentation comes later. But of course, I'm not entirely right here: presentation is important. Mathematical formulas are always presented in a two-dimensional layout.

Fortunately, SGML's philosophy allows us to separate structure from presentation, and the Web DTD, HTML, is no exception. Even in the NeXTStep version of 1990, Tim Berners-Lee provided for style sheets, though at a rudimentary level (we had other things to do then!).

Today, style sheets are becoming a reality again, this time much more elaborate. This is an important milestone for the Web, and we should stop for a minute to reflect on the potential benefits and pitfalls of this technology.

I followed the CSS effort from its inception – mostly over cups of coffee with Håkon at CERN – and I've always had one concern: is it possible to create a powerful enough style sheet "language" without ending up with a programming language?

The CSS described in this book shows that you can create some quite stunning presentations without programming. While the programmer in me may be a little disappointed, the minimalist in me is comforted. In fact, I'll never need this much freedom and special effects, but then I'm not a graphic artist. Anything that needs more complication effectively becomes an image, and should be treated as such. I feel therefore that the middle part of the spectrum between pure ASCII text and full images is effectively covered by the power of CSS, without introducing the complexity of programming.

You have here a book on presentation. But it is presentation of information that should also remain structured, so that your content can be effectively used by others, while retaining the specific visual aspects you want to give it. Use CSS with care. It is the long-awaited salt on the Web food: a little is necessary, too much is not good cooking.

The efforts of the authors have finally brought us what we sorely needed: the author's ability to shape the content without affecting the structure. This is good news for the Web!

Robert Cailliau
CERN, Geneva
January 1999

. . . . .

Preface

This book is about a new way to design Web pages. It's called Cascading Style Sheets (CSS) and it will revolutionize the way authors design Web pages and how readers see them. CSS lets authors specify how they want their documents to appear on screens or paper, for example the fonts and colors to be used.

Ever since the first Web document was written, Web authors have been yearning for more control over their documents. That desire has been so strong that every possible means to influence other people's screens — making text bold, have it blink, being pushed off five pixels to the right or scrolling across your screen — have gathered a following. No matter how absurd the effect, as long as the most popular browsers support it it gets added to the ever-increasing list of accepted HTML extensions. When developing CSS, we made sure it offers people some neat new toys — to satisfy the immediate desires. Also, we were able to sneak in some features that we think will actually help the Web remain a publishing arena for documents beyond sales brochures.

This book is written for people who design Web pages. You will learn how CSS can make your work easier and your pages look better. CSS has been designed to give Web designers the influence they want while retaining the Web's interoperability and accessibility — and a few other "abilities:"

- CSS has been developed in a vendor-neutral consortium (the World Wide Web Consortium, directed by the same Tim Berners-Lee who invented the Web and HTML)
- Chances are that your favorite browser already supports CSS
- CSS does not break current documents, it augments them
- CSS allows readers, as well as authors to define style sheets
- CSS uses common desktop publishing terminology that you probably know from before
- CSS allows organization-wide style sheets: you only need to change one file when your site style changes

This book will tell you all you need to know to start using CSS.

ACKNOWLEDGMENTS

Creating a lasting specification for the Web is not a job for one person. That's why the two authors joined forces. Then we found out two wasn't enough and a W3C Working Group (which includes W3C technical staff and W3C Member representatives) was formed. The CSS2 specification is the product of that Working Group, and we would like to thank its members: Brad Chase (Bitstream), Chris Wilson (Microsoft), Daniel Glazman (Electricité de France), Ed Tecot (Microsoft), Jared Sorensen (Novell), Lauren Wood (SoftQuad), Laurie Anna Kaplan (Microsoft), Scott Furman (Netscape), Scott Isaacs (Microsoft), Mike Wexler (Adobe), Murray Maloney (Grif), Powell Smith (IBM), Robert Stevahn (HP), Steve Zilles (Adobe), Steve Byrne (JavaSoft), Steven Pemberton (CWI), Thom Phillabaum (Netscape), Douglas Rand (Silicon Graphics), Robert Pernett (Lotus), Dwayne Dicks (SoftQuad), Sho Kuwamoto (Macromedia), Eric Meyer (Case Western Reserve University), Tim Boland (NIST), Tantek Çelik (Microsoft), Jeff Veen (HotWired), Todd Fahrner (Verso), Angus Davis (Netscape) and Peter Linss (Netscape). T.V. Raman (Adobe) was responsible for starting and finishing most of the work on Aural Cascading Style Sheets (ACSS).

Through electronic and physical encounters, the following people have contributed to the development of CSS2: Alan Borning, Robert Cailliau, Liz Castro, James Clark, Dan Connolly, Donna Converse, Adam Costello, Al Gilman, Daniel Greene, Jan Kärrman, Vincent Mallet, Kim Marriott, Brian Michalowski, Lou Montulli, Jacob Nielsen, Eva von Pepel, William Perry, David Siegel, Peter Stuckey, and Jason White.

Also, all along, the Web community has been very supportive. The discussions on *www-style@w3.org* have been influential in many key issues for CSS. Especially, we would like to thank Bjorn Backlund, David Baron, Todd

Fahrner, Lars Marius Garshol, Ian Hickson, Sue Jordan, Susan Lesch, Andrew Marshall, MegaZone, Eric Meyer, Russell O'Connor, David Perrell, Liam Quinn, Jon Seymour, Neil St. Laurent, Taylor, Brian Wilson, and Chris Wilson for their participation.

Without implementations, CSS would be quite useless. The programmers responsible for implementing CSS rendering engines are the heroes of this book. They include: Tantek Çelik (Microsoft), Kipp Hickman (Netscape), Geir Ivarsøy (Opera), Sho Kuwamoto (Macromedia), Peter Linss (Netscape), Irène Vatton (W3C) and Chris Wilson (Microsoft).

Implementations, however, sometimes have bugs and it happens that shipping deadlines get in the way of perfection. The samurai group of the WebStandards project have recently done a great job of documenting the state of CSS implementations. The group includes: Todd Fahrner, Ian Hickson, Eric Meyer, David Baron, John Allsopp, Roland Eriksson, Ken Gunderson, Braden McDaniel, Liam Quinn and Sue Sims.

Without the W3C and our colleagues there, CSS would never have happened. Especially, we would like to thank: Chris Lilley (chairman of the CSS2 Working Group and co-editor of the CSS2 specification), Ian Jacobs (co-editor of the CSS2 specification), Martin Dürst, Vincent Quint, Dave Raggett, Jenny Raggett, Philippe Le Hégaret, Arnaud Le Hors, Daniel Dardailler, Judy Brewer, Henrik Frystyk Nielsen, Philipp Hoschka and Irène Vatton.

Lastly, our thanks to Tim Berners-Lee, without whom none of this would have been possible.

Håkon Wium Lie
Bert Bos
Antibes, February 1999

TRADEMARK NOTICE

AltaVista is a trademark or registered trademark of Compaq Computer Corporation

Bitstream and TrueDoc is a trademark or registered trademark of Bitstream Inc.

FrameMaker and PostScript are trademarks or registered trademarks of Adobe Systems Inc.

Internet Explorer, Word and Windows are trademarks or registered trademarks of Microsoft Corporation

Java and JavaScript are trademarks or registered trademarks of Sun Microsystems Inc.

Lycos is a registered trademark of Carnegie Mellon University

Mosaic and NCSA Mosaic are proprietary trademarks of University of Illinois

Netscape Navigator, the Netscape logos are registered trademarks and trade names of Netscape Communications Corporation

TrueType is a trademark or a registered trademark of Apple Computer Inc.

WebReview is a trademark or registered trademark of Songline Studios Inc.

• • • • •
Contents

Chapter 5

FONTS 84

Chapter 1

The Web and HTML

Cascading Style Sheets, CSS for short, represents a major breakthrough in how Web page designers work by expanding their ability to control the appearance of Web pages – the documents that people publish on the Web.

Since the World Wide Web (the Web, for short) was created in 1990, people who wanted to put pages on the Web have had little control over what those pages would look like. In the beginning, authors could only specify structural aspects of their pages, for example, that some piece of text would be a heading or some other piece would be straight text. Also, there were ways to make text bold or italic, among a few other effects, but that's where their control ended.

In the scientific environments where the Web was born, people are more concerned with the content of their documents than the presentation. In a research report, the choice of type faces (or fonts, as we call them in this book) is of little importance compared to the scientific results that are reported. However, when authors outside the scientific environments discovered the Web, the limitations of Web document formats became a source of continuing frustration. Authors often came from a paper-based publication environment where they had full control of the presentation. They wanted to be able to make text red or black, make it look more s p a c e d o u t or more squeezed, to center it or put it against the right margin, or anywhere else they wanted. Many Web designers come from a desktop publishing background, in which they can do all of these things, and more, to improve the appearance of printed material. They want the same capabilities when they design Web pages. However, such capabilities have been slow to develop – slow by Internet speed standards, that is. So designers have devised techniques to sidestep these limitations, but these techniques sometimes have unfortunate side effects. We discuss those techniques and their side effects later in this chapter.

This book is about a new method for designing Web pages. CSS works with HTML (the HyperText Markup Language), which is the primary document format on the Web. HTML describes the document's *structure;* that is, the roles the various parts of a document play. For example, a piece of text may be designated as a heading or a paragraph. HTML doesn't pay much attention to the document's *appearance,* and in fact it has only very limited capability to influence appearance. CSS, however, describes how these elements are to be presented to the reader of the document. Now, using CSS, you can better specify the appearance of your HTML pages as well as make your pages available to more Web users worldwide. The release of CSS greatly enhances the potential of HTML and the Web.

A style sheet is a set of stylistic guidelines that tell a browser how an HTML document is to be presented to users. With CSS, you can specify such styles as the size, color, and spacing of text, as well as the placement of text and images on the page. Plus a whole lot more.

A key feature of CSS is that style sheets can *cascade.* That is, several different style sheets can be attached to a document and all of them can influence the presentation of the document. In this way, the author can create a style sheet to specify how the page should look, while the reader can attach a personal style sheet to adjust the appearance of the page for human or technological limitations, such as poor eyesight or a personal preference for a certain font.

CSS is a simple language that can be read by humans – in contrast to some computer languages. Perhaps even more important, however, is that CSS is easy to write. All you need to know is a little HTML as well as some basic desktop publishing terminology: CSS borrows from that terminology when expressing style. So those of you who have experience in desktop publishing should be able to grasp CSS very quickly. But if you're new to HTML, desktop publishing, and/or Web page design, don't despair. You are likely to find CSS surprisingly easy to grasp. The book includes a brief review of basic HTML as well as tips on page design.

To understand how revolutionary CSS is, you first need to understand Web page design as it has been and the problems that CSS can help solve. In this chapter, we begin with a brief tour of the Web and the problems Web designers and others have faced prior to the introduction of CSS. Then we quickly review the basics of HTML. For those of you who are already publishing on the Web, this all may be old news. For those of you

CSS also works with XML which is another document format for the Web. See Chapter 18 for how to use CSS and XML together.

who are new to the idea of designing Web pages, this should help put things in perspective. In Chapter 2, "Enter CSS," we step you through the basics of how to use CSS. In subsequent chapters, we delve more deeply into CSS, covering how you can specify the text, background, color, spacing, and more in the design of your Web pages.

THE WEB

The Web is a vast collection of documents on the *Internet* that are linked together via *hyperlinks*. The Internet consist of millions of computers worldwide that communicate electronically. A hyperlink is a predefined link between two documents. The hyperlinks allow a user to access documents on various *Web servers* without concern for where they are located. A Web server is a computer on the Internet that serves out Web pages on request. From a document on a Web server in California, the user is just one mouse click away from a document that is stored, perhaps, on a Web server in France. Hyperlinks are integral to the Web. Without them, there would be no Web.

Users gain access to the Web through a *browser*. A browser is a computer program that lets users browse, or "surf," the Web by fetching documents from Web servers and displaying them to the user. To move from one document to another, the user clicks on a <u>highlighted</u> (often underlined) word or image, that represents a hyperlink. The browser then retrieves the document that is at the other end of the hyperlink and displays it on the screen. For example, a user could be in a document about baroque music and click the highlighted words <u>Johann Sebastian Bach</u> which is linked to "Bach's home page" (on the Web, all celebrities – as well as everyone else who wants one – have a home page). When the browser has fetched Bach's home page (instantly in the best case) it will appear on the user's screen.

Development of the Web

The Web was invented around 1990 by Tim Berners-Lee with Robert Cailliau as a close ally. Both of them were then working at CERN, the European Laboratory for Particle Physics. Tim is a graduate of Oxford University and a long-time computer and software expert, and is now Director of the World Wide Web Consortium (W3C) an organization that coordinates the development of the Web. He also is a Principal Research Scientist at Massachusetts Institute of Technology's Laboratory for Computer Science (MIT LCS). And he's our boss. Robert is a 20-year veteran at CERN, where he still works. It was Robert who organized the first Web conference in

Geneva in 1993. Both Tim and Robert were awarded the ACM Software System Award in 1995 because of their work on the Web. Robert wrote the Foreword to this book.

Tim created the language HTML that is used by people to exchange information on the Web. We discuss what HTML is in the next section and give a brief review of its basics later in the chapter. Tim also began work on style sheets soon afterward, but when the Web really started taking off in 1993 the work on them was not complete.

The world outside scientific laboratories discovered the Web around 1994. Since then, the Web's growth has been tremendous. Had style sheets been available on the Web from its beginning, Web page designers would have been spared much frustration. However, releasing CSS1 two years later did offer some advantages. First, in the interim we learned much about what visual effects Web designers want to achieve on their pages. Second, we learned that users also want their say in how documents are presented on their computer screens; for example, the visually impaired may want to make fonts bigger so that they can be read more easily. As a result, we were able to provide functionality to meet as many of these needs of designers and users as possible, and even more was added when CSS2 was issued in 1998. Hence, the CSS of 1999 is a better solution than a style sheet solution years earlier would have been.

MARKUP LANGUAGES

HTML is a *markup language*. A markup language is a method of indicating within a document the roles that the document's pieces are to play. Its focus is on the structure of a document rather than its appearance. For example, you can indicate that one piece of text is a paragraph, another is a top-level heading, and another is a lower-level heading. You indicate these by placing codes, called *tags*, into the document. HTML has around 30 commonly used tags which are reviewed later in this chapter. You could, for example, use a tag that says, in effect: "Make this piece of text a heading."

In contrast, desktop publishing (DTP) programs emphasize the presentation of a document rather than its structure. Authors can select font families, text colors and margin widths and thereby accurately control what the final product – which normally ends up on paper – looks like.

The distinction between structural and presentational systems isn't always as clear cut as described above. HTML, while having its roots in structured documents has some tags that describe presentation rather than structure. For example, you can specify that a text should be presented in **bold** or *italic*. Also, some DTP programs let you describe the structure – in addition to the presentation – of a document. When you create a new

18 point Helvetica bold italic

Figure 1.1 18 point Helvetica bold italic.

document in applications like Microsoft Word or Adobe FrameMaker, there is a standard set of "styles" available. A style is a group of stylistic characteristics that you can apply to a piece of text. For example, you may have a style called *title1* that has the stylistic characteristics that sets the text to *18 point Helvetica bold italic*. (If you're not familiar with what *18 point Helvetica bold italic* means, don't worry; we explain it in Chapter 5, "Fonts.") By applying the style *title1* to selected parts of your document you are effectively marking it up. At the same time, you are also specifying how those pieces of text should be presented. Figure 1.1 shows what "18 point Helvetica bold italic" looks like.

Conceptually, this is very similar to HTML and CSS. In HTML, "title1" would be a tag, and the stylistic characteristics (namely "18 point Helvetica bold italic") would be written in a CSS style sheet. If you already know a DTP program that supports this notion of styles, the transition to HTML and CSS will be easy.

DODGING THE LIMITATIONS OF HTML

The HyperText Markup Language – HTML – is a simple, easy-to-learn markup language designed for hypertext documents on the Web. In fact, a computer-literate person can learn to write basic HTML in less than a day. This simplicity is one reason for the huge success of the Web.

From the beginnings of HTML, Web page designers have tried to sidestep its stylistic limitations. Their intentions have been the best – to improve the presentation of documents – but often the techniques have had unfortunate side effects. Typically, the techniques work for some of the people some of the time but never for all of the people all of the time. They include the following:

- using proprietary HTML extensions
- converting text into images
- placing text into tables
- writing a program instead of using HTML

We discuss these techniques, and their side effects, in the next sections.

Proprietary HTML extensions

One way to sidestep HTML's limitations has been for browser vendors to create their own tags that give designers who use their browser a little more control over the appearance of a Web page. At some point, it seemed that every new version of a browser introduced a few new elements that designers could play with. For example, Netscape introduced the CENTER element in 1994, to allow text to be centered on the screen, and more recently the SPACER element for, among other things, indenting the first line of a paragraph. Microsoft introduced the MARQUEE element in 1995, to make text slide across the screen. (Chapter 17 shows more extensions, with their CSS replacements.)

But these HTML extensions have their problems. First, they are not universal. Although the W3C officially added CENTER to HTML 3.2 to avoid problems with browsers behaving differently at a time when CSS was not ready, the others remain specific to a particular browser.

Another problem is that the extensions are meaningless on non-visual browsers such as speech browsers that read pages out aloud, or Braille browsers. Some of the extensions, such as the FONT element, won't even work on certain visual browsers, such as the text-only browser Lynx or browsers on hand-held devices. The standard HTML elements, on the other hand, are all designed to be device-independent. An element like EM ("emphasis"), which is usually shown as italic text on graphical browsers, can be rendered underlined or in reverse video by Lynx, or with a more emphatic voice by a speech browser.

Luckily, CSS offers more powerful alternatives to these HTML extensions, as we will show in this book. Moreover, the CSS equivalents are standardized by W3C, which means all major browser makers agree on them. CSS also offers control over non-visual presentations, which none of the extensions do.

The availability of CSS has even made possible the removal from HTML of the oldest extensions. Now that there is a better place to put layout information, elements like CENTER and FONT are no longer needed in HTML. In HTML 4.0, which is the current version at the time of writing, they have been relegated to a special "transitional module," and are no longer part of the main standard. In the next version of HTML they may disappear completely.

Converting text into images

A second way by which designers have sought to get around the limitations of HTML has been to make text into images. With an image, the designer can fully control colors, spacing, and fonts, among other features. Then the designer simply inserts in the document the appropriate hyperlink where the image is to appear on the page, thereby linking the image's file to the page. When the browser displays the page, the text – in the form of an image – appears on the page.

This method, too, has downsides: it compromises accessibility to a page, and it requires readers to wait longer for documents to display.

Accessibility is the ability of people or programs to use the information on a page. Accessibility of a page is compromised in two ways when you use images to hold text. First, certain types of software called *robots* (also known as *crawlers* or *spiders*) roam the Web (so to speak) seeking what's out there and then creating and updating indexes that users can use to find Web pages. Indexing services like AltaVista, Hotbot, and Lycos use robots to build their indexes.

Robots work by loading a Web page, and then automatically loading all of the pages that are linked from that page, and then loading all of the pages that are linked to those pages, and so on, usually for the purpose of creating a database of all the words on all of the pages. When a user searches for a particular word or set of words, all the pages containing that selection are made available. Robots, however, cannot read images. So they just skip them. Hence, they simply miss text that is part of an image.

Accessibility of your page is compromised in a second way. Not all users have a browser that provides a GUI – Graphical User Interface – such as that provided by Navigator and Explorer. Some browsers can display only text, not images. Also, some people may have configured their browser to not display images. So the content of those images is lost to the user. And some people *do* have a graphical brower with images, but need to set the fonts to a large size to be able to read them. They will find that the text in the images is too small or doesn't have enough contrast.

Currently, the only way around these accessibility problems, apart from CSS, is to enclose a textual description of the image that robots and text-only browsers can use. In the latter, for example, the user would receive this textual description of the image rather than the image – not a great substitute for the real thing but better than nothing.

The second downside to using images to hold text is that images take longer to load and draw on the screen than text. The user may become impatient and back out of a page before it's had time to load completely. Also, the preponderance of images as a substitute for attractive type can account for much of the reputed slowness of the Web to respond when drawing pages on screens.

Placing text into a table

A third technique designers have used to bypass the limitations of HTML is to put text into a table. Doing this enables the designer to control the layout of the text. For example, to add a margin of a certain width on the left side of a page, you would put the whole document inside a table and then add an empty column along the left side to create the "margin."

The downside (you knew there would be one): not all browsers support tables, so pages that use tables do not display well on those browsers. Depending on how you use tables, the result on such browsers can be somewhere between "weird" and "disastrous."

The use of tables also complicates the writing of HTML. You have to add a lot more tags even for a simple table. The more complex the table or table structure — you can create tables within tables to any depth you want — the more complex your code becomes.

Tables have severe accessibility problems as well. Tables used for layout pose problems to programs that try to read pages without displaying them visually. For example, a browser that gives access to the Web over the phone (by reading the pages out loud), would indicate to the listener that it enters a table and then make some specific sound at the start of every cell; rather disturbing if the text isn't actually made up of tabular data. The voice browser has to do it that way, however, since it has to assume that a table contains data for which it is important to know the precise arrangement in rows and columns, such as price lists or sales figures. Browsers with a limited display area, such as browsers in mobile phones, Braille browsers, or browsers set to display text with a large font, have the same problem. They often display only one table cell at a time. Users will not like it when they have to navigate through the cells of a table that isn't one.

A handy rule of thumb for determining if a table is structural or presentational is to try to "transpose" it (*i.e.*, swap the rows and columns, without rotating the cells, so that a vertical table becomes a horizontal one, and vice versa) and see if it still makes sense. If not, it is probably presentational. Tables printed on a Braille printer often need to be transposed, since a Braille page is relatively narrow, typically no more than 40 characters wide.

Used with care, tables can sometimes be the right solution. CSS can nearly always replace tables, so the designer has a choice: is the arrangement in rows and columns a matter of style (and thus for CSS), or is it an intrinsic part of the structure of the text, that even non-visual browsers need to know about?

Writing a program instead of using HTML

A fourth technique designers use to bypass the limitations of HTML is to create a program that displays pages. Although much more complex than any other alternative, this technique has the advantage of giving designers control over every pixel on the screen — something not even CSS style sheets can do. However, this technique shares some of the drawbacks of the previous three discussed. A program cannot be searched by robots, and it cannot be used by text-only browsers. Further, because it is an actual programming language (which HTML is not), it is more difficult to learn. It may contain a computer virus. And it is questionable whether 15 years from now there will be computers that can run the program. Examples of programming languages for creating Web documents are Java and JavaScript.

Why should all of this matter?

HTML has become a universal data format for publishing information. Thanks to its simplicity, anyone with a computer and Internet connection can publish in HTML without expensive DTP applications. Likewise, on the user side, HTML documents can be shown on a variety of devices without the user having to buy proprietary software. Also, perhaps the strongest point in HTML's favor: it allows for electronic documents that have a much higher chance of withstanding the years than proprietary data formats. The methods of dodging the limitations of HTML described above are undermining these benefits: the "extended HTML" that you all too often find on the Web is a complicated proprietary data format that cannot be freely exchanged. CSS, by allowing authors to express their desire for influence over document presentation will help HTML remain the simple little language it was meant to be.

This is why we developed CSS.

Also, there are aesthetic and commercial reasons for why the Web needs a powerful style sheet language. Today, placing a page on the Web is no longer just a matter of putting up some text and hoping someone will stumble across it. Web pages have become an important means whereby people around the world can get together to share ideas, hobbies, interests, and much more. It also is becoming an increasingly important medium for advertising products and services. A page needs to attract and stimulate as well as inform. It needs to stand out among the enormous and rapidly growing repertoire of pages that make up the Web. Aesthetics have become more important. The current HTML tools simply aren't enough for the Web page designer who wants to make good-looking pages.

Let's get started. In the next section, we review the basics of writing HTML. In Chapter 2, we introduce CSS and show you how it works with HTML. From there, we lead you on an exploration of CSS and explain how to use it to create distinctive and manageable Web pages.

HTML BASICS

CSS was designed to work along with HTML. To take advantage of CSS, you need to know a little HTML. As we said in the Preface, we assume most readers of this book will have had some exposure to HTML. However, to ensure we all are talking about the same thing, we review here the basics of HTML.

Elements

HTML is simple to write. It is essentially a series of elements that define the structure of your document. An *element* normally has three parts:

- start tag
- content
- end tag

The diagram below illustrates the three parts of an element:

Figure 1.2 Anatomy of an element.

All tags in HTML start with a "<" and end with a ">". Between these comes the name of the element. In the above example, the name of the element is SENTENCE. The content of the above element is a string of characters (but we will soon see that the content of an element can be another element). After that comes the end tag. End tags look like the start tag, except they have a "/" (called "slash") before the element name.

Building a simple HTML document

> In this book, all element names are printed using small-cap letters, for example BODY. HTML elements are case-insensitive. That is, any combination of uppercase and lowercase letters can be used. Hence, "TITLE," "Title," and "title" are all the same. XML, however, is case-sensitive.

HTML has around 30 commonly used elements. SENTENCE isn't one of them, in fact, SENTENCE isn't an HTML element at all. We just used it as an example to show the basic structure of all elements. Let's look at a real HTML element.

```
<HTML></HTML>
```

One of the elements in HTML is called "HTML". The HTML start tag (**<HTML>**) marks the beginning of an HTML document, and the HTML end tag (**</HTML>**) marks the end. Everything between these two tags is the content of the HTML element. In the above example there isn't anything between the start and the end tag. In the next example we have added some content:

```
<HTML><TITLE>Bach's home page</TITLE></HTML>
```

What we added from the last example is marked in bold letters (this is a convention we will use throughout this chapter). Unlike the SENTENCE example, the content of the HTML element is not just a string of characters – it's actually another element. The title element contains the title of an HTML document. The title of the document we will be building in this chapter is "Bach's home page." The diagram below maps out the two elements we have so far:

HTML element

```
<HTML><TITLE>Bach's home page<TITLE/><HTML>
```

TITLE element

Figure 1.3 Diagram of an element.

When a browser displays an HTML document in a window on the screen, the content of the title element generally goes into the title bar of the window. The title bar is at the top of the window. Below that is often the browser's control panel. Further below is the most interesting part of the browser window: the canvas. The canvas is that part of the window in which documents are actually displayed. See Figure 1.4.

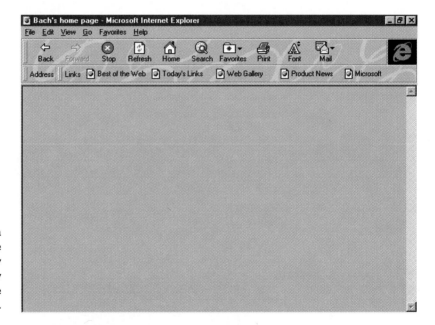

Figure 1.4 The parts of a browser's window. The top line is the title bar, the large grey area is the canvas. CSS only deals with the contents of the canvas.

As you can see, we have yet to put anything in our document that will be displayed in the canvas. To have something actually show up on the canvas, you must place it in the BODY element. The body element is inside the HTML element:

To make it easier to see where elements start and end, we will show the HTML examples over several lines and indent elements that are inside others. We do this because it makes the code easier to read. The browser will ignore the extra space as well as the line breaks that separate one line from another.

```
<HTML>
  <TITLE>My own site</TITLE>
  <BODY>
  </BODY>
</HTML>
```

The content of the HTML element now consists of not one, but two other elements. By themselves, the BODY tags do not add anything to the canvas; we need to give the BODY element some content. Let's start by adding a first-level heading to the sample document. The standard HTML tag for a first-level heading is H1. Here's the HTML code:

```
<HTML>
  <TITLE>Bach's home page</TITLE>
  <BODY>
    <H1>Bach's home page</H1>
  </BODY>
</HTML>
```

(Above, the title of the document is the same as the first-level heading. This will often be the case in HTML document, but doesn't have to be.)

HTML also has other headings you can use: H2, H3, H4, H5, and H6. The higher the number, the less important the heading. If H1 corresponds to a chapter, then H2 is a section, H3 a subsection, etc. Typically, also, the higher the number, the smaller the font size. Here's our document with a couple of extra headings added:

```
<HTML>
  <TITLE>Bach's home page</TITLE>
  <BODY>
    <H1>Bach's home page</H1>
    <H2>Bach's compositions</H2>
    <H3>The keyboard music</H3>
  </BODY>
</HTML>
```

Figure 1.5 Three levels of heading.

However, we don't need those two extra headings right now, so we delete them and add a paragraph of text instead. We do this using the paragraph element, P:

```
<HTML>
  <TITLE>Bach's home page</TITLE>
  <BODY>
    <H1>Bach's home page</H1>
    <P>Johann Sebastian Bach was a prolific
        composer.
  </BODY>
</HTML>
```

Figure 1.6 Adding a paragraph of text.

Bach's home page

Johann Sebastian Bach was a prolific composer.

Note that we left out the ending paragraph tag, **</P>**. Normally, an element begins with a start tag and ends with an end tag. However, for some HTML elements the end tag may be omitted. The end tag is there to notify the browser when the element ends, but in some cases, the browser can figure this out for itself, so the tag is not needed. For example, the P element cannot exist outside of the BODY element. So, when the browser encounters the BODY end tag (**</BODY>**), it knows that the P element also has ended. Still, including the P end tag is perfectly legal. HTML specifies that leaving out the **</P>** has no effect on the way the document is displayed.

You can also see that the browser ignored the spaces and line breaks in the source document. There is only one space between each pair of words and the line breaks are gone.

Next, suppose we want to emphasize a word relative to the surrounding text. Several HTML elements can express this, among them we find STRONG and EM (EM stands for emphasis). The names of these elements do not say anything about how they are to be displayed, but there are some conventions: STRONG elements are normally displayed in **bold**, and EM elements are displayed in *italic*.

The following code shows the use of the STRONG element:

```
<HTML>
  <TITLE>Bach's home page</TITLE>
  <BODY>
    <H1>Bach's home page</H1>
    <P>Johann Sebastian Bach was a
      <STRONG>prolific</STRONG>
      composer.
  </BODY>
</HTML>
```

This is displayed as:

Figure 1.7 An example of using the STRONG element.

Bach's home page

Johann Sebastian Bach was a **prolific** composer.

Notice how the word "prolific" stands out relative to the surrounding text. Also note that while the H1 and P elements start on a new line, the STRONG element continues on the same line where the P element started. H1 and P are examples of *block-level* elements, while the STRONG element is an *inline* element. We discuss block-level and inline elements below.

Block-level and inline elements

In the previous section, the STRONG element was placed in the middle of an element, P, while the P and H1 elements both began and ended a line. You can't insert a P element in the middle of another element, say, an H1 element, or vice versa. But you can insert an element like STRONG in the middle of any other element. This is because the P and H1 elements are *block-level elements,* while the STRONG element is an *inline element.*

Elements can be divided into three groups:

1 block-level
2 inline
3 invisible

A *block-level element* is an element that begins and ends a line or, put another way, that has a line break before and after its content. Examples of block-level elements that you've seen so far in this chapter are H1 and P. Others are given in Table 1.1.

An *inline element* is an element that does not begin and end a line, although it may be placed at either end. Examples of inline elements are STRONG, which you saw in the earlier example, and EM. Others are given in Table 1.1.

An *invisible element* is an element whose content isn't displayed on the canvas. We have seen only one invisible element so far: TITLE. It's not really an invisible element since it appears in the title bar of the window, but it is not displayed on the canvas. HTML only has a few invisible elements and you will find them in Table 1.1.

Element overview

Confused about the different elements? Don't worry. Table 1.1 gives you an overview of the most common HTML elements. We've introduced you to several of these already and will discuss others shortly. We talk about others when appropriate throughout the rest of the book and use them in a lot of examples. Also, we suggest you refer to the table as needed as you work your way through the book. The last column of the table ("Empty?/ Replaced?") will be explained further on in this chapter

Among the elements that are not included in Table 1.1 are the elements to create forms and tables. Also, the non-standard elements have been left out.

Element name	Abbreviation for	Block, inline, or invisible	Typical visual effect	End tag can be omitted?	Empty? Replaced?
A	anchor	inline	highlighted	no	
BLOCKQUOTE		block-level	indented	no	
BODY		block-level	inside canvas	yes	
BR	break	block-level	breaks the line	yes*	empty
DD	definition description	block-level		yes	
DL	definition list	block-level		no	
DIV	division	block-level		no	
DT	definition term	block-level		yes	
EM	emphasis	inline	italic	no	
H1, H2 ... H6	heading levels	block-level	large fonts	no	
HR	horizontal rule	block-level	horizontal rule	yes*	empty
HTML		block-level		yes	
I	italic	inline	italic	no	
IMG	image	inline	as an image	yes*	empty and replaced
LI	list item	block-level	with a list item marker in front	yes	
LINK		invisible		yes*	empty
OBJECT		block-level		no	replaced
OL	ordered list	block-level		no	
P	paragraph	block-level		yes	
PRE	preformatted	block-level	in monospace font	no	
SPAN		inline		no	
STRONG		inline	bold	no	
STYLE		invisible		no	
TITLE		invisible	shown in title bar, not on canvas	no	
TT	teletype	inline	in monospace font	no	
UL	unordered list	block-level		no	

Table 1.1 Common HTML tags. (* indicates that the element is empty and that the end tag doesn't exist.)

In the next several sections, we add to your repertoire of HTML tags by discussing elements that you can use to create lists, add a horizontal rule, force a line break, and link to text and images.

Comments

Most of your document will consist of elements. However, you can also insert HTML *comments* into the document. A comment is anything you want to say about what is going on with your document that you don't want the user to see. The user can't see the contents of a comment because browsers ignore comments; that is, they do not display a comment's contents. Comments can be a helpful way of communicating something about your document to other designers who will see your code.

To ensure the comment really is not viewable by the user, you enclose it between special strings that the browser will recognize as enclosing a comment. You begin the comment with the string **<!--** and end it with the string **-->**. (That's two hyphens in both cases.) Here's a sample comment:

```
<!--CSS is the greatest thing to hit the Web since
hyperlinks-->
```

Lists

Lists are very common in HTML documents. HTML has three elements that create lists:

1 OL, which creates an *ordered* list. In an ordered list, each list item has a label that indicates the order, *e.g.,* a digit (1, 2, 3, 4 or I, II, III, IV) or letter (a, b, c, d). In desktop publishing terminology, ordered lists are often called numbered lists.
2 UL, which creates an *unordered* list. In an unordered list, each list item has a mark that does not indicate order, *e.g.,* a bullet symbol. In desktop publishing terminology, unordered lists are often called "bulleted" lists.
3 DL, which creates a *definition* list. A definition list is a list of terms with their corresponding definitions. For example, a dictionary is a (long!) definition list.

Bach's home page must surely include a list of some of his compositions. Let's add an ordered list:

```
<HTML>
  <TITLE>Bach's home page</TITLE>
  <BODY>
```

```
<H1>Bach's home page</H1>
<P>Johann Sebastian Bach was a
  <STRONG>prolific</STRONG>
  composer. Here are his best works:
<OL>
  <LI>the Goldberg Variations
  <LI>the Brandenburg Concertos
  <LI>the Christmas Oratorio
</OL>
</BODY>
</HTML>
```

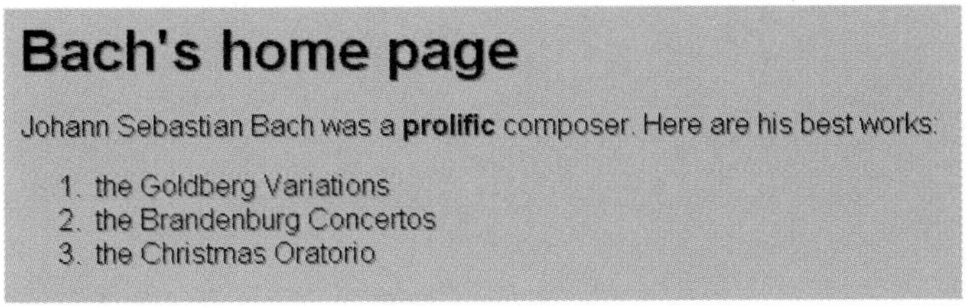

Bach's home page

Johann Sebastian Bach was a **prolific** composer. Here are his best works:

1. the Goldberg Variations
2. the Brandenburg Concertos
3. the Christmas Oratorio

Figure 1.8 An ordered list.

Notice that an LI doesn't need an end tag, but an OL does. Figure 1.8 shows the result.

The ordered list above is unfair to all the other great compositions by Bach. (What about the Mass in B-minor?) Let's change the ordered list into an unordered list. To do this, we simply change the OL to UL:

```
<HTML>
  <TITLE>Bach's home page</TITLE>
  <BODY>
    <H1>Bach's home page</H1>
    <P>Johann Sebastian Bach was a
      <STRONG>prolific</STRONG>composer.
      Among his works are:
    <UL>
      <LI>the Goldberg Variations
      <LI>the Brandenburg Concertos
      <LI>the Christmas Oratorio
    </UL>
  </BODY>
</HTML>
```

Notice that we do not have to change the LI elements to change the list from unordered to ordered: both UL and OL use LI as the list item element. But since the LI elements are now inside the UL element, they will look different.

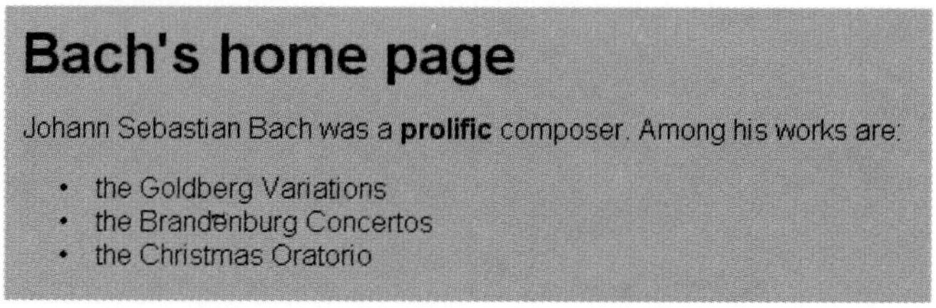

Bach's home page

Johann Sebastian Bach was a **prolific** composer. Among his works are:

- the Goldberg Variations
- the Brandenburg Concertos
- the Christmas Oratorio

Figure 1.9 An unordered list.

A DL, or definition list, is used for lists that have terms and their corresponding definitions. Each term is contained in a DT element, and each definition in a DD element. An example of a DL is a dictionary or glossary. In the next example, we change our OL to a DL. Notice how the LIs change to DTs and that like the LIs, they do not require end tags. Figure 1.10 shows the result.

```
<HTML>
  <TITLE>Bach's home page</TITLE>
  <BODY>
    <H1>Bach's home page</H1>
    <P>Johann Sebastian Bach was a
      <STRONG>prolific</STRONG> composer.
      Among his works are:
    <DL>
      <DT>the Goldberg Variations
      <DD>composed in 1741, catalog number BWV988
      <DT>the Brandenburg Concertos
      <DD>composed in 1713, catalog numbers
          BWV1046-1051
      <DT>the Christmas Oratorio
      <DD>composed in 1734, catalog number BWV248
    </DL>
  </BODY>
</HTML>
```

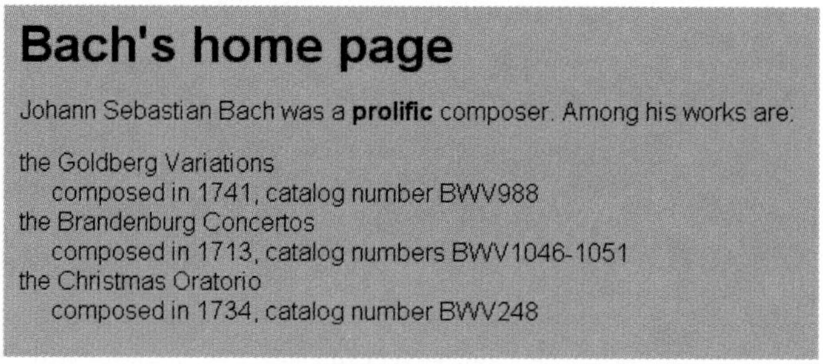

Bach's home page

Johann Sebastian Bach was a **prolific** composer. Among his works are:

the Goldberg Variations
    composed in 1741, catalog number BWV988
the Brandenburg Concertos
    composed in 1713, catalog numbers BWV1046-1051
the Christmas Oratorio
    composed in 1734, catalog number BWV248

Figure 1.10 A definition list.

Empty elements HR and BR

All HTML elements we have discussed so far have had content. HTML also has some elements that do not have content; they are called *empty elements*. One example is the HR element which inserts a horizontal rule in the document. It doesn't need any content. Also, there is the BR element whose sole purpose is to force a line break. Since empty elements do not have any content they don't need any end tags either.

We can add a horizontal rule to a document by using the HR (horizontal rule) element. HR is an empty element, so you should omit its end tag. Here's the code for adding an HR element.

```
<HTML>
  <TITLE>Bach's home page</TITLE>
  <BODY>
    <H1>Bach's home page</H1>
    <P>Johann Sebastian Bach was a
      <STRONG>prolific</STRONG>
      composer. Among his works are:
    <UL>
      <LI>the Goldberg Variations
      <LI>the Brandenburg Concertos
      <LI>the Christmas Oratorio
    </UL>
    <HR>
  </BODY>
</HTML>
```

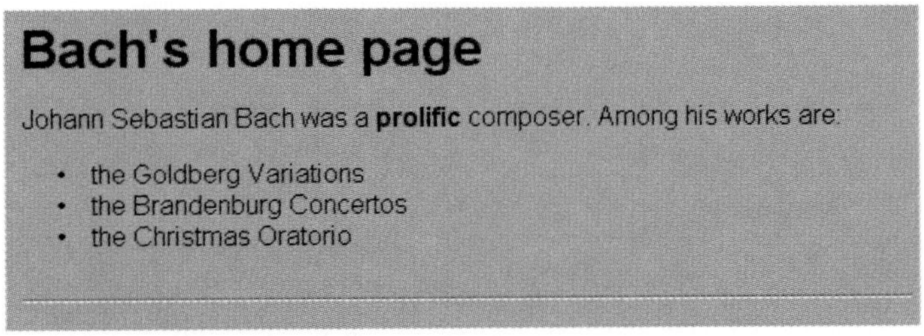

Bach's home page

Johann Sebastian Bach was a **prolific** composer. Among his works are:

- the Goldberg Variations
- the Brandenburg Concertos
- the Christmas Oratorio

Figure 1.11 Adding a horizontal rule.

We can force a line break in the middle of an element by using the BR (break) element. The browser normally ignores line breaks in the HTML document and will automatically break a line when needed when it displays the document. However, if you want to enforce a line break at a certain spot in the document, BR lets you do this. BR is an empty element, so you should omit its end tag.

Here is our example with a BR element added:

```
<HTML>
  <TITLE>Bach's home page</TITLE>
  <BODY>
    <H1>Bach's <BR>home page</H1>
    <P>Johann Sebastian Bach was a
      <STRONG>prolific</STRONG>
      composer. Among his works are:
    <UL>
      <LI>the Goldberg Variations
      <LI>the Brandenburg Concertos
      <LI>the Christmas Oratorio
    </UL>
  </BODY>
</HTML>
```

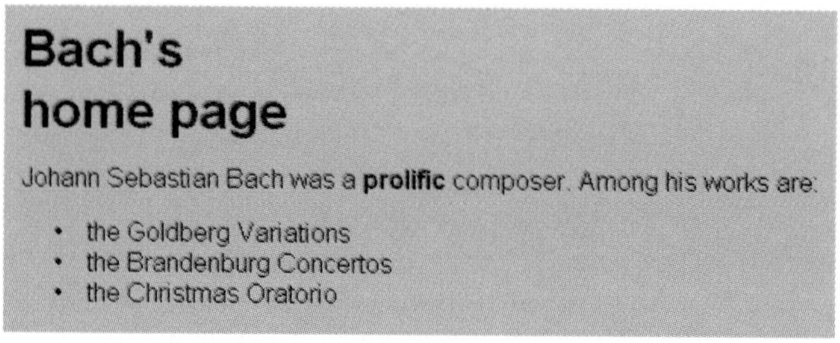

**Bach's
home page**

Johann Sebastian Bach was a **prolific** composer. Among his works are:

- the Goldberg Variations
- the Brandenburg Concertos
- the Christmas Oratorio

Figure 1.12 Adding a line break.

It is usually better to let the browser determine the line breaks, since as an author you cannot know how wide the user's window is, or how large the fonts are. So we'll take out the BR element as we move on.

Maintaining preformatted text

In the previous example, we mentioned that a browser generally ignores line breaks, except for those that you enter using the BR element. The browser also ignores tabs and extra white space. Tabspaces are converted to single white-space characters, while extra white-space characters – any more than one – are collapsed into one white-space character. Generally, this is what we want. This feature enables us to space out our code so that it is more readable and reflects the structure of the document, secure in the knowledge that the browser will ignore all the extra white spaces.

Sometimes, however, you may want to insert white space and have the browser display your text exactly as you formatted it. The PRE (preformatted) element allows you do this. Simply enclose within **<PRE>** tags the information whose formatting you want to preserve. The PRE element is often used for simple tables where columns need to align vertically:

```
<HTML>
  <TITLE>Bach's home page</TITLE>
  <BODY>
    <H1>Bach's <BR>home page</H1>
    <P>Johann Sebastian Bach was a
      <STRONG>prolific</STRONG>
      composer. Among his works are:
    <PRE>
COMPOSITION             YEAR  CATALOG#
Goldberg Variation      1741  BWV988
Brandenburg Concertos 1713  BWV1046-1051
Christmas Oratorio      1734  BWV248
    </PRE>
  </BODY>
</HTML>
```

Notice that the content of the PRE element cannot be aligned with the other elements since the extra whitespace would appear on the canvas. Here is the result (Figure 1.13):

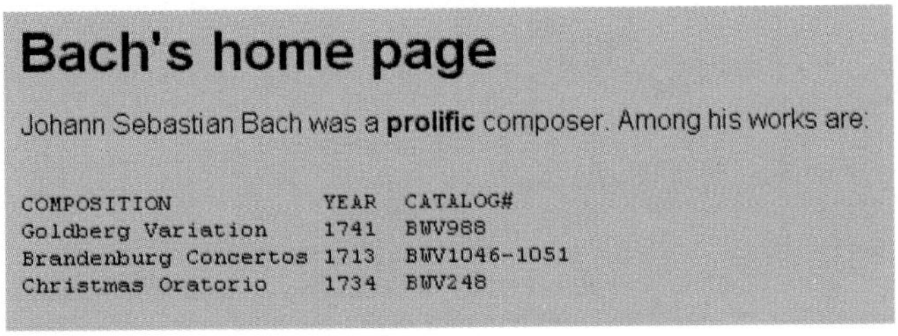

Figure 1.13 Preserving preformatted text.

This is actually not a very good example, since by using PRE we hide the fact that the content is a table. This is a case where using a table is in fact the right thing to do, since it enhances accessibility (see "Placing text into a table" on page 7).

Adding hyperlinks

We can make our document more interesting by adding hyperlinks to it. When hyperlinks are in place, users can click on them to access related documents from somewhere else on the Web. Hyperlinks are integral to HTML and the Web. Without hyperlinks, there would be no Web.

To make a hyperlink, you use the A (anchor) element. When the user clicks on the A element, the browser fetches the document at the other end of the hyperlink. The browser needs to be told where it can find the other document, and this information goes into an attribute on the A element. An *attribute* is a characteristic quality of the element, other than the type or content of an element. The A element uses an attribute called HREF (hypertext reference) to add a hyperlink:

```
<HTML>
  <TITLE>Bach's home page</TITLE>
  <BODY>
    <H1>Bach's home page</H1>
    <P>Johann Sebastian Bach was a
      <STRONG>prolific</STRONG>
      composer. Among his works are:
    <UL>
      <LI>the <A HREF="goldberg.html">Goldberg</A>
        Variations
      <LI>the Brandenburg Concertos
      <LI>the Christmas Oratorio
    </UL>
    <HR>
  </BODY>
</HTML>
```

Let's take a closer look at the newly added A element. Figure 1.14 shows the different parts of the A element.

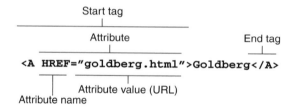

Figure 1.14 The different parts of an A element.

The A start tag is a bit more complicated than the other start tags we have seen so far; in addition to the element name it includes an attribute. Different element types have different attributes, among the most common ones is the HREF attribute on the A element. Attributes can only go into the start tag of the element, after the element name. Most attributes need a value: the HREF attributes always takes a URL as a value. A URL, Universal Resource Locator, is a Web address that the browser uses to locate the hyperlinked document. When URLs are used as values on the HREF attribute, they should always be quoted ("…").

URLs come in two flavors:

- A *relative URL* gives the location of the document relative to the document where it is referenced (that is, the document where the A element is). You can only use relative URLs when you link to a document on the same Web server as the document you are linking from.

- An *absolute URL* gives the location of the document independent of any other document. You must use absolute URLs when you link to a document on a different server. Absolute URLs can be typed into any machine on the Internet and the browser will find it. That's why you see absolute URLs on T-shirts, in TV commercials etc.

In the previous example, the HREF attribute had a relative URL (**goldberg.html**) as value. If the user clicks on the word "Goldberg," the browser will fetch the document called **goldberg.html** from the same location as where our sample document is found.

We can also put an absolute URL into our document:

```
<HTML>
  <TITLE>Bach's home page</TITLE>
  <BODY>
    <H1>Bach's home page</H1>
    <P>Johann Sebastian Bach was a
      <STRONG>prolific</STRONG> composer.
      Among his works are:
    <UL>
      <LI>the <A HREF="goldberg.html">Goldberg</A>
          Variations
      <LI>the Brandenburg Concertos
      <LI>the<AHREF="http://www.noel.org/christmas.html">
          Christmas</A> Oratorio
    </UL>
    <HR>
  </BODY>
</HTML>
```

As you can see above, absolute URLs are slightly more complicated than relative ones. In fact, when Tim Berners-Lee invented the URL scheme, they were only meant to be seen by machines. Figure 1.15 shows the various parts of the above URL.

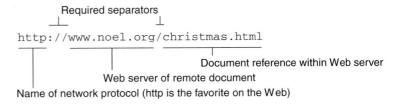

Figure 1.15 The structure of a URL.

The details of URLs are not the main topic for this book and as long as you are aware of the two types of URL you may safely proceed.

Adding images

Images proliferate on the Web. It wasn't until the Mosaic browser added support for images in 1993 that a critical mass of people realized the potential of the Web. You can add images to your documents with the IMG element — IMG is short for image.

IMG is a peculiar element. First, it's empty. That's not so strange, we've seen those before (quick reminder: an empty element is an element without content, e.g., HR, BR). Second, it's a *replaced* element. A replaced element is a placeholder for some other content that is being pointed to from the element. In the case of IMG, it points to an image that is fetched by the browser when the IMG element is encountered. Unlike the A element, which gives the user the option of jumping to a link or not, the browser will automatically fetch the image IMG points to. Also, unlike the A element, IMG uses an attribute called SRC to point to the image.

Let's add an image to the sample document. Not many portraits of Bach are known, but those that exist are on the Web:

```
<HTML>
  <TITLE>Bach's home page</TITLE>
  <BODY>
    <H1><IMG SRC="jsbach.gif" ALT="Portrait of
    J.S.Bach">Bach's home page</H1>
    <P>Johann Sebastian Bach was a
      <STRONG>prolific</STRONG>
      composer. Among his works are:
    <UL>
      <LI>the <A HREF="goldberg.html">Goldberg</A>
         Variations
      <LI>the Brandenburg Concertos
      <LI>the <A HREF="http:/www.noel.org">Christmas
        </A> Oratorio
    </UL>
    <HR>
  </BODY>
</HTML>
```

Let's take a closer look at the attributes on the IMG element:

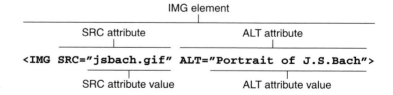

Figure 1.16 The IMG element.

The SRC attribute on IMG is similar to the HREF attribute on A: they both take a URL as a value. The ALT attribute is new. The purpose of ALT is to provide an alternative (from which it gets its name) textual description of the image. Sometimes a browser cannot fetch the image (perhaps the Web server is broken?) or it may be configured to ignore images, for example, in the case of a text-only browser. In these cases, the browser will look for the alternative textual description and display that instead of the image. The ALT text is also essential for people who cannot see. Therefore, you should always try to include a textual description of the image so users can still get a sense of what is going on.

This is how Microsoft Internet Explorer shows the page while the image is being fetched (Figure 1.17):

Figure 1.17 Waiting for an element to be fetched.

When the image is ready, the page looks like this (Figure 1.18):

Figure 1.18 The image has been loaded.

DOCUMENT TREES

In this chapter, we have demonstrated how elements in HTML are placed inside one another. We did this by indenting the code, as shown in all the previous code examples. The HTML element itself is the outermost element that encompasses all the other elements. Inside the HTML element are the TITLE and BODY elements, with the latter encompassing all the other elements, such as H1 and P. And within some of those elements are other elements. For example, within the UL element are the LI elements. If you were to diagram this idea of elements within elements, the result might be as shown in Figure 1.19.

```
<HTML>
  <TITLE>Bach's home page</TITLE>
  <BODY>
    <H1>Bach's home page</H1>
    <P>Johann Sebastian Bach was a
      <STRONG>prolific</STRONG>
      composer. Among his works are:
    <UL>
      <LI>the Goldberg Variations
      <LI>the Brandenburg Concertos
      <LI>the Christmas Oratorio
    </UL>
  </BODY>
</HTML>
```

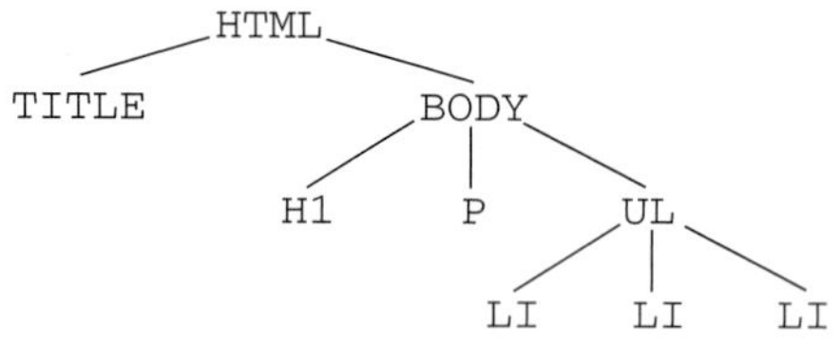

Figure 1.19 Diagram of elements within elements in a tree structure.

Notice how the diagram resembles a person's genealogical chart, with parents and children spread out in a top-to-bottom fashion, where parents can also be children. This is called a *tree structure*. In the tree structure of an HTML document, the HTML element is the earliest ancestor – the top parent. All other elements are children, grandchildren, and great-grandchildren – in short, descendants – of the HTML element. An element can have from zero to many children, but it always has only one parent, with the exception of the HTML element, which is an orphan. In this diagram, note that TITLE and BODY are children of HTML. TITLE has no children, but BODY has three: H1, P, and UL. In turn, UL has three children: the LIs. Also note that in this example, BODY is both a child and a parent, as is UL.

We encounter tree structures in many situations outside HTML and genealogy. Trees – real trees such as spruce and pine – are (not surprisingly) tree structures. Organizational charts for companies are often set out in a tree structure. Books and technical documents, too, are usually set out in a tree structure, where sections and subsections are branches of the whole. (The fact that books are made from trees doesn't seem to have anything to do with it… .) The last example is probably the reason why HTML documents always have a tree structure.

Nested elements

In HTML, there are some restrictions on which elements can be children of which elements. Usually, an element cannot contain children of its own type. That is, a P, for example, cannot be a child element of another P. You would not typically want to put a paragraph inside another paragraph, anyway. Similarly, an H1 cannot be a child element of another H1.

Some elements, however, may contain children of their own type. One example is BLOCKQUOTE, the element that is used to put quoted material within a document. This element can have nested within it quoted material that is the content of another BLOCKQUOTE element, that is, you can put a quote within a quote. This ability of an element to have children of its own type is called *nesting*.

Following is an example using no less than three nested BLOCKQUOTE elements (shown in bold, italic and bold italic, respectively):

```
<HTML>
  <TITLE>Fredrick the Great meets Bach</TITLE>
  <BODY>
    <H1>Fredrick the Great meets Bach</H1>
    <P>In his book "Gödel, Escher, Bach," Douglas
      Hofstadter writes:
    <BLOCKQUOTE>Johann Nikolaus Forkel, one of
      Bach's earliest biographers, tells the story
      as follows:
    <BLOCKQUOTE>One evening, just as he was
        getting his flute ready, and his musicians
        were assembled, an officer brought him a
        list of the strangers who had arrived. With
        his flute in his hand he ran over the list,
        but immediately turned to the assembled
        musicians, and said, with a kind of
        agitation:
      <BLOCKQUOTE>Gentlemen, old Bach is come.
      </BLOCKQUOTE>
    </BLOCKQUOTE>
    </BLOCKQUOTE>
  </BODY>
</HTML>
```

This can be displayed as in Figure 1.20.

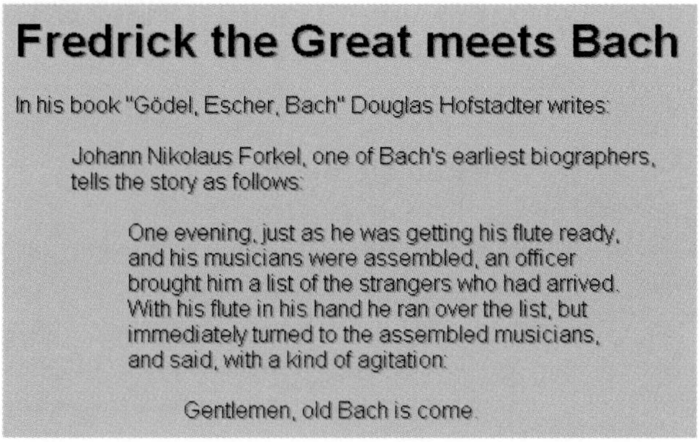

Figure 1.20 Nested BLOCKQUOTE elements.

Notice how with the nested elements, the second element is indented even more than the first is. This is a visual indication that it is a child of the first BLOCKQUOTE.

BLOCKQUOTE marks content as a quote. When you use it for all quotes in your document, you or others, such as robots, can easily extract all of the quotes. It is much used also as a means of indenting material other than quotes. It is common to see stacks of BLOCKQUOTE elements, not because there are so many levels of quotes but because designers think indentation looks good. Here's an example of that (see Figure 1.21):

```
<HTML>
  <BODY>
    <BLOCKQUOTE>
      <BLOCKQUOTE>
        <BLOCKQUOTE>
          <BLOCKQUOTE>
            Indentation is great!
          </BLOCKQUOTE>
        </BLOCKQUOTE>
      </BLOCKQUOTE>
    </BLOCKQUOTE>
  </BODY>
</HTML>
```

Figure 1.21 Using BLOCKQUOTE for indentation.

Unfortunately, when robots or others search for quotes, they find not only quotes but also everything else tagged as quotes.

With the arrival of CSS, this misuse of BLOCKQUOTE should not be necessary anymore. CSS provides easy-to-use methods for indenting text and images, as we will show you in subsequent chapters.

Well, there you have it. The elements we described in this chapter, plus a few others we discuss later where appropriate, form the basics of HTML. With these, you can write and publish many literary gems. Of course, they may not look all that great. But we will fix that with CSS.

Chapter 2

CSS

As we explained in the previous chapter, HTML elements enable Web page designers to mark up a document as to its structure. The HTML specification lists guidelines on how browsers should display these elements. For example, you can be reasonably sure that the contents of a STRONG element will be displayed bold-faced. Also, you can pretty much trust that most browsers will display the content of an H1 element using a big font size... at least bigger than the P element and bigger than the H2 element. But beyond trust and hope, you don't have any control over how your text appears.

CSS changes that. CSS puts the designer in the driver's seat. We devote much of the rest of this book to explaining what you can do with CSS. In this chapter, we begin by introducing you to the basics of how to write style sheets and how CSS and HTML work together to describe both the structure and appearance of your document.

RULES AND STYLE SHEETS

To start using CSS, you don't even have to write style sheets. Chapter 16 will tell you how to point to existing style sheets on the Web.

There are two ways to create CSSs. You can either use a normal text editor and write the style sheets "by hand," or you can use a dedicated tool – for example a Web page design application – which supports CSS. The dedicated tools allow you to create style sheets without learning the syntax of the CSS language. However, in many cases the designer will want to tweak the style sheet by hand afterwards, so we recommend that you learn to write and edit CSSs by hand. Let's get started!

```
H1 { color: green }
```

What you see above is a simple CSS rule that contains one rule. A *rule* is a statement about one stylistic aspect of one or more elements. A *style sheet* is a set of one or more rules that apply to an HTML document. The rule above sets the color of all first-level headings (H1). Let's take a quick look at what the visual result of the rule could be:

Figure 2.1

Bach's home page

We will now start dissecting the rule.

Anatomy of a rule

A rule consists of two parts:

- Selector – the part before the left curly brace
- Declaration – the part within the curly braces

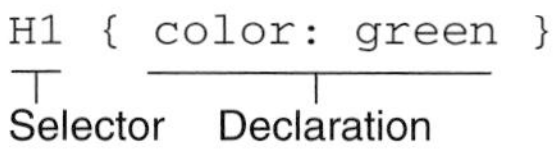

```
H1 { color: green }
```
Selector   Declaration

The *selector* is the link between the HTML document and the style. It specifies what elements are affected by the declaration. The *declaration* is that part of the rule that sets forth what the effect will be. In the example above, the selector is H1 and the declaration is "color: green." Hence, all H1 elements will be affected by the declaration, that is, they will be turned green. (The **color** property just affects the foreground text color, there are other properties for background, border, etc.)

The above selector is based on the *type* of the element: it selects all elements of type "H1." This kind of selector is called *type selector*. Any HTML element type can be used as a type selector. Type selectors are the simplest kind of selectors. We discuss other kinds of selectors in Chapter 4, "CSS selectors."

Anatomy of a declaration

A declaration has two parts separated by a colon:

31 • CSS

- Property – that part before the colon
- Value – that part after the colon

```
H1 { color: green }
       ‾‾‾‾‾  ‾‾‾‾‾
     Property  Value
```

The *property* is a quality or characteristic that something possesses. In the previous example, it is **color**. CSS2 (see separate box) defines around 120 properties and we can assign values to all of them.

<table>
<tr><td>

CSS SPECIFICATIONS

</td><td>

Cascading Style Sheets is formally described in two specifications from W3C: CSS1 and CSS2. CSS1 was issued in December 1996 and describes a simple formatting model mostly for screen-based presentations. CSS1 has around 50 properties (for example **color** and **font-size**). CSS2 was finalized in May 1998 and builds on CSS1. CSS2 includes all CSS1 properties and adds around 70 of its own, such as properties to describe aural presentations and page breaks. In this book we do not try to distinguish between CSS1 and CSS2 and use the term "CSS" unless the distinction is important. Most features described in the first four chapters are part of CSS1. If you would like to read the CSS specifications themselves, you can find them from:

```
http://www.w3.org/TR/REC-CSS1
http://www.w3.org/TR/REC-CSS2
```

</td></tr>
</table>

The *value* is a precise specification of the property. In the example, it is "green," but it could just as easily be blue, red, yellow, or some other color.

The diagram below shows all ingredients of a rule. The curly braces ({ }) and colon (:) make it possible for the browser to distinguish between the selector, property, and value.

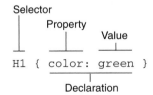

Figure 2.2 Diagram of a rule.

Grouping selectors and rules

In designing CSS, brevity was a goal. We figured that if we could reduce the size of style sheets, we could enable designers to write and edit style sheets "by hand." Also, short style sheets load faster than longer ones. CSS therefore includes several mechanisms to shorten style sheets by way of grouping selectors and declarations.

For example, consider these three rules:

```
H1 { font-weight: bold }
H2 { font-weight: bold }
H3 { font-weight: bold }
```

All three rules have exactly the same declaration – they set the font to be bold. (This is done using the **font-weight** property, which we discuss in Chapter 5.) Since all three declarations are identical, we can group the selectors into a *comma-separated list* and only list the declaration once, like this:

```
H1, H2, H3 { font-style: bold }
```

This rule will produce the same result as the first three.

A selector may have more than one declaration. For example, we could write a style sheet with these two rules:

```
H1 { color: green }
H1 { text-align: center }
```

In this case, we set all H1s to be green and to be centered on the canvas. (This is done using the **text-align** property, discussed in Chapter 5.)

But we can achieve the same effect faster by grouping the declarations that relate to the same selector into a *semicolon-separated list*, like this:

```
H1 {
    color: green;
    text-align: center;
}
```

All declarations must be contained within the pair of curly braces. A semicolon separates the declarations and may – but doesn't have to – also appear at the end of the last declaration. Also, to make your code easier to read, we suggest you place each declaration on its own line, as we did here. (Browsers won't care, they'll just ignore all the extra whitespace and line breaks.)

Now you have the basics of how to create CSS rules and style sheets. However, you're not done yet. In order for the style sheet to have any effect you have to "glue" your style sheet to your HTML document.

"GLUING" STYLE SHEETS TO THE DOCUMENT

For any style sheet to affect the HTML document, it must be "glued" to the document. That is, the style sheet and the HTML document must be combined so that they can work together to present the document. This can be done in any of four ways:

1 Apply the basic, document-wide style sheet for the document by using the STYLE element.
2 Apply a style sheet to an individual element using the STYLE attribute.
3 Link an external style sheet to the document using the LINK element.
4 Import a style sheet using the CSS @import notation.

In the next section, we discuss the first method: using the STYLE element. We discuss using the STYLE attribute in Chapter 4, "CSS selectors," and using the LINK element and the @import notation in Chapter 16, "External style sheets."

Gluing by using the STYLE element

You can glue the style sheet and the HTML document together by putting the style sheet inside a STYLE element at the top of your document. The STYLE element was introduced in HTML specifically to allow style sheets to be inserted inside HTML documents. Here's a style sheet (shown in bold) glued to a sample document by using the STYLE element. The result is shown in Figure 2.3.

```
<HTML>
  <TITLE>Bach's home page</TITLE>
  <STYLE>
    H1, H2 { color: green }
  </STYLE>
  <BODY>
    <H1>Bach's home page</H1>
    <P>Johann Sebastian Bach was a prolific
       composer. Among his works are:
    <UL>
      <LI>the Goldberg Variations
      <LI>the Brandenburg Concertos
      <LI>the Christmas Oratorio
    </UL>
    <H2>Historical perspective</H2>
    <P>Bach composed in what has been referred to as
```

```
                         the Baroque period.
                </BODY>
              </HTML>
```

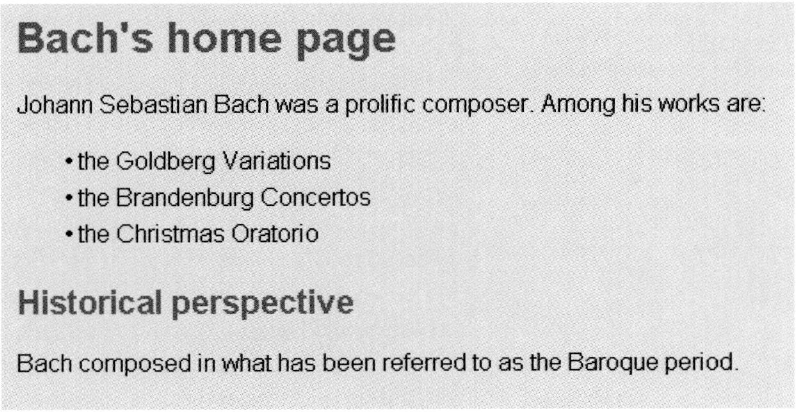

Bach's home page

Johann Sebastian Bach was a prolific composer. Among his works are:

- the Goldberg Variations
- the Brandenburg Concertos
- the Christmas Oratorio

Historical perspective

Bach composed in what has been referred to as the Baroque period.

Figure 2.3 The result of adding to a style sheet a rule to turn H1s green and then gluing the style sheet to the document using the STYLE elements.

Notice that the STYLE element is placed after the TITLE element and before the BODY element. The title of a document does not show up on the canvas, so it is not affected by CSS styles.

The content of a STYLE element is a style sheet. However, whereas the content of such elements as H1, P, and UL appears on the canvas, the content of a STYLE element does not show on the canvas. Rather, it is the *effect* of the content of the STYLE element – the style sheet – that appears on the canvas. So you don't see "{ color: green }" displayed on your screen; you see instead two H1 elements colored green. No rules have been added that affect any of the other elements, so those elements appear in the browser's default color.

BROWSERS AND CSS

For an updated overview of available browsers, see http://www.w3.org/Style/CSS/ #browsers

For CSS to work as described in this book, you must use a CSS-enhanced browser, that is, a browser that supports CSS. A CSS-enhanced browser will recognize the STYLE element as a container for a style sheet and present the document accordingly. Most browsers that are distributed today support CSS, for example Microsoft Internet Explorer 4 (IE4), Netscape Navigator 4 (NS4) and Opera 3.5 (O3.5). Conservative estimates indicate that more than half the people on the Web use a CSS-enhanced browser, and the figures are steadily rising. Chances are that the people you communicate with have CSS-enhanced browsers. If not, give them a reason to upgrade!

The best source for information on how different browsers support CSS is WebReview's charts found from http://webreview.com/wr/pub/guides/style/mastergrid.html

Alas, not all CSS implementations are perfect. When you start experimenting with style sheets, you will soon notice that each browser comes with a set of bugs and limitations. In general, newer browsers behave better than older ones. IE4 and O3.5 are among the best, and Netscape's next offering – code-named Gecko – also promises much improved support for CSS.

Those who don't use CSS-enhanced browsers can still read pages that use style sheets. CSS was carefully designed so that all content should remain visible even if the browser knows nothing about CSS. Some browsers, such as Netscape's Navigator version 2 and 3 don't support style sheets but they know enough about the STYLE element to fully ignore it. Next to supporting style sheets, this is the correct behavior.

However, other browsers that do not know the STYLE element, such as Netscape's Navigator 1 and Microsoft Internet Explorer 2, will ignore the STYLE *tags* but display the *content* of the STYLE element. Thus, the user will end up with the style sheet printed on the top of the canvas. At the time of writing, only a few percent of Web users will experience this problem. To avoid this, you can put your style sheet inside an *HTML comment*, which we discussed in Chapter 1. Because comments don't display on the screen, by placing your style sheet inside an HTML comment, you prevent the oldest browsers from displaying the STYLE element's content. CSS-enhanced browsers are aware of this trick, and will treat the content of the STYLE element as a style sheet.

Recall that HTML comments start with <!-- and end with -->. Here's an excerpt from the previous code example that shows how you write a style sheet in an HTML comment. The comment encloses the STYLE element content only:

```
<HTML>
  <TITLE>Bach's home page</TITLE>
  <STYLE>
    <!--
      H1 { color: green }
    -->
  </STYLE>
  <BODY>
    ..
  </BODY>
</HTML>
```

CSS also has its own set of comments that you can use within the style sheet. A CSS comment begins with "/*" and ends with "*/." (Those familiar with the C programming language will recognize these.) CSS rules inside a CSS comment will not have any effect on the presentation of the document.

The browser also needs to be told that you are working with CSS style sheets. CSS is currently the only style sheet language in use with HTML documents and we don't expect this to change. For XML the situation might be different. But just as there is more than one image format (GIF, JPEG and PNG come to mind), there could be more than one style sheet language. So it's a good habit to tell browsers that they are dealing with CSS. (In fact, HTML requires you to.) This is done with the TYPE attribute of the STYLE element. The value of TYPE indicates what type of style sheet is being used. For CSS, that value is "text/css." The following is an excerpt from our previous sample document that shows you how you would write this (in combination with the use of the HTML comment):

```
<HTML>
  <TITLE>Bach's home page</TITLE>
  <STYLE TYPE="text/css">
    <!--
      H1 { color: green }
    -->
  </STYLE>
  <BODY>
    ..
  </BODY>
</HTML>
```

When the browser loads a document, it checks to see if it understands the style sheet language. If it does, it will try to read the sheet, otherwise it will ignore it. The TYPE attribute (see Chapter 1 for a discussion on HTML attributes) on the STYLE element is a way to let the browser know which style sheet language is being used. The TYPE attribute must be included.

To make examples easier to read, we have chosen not to wrap style sheets in HTML comments, but we do use the TYPE attribute throughout this book.

TREE STRUCTURES AND INHERITANCE

Recall from Chapter 1 the discussion about HTML representing a document with a tree-like structure and how elements in HTML have children and parents. There are many reasons for having tree-structured documents. For style sheets, there is one very good reason: inheritance. Just as children inherit from their parents, so do HTML elements. Instead of inheriting genes and money, HTML elements inherit stylistic properties.

Let's start by taking a look at the sample document:

```
<HTML>
  <TITLE>Bach's home page</TITLE>
  <BODY>
    <H1>Bach's home page</H1>
    <P>Johann Sebastian Bach was a
      <STRONG>prolific</STRONG> composer. Among his
        works are:
    <UL>
      <LI>the Goldberg Variations
      <LI>the Brandenburg Concertos
      <LI>the Christmas Oratorio
    </UL>
  </BODY>
</HTML>
```

The tree structure of this document is:

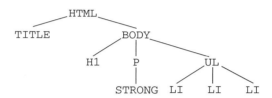

Through inheritance, CSS property values set on one element will be transferred down the tree to its descendants. For example, our examples have up to now set the color to be green for H1 and H2 elements. Now, say, you would like to set the same color on all elements in your document. You could do this by listing all element types in the selector:

```
<STYLE TYPE="text/css">
    H1, H2, P, LI { color: green }
</STYLE>
```

However, most HTML documents are more complex than our sample document, and your style sheet would soon get long. There is a better — and shorter — way. Instead of setting the style on each element type, we set it on their common ancestor, the BODY element:

```
<STYLE TYPE="text/css">
  BODY { color: green }
</STYLE>
```

Since other elements inherit properties from the BODY element, they will all inherit the color green (Figure 2.4).

As you have seen above, inheritance is a transport vehicle that will distribute stylistic properties to descendants of an element. Since the BODY element

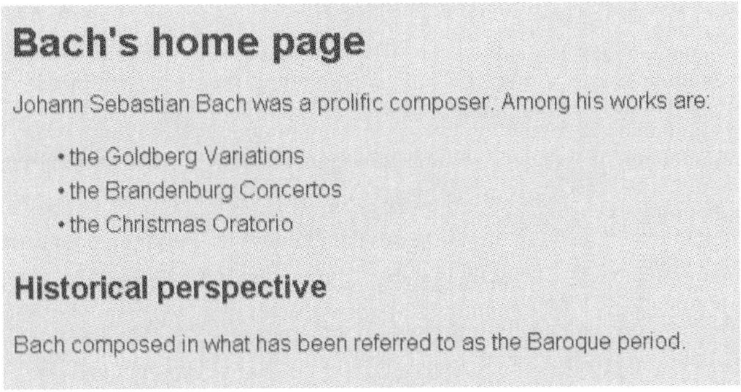

Bach's home page

Johann Sebastian Bach was a prolific composer. Among his works are:

- the Goldberg Variations
- the Brandenburg Concertos
- the Christmas Oratorio

Historical perspective

Bach composed in what has been referred to as the Baroque period.

Figure 2.4 The result of inheritance.

is a common ancestor for all visible elements, BODY is a convenient selector when you want to set stylistic rules for the entire document.

OVERRIDING INHERITANCE

In the previous example, all elements were given the same color through inheritance. Sometimes, however, children don't look like their parents. Not surprisingly, CSS also accounts for this. Say you would like for H1 elements to be blue while the rest should be green. This is easily expressed in CSS:

```
<STYLE TYPE="text/css">
  BODY { color: green }
  H1 { color: navy }
</STYLE>
```

Since H1 is a child element of BODY (and thereby inherits from BODY), the two rules in the above style sheet are conflicting. The first one sets the color of the BODY element – and thereby also the color of H1 through inheritance – while the second one sets the color specifically on the H1 element. Which rule will win? Let's find out:

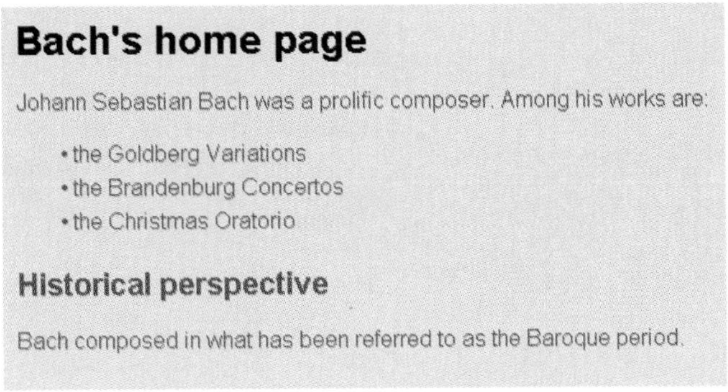

Bach's home page

Johann Sebastian Bach was a prolific composer. Among his works are:

- the Goldberg Variations
- the Brandenburg Concertos
- the Christmas Oratorio

Historical perspective

Bach composed in what has been referred to as the Baroque period.

The reason why the second rule wins is that it is more *specific* than the first. The first rule is very general — it affects all elements on the canvas. The second rule only affects H1 elements in the document and is therefore more specific.

If CSS had been a programming language, the order in which the rules were specified would determine which of them would win. CSS is not a programming language, and in the above example, the order is irrelevant. The result is exactly the same if we use this style sheet:

```
<STYLE TYPE="text/css">
  H1 { color: navy }
  BODY { color: green }
</STYLE>
```

CSS has been designed to resolve conflicts between style sheet rules like the one above. Specificity is one aspect of that. You can find the details in Chapter 15, "Cascading and inheritance."

PROPERTIES THAT DON'T INHERIT

As a general rule, properties in CSS inherit from parent to child elements as described in the previous examples. Some properties, however, don't inherit and there is always a good reason why. We will use the **background** property (described in Chapter 11) as an example of a property that doesn't inherit.

Let's say you want to set a background image for a page. This is a common effect on the Web. In CSS, you can write:

```
<HTML>
  <TITLE>Bach's home page</TITLE>
  <STYLE TYPE="text/css">
    BODY {
      background: url(texture.gif) white;
      color: black;
    }
  </STYLE>
  <BODY>
    <H1>Bach's <EM>home</EM> page</H1>
    <P>Johann Sebastian Bach was a prolific
      composer.
  </BODY>
</HTML>
```

The **background** property has a URL ("texture.gif") that points to a background image as value. When the image is loaded, the canvas looks like:

Bach's *home* page

Johann Sebastian Bach was a prolific composer.

There are a few noteworthy things in the above example:

- The background image covers the surface like a wallpaper – also the backgrounds of the H1 and P element have been covered. This is not due to inheritance, but to the fact that unless otherwise set, all backgrounds are transparent. So, since we haven't set the backgrounds of the H1 or P element to something else, the parent element, BODY, will shine through.
- In addition to the URL of the image, a color (white) has also been specified as the background. In case the image can't be found, you will see the color instead.
- The color of the BODY element has been set to black. To ensure contrast between the text and the background, it is a good habit to always set a **color** when the **background** property is set.

So, exactly why doesn't the **background** property inherit? Visually, the effect of transparency is similar to inheritance: it looks like all elements have the same backgrounds. There are two reasons: first, transparent backgrounds are faster to display (there is nothing to display!) than other backgrounds. Second, since background images are aligned relative to the element they belong to, you would otherwise not always end up with a smooth background surface.

COMMON TASKS WITH CSS

Setting colors and backgrounds – as described above – are among the most common tasks performed by CSS. Other common tasks include setting fonts and white space around elements. This section gives you a guided tour of the most commonly used properties in CSS.

Common tasks: fonts

Let's start with fonts. If you have used desktop publishing applications in the past, you should be able to read this little style sheet:

```
H1 { font: 36pt serif }
```

The rule above sets the font for H1 elements. The first part of the value – **36pt** – sets the font size to be 36 points. A "point" is an old typographic unit of measurement which has survived into the digital age. In the next chapter we will tell you why you should use the "em" unit instead of "pt" but for now we'll stick to points. The second part of the value – **serif** – tells the browser to use a font with serifs (the little hooks at the ends of the strokes, Chapter 5 will tell you all about them). The more decorated serif fonts suit Bach's home page well since the modern sans-serif fonts (fonts without serifs) weren't used in his time. Here is the result:

Bach's home page

Johann Sebastian Bach was a prolific composer. Among his works are:

- the Goldberg Variations
- the Brandenburg Concertos
- the Christmas Oratorio

The **font** property is a shorthand property for setting several other properties at once. By using it, you can shorten your style sheets and set values on all properties it replaces. If you choose to use the expanded version, you would have to set all of these to replace the example above:

```
H1 {
    font-size: 36pt;
    font-family: serif;
    font-style: normal;
    font-weight: normal;
    font-variant: normal;
    line-height: normal;
}
```

Sometimes you only want to set one of these. For example, you may want to slant the text in some elements. Here is an example:

```
UL { font-style: italic }
```

The **font-style** property will not change the font size or the font family, it will only slant the existing font. When set on the UL element, the LI elements inside will become slanted, since **font-style** is inherited. Here is the result when applied to the test page you know by now:

Bach's home page

Johann Sebastian Bach was a prolific composer. Among his works are:

- *the Goldberg Variations*
- *the Brandenburg Concertos*
- *the Christmas Oratorio*

Similarly, the **font-weight** property is used to change the weight – thickness – of the letters. You can further emphasize the list items by setting their ancestor to be **bold**:

```
UL {
    font-style: italic;
    font-weight: bold;
}
```

Which yields:

Bach's home page

Johann Sebastian Bach was a prolific composer. Among his works are:

- ***the Goldberg Variations***
- ***the Brandenburg Concertos***
- ***the Christmas Oratorio***

The last properties, **font-variant** and **line-height**, haven't been widely supported in browsers up to now and are therefore not as commonly used yet.

Common tasks: margins

Setting space around elements is a basic tool in typography. The headline above this paragraph has space above it and (slightly less) space below it. This paragraph, as printed in the book, has space on the left and (slightly less) on the right. CSS can be used to express how much space there should be around different kinds of elements.

By default, your browser knows quite a bit about how to display the different kinds of elements in HTML. For example, it knows that lists and BLOCKQUOTE elements should be indented to set them apart from the rest of the text. As a designer, you can build on these settings while at the same time provide your own refinements. Let's use the BLOCKQUOTE element as an example. Here's a test document:

```
<HTML>
  <TITLE>Fredrick the Great meets Bach</TITLE>
  <BODY>
    <P>One evening, just as Fredrick the Great was
      getting his flute ready, and his musicians
      were assembled, an officer brought him a
      list of the strangers who had arrived. With
      his flute in his hand he ran over the list,
      but immediately turned to the assembled
      musicians, and said, with a kind of
      agitation:
    <BLOCKQUOTE>"Gentlemen, old Bach is come."
    </BLOCKQUOTE>
    <P>The flute was now laid aside, and old Bach, who
      had alighted at his son's lodgings, was immediately
      summoned to the Palace.
  </BODY>
</HTML>
```

The screen-shot below is how a typical HTML browser would display the document:

> One evening, just as Fredrick the Great was getting his flute ready, and his musicians were assembled, an officer brought him a list of the strangers who had arrived. With his flute in his hand he ran over the list, but immediately turned to the assembled musicians, and said, with a kind of agitation:
>
> > "Gentlemen, old Bach is come."
>
> The flute was now laid aside, and old Bach, who had alighted at his son's lodgings, was immediately summoned to the Palace.

As you can see, the browser has added space on all sides of the quoted text. In CSS, this space is called "margins" and all elements have margins on all four sides. The properties are called: **margin-top**, **margin-right**, **margin-bottom**, and **margin-left**. You can change how the BLOCKQUOTE element is displayed by writing a little style sheet:

```
BLOCKQUOTE {
    margin-top: 1em;
    margin-right: 0em;
    margin-bottom: 1em;
    margin-left: 0em;
    font-style: italic;
}
```

The "em" unit will be treated in detail in the next chapter, but we can already now reveal its secret: it scales relative to the font size. So, the above example will result in the vertical margins being as high as the font size (**1em**) of the BLOCKQUOTE, and horizontal margins having zero width. To make sure the quoted text can still be distinguished, it has been given an italic slant. The result is:

> One evening, just as Fredrick the Great was getting his flute ready, and his musicians were assembled, an officer brought him a list of the strangers who had arrived. With his flute in his hand he ran over the list, but immediately turned to the assembled musicians, and said, with a kind of agitation:
>
> *"Gentlemen, old Bach is come."*
>
> The flute was now laid aside, and old Bach, who had alighted at his son's lodgings, was immediately summoned to the Palace.

Just like **font** is a shorthand property to set several font-related properties at once, **margin** is a shorthand property which sets all margin properties. The above example can therefore be written:

```
BLOCKQUOTE {
    margin: 1em 0em 1em 0em;
    font-style: italic;
}
```

The first part of the value – **1em** – is assigned to margin-top. From there it's clockwise: **0em** is assigned to **margin-right**, 1em is assigned to **margin-bottom**, and **0em** is assigned to **margin-left**.

With the left margin set to zero, the quoted text needs more styling to set it apart from the rest of the text. Setting **font-style** to `italic` helps, and adding a background color further amplifies the quote:

```
BLOCKQUOTE {
    margin: 1em 0em 1em 0em;
    font-style: italic;
    background: #EDB;
}
```

The result is:

> One evening, just as Fredrick the Great was getting his flute ready, and his musicians were assembled, an officer brought him a list of the strangers who had arrived. With his flute in his hand he ran over the list, but immediately turned to the assembled musicians, and said, with a kind of agitation:
>
> *"Gentlemen, old Bach is come."*
>
> The flute was now laid aside, and old Bach, who had alighted at his son's lodgings, was immediately summoned to the Palace.

As expected, the background color behind the quote has changed. Unlike previous examples, the color was specified in red/green/blue (RGB) components. RGB colors are described in detail in Chapter 11.

One stylistic problem in the example above is that the background color barely covers the quoted text. The space around the quote – the margin area – does not use the element's background color. CSS has another kind of space, called padding, which uses the background color of the element. In other respects the padding properties are like the margin properties: they add space around an element. Let's add some padding to the quote:

```
BLOCKQUOTE {
    margin: 1em 0em 1em 0em;
    font-style: italic;
    background: #EDB;
    padding: 0.5em;
}
```

The result of setting the padding is added space between the text and the rectangle that surrounds it:

> One evening, just as Fredrick the Great was getting his flute ready, and his musicians were assembled, an officer brought him a list of the strangers who had arrived. With his flute in his hand he ran over the list, but immediately turned to the assembled musicians, and said, with a kind of agitation:
>
> *"Gentlemen, old Bach is come."*
>
> The flute was now laid aside, and old Bach, who had alighted at his son's lodgings, was immediately summoned to the Palace.

Notice that the **padding** property was only given one value (**0.5em**). Just like the **margin** property, **padding** could have taken 4 values which would have been assigned to the top, right, bottom and left padding respectively. However, when the same value is to be set on all sides, listing it once will suffice. This is true both for **padding** and **margin** (as well as some other border properties, which are described in Chapter 9).

Common tasks: links

To make it easier for users to browse in hypertext documents, the links should have a style that distinguishes them from normal text. HTML browsers have often underlined hyperlink text. Also, various color schemes have been used to indicate if the user has previously visited the link or not. Since hyperlinks are such a fundamental part of the Web, CSS has special support for styling them. Here's a simple example:

```
A:link { text-decoration: underline }
```

The above example specifies that unvisited links should be underlined:

Bach's home page

Johann Sebastian Bach was a prolific composer. Among his works are:

- the Goldberg Variations
- the Brandenburg Concertos
- the Christmas Oratorio

The links are underlined, as we have specified, but they are also blue, which we have not. When authors do not specify all possible styles, browsers use default styles to fill in the gaps. The interaction between author styles, browser default styles and user styles (the user's own preferences) is another example of CSS's conflict resolution rules. It is called the cascade (the "C" of CSS). We will discuss the cascade below.

The selector (**A:link**) deserves special mentioning. You probably recognize "A" as being an HTML element, but the last part is new. "*:link*" is one of several so-called pseudo-classes in CSS. Pseudo-classes are used to give style to elements based on information outside of the document itself. For example, the author of the document can't know if a certain link will be visited or not. Pseudo-classes are described in detail in Chapter 4, and we'll only give a few more examples here:

```
A:visited { text-decoration: none }
```

This rule gives style to visited links, just like **A:link** gave style to unvisited links. Here is a slightly more complex example:

```
A:link, A:visited { text-decoration: none }
A:hover { background: cyan }
```

The last rule introduces a new pseudo-class *:hover*. Assuming the user is moving a pointing device (like a mouse), the specified style will be applied to the element when the user moves the pointer over ("hovers" over) the link. A common effect is to change the background color. Here is what it looks like:

Bach's home page

Johann Sebastian Bach was a prolific composer. Among his works are:

- the Goldberg Variations
- the Brandenburg Concertos
- the Christmas Oratorio

The *:hover* pseudo-class has an interesting history. It was introduced in CSS2 after the hover effect became popular among JavaScript programmers. The JavaScript solution requires complicated code compared to the CSS pseudo-class and this is an example of CSS picking up effects that have become popular among Web designers.

A WORD ABOUT CASCADING

A fundamental feature of CSS is that more than one style sheet can influence the presentation of a document. This feature is known as *cascading* because the different style sheets are thought of as coming in a series. Cascading is a fundamental feature of CSS, because we realized that any single document could very likely end up with style sheets from multiple sources: the browser, the designer, and possibly the user.

In the last set of examples you saw that the text color of the links turned blue without that being specified in the style sheet. Also, the browser knew how to format BLOCKQUOTE and H1 elements without being told so explicitly. Everything that the browser knows about formatting is stored in the browser's *default style sheet* and is merged with author and user style sheets when the document is displayed.

We have known for years that designers want to develop their own style sheets. However, we discovered that users, too, want the option of influencing the presentation of their documents. With CSS, they can do this by supplying a personal style sheet that will be merged with the browser's and the designer's style sheets. Any conflicts between the various style sheets are resolved by the browser. Usually, the designer's style sheet will have the strongest claim on the document, followed by the user's, and then the browser's default. However, the user can say that a rule is very important and it will then override any author or browser styles.

We go into details about cascading in Chapter 15, "Cascading and inheritance." Before that, there is much to learn about fonts, space and colors.

Chapter 3

The amazing em unit and other best practices

This chapter is about writing style sheets with style. By showing you case studies and how they are constructed, we hope to give you a sense of how CSS can be used to encode the visual presentation you want to achieve. Also, more importantly, if you follow the guidelines in this chapter your documents will behave well on a wide range of web devices. For example, they will scale gracefully from one screen size to another.

The foremost tool for writing scalable style sheets is the "em" unit, and it therefore goes on top of the list of guidelines that we will compile throughout this chapter: *use ems to make scalable style sheets.* Named after the letter "M," the em unit has a long-standing tradition in typography where it has been used to measure horizontal widths. For example, the long dash often found in American texts (—) is known as an "em-dash" since historically it has had the same width as the letter "M." Its narrower cousin (–), often found in European texts is similarly referred to as "en-dash."

The meaning of "em" has changed over the years. Not all fonts have the letter "M" in them (for example Chinese), but all fonts have a height. The term has therefore come to mean the height of the font – not the width of the letter "M."

In CSS, the em unit is a general unit for measuring lengths; for example, page margins and padding around elements. You can use it both horizontally

Use ems to make scalable style sheets!

and vertically, and this shocks traditional typographers who have always used the em exclusively for horizontal measurements. By extending the em unit to also work vertically, it has become a very powerful unit – so powerful that you seldom have to use other units of length.

Let's look at a simple example where we use the em unit to set font sizes:

```
<HTML>
  <STYLE>
    H1 { font-size: 2em }
  </STYLE>
  <BODY>
    <H1>Movies</H1>
  </BODY>
</HTML>
```

When used to specify font sizes, the em unit refers to the font size of the parent element. So, in the example above, the font size of the H1 element is set to be two times the font size of the BODY element. In order to find what the font size of the H1 element will be, we need to know the font size of BODY. Since this isn't specified in the the style sheet, the browser will have to find it from somewhere else – a good place to look is in the user's preferences. So, if the user has set the normal font size to be 10 points, the size of the H1 element will be 20 points. This will make document headlines stand out relative to the surrounding text. Therefore: *always use ems to set font sizes!*

Designers who come from desktop publishing may be inclined to skip the indirection that em introduces and specify directly that the font size should be 20 points. This is possible in CSS (see the description of the **font-size** property in Chapter 5) but using "em" is a better solution. Say, for example, that a sight-impaired user sets his normal font size to **20pt** (20 points). If the font size of H1 is **2em** – as we recommend – H1 elements will scale accordingly and be displayed in 40 points. If, however, the style sheet sets the font size to be **20pt**, there will be no scaling of fonts and the size of headlines will have the same size as the surrounding text.

The usefulness of the em unit isn't limited to font sizes. Figure 3.1 shows a page design where all lengths – including the padding and margins around elements – are specified in ems.

Let's first consider the *padding*. In CSS, padding is space around an element which is added to set the element apart from the rest of the content. The color of the padding is always the same as the background color of the element it surrounds. In Figure 3.1, the menu on the right has been given a padding with this rule:

```
DIV.menu { padding: 1.5em }
```

Always use ems to set font sizes!

EMS ARE RELATIVE TO USER'S PREFERENCES

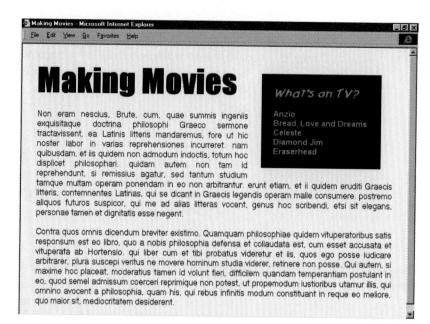

Figure 3.1 All lengths on this page are specified using ems.

EMS ARE RELATIVE

By specifying the padding width in ems, the width of the padding is relative to the font size of the DIV element. As a designer, you don't really care what the exact width of the padding is on the user's screen, what you care about is the proportions of the page you are composing. If the font size of an element increases, the padding around the element should also increase. This is shown in Figure 3.2 where the font size of the menu has increased while the proportions remain constant. (You can learn more about padding in Chapter 9.)

Outside the menu's padding is the margin area. The margin area ensures that there is enough space around an element so that the page doesn't appear cramped. The margin around the menu is set with this rule:

```
DIV.menu { margin: 1.5em }
```

Figure 3.2 identifies the margin area. Again, the use of ems ensures scalable designs.

Another use of ems can be found in this book where the indent of the first line of most paragraphs to is set to **1.8em**. The same value is used for the left margin of code examples, such as this:

```
P { text-indent: 1.8em }
PRE { margin-left: 1.8em }
```

So, if ems are so great, why does CSS have other units as well? There are cases when it makes sense to use other units. For example, here is a case where percentages may work just as well, if not better: setting the margins

padding

Figure 3.2 Since margins and padding are specified in ems they will scale relative to the font size.

margin

of the BODY element. Remember that everything that is displayed in an HTML page is inside BODY, so setting the margins of that element sets the overall shape of the page. You could give the page nice wide margins on both sides with these two rules:

```
BODY {
    margin-left: 15%;
    margin-right: 10%
}
```

This makes the text 75% of the total width, and the left margin a bit wider than the right one. Try it! Your page immediately looks more professional. Percentage values set on the BODY element will typically be calculated with respect to the browser window. So, in the example above, the text will cover 75% of the browser window.

Use relative units for lengths!

Both ems and percentages are *relative units* – which means they are computed with respect to something. We can distill a general rule from this: *use relative units for lengths*. But, how about the *absolute units* in CSS – inches, centimeters, points, picas – why are they in there at all if you never recommend their use?

There are cases when they should be used. Say, for example, that you are doing your wedding invitations using XML and CSS. You have carefully crafted tags such as `<BESTMAN>` and `<RSVP/>` and you plan to distribute the invitations through the Web. However, parts of your families are not yet connected and require printed invitations. On handmade paper, of course. With proper margins. And 12 point fonts, exactly. This is the time for pulling out the obsolete, ehh… absolute length units: *only use absolute length units when the physical characteristics of the output medium are known.* In practice, this only happens when you hand-tailor a style sheet for a specific printer paper size. In all other cases you are better off using relative length units.

A common presentation on the Web is to move elements to the sides of the page. Typically, this is achieved by using a table for layout purposes. Although you can use CSS to describe table layout (see Chapter 19), there is also a simpler way to "put stuff on the side." In HTML, images can be floating, *i.e.*, they move over to the side while allowing text to "wrap around" them. In CSS, all elements – not just images – can be floating. The menu in Figures 3.1 and 3.2 is an example of a floating element that has been set to float to the right side of the page. There are two steps to achieving this effect. First, the element must be declared to be floating using the **float** property. Second, the element must be given an appropriate width (in ems of course). This is done through the **width** property. Here are the two rules needed:

```
DIV.menu {
    float: right;
    width: 15em;
}
```

By using floating text elements instead of tables, your markup can remain simple while achieving many of the visual effects which are often accomplished with tables in HTML. Thus, we have another guideline: *use floating elements instead of tables.* Simpler markup isn't the only reason why floating elements are good replacements for tables. Flexible layout schemes are another. By changing a few lines in the style sheet which generated the page in Figure 3.1 we can, for example move the menu to the left side (see Figure 3.3). Also, many text-only browsers have problems displaying tables since content within the table doesn't come in its logical order.

This brings us to the next guideline: *put content in its logical order.* Even though CSS allows you to move text around on the screen by means of floats and other ways of positioning, you should not rely on that. By putting content in its logical order you ensure that you document will make sense in browsers which don't support CSS. That includes browsers that work in text-mode, such as Lynx, older browsers that date from before CSS,

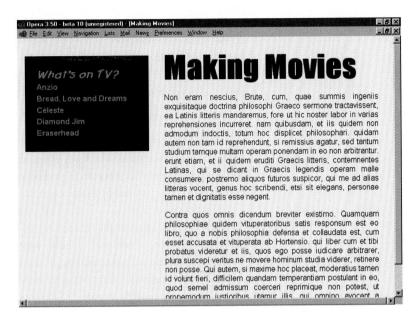

Figure 3.3 By changing a few lines in the style sheets, a different design can be achieved.

browsers whose users have turned style sheets off, or browsers that don't work visually at all: voice browsers and Braille browsers. Voice browsers may actually support CSS, since CSS can also describe the style of spoken pages, but aural CSS (see Chapter 13) doesn't allow text to be spoken out of order.

Make sure your documents are legible without style sheets!

And even a browser that supports CSS may sometimes fail to load the style sheet, due to a network error. Therefore, you should always: *make sure your documents are legible without style sheets.* Legible to humans, but also to Web robots and other software, that try to index, summarize, or translate your documents. And think of the future: in 5 years from now the style sheet may be lost, in 50 years there may not be a browser that knows CSS, and in 500 years... .

Test your documents on several browsers!

A good way to make sure your documents are really legible is to: *test your documents on several browsers.* Alas, not all browsers which claim to support CSS do so according to W3C's specification. How much effort you should put into testing your style sheets depends on the target audience of your documents. If you publish on a closed intranet where everyone uses the same browser, your testing job will be easy. If, on the other hand, your documents are openly available on the Web, testing can be a time-consuming task. One way to avoid doing all the testing yourself is to use one of the W3C Core Styles which are freely available on the Web (see Chapter 16).

Always specify a fallback generic font!

Realize that your document will end up on systems that have different fonts. CSS specifies five so-called *generic fonts* which are guaranteed to exist in all browsers: **serif**, **sans-serif**, **monospace**, **cursive** and **fantasy**.

55 • **The amazing em unit and other best practices**

When specifying a font family in CSS you have the option of supplying a list to increase the chance of finding a specified font at the user's system. The last font family in the list should always be a generic font. So: *always specify a fallback generic font*. This book, e.g., has been set in "Gill Sans." But not everybody has a copy of that font, so we actually specified the font as

```
BODY { font-family: "Gill Sans", sans-serif }
```

which says that the font for the document's body is "Gill Sans" when available, or any other sans-serif font, when not. Depending on your browser and your machine's configuration, you may get Helvetica, or Arial, or something similar. You can learn more about setting fonts in Chapter 5.

Use numbers, not names, for colors!

Color names also vary from one platform to another. CSS supports 16 color names: aqua, black, blue, fuchsia, gray, green, lime, maroon, navy, olive, purple, red, silver, teal, yellow, white. Some browsers have chosen to support additional color names, but there is no definite list. Therefore, you should: *use numbers, not names, for colors*. Color names may seem friendlier than the somewhat cryptic RGB notation introduced in the previous chapter, but the Web has yet to see the ultimate list of color names that work on all platforms. Color numbers, on the other hand, can easily be interpreted by any browser.

You may have to experiment a bit to get the exact color you want, or find some software that helps you mix the right colors. CSS supports the hexadecimal notation ("#FF0000" and "#F00") and also some other notations that may be easier to use. The following two rules both set the color of H1 elements to brown (50% red, 50% green, 0% blue):

```
H1 {color: #808000}
H1 {color: rgb(50%,50%,0%)}
```

You can learn all about colors in Chapter 11.

Know when to stop!

A word of warning at the end: *know when to stop*. Be critical when designing your style sheet. Just because you can use 10 different fonts and 30 different colors on the same page doesn't mean you have to – or should. Simple style sheets will often convey your message better than overloaded ones. That single word of red in a page of black gets much more attention then any of the words on a page with a dozen different fonts and colors. If you think a piece of your text deserves more attention, try giving it larger margins, maybe even on all four sides. A little extra space can do wonders.

Chapter 4

CSS selectors

In the preceding chapters we have already used a number of selectors, most of which select elements by their type; for example, H1 or P. This chapter describes all the possible ways in which elements can be selected, from simple ones, like the type selectors, to advanced, such as selectors that look for elements with a combination of characteristics.

We start with the simple, and most common ones, and show how they can be combined into powerful, but still simple, selectors. The second half of the chapter contains the advanced selectors. See also Chapter 15 for the cascading rules that decide which selector wins in case of conflicts.

SELECTOR SCHEMES

To give you enough freedom to select which elements a style is applied to, CSS2 supports four selector schemes. Each is based on some aspect of an element:

- an element's type
- an element's attributes
- the context in which the element is used
- external information about the element

Also, CSS2 includes a way of attaching style rules to an element without using a traditional selector; the STYLE attribute effectively bypasses the whole selector mechanism.

The four schemes can be combined in a single selector, to put style properties on elements that exhibit a combination of characteristics. For example, the selector "H1 EM" uses element types (H1 and EM) as well as context (EM must be inside H1).

TYPE SELECTORS

The simplest kind of selector in CSS is the name of an element type. Using this kind of selector, which is called a *type selector*, you apply the declaration to every instance of the element type. For example, the selector of the following simple rule is **H1**, so the rule affects all H1 elements in a document:

```
H1 { color: red }
```

We used type selectors in Chapter 2, "CSS."

If you find yourself writing several style rules that are the same except for the selector, for example:

```
H1 { color: red }
H2 { color: red }
H3 { color: red }
```

you can write this more briefly by *grouping* the selectors in a comma-separated list:

```
H1, H2, H3 { color: red }
```

It is a matter of taste whether you want to use this grouping mechanism or not.

When selecting HTML elements, type selectors are case-insensitive. Therefore, the following four rules are equivalent:

```
BLOCKQUOTE { margin-left: 2em }
BlockQuote { margin-left: 2em }
blockquote { margin-left: 2em }
BLockQUoTE { margin-left: 2em }
```

(For now, don't worry about the margin declarations; margins are explained in "Using the padding property" in Chapter 9.)

SIMPLE ATTRIBUTE SELECTORS

One of the most powerful ways on which to base selection is on an attribute. Recall from Chapter 1, "The Web and HTML," that an attribute is a characteristic quality, other than the type or content of an element. In that chapter we discussed the attributes HREF, SRC, and ALT. In this section we will discuss two other attributes: CLASS and ID.

Both these attributes can be used with any HTML element and we will see how they can create powerful selectors. They are not the only attributes that can occur in a selector, but they are very common, and CSS makes using CLASS and ID especially easy. How to refer to other attributes is explained below, in the section "Advanced attribute selectors" on page 73.

The CLASS attribute

The CLASS attribute enables you to apply declarations to a group of elements that have the same value on the CLASS attribute. All elements inside BODY can have a CLASS attribute. Essentially, you *classify* elements with the CLASS attribute, create rules in your style sheet that refer to the value of the CLASS attribute, and then the browser will automatically apply those rules to the group of elements.

For example, say you are an actor rehearsing for the role of Polonius in Shakespeare's *Hamlet*. In your copy of the manuscript you would like all lines by Polonius to stand out. The first step to achieving this is to classify Polonius' lines, that is, set the CLASS attribute on all elements containing lines by Polonius. Here is how you set the CLASS value:

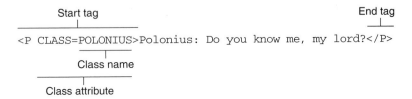

Figure 4.1 Setting a CLASS attribute on an HTML element.

In the above example, the class name chosen is "POLONIUS." Authors pick class names.

Class names must be single words, although you can use digits and dashes. The following are all acceptable class names:

- POLONIUS
- name-10
- first-remark

But the following are not:

- The man   (contains space)
- item+12   (contains plus sign)
- last!!   (contains exclamation mark)

In contrast to element names, class names are case-sensitive. That means you must spell class names in the style sheet with exactly the same uppercase and lowercase letters as in the HTML source file.

The next step is to write style rules with selectors that refers to the class name. A selector that includes a class name is called a *class selector*. Here is a rule with a selector that selects all of Polonius' elements:

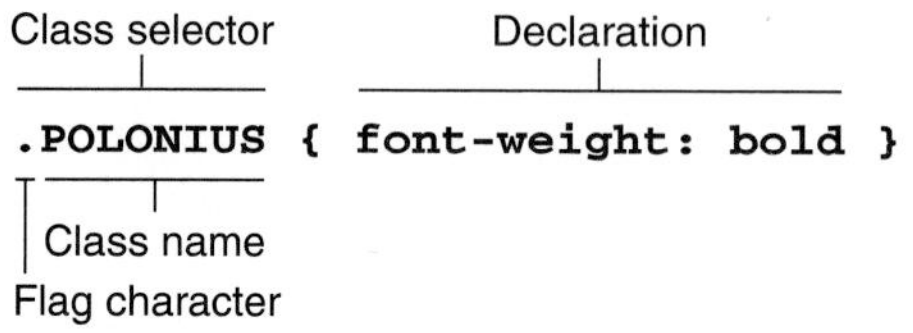

```
Class selector            Declaration
     |              |                    |
.POLONIUS { font-weight: bold }
        |
     | Class name
Flag character
```

Figure 4.2 Anatomy of a rule with a class selector.

The class selector starts with a *flag character* (the period) which signals what type of selector follows. For class selectors, the period was chosen since it is associated with the term "class" in many programming languages. Translated into English, the flag character reads "elements with class name." The whole selector says: "elements with class name POLONIUS." Authors are free to choose class names. Assuming you have consistently classified elements containing lines by Polonius, they will be printed in a bold font.

Let's look at a complete example that introduces a second class:

```
<HTML>
  <TITLE>Hamlet, excerpt from act II</TITLE>
  <STYLE TYPE="text/css">
    .POLONIUS { font-weight: bold }
    .HAMLET { font-weight: normal }
  </STYLE>
  <BODY>
    <P CLASS=POLONIUS>
      Polonius: Do you know me, my lord?
    <P CLASS=HAMLET>
      Hamlet: Excellent well,
      you are a fishmonger.
    <P CLASS=POLONIUS>
      Polonius: Not I, my lord.
    <P CLASS=HAMLET>
      Hamlet: Then I would you
```

Similar to setting anchors within a document (handwritten margin note)

```
                    were so honest a man.
        </BODY>
      </HTML>
```

In the above example, two classes have been defined, HAMLET and POLONIUS. The style sheet in the STYLE element sets the font weight (the "thickness" of the fonts, see Chapter 5, "Fonts") to be different. The result can be seen in the figure below.

Polonius: Do you know me, my lord?

Hamlet: Excellent well, you are a fishmonger.

Polonius: Not I, my lord.

Hamlet: Then I would you were so honest a man.

Figure 4.3 The formatted fragment with Polonius' lines in bold.

As you can see, Polonius' lines stand out: an invaluable tool when you rehearse a role.

One could argue that the same result could be achieved without style sheets. By enclosing Polonius' lines in STRONG or B elements they would also come out in a bold. This is true, but consider the consequences when the actor who is scheduled to play Hamlet catches a cold and you have to replace him. Now you suddenly need Hamlet's lines to stand out and Polonius' lines to use the normal font weight. If you had been using STRONG elements to emphasize Polonius' lines, you'd have to remove them and add them to Hamlet's lines instead. But, if you are using CSS, you simply change two lines in the style sheet:

REASON FOR USING STYLE SHEET!

```
.POLONIUS { font-weight: normal }
.HAMLET { font-weight: bold }
```

This will reverse the effect and Hamlet's lines will stand out:

Polonius: Do you know me, my lord?

Hamlet: Excellent well, you are a fishmonger.

Polonius: Not I, my lord.

Hamlet: Then I would you were so honest a man.

Figure 4.4 The same fragment from Shakespeare, but with the font weights reversed.

The CLASS attribute is a very powerful feature of CSS. We recommend that you use the CLASS attribute to add more information about elements, information that can be used to enhance the presentation of your documents. We do not recommend that you use the CLASS attribute to totally change the presentation of an element. For example, you can easily change an LI element to look like an H1 element by classifying it. If you want an element to look like H1, we would rather recommend that you mark it up as H1. Do not let style sheets replace the structure of your documents; rather, let the style sheets enhance the structure.

The ID attribute

The ID attribute works like the CLASS attribute with one important difference: the value of an ID attribute must be unique throughout the document. That is, every element inside BODY can have an ID attribute, but the values must all be different. This makes the ID attribute useful for setting style rules on individual elements. A selector that includes an ID attribute is called an *ID selector*. The general form of an ID selector resembles that of the class selector in the previous section:

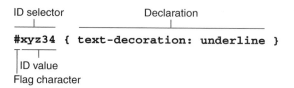

Figure 4.5 Anatomy of a rule with an ID selector.

Notice that the flag character for ID selectors is a hash mark (#). The flag character alerts the browser that an ID value is coming up next. In English, the above selector says "the element with an ID value equal to xyz34." The entire rule reads: "the element with an ID value equal to xyz43 is to be underlined." The author is free to pick the value of the ID attribute, and the chosen value is case-insensitive.

The HTML syntax of the element on which you want to use the ID attribute resembles that of other elements with attributes; for example:

```
<P ID=xyz34>Underlined text</P>
```

Combined with the style sheet rule above, the content of the element will be underlined. Because the value of the ID attribute must be unique, you could not also include in the same document another usage of it, such as:

```
<H1 ID=xyz34>A headline</H1>
<P ID=xyz34>Underlined text</P>    <!-- WRONG! -->
```

Rather, you would have to give the two elements different ID values:

```
<H1 ID=xyz34>A headline</H1>
<P ID=xyz35>Underlined text</P>
```

Here is a complete example using an ID selector:

```
<HTML>
  <TITLE>ID showoff</TITLE>
  <STYLE TYPE="text/css">
    #xyz34 { text-decoration: underline }
  </STYLE>
  <BODY>
    <P ID=xyz34>Underlined text</P>
  </BODY>
</HTML>
```

By using the ID selectors, you can set style properties on a per-element basis. Like CLASS, ID is a powerful feature. It carries the same cautions we set out in the previous section.

THE STYLE ATTRIBUTE

The STYLE attribute is different from the other attributes described in this chapter. Whereas CLASS and ID attribute values can be used in selectors, the STYLE attribute is actually a replacement for the whole selector mechanism. Instead of having a value that can be referred to in a selector (which is what ID and CLASS have), the value of the STYLE attribute is actually one or more CSS declarations.

Normally, using CSS, a designer will put all style rules into a style sheet that goes into the STYLE element at the top of the document (or is LINKed externally as described in Chapter 16, "External style sheets"). However, using the STYLE attribute, you can bypass the style sheet and put declarations directly into the start tags of your document.

Here is one example:

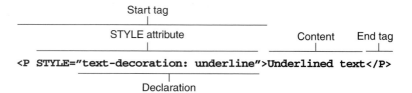

Figure 4.6 An HTML element with style rules embedded in the start tag.

The example above attaches a declaration to a single element and results in underlining the content of the element. You will recall from the example in the previous section that the ID attribute accomplishes the very same thing: setting style on a single element. Whereas the ID attribute involves an indirection, the STYLE attribute bypasses the style sheet and puts the declaration directly into the start tag of the element it applies to. Properties set using the STYLE attribute are treated exactly in the same manner as if the property had been set in a style sheet using an ID selector.

You could conceivably use the STYLE attribute to apply styles to just about anything and everything. For example, you could use the STYLE attribute this way (shown in bold):

```
<HTML>
  <TITLE>Hamlet, excerpt from act II</TITLE>
  <BODY STYLE="color: black; background: white">
    <P STYLE="font-weight: bold">
    Polonius: Do you know me, my lord?
    <P STYLE="font-weight: normal">
    Hamlet: Excellent well,
    you are a fishmonger.
    <P STYLE="font-weight: bold">
    Polonius: Not I, my lord.
    <P STYLE="font-weight: normal">
    Hamlet: Then I would you
    were so honest a man.
  </BODY>
</HTML>
```

This use of the STYLE attribute is legal, but there are two reasons why you should not, in general, use the STYLE attribute. First, it's the long way to go about setting styles. Since the declarations in the STYLE attribute only apply to the element where they are specified, there is no way to reuse your declarations and your documents will get longer. Also, if you later want to change the presentation of your document, you will have to make changes in more places. Second, by interleaving style and content, you miss out on an important advantage of style sheets: the separation of content and presentation. By putting all your style settings into a style sheet, you can make your style sheets apply to more than one document (see Chapter 16, "External style sheets," for how the LINK element can be used for this).

The rather messy use of the STYLE attribute above can be rewritten into:

```
<HTML>
  <TITLE>Hamlet, excerpt from act II</TITLE>
  <STYLE TYPE="text/css">
    BODY { color: black; background: white }
    .POLONIUS { font-weight: bold }
    .HAMLET { font-weight: normal }
  </STYLE>
  <BODY>
```

```
<P CLASS=POLONIUS>
  Polonius: Do you know me, my lord
<P CLASS=HAMLET>
  Hamlet: Excellent well,
  you are a fishmonger.
<P CLASS=POLONIUS>
  Polonius: Not I, my lord.
<P CLASS=HAMLET>
  Hamlet: Then I would you
  were so honest a man.
</BODY>
</HTML>
```

So use the STYLE *element* to apply styles to all of a type of element. Save the STYLE *attribute* for those occasional stylistic changes you want to make to an element while leaving alone the style of all others of the same element type.

COMBINING SELECTOR TYPES

Three kinds of selector have been described in this chapter up to now: type selectors, ID selectors and class selectors. Often, different selector types are combined to form more complex selectors. By combining selectors you can more accurately target elements that you want to give a certain presentation. For example, by combining a type selector and a class selector, an element must fulfill both requirements: it must be of the right type *and* the right class in order to be influenced by the style rule. Let's look at one example:

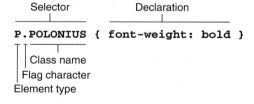

Figure 4.7 A combined type and class selector.

In English the selector above reads: "P elements with class name POLONIUS." That is, an element must be of the right type (P) and it must also be of the right class (POLONIUS). Compare the above example with this selector:

```
.POLONIUS { font-weight: bold }
```

The latter example omits the element type and starts off with the flag character. By doing so, it selects all elements with the right class, no matter what type the element is.

We will see more examples of how to combine different kinds of selectors later in this chapter.

SIMPLE CONTEXTUAL SELECTORS

A *contextual selector* is a selector that takes into account the context in which the style is to be applied. That is, the specified style is applied to an element only if the element is in the specified context. An element's context is formed by its ancestor elements and the elements that precede it. In this section we only look at the ancestors. The section "Advanced contextual selectors" on page 77 describes how other contexts can be added to a selector.

Suppose you were to write these two rules:

```
H1 { color: red }
EM { color: red }
```

These rules will work fine. H1 headings will turn red, and so will EM elements. Now, suppose you have this code in your document:

```
<H1>This headline is <EM>very</EM> important.</H1>
```

You want to emphasize "very" but because both the EM and the H1 are set to red, you will lose the emphasis provided by EM. You want both EM and H1 to stay red for the document as a whole, but for EM elements inside H1, you're going to have to come up with some other way to emphasize "very." You still want to use the EM element. How do you do it?

Using a contextual selector, you can specify a rule that only applies to EMS that are inside H1 elements. No other EM elements will be affected. Consider this rule:

```
H1 EM { color: blue }
```

In English, this rule is saying: "For any EM that is inside H1, make it blue (and not red like the previous rule specified)." Thus the EM will be made blue only in the context of an H1. In all other contexts, it will be red as usual. Hence, the name contextual selector.

Contextual selectors are made up of two or more simple selectors separated by white space. Any type, class or ID selector is a simple selector. Also, combinations of type and class selectors, as described in the previous section, are regarded as simple selectors.

You fine-tune your contextual selector by including more simple selectors. For example:

```
UL UL { list-style: lower-roman }      /* rule 1 */
OL UL { list-style: decimal }          /* rule 2 */
UL UL UL { list-style: lower-alpha }   /* rule 3 */
```

Here we have used three contextual selectors. The first selects all UL elements that appear inside another UL. The second selects all UL elements that appear inside an OL. The third selects all UL elements that have *two* other ULS as ancestors: they are at least the third level of UL lists. Figure 4.8 shows the result of these three rules.

Figure 4.8 The effect of the three contextual selectors on nested OL and UL lists: (a) three nested UL lists; (b) two nested UL lists inside an OL list.

```
1. First item at the first level in a UL list          • First bullet in an OL list
    i. First sub-item: "UL UL"                              1. First sub-item: "OL UL"
        a. Sub-sub-item: "UL UL UL"                            1. Sub-sub-item: "OL UL"
        b. Second sub-sub-item                                 2. Second sub-sub-item
    ii. Second sub-item                                    2. Second item at a sub-level
        a. Another sub-sub-item                                1. Another sub-sub-item
    iii. Third sub-item                                    3. Third item at a sub-level
2. Second item at the first level                      • Second bullet in an OL list
3. Third item at the first level                       • Third bullet in an OL list
                (a)                                                (b)
```

Note that any third-level UL also matches rule 1, since, after all, it is inside at least one UL. But CSS favors longer, more specific selectors over shorter ones, so the **list-style** property will be set by rule 3. The details of these cascading rules are explained in Chapter 15.

EXTERNAL INFORMATION: PSEUDO-CLASSES AND PSEUDO-ELEMENTS

In CSS1, style is normally based on the tags and attributes as found in the HTML source. This works fine for many design scenarios, but it doesn't cover some common design effects designers want to achieve.

Pseudo-classes and pseudo-elements were devised to fill in some of these gaps. Both are mechanisms that extend the expressive power of CSS. In CSS1, using pseudo-classes, you can change the style of a document's links based on whether and when the links have been visited, or based on how the user is interacting with the document. Using pseudo-elements, you can change the style of the first letter and first line of an element, or add elements that were not present in the source document. Neither pseudo-classes nor pseudo-elements exist in HTML, that is, they are not visible in the HTML code. Both mechanisms have been designed so that they can be further extended in future versions of CSS; *i.e.*, fill in more gaps.

This section describes the pseudo-classes to format hyperlinks, and the pseudo-elements to set properties on the first letter and first line of a paragraph. Other pseudo-classes and pseudo-elements will be introduced in the sections "Advanced pseudo-classes" on page 78 and "Advanced pseudo-elements" on page 81.

The anchor pseudo-classes

In HTML, there is only one element that can be a hyperlink: the A (anchor) element. In document formats written in XML there can be others. An *anchor pseudo-class* is a mechanism by which a browser indicates to a user the status of a hyperlink in the document the user is viewing.

A browser typically displays a link in a document in a different color from the rest of the text. Links that a user hasn't visited will be one color. Links the user has visited will be another color.

There is no way for an author to know whether a user has visited a link; this information is known only to the browser. However, you can set in the style sheet the colors that indicate the status of links. This is done by including an anchor pseudo-class in the selector:

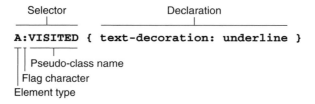

Figure 4.9 Anatomy of a rule with an anchor pseudo-class.

There are several things to note in the above figure:

- The selector is a combination of a type selector and a pseudo-class selector. Since in HTML only A elements can have anchor pseudo-classes, the A could have been omitted, but the selector arguably looks nicer.
- The flag character is a colon (:). Both pseudo-classes and pseudo-elements use the colon as the flag character.

All links in a document (that is, all A elements with an HREF attribute) are automatically classified as either visited (`:visited`) or unvisited (`:link`).

Initially, a link is in pseudo-class "link." If the link has been visited recently, the browser will put it into pseudo-class "visited." (How recent the visit has to be is up to the browser.) The names of pseudo-classes and pseudo-elements are case-insensitive.

Here are some examples:

```
A:link { color: red }      /* unvisited link */
A:visited { color: blue }  /* visited link */
```

The first-letter and first-line pseudo-elements

Pseudo-elements allow you to set style on a subpart of an element's content. Like pseudo-classes, pseudo-elements don't exist in the HTML code. Pseudo-elements have been introduced to allow for designs that would otherwise not have been possible.

Two of these pseudo-elements are "first-letter" and "first-line." The effects of these elements are not related to the structure of the HTML document. Rather, the effects are based on how the element is formatted. They enable you to impose styles on the first letter of a word and on the first line of a paragraph, respectively, independent of any other styles. Both can only be attached to block-level elements (that is, elements with their **display** property set to **block**, see Chapter 7.)

These effects are not new. Traditional printers have been using them for centuries, and you will often find them in use in contemporary magazines. A common usage is to increase the size of the first letter or make the first line use uppercase letters. However, you can also set the properties for color, background, text decorations and case transformation among others.

According to the CSS1 specification, CSS1 browsers are not required to support pseudo-elements. CSS2 makes no such exception, but you may encounter browsers that do not support the first-letter and first-line pseudo-elements.

A pseudo-element has the following general form:

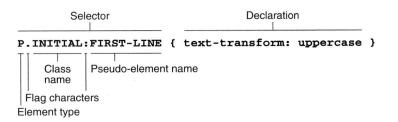

Figure 4.11 Anatomy of a rule with a type selector, a class selector, and a pseudo-element.

a pseudo-element selector will almost always be used in combination with other selectors. this is because you seldom want pseudo-element formatting on all elements in your document. above, the pseudo-element selector

L e 23 juin, le Palace a ér million de francs, à Pie propriétaires de nomb parisiennes. Or le premier c ancien président de chambre Paris, «encore en fonctions le ; date de l'ouverture de la procé

Figure 4.10 The beginning of an article showing a "drop-cap."

is combined with two other selectors: a type selector (P) and a class selector (.INITIAL). the resulting selector reads: "the first line of P elements with class name initial." the above rule is the first step on the way to create a style sheet that replicates the style of articles in magazines like time. let's put the above rule into a complete document:

```
<HTML>
  <TITLE>The style of TIME magazine</TITLE>
  <STYLE TYPE="text/css">
    P.initial:first-line {
      text-transform: uppercase }
  </STYLE>
  <BODY>
    <H1>A sample article</H1>
    <P CLASS=initial>The first line
      of the first paragraph in a TIME
      magazine article is printed in
      uppercase letters.
    <P>The text in the second paragraph
      has no special formatting.
  </BODY>
</HTML>
```

Figure 4.12 shows how this could be displayed.

It doesn't make any difference how long the line is or how many words are on it. Whatever text happens to fall on the first line will be displayed in uppercase. Because browser windows can be resized, there is no way to know how many words will be on the first line of a paragraph, so using a pseudo-element is the only way to achieve this effect.

The style sheet for TIME magazine is still missing a key design feature: the drop-cap initial letter. A drop-cap initial is a common trick in typography: the first letter of a text is enlarged and "dropped" into the formatted paragraph. We can attach style rules to the first letter of an element by using, you guessed it, the "first-letter" pseudo-element:

```
P.initial:first-letter { font-size: 200% }
```

The selector in the above example reads: "The first letter of P elements with class name initial." That is, the style rule will apply to the first letter of lines that were affected in the example above. The whole rule says: "The first letter of P elements with class name 'initial' should have a font size two times bigger than the surrounding text." Formatted, the text now looks as in Figure 4.13.

We're almost there! The first letter now has the right size, but not the right position; it's not "dropped" into the formatted paragraph. By making

---

A sample article

THE FIRST LINE OF THE first paragraph in a TIME magazine article is printed in uppercase letters.

The text in the second paragraph has no special formatting.

Figure 4.12 Rendering of the first TIME example.

A sample article

T HE FIRST LINE OF the first paragraph in a TIME magazine article is printed in uppercase letters.

The text in the second paragraph has no special formatting.

Figure 4.13 Rendering of the TIME example with a large initial.

the first letter "float" (discussed in Chapter 9, we achieve the drop-cap effect. The HTML example becomes:

```
<HTML>
  <TITLE>The style of TIME magazine</TITLE>
  <STYLE TYPE="text/css">
    P.initial:first-line {
      text-transform: uppercase }
    P.initial:first-letter {
      font-size: 200%; float: left }
  </STYLE>
  <BODY>
    <H1>A sample article</H1>
    <P CLASS=initial>The first line
      of the first paragraph in a TIME
      magazine article is printed in
      uppercase letters.
    <P>The text in the second paragraph
      has no special formatting.
  </BODY>
</HTML>
```

Our sample document is formatted as in Figure 4.14.

A sample article

THE FIRST LINE OF the first paragraph in a TIME magazine article is printed in uppercase letters. The text in the second paragraph has no special formatting.

Figure 4.14 Rendering of the TIME example with a drop-cap.

DIV AND SPAN

Before we go on to the advanced selectors, we have to talk a bit about two HTML elements. DIV (division) and SPAN (a span of words) have been added to HTML partly to support style sheets. We have delayed describing them till now since they are mostly used in combination with the CLASS attribute.

The CLASS attribute is a very powerful feature of CSS. Using it, you can in effect create new elements in HTML. Creating new elements through the CLASS attribute is much easier than convincing browser vendors and maintainers of the HTML specification that a new tag is needed and beneficial for everyone.

Using the DIV and SPAN elements you are able to create your own elements. The reason there are two elements for this is that DIV is a block-level element, while SPAN is inline. For example, if you are a poet, you have no way to mark your products as poems in HTML. For this, you would like to have a new POEM tag. It's unlikely that POEM will become an HTML element in the near future, but the DIV element, in combination with the CLASS attribute, offers you an alternative:

```
<DIV CLASS=POEM>
  Roses are red, <BR>
  violets are blue, <BR>
  if you're into poetry, <BR>
  DIV is for you!
</DIV>
```

In this way, you are able to preserve semantics (the fact that the above text is a poem) through the use of the DIV element. In the style sheet, you can set a certain style for the "poem" element:

```
DIV.POEM { font-family: cursive }
```

Using the SPAN element you can make new inline elements:

```
<DIV CLASS=POEM>
  <SPAN CLASS=FLOWER>Roses</SPAN> are red, <BR>
  <SPAN CLASS=FLOWER>violets</SPAN are blue, <BR>
  if you're into poetry, <BR>
  DIV is for you!
</DIV>
```

The new "flower" element can be addressed in the style sheet:

```
SPAN.FLOWER { font-family: fantasy }
```

The complete HTML example thus becomes:

```
<HTML>
  <TITLE>A poem</TITLE>
  <STYLE TYPE="text/css">
    DIV.POEM { font-family: cursive }
    SPAN.FLOWER { font-family: fantasy }
  </STYLE>
  <BODY>
    <DIV CLASS=POEM>
      <SPAN CLASS=FLOWER>Roses</SPAN> are red, <BR>
      <SPAN CLASS=FLOWER>violets</SPAN are blue,<BR>
      if you're into poetry, <BR>
      DIV is for you!
    </DIV>
  </BODY>
</HTML>
```

Which can be displayed as:

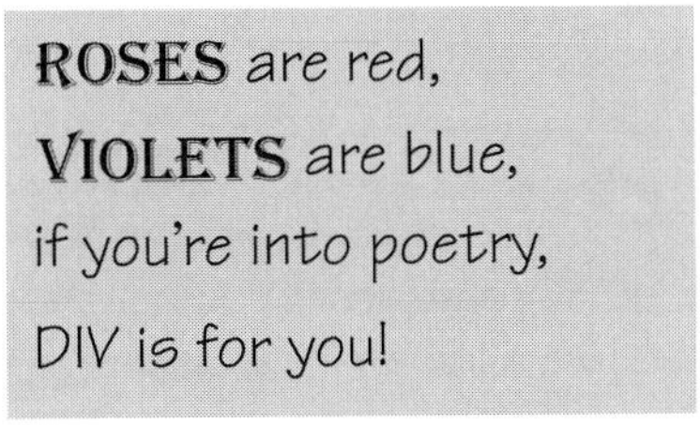

Figure 4.15 The effect of the "poem" and "flower" elements.

ROSES are red,

VIOLETS are blue,

if you're into poetry,

DIV is for you!

ADVANCED ATTRIBUTE SELECTORS

The CLASS and ID attributes are very easy to use, but sometimes it is impossible to add them to the document. For example, if you are writing a style sheet for a set of documents that you are not allowed to edit, then you will have to write selectors that make use of whatever attributes and context there are. If the documents use attributes in a consistent way, it may be possible to select elements based on them.

CSS2 has three different advanced attribute selectors, plus two selectors that are designed for multilingual documents and that select elements based on the language of their contents.

Selecting on the presence of an attribute

A selector that matches elements based on whether they have a certain attribute is constructed by putting the attribute name in square brackets:

```
[COMPACT] { font-weight: bolder }
TABLE[BORDER] { border: thin solid }
```

The first rule matches all elements that have a COMPACT attribute, the second matches all TABLE elements that have a BORDER attribute. The actual value of the attributes is not important, as long as the attribute is present. Here is another example, combining type selectors, contextual selectors and advanced attribute selectors:

```
TABLE[BORDER] TD { border: medium ridge }
```

Note that in HTML, the names of attributes, like the names of elements, are case-insensitive. You can write "BORDER" as well as "border." But in document formats that are written in XML the names of attributes and the of elements are case-sensitive. In style sheets for XML-based documents "BORDER" and "border" are *not* the same.

Selecting on the value of an attribute

A selector that matches on the value of an attribute is written like this:

```
[ALIGN="left"] { text-align: left }
```

This matches all elements that have an ALIGN attribute with the value "left."

In HTML, some attribute values are case-sensitive and others are not. Rather than give a list which is case-insensitive, we recommend that you try to write the attribute values in the selectors with the same case as they appear in the source document. Especially since in XML, *all* attribute values are case-sensitive.

However, the rule of thumb for HTML attributes is that attributes that accept a limited set of keywords, such as the ALIGN and RULES attributes, are case-insenstive, while attributes that accept many different values, such as HREF and ALT, are case sensitive. Thus **[ALIGN="left"]** and **[ALIGN="LEFT"]** are the same, but **[ALT="Diagram"]** and **[ALT="diagram"]** are not. In case of doubt, consult an HTML book, or the official HTML specification.

Selecting on a single word in the value of an attribute

Some attributes may accept space-separated lists of values. The CLASS attribute is an example, as is the REL attribute of A elements. Attributes like the ALT attribute, that typically have a short sentence as value, can also be regarded as a space-separated list of values. A selector that matches single words from such attributes is written as follows:

```
[REL~="home"] { color: green }
```

This matches elements like **<A REL="home">** or **<... REL="up home"...>**. In fact, the class selector can be expressed this way. The following two rules are equivalent:

```
.note { text-decoration: underline }
[CLASS~="note"] { text-decoration: underline }
```

Although you can use this selector with attributes like ALT that contain short phrases, you have to be careful. The selector **[ALT~="Yes"]** will match the element **<IMG ALT="Yes and No"...>**, but not the element **<IMG ALT="Yes, and No"...>**, because of the comma that is attached to the word.

Selecting on the language of an element

Documents are usually written in some human language, at least the documents for which a style sheet makes any sense. Some documents are written in a combination of languages; for example, an English article with French citations, or a manual in four languages.

There are at least two reasons why a selector for language is necessary. The first is the case where you have a set of documents that must all have the same style sheet, but where some documents are in a different language. Although most of the style rules can be the same, there are certain styles that must be different for each language; for example, the quotation marks (see Chapter 7).

The second reason is the case of multilingual documents: documents that contain text in more than one language.

There are two places where a browser can get language data from. One is from the headers that are sent along with the document (but outside the document) when a Web server transfers the document to the browser. The HTTP protocol for transferring information between servers and clients has a special field for the language of the document. This is the default language of the document. An English article with quotations in Russian would be labeled as English, not Russian.

The other place is in attributes on each element. All HTML elements may have a LANG attribute. In XML-based documents the attribute is called "xml:lang," but is otherwise exactly the same.

The value of the LANG attribute and of the HTTP header has a certain structure: it contains a 2-letter language code, and optionally further precisions as to what region of the world (another 2-letter code), or which dialect. Here are some examples:

- en – English
- en-uk – British English
- en-us – American English
- fr-argot – French slang
- no-bok – Norwegian book language ("Bokmål")
- no-nyn – New Norwegian ("Nynorsk")
- i-navajo – Navajo

Navajo (an American Indian language) doesn't have a 2-letter code in the ISO (International Organization for Standardization) list of languages. Instead, it uses a code that is registered with IANA, the Internet Assigned Numbers Authority.

ab	Abkhazian	fr	French	lt	Lithuanian	sd	Sindhi
aa	Afar	fy	Frisian	mk	Macedonian	si	Singhalese
af	Afrikaans	gl	Galician	mg	Malagasy	ss	Siswati
sq	Albanian	ka	Georgian	ms	Malay	sk	Slovak
am	Amharic	de	German	ml	Malayalam	sl	Slovenian
ar	Arabic	el	Greek	mt	Maltese	so	Somali
hy	Armenian	kl	Greenlandic	gv	Manx Gaelic	es	Spanish
as	Assamese	gn	Guarani	mi	Maori	su	Sundanese
ay	Aymara	gu	Gujarati	mr	Marathi	sw	Swahili
az	Azerbaijani	ha	Hausa	mo	Moldavian	sv	Swedish
ba	Bashkir	iw,he	Hebrew	mn	Mongolian	tl	Tagalog
eu	Basque	hi	Hindi	na	Nauru	tg	Tajik
bn	Bengali (Bangla)	hu	Hungarian	ne	Nepali	ta	Tamil
dz	Bhutani	is	Icelandic	no	Norwegian	tt	Tatar
bh	Bihari	in,id	Indonesian	oc	Occitan	te	Telugu
bi	Bislama	ia	Interlingua	or	Oriya	th	Thai
br	Breton	ie	Interlingue	om	Oromo (Afan)	bo	Tibetan
bg	Bulgarian	iu	Inuktitut	ps	Pashto (Pushto)	ti	Tigrinya
my	Burmese	ik	Inupiak	pl	Polish	to	Tonga
be	Byelorussian	ga	Irish	pt	Portuguese	ts	Tsonga
km	Cambodian	it	Italian	pa	Punjabi	tr	Turkish
ca	Catalan	ja	Japanese	qu	Quechua	tk	Turkmen
zh	Chinese	jw	Javanese	rm	Rhaeto-	tw	Twi
co	Corsican	kn	Kannada		Romance	ug	Uighur
hr	Croatian	ks	Kashmiri	ro	Romanian	uk	Ukrainian
cs	Czech	kk	Kazakh	ru	Russian	ur	Urdu
da	Danish	rw	Kinyarwanda	sm	Samoan	uz	Uzbek
nl	Dutch	ky	Kirghiz	sg	Sangro	vi	Vietnamese
en	English	rn	Kirundi	sa	Sanskrit	vo	Volapük
eo	Esperanto	ko	Korean	gd	Scots Gaelic	cy	Welsh
et	Estonian	ku	Kurdish	sr	Serbian	wo	Wolof
fo	Faeroese	lo	Laothian	sh	Serbo-Croatian	xh	Xhosa
fa	Farsi	la	Latin	st	Sesotho	ji,yi	Yiddish
fj	Fiji	lv	Latvian (Lettish)	tn	Setswana	yo	Yoruba
fi	Finnish	ln	Lingala	sn	Shona	zu	Zulu

Figure 4.16 The ISO 2-letter language codes (ISO 639).

The selector that checks for a language has the following form:

```
[LANG|="en-uk"] { background: rgb(90%,90%,0%) }
[LANG|="en-us"] { background: rgb(90%,90%,90%) }
[LANG|="en"] { color: blue }
```

The first matches elements that have an attribute **LANG="en-uk"** or **LANG="en-uk-..."** where the dots stand for arbitrary codes. The third rule matches everything the first two match, and also **LANG="en"**. The result is that every element that is in English (and their child elements, if they don't override it) will have blue text, against either a yellow background (for British English) or a light gray one (for American English).

CSS2 also provides a language selector based on a pseudo-class. It is written like this:

```
P:lang(nl) { font-style: italic }
```

This works differently from the attribute selector, because it selects all elements (all P elements in this case) that are in a certain language, not just those that have a LANG attribute. An element is considered to be in a certain language if:

1. it has a LANG attribute for that language, or
2. it doesn't have a LANG attribute but its parent is in that language, or
3. it is the root element and the HTTP header specifies that language.

The following HTML fragment illustrates the effect of the lang pseudo-class. The document has elements in two languages: English and French. The start tags of the elements that would match **:lang(fr)** are shown in bold:

```
<BODY LANG="en">
  <H1>English title</H1>
  <P>This is a paragraph in English, that leads
    up to the quotation:
  <BLOCKQUOTE LANG="fr">
    <P>Ici commencent les lignes en français.
      Il y a même un mot en <B>gras.</B>
    <P>Encore un peu de français.
  </BLOCKQUOTE>
  <P>And here it is back to English again.
</BODY>
```

ADVANCED CONTEXTUAL SELECTORS

The context of an element consists of all the element's ancestors and all elements that precede it in the document. It is not possible to look at elements that follow an element, because browsers often need to be able to decide on the style of an element before the rest of the document comes in. The most common contextual selector is the one that was explained earlier, in the section "Simple contextual selectors" on page 66. It only checks whether an element is inside some other element, without regard for how far removed that ancestor is.

Two other contextual selectors, the child selector and the sibling selector, give very precise control over the relation between the element to select and its context. In combination with the first-child pseudo-class explained below, these can be used to trace out a path from some element to the element you want to select.

The child selector

To select an element under the condition that its parent matches some other selector, you can use a rule like the following:

```
DIV.chapter DIV.warning > P { text-indent: 0 }
```

This selects any P elements whose parent matches "**DIV.CHAPTER DIV.WARNING**"; in other words, all P elements that are children of a DIV element with class "warning" that is inside a DIV element of class "chapter." Which may be quite different from:

```
DIV.chapter > DIV.warning P { text-indent: 0 }
```

The sibling selector

Sometimes what determines the style of an element is not so much its parent or other ancestors, but the element that precedes it. A typical example is the indentation of the first line of a paragraph. This book uses that device to make it easier to spot where one paragraph ends and the next one begins. The rule is that an indent is only used between paragraphs; in other words, not on a paragraph that follows a heading, a list, or something else that is already visually distinguished. Expressed in CSS, the rule becomes:

```
P + P { text-indent: 2em }
```

This matches a P if it is preceded by another P, and both have the same parent.

Here is a triplet of rules that sets the font size of H1 and H2 elements: by themselves they are set to fairly large letters, but when an H2 immediately follows an H1, it is made smaller. You might do this, for example, because such H2s function as subtitles.

```
H1 { font-size: xx-large }
H2 { font-size: x-large }
H1 + H2 { font-size: medium }
```

ADVANCED PSEUDO-CLASSES

In addition to the two anchor pseudo-classes that were described on page 68, CSS2 has four more pseudo-classes. Three of them allow dynamic effects: the style changes when the user does something. The fourth selects elements that are the first children of their parent.

User-interaction: the active, hover and focus pseudo-classes

CSS2 can describe a few dynamic effects. They are typically used to give the users of a document extra visual feedback on the purpose of various elements. For example, you can change the color of an A element when the mouse moves over it, or indeed you can change the shape of the mouse pointer itself, to give an extra visual clue that the A element is active, and that something more would happen if the user actually clicked, instead of just moved the mouse.

These dynamic effects, because they are dynamic, attract the user's attention much more than static displays of colors and text. But they can easily be overdone, and many people don't like it when their attention is constantly drawn to new areas when all they do is move the mouse a bit. So be careful with these features.

The three pseudo-classes that select elements based on the user's interaction with them represent three common states for elements in an interactive document. They can be applied to the source anchors of hyperlinks, or to elements in forms, and in documents with scripts often to other elements. (But in that last case extra care is called for, since users don't expect elements outside a form to be active.) The three states are:

- hover – the mouse or some other pointing device "hovers" over the element. The user hasn't clicked or otherwise activated the element, but is in a position that he or she *could* click. For example, to change the background of a hyperlink when the mouse enters the element's box, you might use this rule:

```
A:link:hover, A:visited:hover {
    background: yellow }
```

- active – the element has been activated, and some action is being performed, but is not yet complete. The typical application is again for hyperlinks, to indicate that the user's request to fetch a new page has been accepted, but that the page hasn't arrived yet:

```
A:active { color: white; background: black }
```

- focus – when there are elements that accept keyboard input, such as the INPUT and TEXTAREA elements of HTML, at most one of them can accept input at any time. The user has to explicitly select the element he or she wants to send characters to. Depending on the browser that is done by clicking or using the Tab key. The element that currently has the input focus is often indicated with a border-like outline. The CSS rule for that might be as follows:

```
:focus { ouline: solid medium black }
```

The browser may only support a limited number of properties for these pseudo-classes. For example, you should not expect all browsers to be able to change the font size of the active pseudo-class, as this would mean the browser has to reformat the whole document when you click on a link. It's safe to assume that you can change colors and add/remove underlining, since these are purely local changes. But any rule that may change the size of something (for example font or margin) may be ignored by the browser.

Counting elements: the first-child pseudo-class

The contextual rule for siblings described above (page 78) selects elements that have a certain preceding element. The opposite, selecting an element because it has no preceding element, is provided by the first-child pseudo-class. For example:

```
DIV.bio > P:first-child { font-weight: bold }
```

selects P elements that are children of "bio" elements, but only if they are the first child. Combining child selectors, sibling selectors and the first-child pseudo-class leads to very precise selectors. They can sometimes even take the place of an ID selector (page 62), if there is no possibility of adding an ID attribute to the document.

This example picks out the third list item of every UL list:

```
UL > LI:first-child + LI + LI {
    font-style: italic }
```

Applied to this HTML fragment:

```
<UL>
  <LI>horses
  <LI>dogs
  <LI>cows
    <UL>
      <LI>Greta IV
      <LI>Berta II
      <LI>Berta III
    </UL>
</UL>
```

it will cause "cows" and "Berta III" to be put in italic:

Figure 4.17 Using contextual
selectors to put the third item
of every UL list in italic.

- horses
- dogs
- *cows*
  - Greta IV
  - Berta II
  - *Berta III*

ADVANCED PSEUDO-ELEMENTS

The first-line and first-letter pseudo-elements (page 69) select a part of an element. The before and after pseudo-elements go further: they actually add new parts to an element. Here are a few examples (the full discussion can be found in Chapter 7).

The before and after pseudo-elements are used together with the **content** property, that determines what text goes into the pseudo-element. The first example adds the word "Note" in front of every paragraph of class "note:"

```
P.note:before { content: "Note. " }
```

If the element to which the pseudo-element is added is itself a block element, the pseudo-element can also be made a block. In other words, it is possible to add a paragraph. The following example adds a centered line "The end" between two horizontal rules at the end of the document:

```
BODY:after {
    content: "The end";
    display: block;
    border-top: solid thin;
    border-bottom: solid thin }
```

THE "ANY" SELECTOR

The final type of selector in CSS2 is a selector that simply selects all elements. It can be used to set a property on all elements, but that is a rare occurrence. It can also be used in combination with the child selector to count ancestors. Here is an example of the "any" selector used on its own:

```
* { cursor: auto }
```

This resets the shape of the mouse pointer to the browser's default. This is a quick way to undo all changes to the mouse cursor. If the style sheet that comes with a document makes it hard to find the hyperlinks, this might be a useful rule to have in a user's style sheet.

Another place where the "any" selector might come in handy is in selectors that must match only at a certain depth in the document tree. For example, to select all paragraphs except those that are children of the BODY element, this rule will do:

```
BODY * P { font: medium "gill sans", sans-serif }
```

This matches P elements that are descendants of any element which is a descendant of BODY. It therefore excludes P elements that are children of BODY itself.

A final way to use the "any" selector is for purely aesthetic reasons. If you like all your selectors to start with an element name, you can use the "*" in places where the element name doesn't matter:

```
*[BORDER] { border: solid }
*.POLONIUS { font-weight: bold }
*:hover { color: inherit; background: inherit }
```

In these cases the "any" selector is merely used to avoid starting a selector with a flag character. It is a matter of taste.

Table 4.1 gives a summary of all selectors in CSS2.

Pattern	Matches
*	any element
E	any E element (*i.e.*, element of type "E")
F E	any E element that is a descendant of an F element
F > E	any E element that is a child of an F element
F + E	any E element that immediately follows an F element
.class	any element with class "class"
#id	the element with ID "id"
:first-child	any E element that is the first child of its parent
:link :visited	any element that is unvisited, resp. visited hyperlink
:active :hover :focus	any element that is "activated" by the user; resp.: (1) an action has started but not completed, (2) the mouse "hovers" over the element, (3) the element is ready to receive keyboard input.
:lang(c)	any element whose content is in (human) language c
[att]	any element with an "att" attribute
[att="val"]	any element with an "att" attribute with value "val"

Pattern	Matches
`[att~="val"]`	any element with an "att" attribute that includes the word "val"
`[att|="val"]`	any element with an "att" attribute of the form "val-. . ."
`x, y`	grouping: any element that matches x *or* y
`E:first-letter`	the first letter of any (block) element E
`E:first-line`	the first line of any (block) element E
`E:before`	the text inserted at the start of any E element
`E:after`	the text inserted at the end of any E element

Table 4.1 Overview of the building blocks of selectors.

Chapter 5

Fonts

Specifying typesetting properties is one of the most common uses of style sheets. Such properties include a font's size, its width, its weight (is it light or bold?) and its posture (does it slant or stand upright?)

Getting the fonts you want with HTML is difficult, since HTML was designed without any concept of fonts. In HTML, the appearance of the page is the result of the browser's inserting styles it thinks are appropriate. It does this using the HTML structural information in your document. The lack of control over fonts in HTML has led to documents containing pictures of text instead of text. By making pictures of text, designers get total control over fonts. They can pick and choose between any font they have on their own machine and don't have to worry about which fonts are available on the user's machine. The downside of using images is that documents become big and slow to download.

CSS has been designed to give designers the influence over fonts they request without having to resort to images. This is done by setting values on a set of font properties which are defined in CSS. In previous chapters you have seen examples of these properties. For example, the **font-style**, **font-weight** and **font** properties were used in Chapter 2. In this chapter you will find the full definition of all font properties and the values they can take. Also, there are more examples of how they can and should be used in style sheets.

In addition to font *properties*, CSS2 introduced the concept of *font descriptions* which can hold even more detailed information about the requested font than the font properties can. For example, the font description can store the width of characters and the URL from where the font can be downloaded. This is known as WebFonts and is described in the next chapter.

This chapter will give you an introduction to typesetting terminology before moving on to the descriptions of the CSS font properties. Along the way we will also describe the units of measurements used by the font properties. These units are also used by other properties, so pay attention!

TYPESETTING TERMINOLOGY

Typesetting terminology is a difficult field. There exists no universally accepted system for classifying fonts and many of the terms in use mean different things to different people. Traditional printing terminology and that used in desktop publishing and Web design don't always agree.

The word "type" is derived from the Greek word *typos*, which loosely translated means "letterform." Today, "type" refers to letters and other symbols which are used to create words and sentences.

A *typeface*, sometimes called *face*, is all type of a single design and style. All letters and symbols within a typeface share some common characteristics so that they visually fit together. For example, the vertical stems of letters within a typeface will typically have the same thickness.

Several typefaces which share the same basic design form a *type family*. The different typefaces in a type family can vary in *style* by certain attributes, including weight (degree of boldness versus lightness), width (such as narrow versus expanded), and posture (straight versus slanted). Among the most common type families we find Helvetica, Arial, and Palatino. Times Roman (TR) is the name of another very popular type family. *TR Regular*, *TR Italic*, *TR Bold*, and *TR Bold Italic* are typefaces within the TR type family. Figure 5.1 shows a diagram of the TR family and a sample of each typeface.

Aa Bb Cc   TR Regular

Aa Bb Cc   TR Italic

Aa Bb Cc   TR Bold

Aa Bb Cc   TR Bold Italic

Figure 5.1 Four typefaces of the Times Roman type family.

The most common type families usually have at least these four styles: *regular* (also called "roman"), *bold* (also known as "boldface"), *italic*, and *bold italic*. The roman style often forms the basic, most commonly used typeface within the family because in many type families it is very appropriate for running text. However, all type families have their own version of roman, even those whose appearance is inappropriate for running text. Furthermore, not every type family has variations, while other families have many typefaces with these or other characteristics, such as being narrow, expanded or condensed.

The traditional definition of a *font* is one typeface in one size. For example, a 10pt TR Regular is one font, a 12pt TR Regular is another font, as is a 14pt TR Regular. These differ only in their sizes and each is considered to be a font, by the traditional definition. Other fonts could be 10pt TR Bold, 10pt TR Italic, and 10pt TR Bold Italic. These differ only in their style or weight or both.

This definition of font comes from the time when each size and variation of a typeface were cast in lead and stored separately from other fonts so that they wouldn't get mixed up. This also meant the number of fonts was relatively limited (even large printers had only room for so many different fonts). With the introduction of photocomposition (a type technology) and digital computers type can be scaled by very small amounts very easily, thus the number of fonts is potentially much greater. So the consideration of size in the definition of font is no longer useful, and the terms font, typeface, and face are all used synonymously, as is the case in this book. So, we consider TR Italic to be a font, TR Bold to be a font, *etc.*, with no consideration of the size of type.

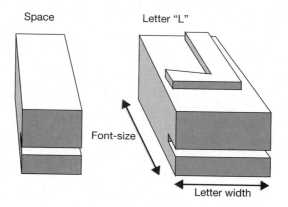

Figure 5.2 Metal type. Small lead or brass blocks all of the same height (the font size) but different widths, each with a raised mirror image of a letter, are assembled on rails to form lines. Spaces bear no letter image. The lines are arranged and locked into a galley to form the pages. After inking, the page is printed onto a sheet of paper.

CLASSIFYING FONT FAMILIES

Font families are often classified into a few general categories. The number and names of categories vary from one typographic tradition to another. Here are the questions CSS asks when classifying a font family:

- does it have *serifs* (defined shortly) or is it *sans-serif*?
- is it proportional-spaced (variable-width) or monospaced (fixed-width)?
- was it designed to resemble handwriting?
- is it intended primarily for decorative purposes rather than for use in running text and headings?

We discuss each of these in the next several subsections.

Serif or sans-serif?

A *serif* is a short cross-stroke that some letters have. A font that has serifs is called *serif*. A font that has no serifs is called *sans-serif* (*sans* is French for "without"). Serifs can differ in appearance, ranging from short feathery strokes to slab-like square strokes. Figure 5.3 shows examples from several serif and sans-serif families. Both sans-serif and serif fonts work well for text and for headings.

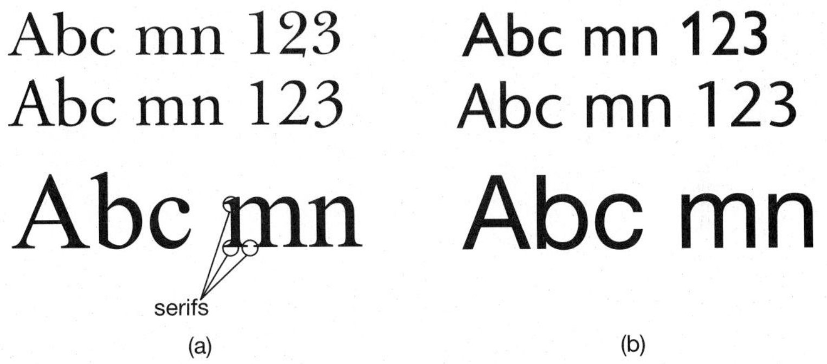

Figure 5.3 (a) Serif fonts; (b) sans-serif fonts.

Proportional-spaced or monospaced?

In a variable-width, or *proportional-spaced*, font each letter takes up just the amount of space it needs. An "I," being naturally skinny, takes up less space than the naturally fatter "M." In a fixed-width, or *monospaced*, font each letter takes up the same amount of space regardless of its width. For example, an "I" and an "M" take up the same amount of space even though they are obviously of different widths.

Proportional-spaced fonts may be either serif or sans-serif and may generally be used both for text and headings. Monospaced fonts are often called *typewriter type*. This is because for a long time, typewriters could produce only monospaced type. Monospaced fonts may be used for both text and headings; however, they are usually reserved for special usages, such as to mimic the effects of a typewriter or to portray computer code. See Figure 5.4 for examples of (a) proportional-spaced and (b) monospaced type.

(a) Aa Bb Ii Mm 0123 !?
The quick brown fox jumps over the lazy dog

(b) Aa Bb Ii Mm 0123 !?
The quick brown fox jumps over the lazy dog

Figure 5.4 (a) Proportional-spaced fonts; (b) monospaced fonts.

Does it resemble handwriting?

A font designed to resemble handwriting is called *cursive*. Cursive characters are usually rounder than serif or sans-serif type, they do not have serifs, and they usually slant to the right. They also may be connected, like handwriting usually is, although this is not necessary. Many italic versions of serif fonts look cursive. They differ from cursive fonts in that a serif font has a roman version, while a cursive form does not. Cursive fonts are often effective when you want to convey a personal touch, since much of it resembles handwriting. Figure 5.5 shows examples of cursive and italic fonts.

This is a cursive font (Zapf Chancery)

This is an italic font (Times italic)

This is a cursive font (Brush Script)

This is an italic font (Palatino italic)

(a)

(b)

Figure 5.5 (a) Cursive fonts; (b) italic fonts.

Is it mainly for decorative purposes?

Some fonts are seldom used for large amounts of text because their appearance is too unique to be read easily in large amounts. Typically they are reserved for display, and to some extent headline, purposes. Some don't even have full alphabets; they just have capital letters. They may be strangely decorated, irregular in shape, or very fancy. Figure 5.6 shows examples of fantasy font families.

Figure 5.6 Some fantasy font families.

On the basis of these factors, CSS classifies font families into five categories, as follows:

- sans-serif
- serif
- monospace
- cursive
- fantasy

In CSS these are known as generic font families. To specify that a document should be printed with a font from a generic font family – or from a specific font family like *Helvetica* – the **font-family** property is used. The next section is devoted to **font-family**.

THE FONT-FAMILY PROPERTY

The **font-family** property lets you specify the font families which will be used in your documents. Here is the formal definition of the property:

IE3   NS4   IE4   O3.5

Name:	**font-family**
Value:	[*<specific-family>* ,]*
	[*<specific-family>*	*<generic-family>*]
Initial:	UA specific
Applies to:	all elements, except replaced elements
Inherited:	yes
Percentages:	N/A

Each CSS property has a "data sheet" like the above which describes, in a formal way, key characteristics of the property. Also, on the left there is a "button bar" which gives you an overview of how widely supported the property is. Throughout this book, you will find definitions like the above for each CSS new property which is introduced. Learning what the different fields represent will save you time when encountering new properties or reviewing old ones. The box on page 91 describes how to read the property definitions.

Even when you learn to read the property data sheet you need to read the textual description of the property in order to understand how the property changes the presentation of a document.

The **font-family** property accepts a list of font families as value. The font families are separated with a comma, and there are two different kinds:

* specific font families (*e.g.* **Arial** or **Courier**)

* generic font families (one of: **serif**, **sans-serif**, **monospace**, **cursive**, **fantasy**)

For example, a document that is to be displayed in Times might have a style sheet like this:

```
BODY { font-family: Times }
```

A document that is to be displayed in Garamond, if possible, and Times if Garamond is not available would have a style sheet like this:

```
BODY { font-family: Garamond, Times }
```

where Garamond and Times are both family names.

It's important to remember the comma when specifying a list of font families. Some font family names have spaces in them (for example, "New Century Schoolbook") and the space character is therefore not

HOW TO READ PROPERTY DATA SHEETS (1)

The "button bar" on the left side indicates how major browsers support each property. The browser categories are: IE3 (Microsoft Internet Explorer 3), NS4 (Netscape Navigator 4), IE4 (Microsoft Internet Explorer 4), and O3.5 (Opera 3.5). The buttons have the following meaning:

- ○ the property is not supported by the browser
- ⊙ the property is partially supported by the browser
- ● the property is fully supported by the browser

For more detailed information about browser support, WebReview's CSS Charts (http://www.webreview.com/wr/pub/guides/style/mastergrid.html) is the best source. For example, it will tell you how the Mac version of IE4 differs from the Windows version.

Name: This is the first field in the formal definition. It simply lists the name of the property.

Value: This field specifes the possible values of the property. You may find one or many values. Words written in italics refer to a group of values which are described elsewhere, while upright words are literal keywords. If a property offers many possible values or many possible complex combinations of values, you may find square brackets, vertical bars, and other symbols in this area. An appendix called "Reading property value definitions" describes in detail how to read the special symbols. We know from experience, however, that many designers do not feel comfortable reading formal grammars, but they still write excellent style sheets. Instead of reading this field you can learn about the possible values by reading the text and examples that follow the data sheet.

Initial: This field gives the *initial value* of the property. If the property is inherited, this is the value that is given to the first element of the document, which is HTML. Otherwise, it is the value that the property will have if there are no style rules for it in the style sheets. Initial values make life easier for designers since they most often make sense and don't need to be changed. The initial value can be either a specific value for a property or "UA-specific," which means that CSS does not define an initial value. Instead, it leaves that definition to the "UA" or *User Agent*: that is, the browser (or other program) that processes CSS on behalf of the user.

Applies to: This field describes what kinds of elements the property applies to. All elements have all properties, but some properties have no effect on some types of elements. For example, **font-family** has no effect if the element is a replaced element (*e.g.,* an image).

continued

sufficient for separating different font families. In addition, you may use quotation marks around family names, as in this example rule:

```
BODY { font-family: "new century schoolbook", serif }
```

The quotation marks are necessary if the name contains characters other than letters, digits, dashes and spaces. For example, if a font were named "Dollar$," the browser might get confused by the dollar-sign.

The value can also be the name of a generic font family — instead of or in addition to the specific font families. Use of generic font families is a partial solution to the problem of dealing with unavailable fonts. A browser may not have any of the fonts listed in the value. To make sure that something will be displayed in the worst case of no match, you can add a generic font family like **serif** to the list. In this case, if the browser does not have any of the given families, it will have to use any font it has that has serifs. Here are the generic names:

- **serif**
- **sans-serif**
- **monospace**
- **cursive**
- **fantasy**

Look familiar? They correspond to the font categories we defined earlier in the chapter. Here's an example rule that includes a generic family name:

```
BODY { font-family: Garamond, Times,
    "New Century Schooolbook", serif }
```

In this example, the browser will first check to see if it has Garamond. If it doesn't, it will check for Times. If it doesn't have Times, it will search all the fonts it has until it finds one in a serif style (if any) that it can use to display the document.

The use of generic font families is encouraged. Each browser has a list of fonts that it can display. Those lists usually differ among browsers. However, all browsers must understand the previous five category names. Hence, when a requested font is not available on a particular browser, and you told the browser which category the font is in, the browser is expected to substitute a font from the same category. Although the resulting translation may be a bit rough, it will usually be a font that looks at least somewhat like the one intended. Figure 5.7 shows sample fonts from the five generic type families.

serif	Ggm	Ggm	Ggm
sans-serif	Ggm	Ggm	Ggm
monospace	Ggm	Ggm	Ggm
cursive	*Ggm*	*Ggm*	*Ggm*
fantasy	**Ggm**	**GGM**	**Ggm**

Figure 5.7 Examples of the five generic font families.

Don't put quotes around the generic name! The generic family names are special keywords in CSS, not real font families. If you write `font-family: "serif"` the browser will think you really meant a font named "serif."

Design tips using font families

Good document design generally involves the use of just two or three different font families. When there are more, finding ones that look good together can soon become a problem. Unless you are a skilled graphics designer, restricting your creative urges to two or three families will give your document a more professional look. Unless you want a document that looks like a *RaNSOm* letter... .

A typical, time-proven scheme is to have all text in a serif font and the headings in a sans-serif font. Popular choices are Times Roman and Helvetica, respectively, and their clones such as Times New Roman and Arial. You may want to use a monospace font for some parts if you are writing about computer software. For example, code is often set in a monospaced font, as may be filenames, function names, method names, and the like. The rest of the variation in your document should be created by using different font styles, weights, and sizes within the same two or three families.

People writing multilingual documents, in which they may be using two or more alphabets, know that it is very hard to find two fonts that look well together, let alone three or more. Some alphabets such as Thai and Devanagari (a script from India) have very different conventions for a letter's baseline and therefore of its height and depth. For example, a 12pt Devanagari font may look too big next to a 12pt Latin font. But since there are only a very few multilingual fonts, there is often not much choice. Figure 5.8 shows a sample of Bitstream Cyberbit, a family with over 8,000 characters. The normal style and weight is free; for italic and bold, you'll have to pay. See URL http://www.bitstream.com/

abpmnABCD1234&!àá âÈÉËþýßÆÞðÐşıŞğĞ™ ¾«""•אתשרבגגזנחטטῠαβ πρςΓΔΘΙΛώύίΖήπΠабв ИЙЛюэЯЖЮрРŕČţĆŢđ ąįāĖžżĘŽšŠ

Figure 5.8 Sample of Bitstream Cyberbit family, which has over 8,000 characters.

Restraint is the key to good design. There are so many possibilities in CSS that it is easy to overdo and spoil your design.

FONT METRICS

Fonts are typically measured in a unit specific to the printing industry called the *point*. A point (abbreviated "pt") is the traditional printer's typographer's unit for specifying the size of fonts, the spacing between adjacent lines, and the thickness of rules — among other things. It is still used a lot, although some countries and some publishers now prefer to use the metric system (specifically, the millimeter — mm — and centimeter — cm). There are three variants of the point:

- The continental European point (the Didot point = 0.376065mm)
- The Anglo-American point (the pica point = 0.351461mm)
- Another Anglo-American point (defined as 1/72 in. = 0.352778mm)

CSS uses only the last one. It does so because that point's value is in between the other two values. Also, it conforms to the point size used in PostScript printers, the most common type of printer.

To understand how type is sized, you first need some information about what makes up a letter. The *x-height* is the size of the body, or main part, of the letter and is approximately equal to the height of the x of the font. The *ascender* is that part of the lowercase letter that extends above the x-height. The *descender* is that part of the lowercase letter that extends below the x-height.

Type sits on an imaginary horizontal line called the *baseline*. For example, notice this line of type you are now reading. All of it is sitting on the baseline. Figure 5.9 shows the parts of a letter sitting on a baseline.

Figure 5.9 The parts of a letter.

The size of type is usually obtained by measuring from roughly the top of its ascenders to the bottom of its descenders. (In the days of metal type, the font size was the size of the letter body, see Figure 5.2.) The measurement is expressed in points. The difference of a point is more noticeable in smaller sizes than in larger sizes. Text type, type used for running text, is generally 14 pt or less. Common sizes are 10 pt and 12 pt. Display type, type used for headings, is generally bigger than 14 pt.

Even though different fonts may be of the same point size, they may appear to be different sizes. This is typically because the x-heights of fonts vary. Some may have a large x-height, while others in comparison have a small x-height. Because type of one size has just so much height it can work with, a large x-height will often be combined with short descenders and ascenders, while a small x-height will be combined with long descenders and ascenders. So the visual impression of size that a font makes is largely due to the font's x-height in combination with the size of its ascenders and descenders. As Figure 5.10 shows, Times Roman has a relatively large x-height and therefore relatively short descenders and ascenders in comparison to Garamond, which has a relatively small x-height and relatively long descenders and ascenders. Notice that the Times Roman sample appears bigger than the Garamond sample even though both are the same point size.

Figure 5.10 Because of differences in x-heights, the Times Roman sample (a) looks bigger than the Garamond sample (b) even though both are the same point size.

Because of differences in x-heights, the Times Roman sample (a) looks bigger than the Garamond sample (b) even though both are the same point size

(a)

Because of differences in x-heights, the Times Roman sample (a) looks bigger than the Garamond sample (b) even though both are the same point size

(b)

This relationship is important because it is one factor that affects the readability of your font on a user's screen. A font with a large x-height is often easier to read in smaller sizes than one with a small x-height. As the font size increases, this difference lessens.

LENGTH UNITS

The point unit is the traditional measurement of length in typography, but not always the best for Web design. CSS accepts a range of different units which fall into three categories:

- absolute units – this category includes the point unit described above as well as other units (mm, cm, in, pc) which describe physical distances that can be measured with a measuring band.
- relative units – these units describe distances relative to other distances. The "em" unit, described in Chapter 3, is the foremost member of this group which also includes the "ex" unit.
- the pixel unit – the pixel unit, as defined in CSS, forms a group of its own since it has some unique characteristics. On normal computer screens, the pixel unit will do what you expect. On printers and other high-resolution devices it will do what you hope!

The three groups and their units are described in more detail below. Common for all the units is the way they are combined with numbers to form values. Here are some examples: `12pt`, `0.9in`, `2.54cm`, `-3px`.

To form a value, a number is combined with a unit. The number can be a whole number (0, 1, 2, . . .), a fractional number (0.5, 2.57, 1.04, . . .), or a negative number (–1, –3.14, –0.25, . . .). If the integer part of the fractional number is zero, it can be omitted (.25, –.61). The unit of measure is added directly after the number with no space between the number and the unit. All units are two-letter abbreviations, with no period at the end.

Properties may restrict the numbers and lengths they accept. For example, the **font-size** property cannot be set to a negative length. All CSS properties that accept lengths also accept the number 0 without a unit of measure. (If a length is 0, it doesn't matter whether it is points or inches.)

Absolute units

An *absolute unit* is a unit of measure that specifies a fixed length – a length which can be measured with a measuring band. The units are:

- millimeter: mm
- centimeter: cm (1cm = 10mm)
- inch: in (1in = 25.4mm)
- point: pt (72pt = 1in)
- pica: pc (1pc = 12pt)

The mm and cm units come from the metric system of measurements. The other units are all defined as fractions of an inch. A *pica* is 12 points. Six picas equal one inch.

Absolute units have limited usefulness because they cannot be scaled. In general, they should only be used if you know the physical properties of the output medium. For example, if you write a style sheet for a document you know will only be printed on A4-sized paper, absolute units may be the right choice. In most cases, however, you will be better off using relative units.

Relative units

A *relative unit* is a unit of measure that specifies a value that is relative to the font size. There are two relative units in CSS: "em" and "ex." Usually the font size they refer to is the font size of the element itself. (The only exception is the **font-size** property, which we discuss later in the chapter, where the value scales to the font size of the element's parent.) Relative units have the advantage over absolute units in that they scale automatically. When you choose a different font, all properties that were expressed in em or ex don't have to be changed.

The em unit was heavily promoted in Chapter 3 and we will not repeat all the good arguments for using the em unit here, but merely state the facts. In CSS, the em is exactly equal to the font size (*i.e.,* the height of the font). For example, in a 12pt font, the em is 12pt wide, while in a 15pt font, the em is 15pt wide. (There are other historical definitions of em that we don't go into. We chose for CSS the one that appeared to be the most convenient.)

The ex unit is also relative to the font size but in a different way. It is called "ex" because it is defined as the x-height (see Figure 5.11). The em can be set explicitly in CSS1, but the ex is a characteristic of the font, so it cannot be set explicitly. This means you can determine how big it is only by inspecting the font. For example, Times Roman has a relatively large ex (x-height) compared to Baskerville. So even though a 12pt Times Roman and a 12pt Baskerville both have an em of 12pt, their ex values will vary because their x-heights vary. Times Roman's will be somewhat larger than Baskerville's. Figure 5.11 illustrates this.

The pixel unit

The term *pixel* is derived from Picture Element. The pixel is the smallest element on a video display screen, such as a computer monitor or a television.

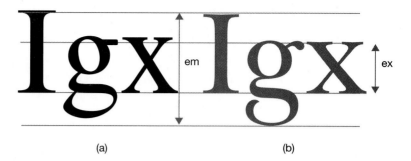

Figure 5.11 Times Roman (a)
and Baskerville (b) with the
same em values have different
ex values.

(a)   (b)

It also applies to the output from certain types of printers, such as laser printers. The pixel unit in CSS is based on pixels, but is slightly more refined than the name implies.

On computer screens, the pixel unit behaves as you expect it to. Consider these two rules:

```
H1 { border-width: 4px }
H2 { border-width: 3px }
```

In the example above, the width of the border surrounding H1 elements is set to four pixels and the border around H2 elements is set to three pixels. On a normal computer screen, these values will be used as specified. That is, the border around H1 elements will actually be four pixels wide, and the border around H2 elements will be three pixels wide. Another seemingly obvious fact is that the H1 border will be exactly one pixel thicker than the H2 border.

When we try to print the document, things get more complicated. Typically, the resolution – the density of pixels – on a laser printer is much higher than the resolution on a computer screen. Therefore, a four-pixel border on a laser printer will appear much thinner than a four-pixel border on a computer screen. CSS deals with this problem by saying that pixel measurements should always appear as they would on a computer screen. When printing, the browser should therefore replicate pixels so that, *e.g.,* the borders specified above will be roughly as thick as they would on a computer screen.

For example, a 600dpi laser printer has six times more pixels per inch than a typical computer monitor does. Most often, however, the paper that it prints is held closer to the eyes than a computer screen, so to get the same perceived effect on screen and on paper, the laser printer could use a square of 4 by 4 pixels to emulate one screen pixel.

Pixels are a useful unit of measure because on any medium it is guaranteed that a difference of 1 pixel will actually be visible. On the other hand, the difference between **0.5em** and **0.6em** may disappear on a computer screen because the screen is not able to show differences of less than 1 pixel.

PERCENTAGES AS VALUES

Many properties that accept a number or a length as a value also accept a percentage, such as **50%**, **33.3%**, and **100%**. Although not a unit of measure, percentages offer similar advantages that relative units do, that is, they automatically scale.

What the percentage is a percentage of – that is, what it is relative to – depends on the property. Usually, it is a percentage of the value that the property has in the parent element. For example, an H1 with a font size of **80%** means the font is **80%** of the font size of its parent (often the BODY element). The only exception is the **line-height** property. (Line height is also known as interline spacing.) We discuss this property in depth in Chapter 8, "Space inside boxes."

KEYWORDS AS VALUES

Keywords are not units of measure, but some have connotations of being relative. In this case, they have the same advantage as relative units and percentages in that they can be scaled. For example the keywords **bolder** and **lighter**, which are for the **font-weight** property, are clearly relative: they are relative to the font weight of the parent. The same applies to **larger** and **smaller** for the **font-size** property, which we get to next.

THE FONT-SIZE PROPERTY

The **font-size** property specifies the size of the font:

IE3	NS4	IE4	O3.5		
⊙	●	●	●		

Name:	**font-size**
Value:	*<length>* | *<percentage>* | *<absolute-size>* | *<relative-size>*
Initial:	medium
Applies to:	all elements
Inherited:	yes
Percentages:	relative to parent's font size

This property has four possible types of values:

- length
- percentage
- absolute size
- relative size

The first two types are general types of values which can be used on many CSS properties. The last two types are sets of keywords which are particular to the **font-size** property.

The "length" value

When a property accepts length values, all units described in the "Length units" section above can be used. This includes absolute units (mm, cm, in, pt, pc), relative units (em, ex) and the pixel unit (px). Here are some examples:

```
BODY { font-size: 12pt }
PRE { font-size: 0.4mm }
H1.chapter { font-size: 16px }
```

Traditional paper-based design specifies the size of a font in absolute units, most often in points, but when working with Web pages, the use of absolute units for specifying sizes is not advised, since, for example, quality differences in screens will make some sizes hard to read and the font size you request may not be available on a particular browser. (Scaling may cause them not to align perfectly with the screen pixels.) It's better to use one of the relative units instead:

```
H1 { font-size: 1.2em }
```

On all properties except **font-size**, the em unit refers to the font size of the element itself. This makes it possible, e.g., to make the border as thick as the size of the font. However, when used on the **font-size** property the em unit has to refer to something else — otherwise it would be referring to itself. So, instead of referring to the font size of itself, the em unit refers to the font size of its parent. In the above example, the font size of H1 elements is set to be 1.2 times the font size of its parent. A similar example is given in Chapter 3 (where the em unit is the hero).

The "percentage" value

On the **font-size** property, using percentages is equivalent to using the em unit. Since the em in this case is the font size of the parent element, a value of 120% is exactly the same as a value of 1.2em. Another context-dependent method for specifying the font size is thus to use percentages. Like the relative value, the percentage is relative to the parent's font size, not the child (current) element's font size as in other properties. A percentage value gives an element the size of the parent's font times the percentage. Thus 120% gives a size that is 20% more than the size of the parent element, while 80% gives a size that is 80% of the parent element's size. For example, if the parent element size is 12pt, a 120% value will result in a size of 14.4pt, while an 80% value would result in a size of 9.6pt. Here is an example:

```
H1 { font-size: 120% }
```

The example above is equivalent to the previous example using the em unit.

The "absolute-size" value

The "absolute-size" value is an index to a table of font sizes that is computed and kept by the browser. These sizes are expressed as keywords, as follows:

- xx-small
- x-small
- small
- medium
- large
- x-large
- xx-large

These sizes form an increasing range. For computer screens, the CSS2 specification suggests that each of them is 1.2 times bigger than the previous one. That is, if the "medium" version of a font is **10pt**, the "large" version would be 1.2 times that size, or **12pt**. Different media may use or need different scaling factors. When the browser is computing the table of size values, it takes into account the quality and availability of fonts. Figure 5.12 gives the table's keywords and a representative example of each. The actual size will vary a little depending on the font.

xx-small	abcdefghijklmnopqrstuvwxyz
x-small	abcdefghijklmnopqrstuvwxyz
small	abcdefghijklmnopqrstuvwxyz
medium	abcdefghijklmnopqrstuvwxyz
large	abcdefghijklmnopqrstuvwxyz
x-large	abcdefghijklmnopqrstuvwxyz
xx-large	abcdefghijklmnopqrstuvwxyz

Figure 5.12 Comparison of the values of the size table.

Here's an example usage of the "absolute" value of the **font-size** property:

```
H1 { font-size: xx-small }
```

The "relative-size" value

The "relative-size" value lets you specify the size in a context-dependent manner. Recall from earlier in the chapter that relative values usually are relative to the font size of the element itself. The only exception is the **font-size** property. For that property, the value scales in relation to the font size of the element's parent.

The value has two keywords: **larger** and **smaller**. The keywords are interpreted relative to the table of font sizes mentioned in the previous section and the font size of the element's parent element. Specifying one of these keywords is a safe way to provide for context-dependent size changes. For example, suppose the parent element has a font size of "medium." If you then set the **font-size** property on the child element to **larger**, that is, larger than **medium**, the resultant size of the child will be **large**, which is the next value in the table of size values. Here's the code for doing this:

```
BODY { font-size: medium }
H2 { font-size: larger }
P { font-size: smaller }
```

BODY has a font size of **medium**. H2, as a child element of BODY, will be one size larger than BODY; that is, **large**. P will be one size smaller than BODY; that is, **small**.

THE FONT-STYLE PROPERTY

The **font-style** property lets you specify an oblique or italic style within the current type family.

IE3	NS4	IE4	O3.5
●	●	●	●

Name:	**font-style**
Value:	normal | italic | oblique
Initial:	normal
Applies to:	all elements
Inherited:	yes
Percentages:	N/A

This property has three keyword values:

- **normal** (also known as "roman", "regular", or sometimes "upright"). This is the default value
- **italic**
- **oblique**

Italic and oblique styles are similar, but not the same. Sans-serif families usually consider the two to be the same. Both are a variant that looks slanted to the right. For some families, that is indeed how they are produced: by mechanically slanting the roman letters. Usually, however, that doesn't lead to beautiful letters, and for most fonts the italic and roman forms are designed separately.

Serif families usually distinguish between the two. The italic form looks very different from the oblique form. The two differ in the shape of their serifs and often look like completely different letter forms. Oblique refers to a version that looks like slanted roman. Figure 5.13 compares roman, oblique and italic style.

Figure 5.13 (a) Sans-serif roman, oblique, and italic; (b) serif roman, oblique, and italic.

	roman	oblique	italic
(a) sans-serif	Aa	Aa	Aa
(b) serif	Aa	Aa	Aa

Font designers have used all kinds of names for their fonts without much consistency. Two other names that usually refer to what we described as oblique are *inclined* and *slanted*. Fonts with Oblique, Inclined, or Slanted in their names will usually be labeled "oblique" in a browser's font database and will be selected by the **oblique** value. Other names that usually refer to what we described as italic are *cursive* and *kursiv*. Fonts with Italic, Cursive, or Kursiv in their names will usually be labeled "italic" in a browser's font database and will be selected by the **italic** value.

If a type family has only an oblique style font, that font will be used as the italic as well. However, if you ask for oblique and the family has only an italic variant, you won't get the italic as a substitute for the oblique. Instead, the next family in the list will be tried to see if it has an oblique variant.

Here are example rules using the **font-style** property:

```
H1, H2, H3 { font-style: italic }
P { font-style: oblique }
H1 EM { font-style: oblique }
```

THE FONT-VARIANT PROPERTY

The **font-variant** property lets you specify a small-caps style within the current font family.

Name:	**font-variant**
Value:	normal | small-caps
Initial:	normal
Applies to:	all elements
Inherited:	yes
Percentages:	N/A

This property has two values:

- `normal`
- `small-caps`

A small-caps font style, despite its name, does not really consist of small capital letters. It is a differently shaped letter entirely that resembles capital letters. They are a little smaller and have slightly different proportions. Figure 5.14 compares small-caps and regular capital letters. The first line of the figure shows a true small-caps font. The second line shows uppercase letters from a roman font that have been reduced by 80% to simulate small-caps.

(a) capital - lowercase small-caps - lowercase

(b) capital - reduced capital - lowercase

Figure 5.14 (a) A true small-caps font; (b) The same font where the small-caps characters are simulated from capitals. The font used in the example is BaseNine.

Notice that the stems of the small caps are the same width as the stems of the lowercase letters around them while the reduced uppercase letters are too thin. The small caps are also wider than the reduced uppercase letters.

The value **normal** selects a font that is not a small-caps font, while **small-caps** selects a small-caps font. In the absence of a small-caps font, the browser may try to create one from an available normal font by scaling down and then stretching some uppercase letters. As a last resort, the browser may even use a normal font's uppercase letters, without reducing them. On the screen in low resolutions, as well as on low-grade printers, the difference between this adaptation and true small-caps will be hard to discern. On paper or a higher-quality output device, where the resolution is normally much higher, the difference will be noticeable.

If there is no small-caps style and the browser hasn't been configured to fake one, it will try the next family in the list of font families to see if it has a small-caps style. The following is an example rule that sets the **font-variant** property value:

```
H3 { font-variant: small-caps }
```

THE FONT-WEIGHT PROPERTY

The **font-weight** property specifies the weight of the desired font within the current family.

IE3   NS4   IE4   O3.5
 ●   ●   ●   ●

Name:	**font-weight**
Value:	normal | bold | bolder | lighter |100 | 200 | 300 | 400 | 500 | 600 | 700 | 800 | 900
Initial:	normal
Applies to:	all elements
Inherited:	yes
Percentages:	N/A

This property has nine levels of weight:

- The nine values **100** to **900** form an ordered sequence, where each number indicates a weight that is at least as dark as it predecessor, 100 being the lightest
- `normal` is the same as **400**
- `bold` is the same as **700**

Two of the values — bolder and lighter — select a weight that is relative to the parent's weight. These are discussed below.

The **font-weight** property is a superset of what is available for most families. Very few families have the equivalent of all nine different weights. Hence, many of the CSS weight values will result in the same font. On the other hand, some families, such as the Adobe's Multiple Master fonts, have an almost unlimited range. For those families, the browser will select nine of the possible weights and assign them to the nine values.

Numerical values are used because we felt that descriptive words, other than **normal** and **bold**, could be potentially confusing. This is because there is no universal naming system for fonts. For example, a font that you might consider bold could be described, depending on the font, as Roman, Regular, Book, Medium, Semi-Bold, Demi-Bold, or a number of other names. These names are generally meaningful mainly within the family that uses them and are used to differentiate fonts within that family. Outside that family, a name may have a different meaning. So you cannot necessarily gauge the weight of a font from its name. In CSS1, the value **normal** (**400**) will have the weight that is normal *for the specified font*. What it means for another font may differ.

Figure 5.15 gives examples of the nine weights. These are only samples. Exactly what you will get if you select a value of, say, **300** will depend on the font you are using. But the figure should help you get some idea of how the weights vary.

100   Font weight sample
200   Font weight sample
300   Font weight sample
400   Font weight sample
500   **Font weight sample**
600   **Font weight sample**
700   **Font weight sample**
800   **Font weight sample**
900   **Font weight sample**

Figure 5.15   Numerical values of the font-weight property.

The following are descriptions of the nine numerical values:

- **100** – this is the lightest weight. Not many fonts have weights lighter than **400** ("normal"). Those that do, for which the browser would select the **100** value, will often have Thin, Light, or Extra-light in their names. But font names are very inconsistent in their descriptions, so we suggest you don't rely on them. Let the browser figure out which weight a font is.
- **200** – this is not usually any different from **100**. However, it is included because some fonts, such as the Multiple Master fonts, have very many weights.
- **300** – this is a little heavier than the **100** and **200**.
- **400** – this is available for all fonts. It corresponds to the "normal" keyword that the property offers. You can choose either the number or keyword.

- **500** – this is a little bolder than **400**, but not by much. Some fonts have a weight called Medium that is just a little bolder than the normal weight; **500** would result in that weight. If there is no such font, 500 will be the same as **400**.
- **600** – this is a little bolder than **500**. A weight name of Demi-bold or Semi-bold would correspond to the **600** weight.
- **700** – this is available for most fonts. It corresponds to the "bold" keyword that the property offers. You can choose either the number or keyword.
- **800** – this is heavier than the usual bold. Fonts that have such a weight may have Extra-bold, Black, or Heavy in their names. Other possibilities are Poster and Ultra.
- **900** – this is the very heaviest weight available in a font. Fonts with this weight often have rather strange names, such as Nord or Ultima. Or they may have cryptic numbers, often the case with Multiple Master fonts. Most fonts on the typical computer don't go beyond bold (**700**), so choosing either 800 or **900** will result in the same effect as choosing **700**.

The **bolder** and `lighter` values select a weight that is relative to the parent's weight. For example, consider this style sheet:

```
P { font-weight: normal } /* same as 400 */
H1 { font-weight: 700 } /* same as "bold" */
STRONG ( font-weight: bolder }
```

In this example, a STRONG element that appears in either the P or H1 element will be bolder than its parent. However, the weight of STRONG when it appears in the P element may be less than its weight in the H1 element. This is because the parent elements' weights differ. We say "may" in this case because, as mentioned above, the font used also plays a role in how bold type looks.

For more information on how fonts are assigned to the numerical scale for each font, we recommend you check the CSS specifications.

THE FONT PROPERTY

The **font** property lets you to specify, in one action, all the other font properties described above plus **line-height** (which we discuss in Chapter 8, "Space inside boxes").

Name:	**font**
Value:	[[*<font-style>* || *<font-variant>* || *<font-weight>*]? *<font-size>* [/ *<line-height>*]? *<font-family>*]|caption | icon | menu | message-box | small-caption | status-bar
Initial:	see individual properties
Applies to:	all elements
Inherited:	yes
Percentages:	allowed on *<font-size>* and *<line-height>* only

The **font** property is the first of the so-called *shorthand properties* we describe in detail. Shorthand properties let you set a group of properties which naturally belong together. The font properties described in this chapter (**font-style**, **font-variant**, **font-weight**, **font-size**, **font-family**) form one such group and the **font** property sets all of them in one statement. Also, the **line-height** property (described in Chapter 8) is set by the **font** property, but note that **font-stretch** and **font-size-adjust** (described below) are not included in this group since they were added in CSS2.

The **font** property is one of the most common CSS properties, and a simple example of its use was given in Chapter 2. Here is another example:

```
H1 { font: 1.3em sans-serif }
```

The font property requires that you always specify a font size and a font family – all other values are optional. The example above is equivalent to writing:

```
H1 {
    font-style: normal;
    font-weight: normal;
    font-variant: normal;
    font-size: 1.3em;
    line-height: normal;
    font-family: sans-serif;
}
```

(Except for **font-size** and **font-family**, all properties in the above example are set to their initial values. Since the browser will do this automatically, it is normally not necessary to set them. Still, if you write your style sheets "by hand" – using a normal text editor rather than a dedicated tool – you will appreciate the brevity of shorthand properties.)

In principle, all values that are legal on the individual properties are also legal on the **font** property. There are restrictions, however, on the order the values must come in. First comes the **font-style**, **font-weight** and **font-variant** values, in any order. These are optional and will be set to their initial values if they are omitted. Then comes the **font-size** value which is required. It may optionally be followed by a "/" and a **line-height** value. Finally comes the **font-family** value which is required.

The syntax resembles a shorthand common in traditional typography, for example "12/14 Times bold italic." Here is an example of how to write a rule that reflects this shorthand:

```
P { font: italic bold normal 12pt/14pt Times, serif }
```

For demonstration purposes, we set every property, including **font-variant**, which has its initial value of "normal." Specifying initial values is not necessary. The browser will automatically use the initial values for those properties not explicitly set. For example:

```
P { font: italic bold large palatino, serif }
```

sets all properties except **font-variant** and **line-height**, whose initial values will be used. In other words, the above is equivalent to:

```
P {
    font-style: italic;
    font-weight: bold;
    font-variant: normal; /* default */
    font-size: large;
    line-height: normal; /* default */
    font-family: palatino, serif;
}
```

Here are some more examples:

```
P { font: italic 12pt/14pt bodoni, bembo, serif }
P { font: normal small-caps 120%/120% fantasy }
P { font: x-large/100% "new century schoolbook", serif }
```

The keyword "message-box" refers to the font used in user interface dialog boxes. The rule above will set all six properties to the values used in dialog boxes. The system font keywords are:

- **caption**: the font used for captioned controls (e.g., buttons, drop-downs, etc.).
- **icon**: the font used to label icons.
- **menu**: the font used in menus (e.g., dropdown menus and menu lists).

- **message-box**: the font used in dialog boxes.
- **small-caption**: the font used for labeling small controls.
- **status-bar**: the font used in window status bars.

System fonts may only be set as a whole; that is, the font family, size, weight, style, etc., are all set at the same time. These values may then be altered individually. For example;

```
BODY {
    font: message-box;
    font-size: x-large;
}
```

THE FONT-STRETCH PROPERTY

IE3	NS4	IE4	O3.5
○	○	○	○

Name:	**font-stretch**
Value:	normal | wider | narrower | ultra-condensed | extra-condensed | condensed | semi-condensed | semi-expanded | expanded | extra-expanded | ultra-expanded
Initial:	normal
Inherited:	all elements
Inherited:	yes
Percentages:	N/A

The **font-stretch** property selects a normal, condensed, or extended face from a font family. The property accepts two keywords which make the text **wider** or **narrower** than the text in the parent element. Also, nine keywords which express stretching in absolute terms are allowed. They have the following order, from narrowest to widest: **ultra-condensed, extra-condensed, condensed, semi-condensed, normal, semi-expanded, expanded, extra-expanded, ultra-expanded.**

It's up to the font designer to decide exactly how wide, say, the **extra-expanded** font is. Browsers can also synthesize condensed or expanded fonts from normal fonts and the example below shows how a browser might interpret the keyword values.

ultra-condensed:

Letters are letters. A is A. B is B.

extra-condensed:

Letters are letters. A is A. B is B.

condensed:

Letters are letters. A is A. B is B.

semi-condensed:

Letters are letters. A is A. B is B.

normal:

Letters are letters. A is A. B is B.

semi-expanded:

Letters are letters. A is A. B is B.

expanded:

Letters are letters. A is A. B is B.

extra-expanded:

Letters are letters. A is A. B is B.

ultra-expanded:

Letters are letters. A is A. B is B.

Figure 5.16 The figure shows how a browser might stretch and condense 14pt Gill Sans. Eric Gill, the font designer, also made the statement about letters.

NUMBERS AS VALUES

Some properties accept numbers without unit identifiers as values. The **font-size-adjust** property (described next) is one example and line-height (described in Chapter 8) is another. The syntax of number values are very simple: the number can be a whole number (0, 1, 2, ...), a fractional number (0.5, 2.57, 1.04, ...), or a negative number (–1, –3.14, –0.25, ...). If the integer part of the fractional number is zero, it can be omitted (.25, –.61).

THE FONT-SIZE-ADJUST PROPERTY

IE3   NS4   IE4   O3.5
○   ○   ○   ○

Name:	**font-size-adjust**
Value:	*<number>* | none
Initial:	none
Applies to:	all elements
Inherited:	yes
Percentages:	N/A

The font-size property was added to in CSS2 to correct a problem that occurred when using very legible fonts. How can very legible fonts be a problem? Recall the discussion about varying x-heights in the "Font metrics" section above. When the font size is the same, fonts with large x-heights (for example, Verdana) are more legible than fonts with smaller x-heights. Designers who are using Verdana are therefore likely to specify smaller font sizes. For example, 10pt Verdana might be just as legible as 12pt Times New Roman. So, in the style sheet we find:

```
BODY { font: 10px Verdana, Times New Roman }
```

Now, consider what happens when the document is displayed on a computer which doesn't have Verdana installed. The browser must then find a substitute and chances are that the substitute font isn't as legible. The result is a page which isn't as the designer intended – it might be downright illegible. The **font-size-adjust** property describes how the font size must be adjusted to preserve legibility if a substitute font is used instead of the designer's first choice. In effect, it allows designers to specify a certain x-height rather than a certain font size.

The value of the font-size-adjust property is either **none** (in which case no adjustments will be made and the value of **font-size** will be used as specified) or a number. The number is the ratio between the x-height and the font size. We call that ratio the *aspect value* of the font. For example, Verdana has an aspect value of 0.58; when Verdana's font size is 100 units, its x-height is 58 units. For comparison, Times New Roman has an aspect value of 0.46. Verdana will therefore tend to remain legible at smaller sizes than Times New Roman. Conversely, Verdana will often look "too big" if substituted for Times New Roman at a chosen size. To fix that, we add to our example:

```
BODY {
    font: 10px Verdana, Times New Roman;
    font-size-adjust: 0.58;
}
```

If the Verdana font isn't available, the substitute's font size will be adjusted so that its x-height becomes the same as Verdana's x-height. Here is the formula:

$$c = y(a/a')$$

where:

c = adjusted value of **font-size**

y = original value of **font-size**

a = specified aspect value

a' = aspect value of available font

For example, if 10px Verdana (with an aspect value of 0.58) was unavailable and an available font had an aspect value of 0.46, the font-size of the substitute would be 10px*(0.58/0.46) = 12.61px.

Figure 5.17 shows several fonts rasterized at a common size together with their aspect values. Note that faces with higher aspect values appear larger than those with lower. Faces with very low aspect values are illegible at the size shown. Figure 5.17 shows the results of **font-size-adjust** where all fonts have been adjusted to have the same x-height as Verdana. When adjusted, the fonts look as if they all were the same size, although the actual sizes vary by more than 100%.

Todd Fahrner of Studio Verso first proposed the **font-size-adjust** property and he also made Figures 5.17 and 5.18.

THE TEXT-DECORATION PROPERTY

The **text-decoration** property does not specify a font property, though it seems to fit best in this chapter because it affects type. The property is used to add underlining, overlining, strike-out or a blinking effect to the text.

IE3	NS4	IE4	O3.5		
⊙	⊙	●	●		

Name:	**text-decoration**
Value:	none | [underline || overline || line-through || blink]
Initial:	none
Applies to:	all elements
Inherited:	no (but see below)
Percentages:	N/A

Verdana: .58

xylophone synergy diaphragm partially hydrogenated
vegetable shortening or lengthening or resting

Comic Sans MS: .54

xylophone synergy diaphragm partially hydrogenated
vegetable shortening or lengthening or resting

Trebuchet MS: .53

xylophone synergy diaphragm partially hydrogenated
vegetable shortening or lengthening or resting

Georgia: .5

xylophone synergy diaphragm partially hydrogenated
vegetable shortening or lengthening or resting

Myriad Web: .48

xylophone synergy diaphragm partially hydrogenated
vegetable shortening or lengthening or resting

Minion Web: .47

xylophone synergy diaphragm partially hydrogenated
vegetable shortening or lengthening or resting

Times New Roman: .46

xylophone synergy diaphragm partially hydrogenated
vegetable shortening or lengthening or resting

Gill Sans: .46

xylophone synergy diaphragm partially hydrogenated
vegetable shortening or lengthening or resting

Bernhard Modern: .4

xylophone synergy diaphragm partially hydrogenated
vegetable shortening or lengthening or resting

Caflisch Script Web: .37

xylophone synergy diaphragm partially hydrogenated
vegetable shortening or lengthening or resting

Flemish Script: .28

xylophone synergy diaphragm partially hydrogenated
vegetable shortening or lengthening or resting

Figure 5.17 Several fonts rasterized at the same size together with their aspect values. Note that typefaces with higher aspect values appear larger than those with lower. Faces with very low aspect values are illegible at the size shown.

Verdana: 1

xylophone synergy diaphragm partially hydrogenated
vegetable shortening or lengthening or resting

Comic Sans MS: 1.07

xylophone synergy diaphragm partially hydrogenated
vegetable shortening or lengthening or resting

Trebuchet MS: 1.09

xylophone synergy diaphragm partially hydrogenated
vegetable shortening or lengthening or resting

Georgia: 1.16

xylophone synergy diaphragm partially hydrogenated
vegetable shortening or lengthening or resting

Myriad Web: 1.2

xylophone synergy diaphragm partially hydrogenated
vegetable shortening or lengthening or resting

Minion Web: 1.23

xylophone synergy diaphragm partially hydrogenated
vegetable shortening or lengthening or resting

Times New Roman: 1.26

xylophone synergy diaphragm partially hydrogenated
vegetable shortening or lengthening or resting

Gill Sans: 1.26

xylophone synergy diaphragm partially hydrogenated
vegetable shortening or lengthening or resting

Bernhard Modern: 1.45

xylophone synergy diaphragm partially hydrogenated
vegetable shortening or lengthening or resting

Caflisch Script Web: 1.57

xylophone synergy diaphragm partially hydrogenated
vegetable shortening or lengthening or resting

Flemish Script: 2.07

xylophone synergy diaphragm partially hydrogenated
vegetable shortening or lengthening or resting

Figure 5.18 The figure shows the effect of the font-size-adjust property. The font sizes have been adjusted to have the same x-height as Verdana.

The value is either **none**, meaning no decoration, or any combination of these:

- **underline** – an underline is added below the text
- **overline** – an overline is added above the text
- **line-through** – a horizontal line is inserted through the text (also known as strike-out)
- **blink** – the text is made to blink

In many browsers, underlining is used with the A element to mark the status of hyperlinks. The default style sheet for those browsers includes a rule like this:

```
A:link, A:visited, A:active {text-decoration: underline}
```

You cannot specify the exact position and thickness of the decorations. Many fonts come with indications of the preferred thicknesses of an overline, underline, and line-through and their distances from the baseline, and the browser will try to use those thickness and distance values. Otherwise, it will compute appropriate values based on the size of the font. The color of the lines will be the same as the color of the text.

You have a similar lack of precise control over the blink decoration. The blinking text will be shown in its own colors about half of the time; how it looks the other half is not specified. It may be invisible, or it may be shown in a different color so that the two colors show alternately. Most browsers will blink at a rate of approximately half a second on and half a second off. Not all browsers can blink, and, of course, blink will have no effect when the document is printed.

The **text-decoration** property is not inherited. However, a decoration on a parent will *continue* in child elements. The effect of this continuation differs from the effect that would result if we were to give the child element its own decoration. For example, suppose you added this rule to your style sheet:

```
EM { text-decoration: underline }
```

In the following, the underline decoration will affect all of the EM element, even the child element, STRONG:

```
Some <EM>very, <STRONG>very</STRONG>important things</EM>
resulted from this effort.
```

The result would look like this:

Some <u>very, **very** important things</u> resulted from this effort.

The color of the decoration (if any) also will continue across child elements. Thus even if STRONG had a different color value, its underline would still have been black.

The reason **text-decoration** is not inherited has to do with possible future additions to this property. For example, suppose the decoration were a fancy border (see Figure 5.19). The EM rule in the style sheet would change from text-decoration: underline to, say, text-decoration: deco-border (note, this value is not yet available in CSS). The child element is included as part of the decoration of its parent. Figure 5.19(b) shows the effect if the child element were to inherit the fancy box value of its parent. The child would have a fancy border of its own in addition to that of its parent.

Figure 5.19 (a) The decoration continues across the embedded element. (b) The embedded element has its own decoration.

(a)
Some (very, **very** important things)resulted from this effort.

(b)
Some (very, (**very**) important things)resulted from this effort.

There is another type of decoration that can be applied to text: shadows. But for how to draw shadows we first need to know about colors, so we postpone the description of the **text-shadow** property to the colors chapter (Chapter 11).

THE TEXT-TRANSFORM PROPERTY

The **text transform** property, like the **text-decoration** property, does not specify a font. However, it too seems to fit best in this chapter because it affects the case of text.

IE3	NS4	IE4	O3.5
○	●	●	●

Name:	**text-transform**
Value:	capitalize | uppercase | lowercase | none
Initial:	none
Applies to:	all elements
Inherited:	yes
Percentages:	N/A

This property has four values:

- `capitalize`
- `uppercase`
- `lowercase`
- `none`

The `capitalize` value capitalizes The First Letter Of Each Word, To Give An Effect Like This. **Uppercase** converts everything to UPPERCASE LETTERS, like these; **lowercase** does the opposite. **None** neutralizes an inherited value. These effects are often used in headings and titles but seldom in running text.

Here are some example usages:

```
H1 { text-transform: uppercase }
H1 { text-transform: capitalize }
```

The rules for converting from uppercase to lowercase and vice versa depend on the language used and on the browser. For example, the French typically remove accents when they write in uppercase so that, for example, téléphone becomes TELEPHONE. The Dutch have a special letter that is usually written "ij," although it is really a single letter. So a word like ijstijd would be capitalized as IJstijd.

The property also is useful for converting acronyms, like NATO, BASIC, PIN, and NASA to small-caps, as in, NATO, BASIC, PIN, and NASA. Acronyms in standard uppercase letters look too large. So in the next example (Figure 5.20) we use small-caps instead. We use **font-variant** to change the font to small-caps. But we don't use the uppercase version of small-caps, since our intent is to make the acronym look smaller, as shown earlier in the paragraph. So we use the lowercase version of small-caps (text-transform: lowercase) to achieve the right effect, as shown in Figure 5.20.

```
.acronym {
    text-transform: lowercase;
    font-variant: small-caps;
}
```

Success for NASA	Success for NASA	Success for NASA

`/* no rules */`	`.acronym {`
	`  font-variant: small-caps`
	`}`
		`.acronym {`
		`  font-variant: small-caps;`
		`  text-transform: lowercase`
		`}`

(a)	(b)	(c)

`Success for <SPAN CLASS="acronym">NASA</SPAN>`

Figure 5.20 Converting acronyms from standard uppercase letters into lowercase small-caps: (a) the acronym in standard uppercase letters; (b) the acronym in uppercase small-caps – this is not the effect we want; (c) the acronym in lowercase small-caps – this is the effect we want.

There is often confusion about the effects of **text-transform**'s uppercase and **font-variant**'s small-caps. However, as stated earlier in the chapter, selecting a small-caps font doesn't change the characters. A text transform, on the other hand, does. **Font-variant** selects a font, but **text-transform** doesn't. There is still a connection between them, though.

The fact that small-caps relies on the availability of a small-caps font also means that it can fail, if there is no such font available. For example, if the style sheet reads:

```
P {
    font-family: "Zapf Chancery", cursive;
    font-variant: small-caps;
}
```

the small-caps will fail, since the Zapf Chancery family doesn't have a small-caps variant. The browser may be able to synthesize one by taking the capitals and reducing them in height, but if it is not able to do that, it will show the P in all capitals instead, exactly as if the rule had read `text-transform: uppercase`. In other words, uppercase is a fallback strategy for browsers that don't have access to small-caps fonts.

MORE INFORMATION ABOUT FONTS

The Internet offers a lot of information about fonts. A good place to start is Yahoo's collection of typography links, at URL http://www.yahoo.com/Arts/Design_Arts/Graphic_Design/Typography/

Chapter 6

WebFonts

In CSS1 (the first level of CSS, which is what most current browsers support) all fonts are assumed to be present on the user's computer. When you buy a computer today, it typically comes with a long list of pre-installed fonts. Still, this is only a small fraction of the very long list of fonts that are available, and that list is growing every day. CSS2, the second level of CSS, therefore adds support for WebFonts – fonts that browsers automatically download from the Web. Unless you are particularly interested in downloadable fonts, you should probably skip this chapter in the first reading. If you *are* particularly interested in WebFonts, this chapter will tell you how to use them.

PREREQUISITES FOR WEBFONTS

By putting text into images, a common practice on the Web today, designers get total control over fonts. They can pick and choose between any font they have on their own machine (the list is often long) and don't have to worry about which fonts are available on the user's machine. As we know, however, this use of images is troublesome and should be avoided (Chapter 1 will remind you why). WebFonts are an attempt to give the same – if not higher – richness in fonts without sacrificing accessibility and printability.

Unfortunately, the examples provided in this chapter do not work in current browsers. We expect WebFonts to become widely available at some point in the future, but it's hard to say exactly when. Several things must happen before WebFonts become a solution designers can depend on:

- Browsers must be upgraded to support CSS2. Alas, supporting CSS2 isn't sufficient for making WebFonts work. That's because CSS only stores information *about* fonts, not the fonts themselves.

- A common storage format for WebFonts must be established. A style sheet can refer to a font in any format, but browsers are unlikely to support more than one or two different font formats. On users' machines, fonts are typically stored in TrueType or PostScript. These font formats were developed before the Web and are not necessarily suitable as a storage format for WebFonts. Therefore, Microsoft and Adobe have jointly developed OpenType which encapsulates TrueType and PostScript technology in a new format. Also, Bitstream's TrueDoc format has been developed in the context of the Web. It's still too early to tell which of these, if any, becomes the preferred storage format for WebFonts.

- A critical mass of WebFonts must be made available on the Web. Font designers are hesitant to put their creations on the Web until there is a way of ensuring legal protection of their works. The current protection is limited to the *names* of the fonts and does not cover the font data themselves. (That is, you are not allowed to create a font and publish under the name of "Helvetica," but you *are* allowed to publish a font that looks the same as Helvetica, but is called, say, "Switzerland;" however, the legislation isn't completely clear, and different countries may have different rules.)

FONT DESCRIPTIONS

WebFonts are fonts stored on the Web. In principle, the users themselves could download these fonts and manually install them on their machines – similar to the way in which browser plug-in programs are distributed. However, CSS2 makes the font download and installation process invisible and WebFonts can therefore be gracefully introduced on the Web without alarming users with dialog boxes or other user interaction. The user doesn't have to do any extra work for WebFonts to work, and most often the user will not even know that the fonts used are fetched from the Web.

In order for the browser to download a font from the Web it needs a URL pointing to the font. However, before it starts downloading it's useful to know a few more things about the font. For example, is the font in a format which the browser understands? Does the font have the characters needed to display the document? What if the document is in Chinese? Also, if it turns out that the font isn't available after all (perhaps the font server is down or the font costs money but the user refuses to pay for it) the browser must have information to find the best replacement font.

CSS *font descriptions* provide a way to store this kind of information about WebFonts so that browsers can find the most suitable font without having to download all of them to check. Here is an example of a font descriptor:

```
<HTML>
  <TITLE>Font test</TITLE>
  <STYLE TYPE="text/css">
    @font-face {
      font-family: "Tapered Norse";
      src: url("http://fonts.org/tapered-norse");
    }
    H1 {
      font-family: "Tapered Norse", serif;
      font-weight: bold;
    }
  </STYLE>
  <BODY>
    <H1>This heading is Tapered Norse</H1>
  </BODY>
</HTML>
```

The style sheet in the above example contains one *font description* (printed in bold) with two *font descriptors* (**src** and **font-family**). A font description always starts with **@font-face** followed by curly brackets with font descriptors inside. In the example above, the font descriptors give information about where to find the **Tapered Norse** font.

After the font description comes a rule which sets all H1 elements to use the **Tapered Norse** font family. A browser which only supports CSS1 will ignore the font descriptor, but it will read the H1 rule. Unless **Tapered Norse** is found on the user's computer, the next value (**serif**) will be used instead. This way, WebFonts can be introduced without breaking older browsers.

A CSS2 browser will first examine **@font-face** rules in search of a font description defining **Tapered Norse**. In the example above there is such a font description. Although it doesn't contain much information about the font, it does have a URL where the font can be found. The font will be downloaded from that address and be used when displaying H1 elements. If there had been no font description describing **Tapered Norse**, the user agent would behave exactly like the CSS1 browser.

If the font **Tapered Norse** had been installed on the user's computer, the installed copy would have been used instead of the downloadable font. This ensures that fonts aren't downloaded unless necessary.

FONT DESCRIPTORS

The *font-family* and *src* font descriptors used in the previous example are among the 24 font descriptors defined in CSS2. Font descriptors can be classified into several categories:

- Basic font descriptors: *font-family*, *font-style*, *font-variant*, *font-weight*, *font-stretch*, *font-size*. These descriptors provide the link between the CSS properties and the font description; in order for the fonts to be considered, the values of the font properties must match the values of the font descriptor with the same name. In the above example, "font-family" was used both as a font descriptor and as a property and this resulted in a successful font matching.
- Resource descriptors: *src*, *definition-src*. These descriptors point to font resources on the Web.
- The range descriptor: *unicode-range*. This descriptor indicates the range of characters a font contains. For example, the value can declare that a font contains only Chinese characters, or only uppercase.
- Matching descriptors: *units-per-em*, *panose-1*, *stemv*, *stemh*, *slope*, *cap-height*, *x-height*, *ascent*, *descent*. These descriptors provide additional information about the appearance of a font. If the font cannot be downloaded (e.g., if the user doesn't want to pay for additional fonts or if the font server isn't available), the additional information can be used to find the best match among the fonts that are available locally.
- Synthesis descriptors: *widths*, *bbox*. These descriptors are used if the browser temporarily doesn't have the font but expects it to arrive shortly. The descriptors provide key metric about a font – information which can be used to synthesize a font temporarily and avoid reflowing the document when the font comes in.
- Alignment descriptors: *baseline*, *centerline*, *mathline*, *topline*. These descriptors provide additional information about the font metrics. They are used to align text from different languages, for example when quoting Chinese within an English text.

BASIC FONT DESCRIPTORS

The basic font descriptors provide the link between the CSS properties and the font description; in order for the fonts to be considered, the values of the font properties must match the values of the font descriptor with the same name. Since a single font resource can contain more than one font face, these descriptors accept a comma-separated list of values. Also, the additional keyword "all" is permitted (except on *font-family*) which means that the font will match for all possible values; either because the font contains multiple weights, or because that face only has a single weight. Here is an example:

```
@font-face {
    font-family: Norse;
    font-weight: 300, 400, 500;
    font-stretch: all;
    src: url(http://www.fonts.org/norse-light);
}
```

The list of values on the *font-weight* descriptor indicates that the font resource found behind the attached URL contains three different font weights (**300**, **400** and **500**). The **all** value on the *font-stretch* descriptor indicates that the full range of different stretches are contained in the font resource.

Name:	***font-family***
Value:	[*<family-name>* | *<generic-family>*] [, [*<family-name>* | *<generic-family>*]]*
Initial:	depends on user agent

This is the descriptor for the font family name of a font and takes the same values as the **font-family** property.

Name:	***font-style***
Value:	all | [normal | italic | oblique] [, [normal | italic | oblique]]*
Initial:	all

This is the descriptor corresponding to the **font-style** property.

Name:	**font-variant**
Value:	all | [normal | small-caps] [,[normal | small-caps]]*
Initial:	normal

This is the descriptor corresponding to the **font-variant** property.

Name:	**font-weight**
Value:	all | [normal | bold | 100 | 200 | 300 | 400 | 500 | 600 | 700 | 800 | 900] [, [normal | bold | 100 | 200 | 300 | 400 | 500 | 600 | 700 | 800 | 900]]*
Initial:	all

This is the descriptor corresponding to the **font-weight** property. The relative keywords accepted by the property (**bolder** and **lighter**) are not permitted on this descriptor.

Name:	**font-stretch**
Value:	all | [normal | ultra-condensed | extra-condensed | condensed | semi-condensed | semi-expanded | expanded | extra-expanded | ultra-expanded] [, [normal | ultra-condensed | extra-condensed | condensed | semi-condensed | semi-expanded | expanded | extra-expanded | ultra-expanded]]*
Initial:	normal

This is the descriptor corresponding to the **font-stretch** property. The relative keywords accepted by the property (**wider** and **narrower**) are not permitted on this descriptor.

Name:	**font-size**
Value:	all | <length> [, <length>]*
Initial:	all

This is the descriptor for the sizes provided by this font. Only absolute length units are permitted, in contrast to the **font-size** property, which allows both relative and absolute lengths and sizes. A comma-separated list of absolute lengths is permitted. The initial value of **all** is suitable for most scalable fonts, so this descriptor is primarily for use in an **@font-face** for bitmap fonts.

RESOURCE DESCRIPTORS

The *src* and *definition-src* font descriptors point to font resources on the Web.

Name:	***src***
Value:	[<uri> [format(<*string*> [, <*string*>]*)]? | local(<*font-face-name*>)] [, <*uri*> [format(<*string*> [, <*string*>]*)]? | local(<*font-face-name*>)]*
Initial:	undefined

This descriptor is used to point to the source of a font face. The source can either be a URL, in which case the font can be downloaded from the Web, or it can be the name of a locally installed font.

Let's look at a few examples:

```
@font-face {
    font-family: "Steinbach";
    src: url("http://www.fonts.net/steinbach");
}
```

The above example shows the most basic use of WebFonts where the font description only contains the name of a font family and a URL from where it can be fetched. If a font becomes very popular, it might be a good idea to offer the font from several servers. You can specify several URLs in a comma-separated list:

```
@font-face {
    font-family: "Steinbach";
    src: url("http://www.fonts.net/steinbach"),
        url("http://www.type.net/steinbach");
}
```

To avoid fetching fonts in a format that the browser cannot decode, an optional format description can be added after the URL:

```
@font-face {
    font-family: "Steinbach";
    src: url("http://www.fonts.net/steinbach")
        format(truetype),
```

```
            url("http://www.type.net/steinbach")
            format(type-1);
    }
```

The list of potential formats include **truedoc-pfr** (TrueDoc™ Portable Font Resource), **embedded-opentype** (Embedded OpenType), **type-1** (PostScript™ Type 1), **truetype** (TrueType), **opentype** (OpenType, including TrueType Open), **truetype-gx** (TrueType with GX extensions), **speedo** (Speedo), and **intellifont** (Intellifont).

The *src* font descriptor can also take the name of a locally installed font as a value. For example, a user style sheet can provide a mapping from a generic font family to a locally installed font:

```
@font-face {
    font-family: sans-serif;
    src: local("Gill Sans");
}
```

Note that browsers are required always to provide a substitute font, if the specified font turns out not to be available. In other words, generic fonts cannot fail. In the example above, if the Gill Sans font is not installed, the browser will use some other font.

Name:	***definition-src***
Value:	*<uri>*
Initial:	undefined

There can be cases where font descriptions get very long and this descriptor provides a way to point to an external font description. You can achieve the same functionality by using the well-established **@import**, so we don't recommend using this descriptor.

THE UNICODE-RANGE DESCRIPTOR

The *unicode-range* descriptor is used to avoid checking or downloading a font that does not have the glyphs needed.

Name:	**unicode-range**
Value:	<urange> [, <urange>]*
Initial:	U+0-7FFFFFFF

The value is a comma-separated list of character ranges that are likely to be found in a script. You will need to know about Unicode to understand what a character range is.

Unicode (also known as ISO10646) contains a long list of character sets from all sorts of languages, including historical ones. Each character in Unicode has a number, called a *code point,* which uniquely distinguishes it from other characters. For example, the character "A" has code point number 65. Written in hexadecimal (see Chapter 11) this becomes 0041. If you have a font which only contains the letter "A," you could write:

```
@font-face {
    font-family: "just-a-font";
    unicode-range: U+0041;
    src: url(http://www.fonts.net/just-a-font);
}
```

Fonts with only one character aren't very useful, although they *do* exist. For example, there are several "fonts" containing just the Euro character (€).

To describe a range of characters, a question mark (?) can be used:

```
unicode-range: U+215?
```

The question mark can be thought of as a "wildcard" which can represent the hexadecimal digits from 0 to F. So, the above example describes the range from 2150 to 215F, which is where the mathematical fraction symbols are found in Unicode.

Using two wildcards, the range 0000 to 00FF can be described:

```
unicode-range: U+00??
```

This range is where all the Latin-1 characters (which include most characters in western languages) are found.

A pair of numbers in this format can be combined with the dash character to indicate larger ranges. For example:

```
unicode-range: U+AC00-D7FF
```

starts at AC00 and continues to D7FF, which is where the Hangul syllables are found. (Hangul is the script of Korea.)

Multiple, discontinuous ranges can be specified, separated by a comma. For example:

```
unicode-range: U+370-3FF, U+1F??
```

Unicode is a truly fascinating standard which will provide you with endless dinner-table conversations when dining with I18N ("Internationalization") geeks. You can find out more from http://www.unicode.org.

This covers the range 0370 to 03FF (Modern Greek) plus 1F00 to 1FFF (Ancient polytonic Greek).

MATCHING DESCRIPTORS

Matching descriptors provide additional information about the appearance of a font. If the font cannot be downloaded, the additional information can be used to find the best match among the fonts that are locally available.

Name:	**units-per-em**
Value:	<number>
Initial:	undefined

This descriptor specifies the number of "units" per em. In itself, it does not describe anything about the appearance of the font, but without this descriptor, some other descriptors become meaningless.

Certain font descriptors, e.g., **stemv** and **stemh**, are expressed in units that are relative to an abstract square whose height is the intended distance between lines of type in the same type size. This square is called the *em square* and it is the design grid on which the glyph outlines are defined. The value of this descriptor specifies how many units the em square is divided into.

Name:	**panose-1**
Value:	[<integer>]{10}
Initial:	0 0 0 0 0 0 0 0 0 0

For more information on Panose-1 (and Panose-2!) see http://www.fonts.com/panose/graybook.

Panose-1 is a classification system for fonts and each of the ten numbers in a Panose-1 specification characterizes the font in some way. For example, the fourth number describes the weight of the font. Potentially, Panose-1 can also be used when synthesizing fonts.

Name:	**stemv**
Value:	<number>
Initial:	undefined

Stemv describes the vertical stem width of the font. If the value is undefined, the descriptor is not used for matching. If this descriptor is used, the **units-**

per-em descriptor must also be used. For example, `stemv: 50` indicates that the vertical strokes of the letters are **50** units thick. If *units-per-em* is **1000**, that means the stems are **50/1000**ths of an em thick.

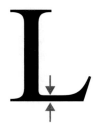

Name:	**stemh**
Value:	*<number>*
Initial:	undefined

Stemh desribes the horizontal stem width of the font. If the value is undefined, the descriptor is not used for matching. If this descriptor is used, the *units-per-em* descriptor must also be used.

Name:	**slope**
Value:	*<number>*
Initial:	0

Slope describes the vertical stroke angle of the font. The value is given in degrees counterclockwise from the vertical. The value is negative for fonts that slope to the right, as almost all italic and oblique fonts do.

```
@font-face {
    font-family: "Univers";
    src: url("http://univers.net/oblique");
    font-style: oblique;
    slope: -18;
}
```

Name:	**cap-height**
Value:	*<number>*
Initial:	undefined

Cap-height describes the height of uppercase glyphs of the font. The value is the distance from the baseline to the top of flat uppercase letters.

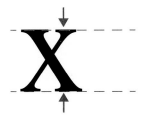

Name:	**x-height**
Value:	<number>
Initial:	undefined

X-height describes the height of lowercase glyphs of the font. This descriptor is useful together with the **font-size-adjust** property, because computation of the aspect value of candidate fonts requires both the font size and the x-height. For example, the x-height of Verdana (*see* Figure 5.17 on page 114) could be described as:

```
@font-face {
    font-family: "Verdana";
    font-style: normal;
    units-per-em: 1000;
    x-height: 580;
}
```

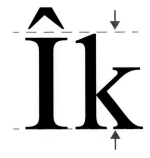

Name:	**ascent**
Value:	<number>
Initial:	undefined

Ascent describes the maximum unaccented height of the font, *i.e.*, the height of the tallest letter, excluding any accents. If the value is undefined, the descriptor is not used for matching.

Name:	**descent**
Value:	<number>
Initial:	undefined

Descent describes the the maximum unaccented depth of the font. If the value is undefined, the descriptor is not used for matching.

SYNTHESIS DESCRIPTORS

In the previous section we described how the browser could find the best locally installed font when the WebFont isn't available. Synthesizing a font is another, arguably more ambitous, replacement strategy for unavailable fonts. CSS2 does not describe *how* the font is to be synthesized, but it provides a way for style sheets to store the *width* of each letter. Once the width is known, the document can be laid out. When the WebFont arrives it can take the place of the synthesized font without having to reflow the document.

Name:	**widths**
Value:	[*<urange>*]? [*<number>*]+ [,[*<urange>*]? *<number>*]+]
Initial:	undefined

Width describes the glyph widths. The value is a comma-separated list of Unicode range values (see the **unicode-range** descriptor) each followed by one or more glyph widths. Here is an example:

```
widths: U+4E00-4E1F 1736 1874 1692
```

In the above example a range of 32 characters is given, from 4E00 to 4E1F. The glyph corresponding to the first character (4E00) has a width of 1736, the second has a width of 1874 and the third, 1692. Because not enough widths have been provided, the last width replicates to cover the rest of the specified range. Here is another:

```
widths: U+1A?? 1490, U+215? 1473 1838 1927 1684 1356 1792
        1815 1848 1870 1492 1715 1745 1584 1992 1978 1770
```

In this example, a single width (1490) is set for an entire range of 256 glyphs and then explicit widths are set for a range of 16 glyphs.

If the Unicode range is omitted, a range of U+0-7FFFFFFF is assumed which covers all characters in Unicode. If this descriptor is used, the **units-per-em** descriptor must also be specified.

Name:	**bbox**
Value:	*<number>*, *<number>*, *<number>*, *<number>*
Initial:	undefined

This is the descriptor for the maximal bounding box of the font. The maximal bounding box is the smallest rectangle enclosing the shape that results if all glyphs in the font are placed with their origins coincident, and then painted. The value is a comma-separated list of exactly four numbers specifying, in order, the lower left x, lower left y, upper right x, and upper right y of the bounding box for the complete font.

ALIGNMENT DESCRIPTORS

These descriptors are used to align runs of characters from different scripts with one another. A *script* is a group of written languages which share key characteristics including letterforms and writing direction.

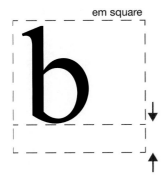

Name:	*baseline*
Value:	*<number>*
Initial:	0

Baseline describes the lower baseline of a font. The lower baseline is used by Latin, Greek, and Cyrillic scripts for alignment, just as the upper baseline is used for Sanscrit-derived scripts. If this descriptor is given a non-default (non-zero) value, the **units-per-em** descriptor must also be used.

Name:	*centerline*
Value:	*<number>*
Initial:	undefined

Centerline describes the central baseline of a font. The central baseline is used by ideographic scripts for alignment, just as the bottom baseline is used for Latin, Greek, and Cyrillic scripts. If the value is undefined, the UA may employ various heuristics such as the midpoint of the ascent and descent values. If this descriptor is used, the **units-per-em** descriptor must also be used.

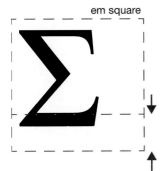

Name:	*mathline*
Value:	*<number>*
Initial:	undefined

Mathline describes the mathematical baseline of a font. The mathematical baseline is used by mathematical symbols for alignment, just as the lower baseline is used for Latin, Greek, and Cyrillic scripts. If undefined, the UA may use the center baseline. If this descriptor is used, the **units-per-em** descriptor must also be given.

Name:	**topline**
Value:	*\<number\>*
Initial:	undefined

topline describes the top baseline of a font. The top baseline is used by Sanscrit-derived scripts for alignment, just as the bottom baseline is used for Latin, Greek, and Cyrillic scripts. If undefined, the UA may use an approximate value such as the ascent. If this descriptor is used, the **units-per-em** descriptor must also be used.

Chapter 7

The fundamental objects

When a document displays on the user's screen, what shows up is not the underlying HTML code. Rather it is the browser's interpretation of that code. In the absence of any explicit instructions to the contrary, the browser will display the document using a set of default parameters. In HTML, for example, the browser will put P elements in separate blocks of text, and LI elements in blocks with a label on the side, but it will not create a separate block for EM elements.

You can affect the basic shape of elements on the screen by using the **display** property. With this property, you can specify that each element be displayed on the screen as one of the following:

- a block of text – for example, paragraphs and headings – are usually (but not always) displayed as a text block
- as part of a line of text – for example, inline elements such EM and SPAN
- a list item, a block with a label (number or bullet) on the side – for example, an LI
- a "run-in" header: a header that starts a new block of text, but doesn't have a line break after it (see page 139)
- a compact label in the margin, like the DT element in some types of list
- a cell or row in a table (table layout is explained in Chapter 19, "Tables")

In this chapter, we show how to use the **display** property to influence the form of elements on the screen. You may be thinking that a heading will always be displayed in a block of its own or that a list item will always be part of a stepped-out list, with list item on top of list item, but this is not the case. By changing the **display** property, you can create entirely different effects. We give some examples of how this is done.

We also discuss in this chapter two related properties:

- **List-style** property (actually a set of four properties), which enables you to create lists with different types of numbers or bullets
- **White-space** property, which lets you control how tabs, newlines, and extra white spaces are handled

The chapter also explains how to insert extra text before and after elements. This is useful if the standard list bullets and numbers are not sufficient, but it can do much more.

THE BOX MODEL

An HTML or XML document consists of elements inside other elements. For example, an EM can be inside a P, which is inside BODY, which is inside HTML. In earlier chapters, we pictured this as a tree structure, a model that helps when we deal with inheritance. This arrangement also could be visualized as a box model, whereby smaller boxes fit inside increasingly larger boxes, as illustrated in Figure 7.1.

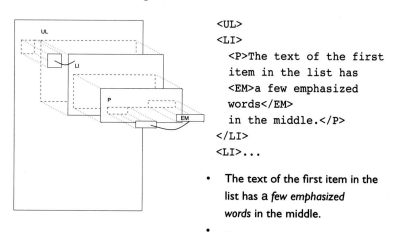

```
<UL>
<LI>
  <P>The text of the first
  item in the list has
  <EM>a few emphasized
  words</EM>
  in the middle.</P>
</LI>
<LI>...
```

- The text of the first item in the list has a *few emphasized words* in the middle.
- ...

Figure 7.1 The box model.

The box model can be used to depict the structure of an HTML document. The outermost box is HTML. The last box contains either text, such as "a few emphasized words" in Figure 7.1, or nothing, such as an empty element like BR. In between is everything else — BODY, P, H1, DIV, IMG, *etc.* A block-level element, like DIV and P, is normally shown as a box on its own. An inline element, like EM and SPAN, may be broken into several small boxes, if it is broken across lines. LI is commonly displayed as a box with a marker called a *label* — a bullet or number — on the side. The size and position of each element is relative to the enclosing box.

Although it looks in CSS as if the style properties are added to elements, what happens in fact is that the browser creates a parallel structure: for each element in the source, there is an object, called a *formatting object*, that gets all the properties. The **display** property determines the type of object, and thus the type and number of boxes that are created.

The fact that there is a difference between the elements and the formatting objects created from them can safely be ignored by users of CSS, but people creating browsers will encounter the objects. Formatting objects also play a role when you're dealing with highly complex design tasks, where simply formatting the document is no longer enough, and the document will have to be transformed in some ways. In that case, you will have to switch to another language other than CSS, for example XSL. At the time of writing, XSL was unfinished, but in time it will become a W3C Recommendation, like CSS. XSL has the same formatting objects and the same properties as CSS, but it also provides ways to create more than one formatting object per element, and to rearrange the order of the formatting objects. XSL is also much more difficult to use.

THE DISPLAY PROPERTY

The **display** property determines whether an element is displayed as a block, inline, list item, or other type of element.

IE3	NS4	IE4	O3.5		
○	⊙	⊙	⊙		

Name:	**display**
Value:	inline | block | list-item | run-in | compact | marker | table | inline-table | table-row-group | table-header-group | table-footer-group | table-row | table-column-group | table-column | table-cell | table-caption | none
Initial:	inline
Applies to:	all elements
Inherited:	no
Percentages:	N/A

This property has many possible values, but the most common are "block" and "inline." The table values will be explained in Chapter 19, "Tables," the others in the sections below.

The block value

An element with a "block" value starts and ends on a new line. For example, the start tag **<h1>** starts a box that contains the H1 element and the end tag **</h1>** ends the box. Here are some examples from HTML:

```
P { display: block }
H1 { display: block }
DIV { display: block }
```

The inline value

An element with an "inline" value does not start and end on a new line. It will be displayed in a box set on the same line as the previous content. The dimensions of the box depend on the size of the content. If the content is text, it may span several lines and there will be a box of text on each line. Familiar examples are EM, STRONG, and SPAN:

```
EM { display: inline }
STRONG { display: inline }
SPAN { display: inline }
```

All elements have a value for the **display** property in the browser's default style sheet and for HTML that is usually the one you want, so you don't often have to use the **display** property yourself. But occasionally you may want to make an LI inline, or a SPAN block. Or you may want to set an element back to its normal display type if you cascade off a style sheet that changes the display of the element.

For XML-based documents the situation is different. The browser probably doesn't have a default style sheet for them, and thus all elements will be "inline," unless you write **display** properties for them.

The list-item value

An element with a "list-item" value is displayed as a box with a label. This value typically applies to the LI element of HTML. A series of LIs with this value forms either an OL or UL list.

The LI may or may not have a visible label: a bullet or number that appears to the left of the list item. Whether it has a label, as well as the properties of the label are set with the **list-style** property, which we discuss in a later section, "More about lists."

The none value

To hide an element from view completely, you can set **display** to "none." The element will not be displayed at all. An example would be a document with questions and answers interleaved: first you display the document with the answers hidden and after you've tried to answer the questions you change to a different style sheet which shows the answers. The first style sheet could contain something like this:

```
.answer { display: none }
```

No boxes are created; not for the element itself, and not for its children either.

The run-in value

Although headings of sections are normally displayed in a block of their own, like the heading above this section, it is also possible to put them on the first line of the first paragraph in the section. The effect will be like this:

The run-in value. Although headings of sections are normally displayed in a block of their own, it is also possible to put them on the first line of the first paragraph in the section.

This is called a "run-in header." The effect is achieved with two style rules such as the following:

```
H3 { display: run-in }
H3:after { content: ". " }
```

The **content** property and the ":after" pseudo-element are explained in detail later in the chapter. They are used here to insert a period and a space after the run-in header.

An element can only be displayed run-in, if the next element is a block or an inline element. If there is, for example, a list item or a table after the heading, the run-in heading will be displayed as a normal block instead.

The compact value

Very short headers, or, more commonly, terms in a glossary, can be displayed in the margin of the following block. This is often done with the DT elements of the DL list in HTML. Figures 7.2(a) and (b) show two ways to format a glossary. In Figure 7.2(a), the terms (DT elements) are set as "block," in Figure 7.2(b) they are set as "compact."

A "compact" element will be put in the margin of the next block, if the margin is wide enough, otherwise it will be formatted as a block by itself. The figures show why it is called "compact."

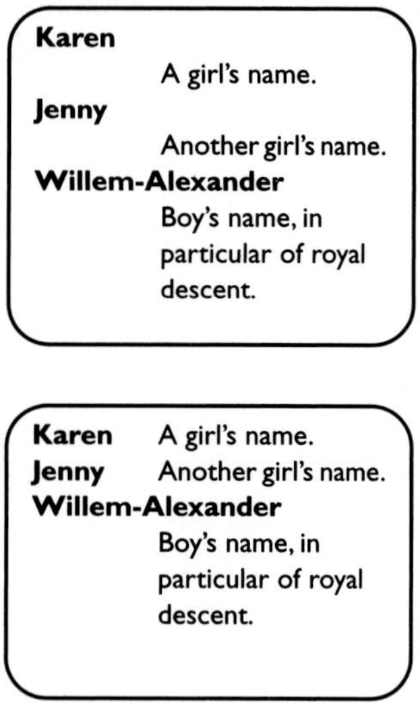

Figure 7.2 (a) A glossary list with "DT {display: block}." (b) Glossary list with "DT {display: compact}."

CREATING SIDE-HEADS

A "side-head" is a heading that is not put above the first paragraph of a section, but in the margin, next to the first paragraph. In CSS, there are two different ways to create side-heads, depending on the desired effect. One of them has already been explained above: "compact." The third relies on the **float** property that will be explained in detail in "Using the padding property" in Chapter 9.

The two different ways of creating side-heads can best be illustrated by how they handle long and short headings. Figure 7.3 shows the differences. For short headings, those short enough to fit in the margin without line breaks, there is no difference, but a long header can either be broken into multiple short lines in the margin (**float**), or changed into a normal block ("compact").

```
H3 {
   float: left;
   width: 5em}
P {margin-left: 5.5em}
```

```
H3 {
   display: compact;
   margin-right: 0.5em}
P {margin-left: 5.5em}
```

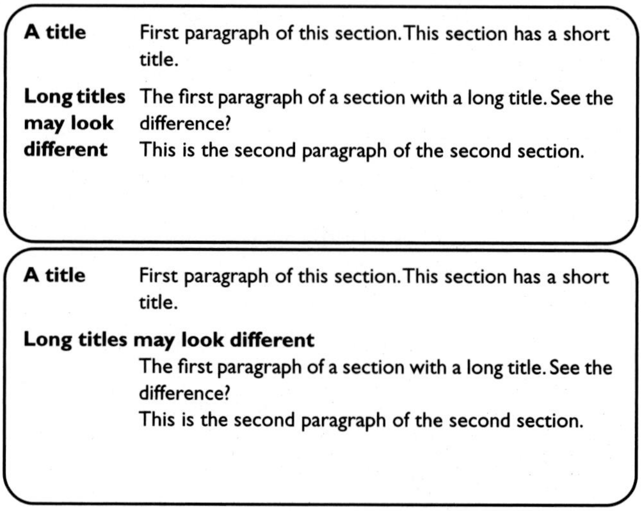

Figure 7.3 Two styles of side-heads.

ACHIEVING DIFFERENT EFFECTS

An element needn't be displayed using the value you might assume. You can change the value depending on the effect you want to achieve. An inline element can be "block," a block-level element can be "inline."

For example, instead of placing LI elements in separate blocks below each other with the "list-item" value, you could string them together in a running sentence and separate them by commas or semicolons. You would do this using the value "inline."

Figure 7.4(a) shows a typical UL list. The UL has its LIS set to "list-item." The labels, square bullets, were set via the **list-style** property discussed in the next section. Here are the rules:

```
LI {
    display: list-item;
    list-style: disc
}
```

Figure 7.4(b) shows the same list, but now with all items following each other on the line (inline). In this case, the LIS have the value "inline" and there are no labels. Since LIS normally contain P elements, we've set the display for P elements inside LIS as well. Here are the rules:

```
LI { display: inline }
LI P { display: inline }
```

Figure 7.4 (a) Using **list-item** to format a list; (b) using **inline** to format a list; (c) the HTML source.

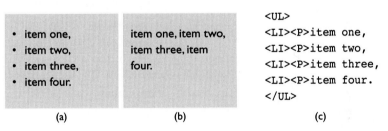

In another example, you can change an IMG that is inline to block. With this **display** property value:

```
IMG { display: inline }
```

and code like this example within the text:

```
<P>Text of a paragraph that is
interrupted <IMG SRC="http://www.image.file"> by this
image.
```

you get the result shown in Figure 7.5(a).

To make the image block-level instead, write this rule:

```
IMG { display: block }
```

to get the effect shown in Figure 7.5(b).

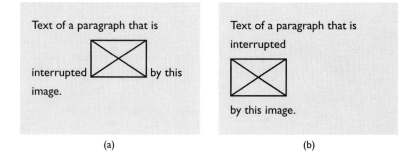

Figure 7.5 (a) An image with the value `inline`; (b) an image with the value `block`.

(a)   (b)

MORE ABOUT LISTS – THE LIST-STYLE PROPERTIES

List items may or may not have a label. If they do, the label will usually be a bullet: for example, ● ○ □ ; or a series of numbers; for example, I, II, III or 1, 2, 3. Lists also may be *nested, i.e.,* there can be lists within lists, with each level of list having a different type of number or bullet. Labels may be displayed:

- outside the box that encloses the LI, or
- to the left of the first line of the LI inside the box.

The **list-style** properties specify whether a list-item has a label, what kind of label (if the list item has one), and where it is placed. And, as mentioned earlier in the chapter, a list may be either stepped-out or run-in depending on the display property value you choose. The style and position of labels applies only to list items with the **display** property value of "list-item."

List-style is the most convenient property to use, since it sets all aspects of the label together, but you can also use **list-style-type**, **list-style-image** and **list-style-position** for setting individual aspects of the label.

THE LIST-STYLE-TYPE PROPERTY

The **list-style-type** property sets whether there is a label and, if so, its appearance.

Name:	**list-style-type**
Value:	disc | circle | square | decimal | decimal-leading-zero | lower-roman | upper-roman | lower-alpha | lower-latin | upper-alpha | upper-latin | lower-greek | hebrew | armenian | georgian | cjk-ideographic | hiragana | katakana | hiragana-iroha | katakane-iroha | none
Initial:	disc
Applies to:	elements with **display** property value "list-item"
Inherited:	yes
Percentages:	N/A

You can set the style of the label by specifying either a keyword or a URL. The property has nine values that are keywords. They can be divided into groups as follows.

To set the label to a predefined symbol:

*   disc (●) – this is the default
*   circle (○)
*   square (□)

To set the label to a number:

*   decimal (1, 2, 3,...)
*   decimal-leading-zero (01, 02, 03,...)
*   lower-roman (i, ii, iii,...)
*   upper-roman (I, II, III,...)
*   lower-alpha/lower-latin (a, b, c,...)
*   upper-alpha/upper-latin (A, B, C,...)
*   hiragana, katakana, hiragana-iroha, katakana-iroha – four different Japanese numbering styles
*   cjk-ideographic – numbering with Chinese characters
*   lower-greek – classical Greek numbers (α, β, γ)
*   armenian, georgian – traditional numbering systems using the Armenian and Georgian scripts, respectively

The final keyword, "none," suppresses the label.

However, "none" does not suppress the counting in a numbered list. If the next list item has a visible label, it will be two numbers higher than the item before the invisible label. For example, suppose you have a list of three list items and the value of the second item is set to "none." The first item will be numbered 1 and the last item will be numbered 3, even though there is no visible number 2 next to the second item. It will look like this:

1   Item with **list-style-type**: decimal
    Item with **list-style-type**: none
3   Item with **list-style-type**: decimal

The following are several examples of rules that set labels:

```
OL { list-style: lower-alpha }/* a b c d... */
OL { list-style: lower-roman }/* i ii iii... */
UL UL { list-style: square }/* square bullet */
LI.nolabel { list-style: none }/* no label */
UL UL.compact { list-style: circle }/* circle */
```

THE LIST-STYLE-IMAGE PROPERTY

Instead of a number or a predefined symbol, you can also use a (small) image as the label. That is done with the **list-style-image** property.

IE3	NS4	IE4	O3.5
○	○	●	●

Name:	**list-style-image**
Value:	*<url>* | none
Initial:	none
Applies to:	elements with **display** property value "list-item"
Inherited:	yes
Percentages:	N/A

For example:

```
UL { list-style-image:
      url("http://png.com/ellipse.png") }
```

Which might look like this:

 the first item

 the second item

 the third item

If there is a **list-style-image** other than none, it will be used as the label, instead of the **list-style-type**. However, if for some reason the browser is unable to download or display the image, it will use the **list-style-type** again.

THE LIST-STYLE-POSITION PROPERTY

The **list-style-position** property specifies the position of the list item label: inside or outside the list box.

IE3 NS4 IE4 O3.5
 ○   ○   ●   ●

Name:	**list-style-position**
Value:	inside | outside
Initial:	outside
Applies to:	elements with **display** property value "list-item"
Inherited:	yes
Percentages:	N/A

This property has two values:

· **inside**

• **outside** – this is the default

"**Outside**" places the label outside the list-item box aligned with the first line of text. "**Inside**" places the label inside the list item box aligned with the first line of the text. The latter value creates a more compact list. Figure 7.6 shows a comparison of the results of the two methods, along with the code that produced the results.

```
UL {list-style-position:        UL {list-style-position:
       outside }                       inside }
```
                ↓   ↓

- First item of a list with labels on the outside. Note that the label is positioned at the same height as the first line of the text, outside the text block.
- The second item in this list. Notice also how the text aligns under the first word of the first line, not under the label.
- Third item of a list with labels on the outside.

(a)

• A list with labels on the inside. The text forms a box and encloses the label as well as the text. The label is the first thing inside that box.
• The second item in this list. Notice how the text aligns under the label, not under the first word of the first line, thus making the list look more compact.
• Third item of a list with labels on the inside.

(b)

Figure 7.6 (a) A list with labels outside the box; (b) a list with labels inside the box.

THE LIST-STYLE PROPERTY

The **list-style** property is a shorthand means of setting both the label and its position at the same time. Its values are the legal values of the **list-style-type**, **list-style-image** and **list-style-position** properties. The following are examples:

```
UL { list-style: disc inside }
OL OL { list-style: circle outside }
```

When you set a URL, it's a good idea to also set a keyword so that if the image cannot be displayed, the browser can display the symbol indicated by the keyword; for example:

```
UL.files {
    list-style: url("images/file.png") square }
```

Using the **list-style** properties, you can create nested lists with a different numbering style at each level. Suppose you want to create a set of three nested lists. The labels of the first list are "decimal": 1, 2, 3, and so on. The labels of the first nested list are "upper-alpha": A, B, C, and so on. The labels of the second nested list are "upper-roman": I, II, III, and so on. You would write three rules, two of which use contextual selectors:

```
OL { list-style: decimal }
OL OL { list-style: upper-alpha }
OL OL OL { list-style: upper-roman }
```

Here is the resulting list:

1   First item of the first list
2   Second item of the first list
3   Third item of the first list; start of the first nested list
    A   First item of the first nested list
    B   Second item of the first nested list; start of the second nested list
        I   First item of the second nested list
        II   Second item of the second nested list
        III   Third item of the second nested list
    C   Return to the first nested list; back to uppercase letters
4   Back to the first list; back to decimal numbers
5   Fifth and last item of the first list

Note how the numbers align. You cannot change the alignment of the numbers. Nor can you specify the distance between the number and the text. (But see "Markers and the marker-offset property" page 155.) However, you can control the distance of the text from the left margin by using the **margin-left** property, which we describe in Chapter 9, "Space around boxes."

GENERATED TEXT, COUNTERS AND QUOTES

Sometimes text needs to be added that is not in the original source. Examples are texts like "Figure 7" or "Chapter XI," quote marks that are automatically inserted around citations, but also, of course, the list bullets and numbers of the previous section.

List bullets and numbers are the most common, and are also the easiest to specify. Numbering for list items is implicit: there is no explicit mention of a counter in the style sheet. But sometimes the **list-style** properties are not enough, for example, when lists must be numbered as A1, A2, etc. For those cases CSS provides explicit counters. The same explicit counters are also used to number chapters and sections, figures, tables, etc.

Fixed texts, such as the word "Figure" in "Figure 7," can be inserted together with the counters, or even on their own. A typical case is the insertion of the word "Note:" in front of all paragraphs that constitute notes.

Quotation marks are a special case. Although it is possible to just insert quote marks as fixed texts, in many cases it is desirable to use different quote marks based on whether the quote is nested inside some other quote or not. CSS has a property **quotes** that automatically tracks the nesting level of quotations and inserts the quote marks for that level.

The :before and :after pseudo-elements and the content property

One example where you might want to use the style sheet to insert text is in the case of notes. Say you have a paragraph with class "note" that looks like this in the source document:

```
...
<P CLASS="note">Steps 22 to 24 should be repeated for
each B-channel.
...
```

The way this should look in the formatted output is like this:

Note: Steps 22 to 24 should be repeated for each B-channel. [end of note]

The text "Note:" is inserted at the start, and "[end of note]" at the end. Here are the style rules to achieve this:

```
P.note:before {
    content: "Note: ";
    font-weight: bold }
P.note:after {
    content: " [end of note]" }
```

The ":before" and ":after" are two pseudo-elements. They refer to "elements" that do not exist in the source document. You can think of them as elements that, had they existed, would have been just after the start tag and just before the end tag:

```
<P CLASS="note">
  <:before>Note: </:before>
  Steps 22 to 24 should be repeated
  for each B-channel.
  <:after> [end of note]</:after>
</P>
```

The **content** property specifies the text that is in the pseudo-element. This property can only occur in rules for the ":before" and ":after" pseudo-elements, since all other elements already have content.

Name:	**content**
Value:	[*<string>* | *<counter>* | open-quote | close-quote | no-open-quote | no-close-quote]+
Initial:	(empty)
Applies to:	:before and :after pseudo-elements
Inherited:	no
Percentages:	N/A

The value of the **content** property is a sequence of text strings and/or counters and/or quote marks. For example:

```
BLOCKQUOTE:before {
    content: open-quote "quote " counter(bq) ". " }
BLOCKQUOTE:after {
    content: close-quote }
```

The next sections explain the keywords for the quote marks and the counters.

The :before and :after pseudo-elements are by default inline elements. They are put just before the first content of the element, or just after the last content. But sometimes you may to want to put them on a separate line, in a block of their own. If their parent element is a block element, then the ":before" and ":after" pseudo-elements may themselves also be block elements. That is done with the **display** property. For example, to end an HTML document with the words "The End" centered on a line by themselves, all that is required is:

```
BODY:after {
    content: "The End";
    display: block;
    text-align: center;
    margin-top: 1em }
```

The **margin-top** is thrown in to put a little space between the last line of the document and the words "The End."

Generating quote marks

Name:	**quotes**
Value:	[<string> <string>]+	none	inherit
Initial:	browser dependent
Applies to:	all elements
Inherited:	yes
Percentages:	N/A

The simplest way to add quotes elements like BLOCKQUOTE and Q is with a rule like **Q:before {content: '"'}**. However, most designers will want to change the double quotes to single quotes if the Q occurs inside another citation. You can usually do that with contextual selectors (**Q Q:after {...}**), but CSS2 has an easier solution.

The solution has two parts. The first part is to declare all the quote marks you want to use at each nested level of quotations. A good place to put them is on the BODY element in HTML, or on the document's root element in XML-based documents:

```
BODY { quotes: '"' '"'  "'" "'"  "‹" "›" }
```

This defines that the sequence of quote marks for progressively nested levels of quotations is "..." for the first citation, then '...' for quotes inside quotes, and ‹...› for the third level of quotations and beyond. After declaring the quotes, all that remains is to write the rules that say which elements get quotes, without saying which quotes, because that will be handled automatically:

```
BLOCKQUOTE:before, Q:before { content: open-quote }
BLOCKQUOTE:after, Q:after { content: close-quote }
```

Now a BLOCKQUOTE that is not inside another BLOCKQUOTE will get the "..." quotes, and if a Q or another BLOCKQUOTE occurs inside it, it will automatically get the '...' quotes, because the browser counts how many quotes have been opened.

If you look closely at the rule for the **quotes** property in the example above, you will see that there are no less than eight different quote marks in that one line. On the keyboard of a typical computer you won't find that many different keys. The program that you use to type in the style sheets may have special functions for generating them, but if it doesn't, there are other ways to put them in the style sheet. For example, even the simplest text editor will allow you to write the rule like this:

```
BODY { quotes: '\201C' '\201D'
    '\2018' '\2019'  '\2039' '\203A' }
```

It may not be immediately clear that `\201C` is the left double quotation mark ("), but when you are in a bind, this may be the only way out. Here is a table of the most common quote marks with their hex-codes:

Mark	Hex-code	Description
"	\22	Straight double quotation mark
'	\27	Straight single quotation mark ("apostrophe")
"	\201C	Left double quotation mark ("double high 6")
"	\201D	Right double quotation mark ("double high 9")
'	\2018	Left single quotation mark ("single high 6")
'	\2019	Right single quotation mark ("single high 9")
«	\AB	Left-pointing double angle quotation mark ("left guillemets")
»	\BB	Right-pointing double angle quotation mark ("right guillemets")
‹	\2039	Single left-pointing angle quotation mark
›	\203A	Single right-pointing angle quotation mark
„	\201E	Double low-9 quotation mark

Table 7.1 Common quote marks and their hex-codes.

Most programs give you the straight quote marks ("..." and '...') when you type the corresponding keys on the keyboard. But look carefully, because there are programs that interpret the keys differently.

Different typographic traditions prefer different quotation marks. Here are some examples in different languages, using the quotes from the table above.

English:

> When I read: "The double angle quotation marks are also called 'guillemets'," I knew that they must be French.

```
BODY { quotes: '"' '"'  ''' ''' }
```

Dutch:

> In een geschiedenisboek las ik: „Van Speyk wilde van overgeven niet horen. 'Dan liever de lucht in,' zei hij."

```
BODY { quotes: '„' '"'  ''' ''' }
```

German:

> Er sagte: ›Wie wär's mit »Gutentag«?‹

```
BODY { quotes: '›' '‹'  '»' '«' }
```

French:

> Dans un interview, Emmanuel a expliqué: « Je ne peux pas dire "Oui, je sais comment cela ce passe". Tout cela est ecrit. »

```
BODY { quotes: '«' '»'  '"' '"' }
```

In high-quality French typesetting, the guillemets and the single angle marks have half a space between them and the quoted words. The hex-code for a "thin space" (which is half the width of a normal space) is 2009, so you can make French graphic designers really happy if you change that last example to:

```
BODY { quotes: '«\2009' '\2009»'  '"' '"' }
```

In fact, if you look closely, you can see that the French example did actually use this rule; for French, it just looks better. If the half space is not supported by your software, the French will be almost as happy with a non-breaking space:

```
BODY { quotes: '«\A0' '\A0»'  '"' '"' }
```

A final note about the "thin space," for people interested in the details. Typography is always a bit more subtle than you think, and the thin space isn't exactly equal to half a normal space, or at least not always, although it is close enough for our purposes. On most systems a thin space is equal to 1/6 of an em, which works out to be close to half of a normal space for most fonts. But it depends a bit on the font. For proportional fonts, the normal space is usually between 0.30 and 0.36em (so the thin space is between 46% and 56% of the normal space), but for monospace fonts a space may be as wide as 0.5em (and a thin space is thus no more than 33% of a normal space).

Counters

If the numbering provided by the **list-style** property is not enough, you will have to resort to explicit counters. For numbering chapter and section titles, or tables, there is no other way. Three things can happen to counters: they are used somewhere, they are incremented, or they are reset to zero.

Using counters is only possible in the **content** property. For example, to number notes, you could do:

```
P.note:before {
    content: "Note " counter(note) ". " }
```

This will insert the fixed texts "Note " and ". " before every note paragraph, with the value of the "note" counter in between.

For incrementing counters, there is the **counter-increment** property. So if the note counter must be incremented every time there is a note paragraph, the rule would be:

```
P.note { counter-increment: note }
```

This is enough to number all notes in the document. But sometimes the style calls for a more sophisticated way of numbering. For example, if notes must be numbered within chapters only. Then every new chapter must reset the counter to zero. If we assume that chapters start with an H1 element, then this rule will suffice:

```
H1 { counter-reset: note }
```

IE3	NS4	IE4	O3.5
○	○	○	○

Name:	**counter-increment**
Value:	none | *<counter-name>*+
Initial:	none
Applies to:	all elements
Inherited:	no
Percentages:	N/A

IE3	NS4	IE4	O3.5
○	○	○	○

Name:	**counter-reset**
Value:	none | *<counter-name>*+
Initial:	none
Applies to:	all elements
Inherited:	no
Percentages:	N/A

Counter-increment and **counter-reset** become a bit more difficult if there is more than one counter that needs to be incremented or reset. For example, if the H1 element resets not only the note counter, but also the counter for subsections and for figures, then the rule would have to be similar to this:

```
H1 { counter-reset: note subsection figure }
```

This means you have to be careful when cascading several style sheets together. If one rule said **H1 {counter-reset: figure}** and later on there is a style rule **H1 {counter-reset: note}**, then the value of the **counter-reset** property will be just **note**, and the figure counter will not be reset.

Here is an example that numbers chapters and sections as 1., 1.1, 1.2, … 2., 2.1, etc.:

1. Life on the ground

...

1.1 Black and red ants

...

1.1.1 Ant heaps

...

1.1.2 What ants eat

...

The style rules that produce this are:

```
H1:before {
    content: counter(chapter) ". ";
    counter-reset: section;
    counter-increment: chapter }
H2:before {
    content: counter(chapter) "." counter(section);
    counter-reset: subsection;
    counter-increment: section }
H3:before {
    content: counter(chapter) "." counter(section)
        "." counter(subsection);
    counter-increment: subsection }
```

Styles for counters

By default, counters are shown as decimal numbers: 1, 2, 3,... . But just like list numbers, counters can also use roman numerals, letters, or various non-western numbering styles. The way the style is indicated is by adding a style keyword after the counter name:

```
counter(chapter, upper-roman)
```

will produce chapter numbers I, II, III, IV,... . All the styles that are available for **list-style** can also be used inside counter. For example, if the appendices of an article have to be numbered "Appendix A," "Appendix B," "Appendix C," etc. and the appendices all start with **<H1 class="appendix">**, then this rule will make that possible:

```
H1.appendix:before {
    content: "Appendix "
        counter(app, upper-alpha) " ";
    counter-increment: app }
```

Self-nesting counters

Numbering schemes like 1, 1.1, 1.2, 1.2.1,... are very common. To number the section headings in HTML this way is not very hard. There will be a counter associated with each of H1, H2, H3 to H6. The example on page 152 shows how it works. But sometimes things have to be numbered that can nest to arbitrary depth. In HTML, H6 is as far as you can go with subsections, but lists, for example, can nest to any depth, and all of them are called OL and LI.

CSS handles that by automatically creating a new counter when an element resets a counter that is already in use. For example, to create lists that look like this:

> 1 first item in first list
> 2 second item in first list
>> 2.1 first item in first sub-list
>> 2.2 second item in first sub-list
>>> 2.2.1 first item in sub-sub-list
>>> 2.2.2 second item in sub-sub-list
>> 2.3 third item in sub-list
>> 2.4 fourth item in sub-list
> 3 third item in first list

and that can go on to any depth, it is enough to create one counter, say "itemnr," and reset it on every OL element. The first OL creates the first "itemnr," the second OL creates a new "itemnr," etc. Each counter can only be used on element at the same depth on the document tree, or deeper, than the element that reset it. Therefore the last item in the list above uses the counter created by the topmost OL, all the others are "out of scope."

But how do you insert the number "1.1" into the formatted output? A declaration like:

```
content: counter(itemnr) "." counter(itemnr)
```

will not work, because both counters refer to the same instance of the "itemnr" counter. Instead, CSS provides a variation of the counter function, spelled **counters** with an "s." The correct rule, then, is as follows:

```
LI:before { content: counters(itemnr, ".");
    counter-increment: itemnr }
OL { counter-reset: itemnr }
```

The second argument of **counters** is the fixed text to put between the numbers. At the first level, the number will be "1," at the second "1.1," at the third "1.1.1," etc.

Of course, **counters** also accepts a style argument. If the numbers should be C.B.D, or III.II.IV, the value becomes **counters(itemnr,**

`".", upper-alpha)` or `counters(itemnr, ".", upper-roman)`.

Markers and the marker-offset property

The style rule above generated a counter in the ":before" pseudo-element of the LI element. But what if the LI is a list item (`display: list-item`), as is normally the case? Will it get two numbers, one from the automatic list label and one from the inserted text?

Yes, indeed it will. But of course there is a solution: tell the browser to use the inserted text *instead of* the normal list label. This is done by setting the **display** property to **marker**:

```
LI:before {
    content: counters(itemnr, ".");
    counter-increment: itemnr;
    display: marker }
```

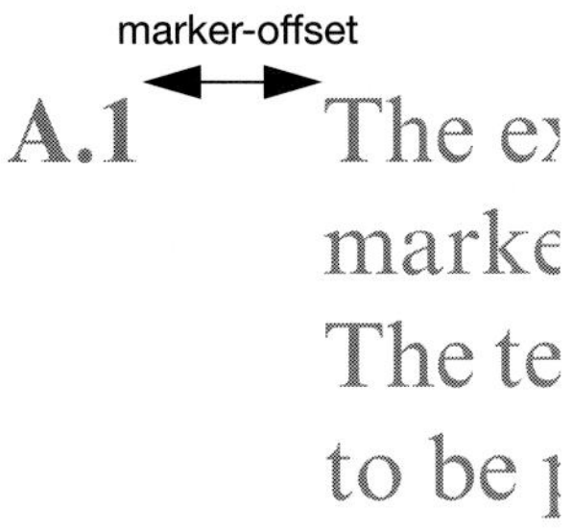

This tells the browser that the ":before" pseudo-element is neither **inline** (the initial value), nor **block**, but is in fact the label part of a list item. If the element in question is not a list item but a block, **marker** will also work, although there is no existing label to replace.

The exact position of a marker can be specified. The **marker-offset** property gives the distance between the marker and the text of the element, or to be precise: between the element's border and the marker. (If there is no border, the edge of the padding is used, and if there is no padding either, it is the edge of the content.) Figure 7.7 shows how it is measured.

marker-offset

A.1 The e:
marke
The te
to be

Figure 7.7 The **marker-offset** property.

IE3 NS4 IE4 O3.5
○   ○   ○   ○

Name:	**marker-offset**
Value:	*<length>*	auto
Initial:	auto
Applies to:	elements with `display: marker`
Inherited:	no
Percentages:	N/A

The value **auto** means that the browser chooses a suitable distance automatically.

Marker boxes can be given a padding and a border (and a background, color, font, and many other properties). Margins have no effect, since **marker-offset** takes over that role.

Normally, the **width** property of a marker is **auto**, meaning the marker box is the minimum size that encloses the marker. But the width can also be set explicitly. That is especially useful in combination with the

text-align or **background** properties. The following figure (Figure 7.8) shows an example that uses both:

I	Use "content: counter(li, upper-roman)" in the ":before"
II	Set display to "marker" in the ":before" pseudo-element
III	Set width to "3em"
IV	Set background to black
V	And color to white
VI	Use "text-align: center" to center the label in its box
VII	Use the top margin of the LI to create some space
VIII	Make the markers bold

Figure 7.8 The labels of the list have been centered in a colored box, by using an explicit counter, a marker box, and a set width for the marker.

The style rules in this case were:

```
LI:before {
    content: counter(li, upper-roman);
    counter-increment: li;
    display: marker;
    marker-offset: 4em;
    width: 3em;
    background: black;
    color: white;
    text-align: center;
    font-weight: bold }
LI { margin-top: 1.2em }
```

THE WHITE-SPACE PROPERTY

The **white-space** property specifies how tabs, newlines (also known as line breaks), and extra white space in an element's content are handled.

IE3	NS4	IE4	O3.5
○	⊙	○	○

Name:	**white-space**
Value:	normal | pre | nowrap
Initial:	normal
Applies to:	block elements
Inherited:	yes
Percentages:	N/A

This property has three values:

- normal
- pre
- nowrap

An HTML document may contain unwanted tabs, newlines, and additional white spaces (more than the normal one white space between words). These can be called collectively *white-space characters*. Usually, you'll want those extra white-space characters to be ignored. The browser will do this automatically for you and lay out the text in a way that fits the window. It will throw away any extra white spaces at the beginning and end of a paragraph and *collapse* (combine) all tabs, newlines, and extra white space between words into single white-space characters. In addition, as the window is resized larger or smaller by the user, the browser will reformat the text as needed to fit it in the new window size.

For some elements, you may have specifically formatted the text in such a way that includes extra white-space characters. You don't want those characters thrown away or collapsed. One way to ensure preformatted text stays formatted is to use the PRE element, which we discussed in Chapter 1, "The Web and HTML."

Note: to ensure an extra white space stays where you put it, you can also use a nonbreaking space, written with the " " entity. For example:

```
<P>There will be   three spaces before the
word "three" no matter what the value of the display
property is. Also, there will never be a line break
between "be" and "three."
```

There will be   three spaces before the word "three" no matter what the value of the display property is. Also, there will never be a line break between "be" and "three."

If you wonder why tabs are interpreted in this strange way: it has to do with the traditional way tabs are displayed on computer terminals. Apart from word processors, most programs that manipulate text interpreted tabs this way (and many still do). Especially in the first pages on the Web, the PRE element was mostly used for displaying computer code; that's why it made sense to interpret a tab as a jump to the next multiple of eight.

The value "normal" of the **white-space** property causes all extra white-space characters in the element to be ignored or collapsed. The "pre" value causes all extra white space to be retained and newlines to cause line breaks. It also causes tabs to be converted into spaces according to a certain formula. The tab is replaced by from 1 to 8 spaces so that the last one is at a column that is a multiple of 8. For example, suppose there are 52 characters to the left of the tab. The browser will insert 4 spaces to reach the nearest multiple of 8, that is, 56. So the next character after the tab will end up as the 57th character of the line. This effect is all right when you use a monospaced (fixed-width) font, but it looks strange when used with a proportional-spaced (variable-width) font. Here is how it looks with a monospaced font:

```
These words      have been aligned      with
tabs so that     the letters align      nicely?
```

And this is with a proportional font. The number of spaces that are inserted is the same, but that doesn't cause the words to be aligned:

These words   have been aligned   with
tabs so that   the letters align   nicely?

The **pre** value also suppresses justification. We discuss justification in Chapter 8, "Space inside boxes."

Figure 7.9 compares the results of the **normal** and **pre** values on an example paragraph of text. Assume the HTML code looked like this:

```
<P> This is a paragraph
with some random    tabs
        and         lots of       spaces. (It may
    have      been
the result of     some hasty copying and
    pasting.)
```

This is a paragraph with some random tabs and lots of spaces. (It may have been the result of some hasty copying and pasting.)

This is a paragraph
with some   random   tabs
        and   lots of   spaces. (It may
    have   been
the result of   some hasty copying
and
        pasting.)

↑

↑

Figure 7.9 The result of formatting the example paragraph with two values for the white-space property. In (a) with value "normal"; in (b) with value "pre."

P {white-space: normal}

(a)

P {white-space: pre}

(b)

The **nowrap** value will collapse extra white space like **normal**, but it will not automatically break lines that are too long. Line breaks only occur when there is a **
** in the text. The example paragraph would be all on one line, too long to show on this page.

Although the value "pre" made the example above look strange, it can be a very useful value in other cases. Here is an example that uses the **pre** element and a *class* attribute to create an element that is specialized for simple poems.

```
<HEAD>
  <TITLE>A poem</TITLE>
  <STYLE>
    PRE.poem {
      white-space: pre;
      font-family: sans-serif
    }
  </STYLE>
</HEAD>
<BODY>
  <H1>A poem</H1>
```

```
<PRE CLASS="poem">
In this little poem
all white space counts
    therefore this line
    and also this
were indented with four spaces
exactly as much
as between this word    and this.</PRE>
</BODY>
```

Here is the result:

A poem

```
In this little poem
all white space counts
    therefore this line
    and also this
were indented with four spaces
exactly as much
as between this word    and this.
```

Chapter 8

Space inside boxes

Extra space in and around elements on a page can enhance your presentation and help get your message across to the reader. Along with influencing color (Chapter 11) and fonts (Chapter 5), influencing spacing has been high on the wishlists of Web page designers.

Before CSS, there were three ways to control space in HTML: with elements, images, and tables:

1 *Elements.* Recall that browsers normally throw away white-space characters – newlines, tabs, and extra white spaces (any more than the usual one space between words). However, inside the PRE element, these characters are preserved with their original meanings. (See "The white-space property" on page 156) By using PRE, designers have used white-space characters to achieve, for example, a very crude, multicolumn layout. Other HTML tags also have been used in unexpected ways. For example, some designers rely on empty P elements or BR elements to increase vertical spacing and on BLOCKQUOTE to indent paragraphs. Often, the results are different in different browsers.

2 *Images.* Recall from Chapter 1 that we talked about the use of images as substitutes for text. Text has often been rendered as an image because in this way every pixel can be controlled. Also, to make minor spacing adjustments, some designers insert transparent images into the text. For example, they indent a paragraph by placing five 1-pixel images

at the beginning of each paragraph. However, using images has a downside: they are not scalable from one screen resolution to another, they are not very accessible, and they make the page download slower.

3 *Tables*. The use of tables is the most recent and most "advanced" method for controlling space in HTML. Tables offer layout capabilities beyond CSS1 (though not beyond CSS2). Unlike images, they are scalable from one screen resolution to another. The downside of tables is that the HTML markup is complicated. Tables also take longer to render and are very bad for accessibility. We talked about the use of tables also in Chapter 1.

Occasionally, there may still be no other way to realize a certain effect. However, these methods do not offer the depth of functionality for influencing space in your documents that CSS does. By using CSS, you can greatly expand your control of spacing in and around block-level elements as well as replaced elements. In this chapter, we will show you how you control spacing inside a box: between letters, between words, between lines. In the next chapter, we will deal with spacing around the box: margins, padding, floating boxes.

SPACE INSIDE BLOCK-LEVEL ELEMENTS

You can affect the space inside a block-level element by changing the amount of space between letters, words, lines, and/or paragraphs as well as by varying the alignment of text. Six properties help you influence space inside paragraphs:

- **text-align**
- **text-indent**
- **line-height**
- **word-spacing**
- **letter-spacing**
- **vertical-align**

These plus the font properties discussed in Chapter 5, "Fonts," give you significant amount of control over your document's appearance.

Among these six properties, **text-align**, **text-indent**, and **line-height** are used most often, because they are the primary means of expressing the character of the text and of safeguarding readability. The other three, **word-spacing**, **letter-spacing**, and **vertical-align**, are usually used only to achieve special, localized effects. In the following sections, we discuss each of the six properties.

THE TEXT-ALIGN PROPERTY

The **text-align** property sets the way the lines are adjusted horizontally between the left and right margins of the element.

IE3 NS4 IE4 O3.5
⊙   ●   ●   ●

Name:	**text-align**
Value:	left	right	center	justify	<string>
Initial:	UA-specific
Applies to:	block-level elements
Inherited:	yes
Percentages:	N/A

This property has five values:

- **left** – lines are aligned at the left margin; the right margin is ragged (uneven). Sometimes called *left-justified*.
- **right** – lines are aligned at the right margin; the left margin is ragged. Sometimes called *right-justified*.
- **center** – lines are individually centered in the middle of the box; both the right and left margins are ragged.
- **justified** – lines are aligned on both the left and right margins; text is spread out between the margins as evenly as possible. Sometimes called *fully justified*.
- a string – used to align table columns (see Chapter 19, page 347).

Figure 8.1 shows each type of alignment.

Figure 8.1 The four types of horizontal alignment with **text-align**.

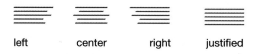

left   center   right   justified

Here's an example rule for changing the alignment of a P element from the default to **center**:

```
P { text-align: center }
```

The **text-align** property is inherited, so you can set the alignment of the whole document by using the BODY element as follows, where we change the alignment from the default to **justify**:

```
BODY { text-align: justify }
```

Note: alignment of text is relative to the width of the element, not the width of the canvas. For example, the text of an element with **text-align** set to **center** will be centered between the margins of the element, regardless of where the element is positioned on the canvas. Hence, the text may not appear centered on the canvas.

RIGHT ALIGNING TEXT

The most common alignments are left, justified, and centered. Right-aligning text – placing it against the right margin – is seldom done in languages that are written and read from left to right, such as English, at least not for long stretches of text. It is too difficult to read in large amounts. Its use is usually reserved for titles, cells in a table, and special type design effects. Examples of these three are shown in Figure 8.2(a)–(c).

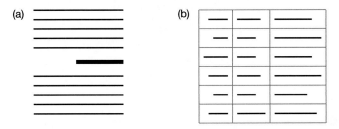

Figure 8.2 Examples of right-aligned text: (a) a right-aligned heading; (b) a table with right-aligned text in the first column; (c) right-aligned "side-heads;" (d) a letter with a right-aligned date and signature.

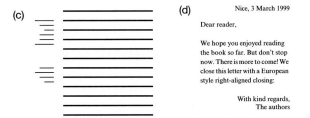

Nice, 3 March 1999

Dear reader,

We hope you enjoyed reading the book so far. But don't stop now. There is more to come! We close this letter with a European style right-aligned closing:

With kind regards,
The authors

Another use for **right** is the signature below a letter. The traditional layout of letters in many languages is for a signature to aligned against the right margin. Here's how you would code this. Figure 8.2(d) shows the result.

```
<STYLE>
  P.date, P.closing, P.signature {
    text-align: right }
  P.opening, P.closing { margin-top: 1.2em }
  P.opening { margin-bottom: 1.2em }
</STYLE>

<P CLASS="date">Nice, 3 March 1999
<P CLASS="opening">Dear reader,
<P>We hope you enjoyed reading the book so far. But don't
stop now. There is more to come! We close this letter
```

```
with a European-style, right-aligned closing:
<P CLASS="closing">With kind regards,<BR>
The authors.
```

JUSTIFYING TEXT

Justified text is text that is spaced out from left to right margin so that the texts fills the space between the margins. For the value `justify`, CSS does not specify how text is stretched, or spaced out, as part of distributing it between the margins. Some implementations will stretch only the spaces between the words. Others may stretch the spaces between the letters as well. Yet others may occasionally shrink spaces instead (and thus put more words on a line). Which method is used depends on the browser as well as on the language in which the text is displayed.

In languages with long words, you may want to avoid justifying lines, unless the lines are relatively long. Long words often will be stretched out to fill the line, sometimes resulting in too much space between the letters. You may have noticed this effect in newspapers, in which full justification can create rivers of white running down through a column of type. One alternative is to use hyphens. CSS2 doesn't do anything with hyphenation – it doesn't turn it on or off. But then, most browsers don't do automatic hyphenation anyway. Future versions of CSS may allow you to control hyphenation. At that time, justifying such languages would be feasible, although perhaps at the trade-off of splitting words. In the meantime, you can manually insert hyphens if you want in order to achieve a better-looking justified appearance.

Not all browsers support `justify`. Those that don't will usually supply a replacement, typically `left` in western languages.

THE TEXT-INDENT PROPERTY

The **text-indent** property specifies the indentation of the first line of a paragraph. In a left-to-right language such as English or French, the indentaion is added to the left of the first line. In a right-to-left language such as Arabic or Hebrew, it is added to the right of the first line.

HTML has a special *entity* for manually hyphenating words: **­** ("soft hyphen"). When you insert it in the middle of a word, like this: "**hy­phen­ate**", a browser may break the word at the position of the entity. A browser that cannot break words should ignore the entity. Unfortunately, at the time of writing (end of 1998), all the major browsers still have a bug that causes them to insert a hyphen for *every* **­** without breaking the word.

Name:	**text-indent**
Value:	*<length>*	*<percentage>*
Initial:	0
Applies to:	block-level elements
Inherited:	yes
Percentages:	refer to parent element's width

This property has two values:

- a length – an absolute or relative number
- a percentage – a percentage of the width of the paragraph; for example, 10% means indent the first line by 10% of the width of the paragraph

Text-indent is an inherited property. Only the computed value is passed on. That is, the amount of indentation is computed once for the parent element and the *result* is inherited by all of its children. The value is not computed again in its child elements even if they have a different font size. For example, if the current font size of the parent element is 10pt and the amount of indentation is set to 2em, child elements will inherit an indent of 20pt, no matter what their own font size is (10pt $\times$ 2 = 20pt). Negative values are allowed, although some browsers may not be able to display them.

USING THE TEXT-INDENT PROPERTY

Indenting first lines is more common in fiction than in technical texts. Some people consider it old-fashioned, although a very large indent may look quite modern again. At the same time, a too-large indent can hamper readability.

Perhaps the best and most common reason for choosing to indent the first line is that it is a good way to indicate the start of a paragraph. That's why we used it in this book. Also, when used in this way, you can save space within the document. Without the indent, paragraphs must have extra space between them so that one paragraph can be distinguished from another. This adds to the length of the document. See Figure 8.3(b), which was achieved using this rule:

```
P { text-indent: 1em }
```

Interesting effects can be achieved with *negative* indents. A negative indent causes the first line to stick out, outside the bounding box of the paragraph. Some newspapers use this effect to distinguish commentaries from news articles, or in order to give a distinct visual appearance. Figure 8.3(c) shows a well-done negative indent, achieved using this rule:

```
P { text-indent: -1em }
```

However, you have to be careful when using negative indents; otherwise, unexpected effects may result. The figure on page 184 in Chapter 9 shows an example of a negative indent that is too large: part of the first word ends up outside the window. This resulted from input like this:

```
BODY { margin-left; 2em }
P { text-indent: -4em }
```

Similarly, an effect that may actually be desirable from a design perspective, is when the first word overlaps something that is to the left of the text, such as a floating image. Code like this could produce that result:

```
P { text-indent: -4em }
IMG { float: left; margin: 2em }
```

This effect is shown in Figure 8.3(d).

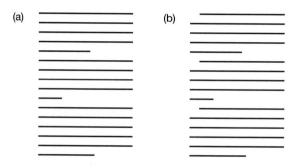

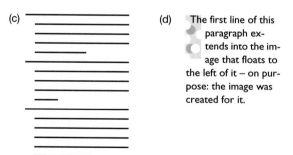

Figure 8.3 Using the **text-indent** property to indent paragraphs: (a) a nonindented paragraph; (b) a regular indented paragraph; (c) a well-done negative indented paragraph; (d) a negative indent with a large indent that was done intentionally to achieve a particular design effect.

(d) The first line of this paragraph extends into the image that floats to the left of it – on purpose: the image was created for it.

Text-indent indents only the first line of any element. However, some elements have a first line that is actually inside another element. In this case, **text-indent** may not be able to indent the first line. Here's an example of how this works. A style sheet with these specifications:

```
DIV { text-indent: 2em }
P { text-indent: 0em }
```

and a document with this text:

```
<DIV><P>A nonindented paragraph...</DIV>
```

will result in the paragraph's not having any indentation. This is because the first line of DIV occurs *inside* another element, P, that has a **text-indent** of 0. The 0em value of P overrides the 2em value of DIV.

On the other hand, an element may appear to consist of several paragraphs, but it actually is a paragraph that is interrupted by another element. It will still have only one first line and hence only that first line will be indented by **text-indent**. For example, suppose you were to specify this style sheet:

```
P { text-indent: 2em }
```

and interrupt a paragraph element with a BR element, this would be the result:

```
<P>This is a paragraph broken
by another element.<BR><BR>
This line is not indented.
```

This is a paragraph broken by another element.

This line is not indented.

THE LINE-HEIGHT PROPERTY

The **line-height** property specifies how far apart the lines in a paragraph are. Or more precisely, it specifies the *minimum* distance between the baselines of the adjacent lines.

Figure 8.4 shows schematically what the line-height specifies.

IE3	NS4	IE4	O3.5
☉	☉	●	●

Name:	**line-height**
Value:	*<number>* | *<length>* | *<percentage>*
Initial:	UA-specific
Applies to:	all elements
Inherited:	yes
Percentages:	relative to the font size of the element itself

This property has three values:

- a number
- a length
- a percentage

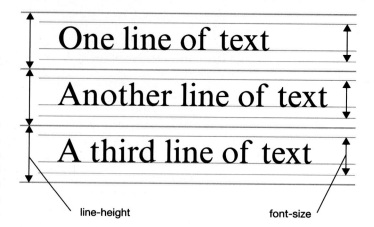

Figure 8.4 What the **line-height** property measures. The added space in addition to the font size is often called the *leading*. In CSS, half of the leading is inserted above the text and half of it below.

line-height

font-size

The "length" value is either an absolute value (e.g. 1 cm, 0.5 in, 15 mm, 20 pt, 2.3 pc) or a relative value (e.g. 1.2em). A common absolute value for **line-height** is 12 pt for a 10 pt font.

The "number" and "percentage" values, as well as a "length" value with an em unit, operate similarly to each other, with an important difference. In principle, all three are interpreted as relative to the font size; if we assume a font size of 10 pt, a line height of 1.2 means the line height is set to 12 pt (1.2 times the font size). A percentage value works similarly: if the value is set to 120%, the resulting line height of a 10 pt font is again 12 pt (120% × 10 pt). In the same manner, a value of 1.2em means 1.2 × 10 = 12 pt.

However, they differ in how they handle inheritance. A line height specified as a number is computed for the parent *and also for each child*. The line height corresponding to the percentage and the em is computed once and *the result* is inherited by all children. (This is true for all properties that allow a percentage or em unit as the value.) Of the three methods for calculating the value, the number method is preferred.

Figure 8.5(a) shows the effect of using the "percentage" value. Figure 8.5(b) shows the effect on the same text using the "number" value. In (a), the paragraph has a line height of 120% times the font size of the body (10 pt), which computes to a line height of 12 pt. The quote is printed in a smaller font, but the line height is not changed. The value of 12 pt is inherited, which may be what the author wanted, but then again, it may not be. In Figure 8.5(b), the paragraph has a line height of 1.2 times its own font size, which again computes to 12 pt. The quote is printed in a smaller font, but this time the line height is changed with it, since the line height is inherited as a factor, not as a fixed size.

A rule of thumb in calculating line height is to start with a value that is 20% more than the font size, either a number value of 1.2, or a percentage value of 120%. You can then adjust from there to create whatever effect you seek.

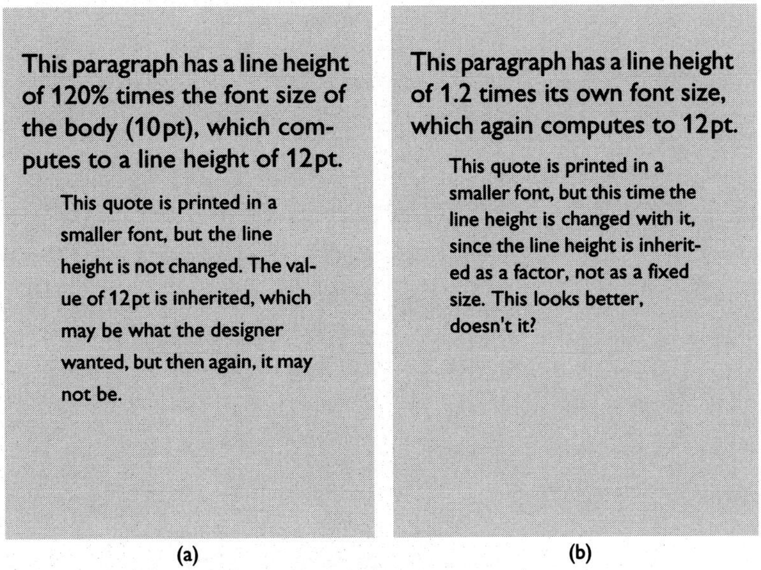

This paragraph has a line height of 120% times the font size of the body (10pt), which computes to a line height of 12pt.

> This quote is printed in a smaller font, but the line height is not changed. The value of 12pt is inherited, which may be what the designer wanted, but then again, it may not be.

(a)

This paragraph has a line height of 1.2 times its own font size, which again computes to 12pt.

> This quote is printed in a smaller font, but this time the line height is changed with it, since the line height is inherited as a factor, not as a fixed size. This looks better, doesn't it?

(b)

Figure 8.5 (a) The effect of seting the **line-height** of the body with a percentage; (b) setting the same **line-height**, but with a number.

```
<STYLE>
  BODY { font-size: 10pt; line-height: 120% }
  BLOCKQUOTE { font-size: 8pt }
</STYLE>
<BODY>
<P>This paragraph has a line height of 120% times the
font size of the body (10 pt), which computes to a line
height of 12 pt.
<BLOCKQUOTE>
<P>This quote is printed in a smaller font, but the line
height is not changed. The value of 12 pt is inherited,
which may be what the designer wanted, but then again, it
may not be.
</BLOCKQUOTE>
</BODY>
```

and:

```
<STYLE>
  BODY { font-size: 10pt; line-height: 1.2 }
  BLOCKQUOTE { font-size: 8pt }
</STYLE>
<BODY>
<P>This paragraph has a line height of 1.2 times its own
font size, which again computes to 12pt.
<BLOCKQUOTE>
<P>This quote is printed in a smaller font, but this time
the line height is changed with it, since the line height
```

```
is inherited as a factor, not as a fixed size. This looks
better, doesn't it?
</BLOCKQUOTE>
</BODY>
```

USING THE LINE-HEIGHT PROPERTY

The line height has a large effect on the character and the readability of text. Specifying a line height is often not just a matter of plugging in a standard value. Many factors go into deciding how large or small a line height should be for a given situation. These factors include the font's size, its appearance (e.g., fancy versus plain), its x-height, the lengths of its ascenders and descenders, and the length of the line of text.

For example, large line heights are sometimes used in advertisements, where a profoundly modern look is called for, even if the result is reduced readability. In comparison, titles, which typically are of a larger font and usually short in length, often look better with a smaller line height. A font with relatively long ascenders and a small x-height introduces a lot of visual space between lines, so you can use a smaller line height. In contrast, relatively short ascenders and large x-height can seem to reduce the visual space between lines. Thus you can use a larger line height.

On the other hand, small line heights may force lines too close together, thereby interfering with readability. Longer lines often need extra space between them to guide the eyes on their way back from the end of one line to the start of the next. Shorter lines can often tolerate a smaller line height. An effect much like double spacing can be achieved by setting the line height to 2.0. This is too much for most cases, but it is sometimes required.

Because this property specifies the *minimum* distance between the baselines of the lines, an inline element with a larger line height or an inline image may cause lines to be further apart than expected.

THE WORD-SPACING PROPERTY

The **word-spacing** property enables you to adjust the amount of spacing between words. Each font has a normal word spacing – the amount of space that is put between words – that should be used in the "ideal" situation (ideal according to the font's designer). Browsers will try to use this value. However, you may sometimes want to achieve certain effects with your text by expanding or shrinking the word spacing.

Name:	**word-spacing**
Value:	normal | *<length>*
Initial:	normal
Applies to:	all elements
Inherited:	yes
Percentages:	N/A

There are two values:

- normal – word spacing is left up to the browser. This is the default
- a length – either an absolute or relative value

Any length value is added to the normal word spacing, thus 0 and **normal** mean the same thing.

Word-spacing is an inherited property. The amount of word spacing is computed once for the parent element and the *result* is inherited by all of its children. The value is not computed again for its child elements even if they have a different font size. For example, if the current font size of the parent element is 10pt and the word spacing is set to 1em, its child elements will inherit a word spacing of 10pt no matter their font size.

The value can be negative, provided the resulting amount of word spacing is not negative. What happens if the original word spacing minus the set value of word-spacing is less than 0 is undefined. Some browsers will act as if the resulting space is 0; others may actually overlap the words.

Here are example rules of the use of the **word-spacing** property:

```
H1 { word-spacing: 15mm }
P {word-spacing: 0.4em }
```

In the first case, the space between words will be increased by 15mm and in the second by 0.4ems.

USING WORD SPACING

To make the text appear a bit more open or dense, or to waste or gain some space, you use the **word-spacing** property to specify the amount of space to be added or subtracted from the normal word spacing. Figure 8.6 shows an example of text with normal word spacing and the same text with extra word spacing and less word spacing. Increasing or decreasing the distance between words should be done with moderation. Generally, only small changes should be made if your intention is to improve readability.

(a) A text with some word spacing
(`word-spacing: normal`)

(b) A text with some word spacing
(`word-spacing: 0.25em`)

(c) A text with some word spacing
(`word-spacing: -0.125em`)

Figure 8.6 Three different levels of word spacing: (a) Normal; (b) more than normal word spacing; (c) less than normal word spacing.

Justifying a line with **text-align** set to **justify** often causes the word spacing to stretch or shrink. Text is justified starting from the adjusted word spacing. A browser may use any of many different algorithms to justify text, but the better algorithms will ensure that the average space in the paragraph is close to the adjusted word spacing. You may want to adjust the word spacing to improve the text's appearance.

THE LETTER-SPACING PROPERTY

The **letter-spacing** property lets you adjust the amount of spacing that occurs between letters. Similarly to word spacing, each font has a normal *letter spacing* – the amount of space that is put between letters – that should be used in the "ideal" situation (as determined by the font's designer). Although browsers will try to use this value, you may sometimes want to achieve certain effects with your text by expanding or shrinking the letter spacing.

IE3	NS4	IE4	O3.5
○	○	●	●

Name:	**letter-spacing**
Value:	normal | *<length>*
Initial:	normal
Applies to:	all elements
Inherited:	yes
Percentages:	N/A

This property has two values:

- normal – letter spacing is left up to the browser. This is the default.
- a length – either absolute or relative.

Letter-spacing is an inherited property. The actual value is passed on. That is, the amount of letter spacing is computed once for the parent element and *the result* is inherited by all of its children. The value is not computed again for its child elements even if they have a different font size. For example, if the current font size of the parent element is 10pt and the letter spacing is set to 0.5em, its child elements will inherit a letter spacing of 5pt regardless of their font size.

The value can be negative, provided the resulting amount of letter spacing is not negative. What happens if the original letter spacing minus the set value of letter spacing is less than 0 is undefined. Some browsers will act as if the resulting space is 0; others may actually overlap the letters.

Here are examples of the use of the **letter-spacing** property:

```
BLOCKQUOTE { letter-spacing: 0.04in }
P { letter-spacing: 0.1em }
```

In the first case, the space between letters will be increased by 0.04in. and in the second, by 0.1em.

USING THE LETTER-SPACING PROPERTY

As with word spacing, increasing or decreasing the distance between the letters in a word should be done with moderation. Begin with small amounts if the intention is to improve readability.

Adjusting the letter spacing is seldom done in running text. When it is used, it is often because tradition calls for it. For example, a publisher producing a "critical edition" (a book comparing different versions of some other book) will often demand that letter spacing be used in certain types of footnotes. Professional designers often frown on the use of letter spacing for anything other than titles because it interferes with the spacing between the letters of a font. The font's designer has usually carefully determined the optimal distance between each pair of letters – ab, bo, bi, Bl, and so on – to achieve a uniform look for all pairs. Some pairs such as VA require less space between them, otherwise they look too spaced. Simply adding or subtracting a fixed amount of space is likely to give less than pleasing results. Increasing the spacing may cause nonuniform distribution of white space. Decreasing the spacing may cause some letters to touch each other while others don't. Also, if the shapes of certain combinations of letters don't match very well, the font designer may have provided ligatures to replace them. However, when a nonzero letter spacing value is requested, those ligatures must be abandoned and you end up with a displeasing match of characters.

Letter spacing may also be affected by justification. With the "normal" value, the browser is free to change the letter spacing in order to justify text. By setting letter spacing explicitly to 0 or another "length" value, you prevent the browser from doing this. A 0 value means the letter spacing will not be changed, while any other "length" value means the browser must change the letter spacing by that exact amount.

Figure 8.7 shows examples of two fonts, each with normal letter spacing, less than normal letter spacing, and more than normal letter spacing.

Figure 8.7 Examples of **letter-spacing**, using Helvetica and Times as examples: (a) normal text; (b) positive letter spacing; (c) negative letter spacing. As the examples show, letter spacing is useful for uppercase, but much less for lowercase text.

(a) A normal line of text – AND UPPERCASE
A normal line of text – AND UPPERCASE

(b) A stretched line of text – AND UPPERCASE
A stretched line of text – AND UPPERCASE

(c) A condensed line of text – AND UPPERCASE
A condensed line of text – AND UPPERCASE

You may sometimes want to adjust the letter spacing to achieve a certain dramatic or other effect. For example, stretching a word is an alternative way of emphasizing it. This was done quite commonly in the nineteenth century, especially in German books, primarily because the font used in them didn't have an italic variant. (On the screen, there are many other ways to emphasize a text besides italicizing it; for example, by using color.) Figure 8.8 shows text in German Fraktur font with the word "emphasizing" stretched to draw attention to it.

Figure 8.8 Example of stretching a word for emphasis. This used to be quite common with the German Fraktur font, which is shown here.

Stretching a word can sometimes be used as an alternative way of e m p h a s i z i n g it. It used to be a quite common device in the nineteenth century, especially in German books. One of the main reasons being that the font they used did not have an italic variant.

Today, explicit letter spacing is still used in titles; often extreme values are used to achieve extreme effects. Figure 8.9 shows examples.

Figure 8.9 Examples of letter spacing: (a) 1em; (b) 0.7em; (c) –0.25em for the word "NARROW" and 0.3em for "WIDE."

New! bubble-gum that lasts *l o n g e r . . .*
(a)

T O O   L A T E

(b)

This new wall-to-wall carpet will fit in NARROW and also in W I D E rooms

(c)

THE VERTICAL-ALIGN PROPERTY

The **vertical-align** property lets you raise or lower letters, as well as images, above or below the baseline of text.

Name:	**vertical-align**
Value:	baseline | sub | super | top | text-top | middle | bottom | text-bottom | <percentage> | <length>
Initial:	baseline
Applies to:	inline elements
Inherited:	no
Percentages:	refer to the line height of the element itself

Text is normally aligned on an invisible baseline. The bottoms of the letters are on the baseline no matter what the style, weight, or even size of the letters. Sometimes a letter or a word has to be raised above the baseline or lowered below the baseline. This is the case with abbreviations that must be superscripted, such as N° (numero), Mme (Madame), and Mlle (Mademoiselle) and for simple mathematics that must be superscripted or subscripted, such as y^2 or x_i.

Vertical-align applies to inline elements, including replaced elements (images) that are inline. These images can be put on the baseline, centered vertically between lines, aligned with the top of the letters, or any of several other possibilities.

This property has three types of values: a keyword, a length and a percentage. Six of the eight available keywords are relative to the parent:

- **baseline** – aligns the baseline of the child element with the baseline of its parent. This is the default. An element without a baseline, such as an image or object, will have its bottom aligned with the parent's baseline.
- **sub** – subscripts the element, that is, aligns the baseline of the element with its parent's preferred position for subscripts. That position normally depends on the font of the parent. If the font does not explicitly define those positions, the browser chooses a "reasonable" (browser-specific) position.
- **super** – superscripts the element, that is, aligns the baseline of the element with its parent's preferred position for superscripts. That position normally depends on the font of the parent. If the font does not explicitly define those positions, the browser chooses a "reasonable" (browser-specific) position.

- **text-top** – aligns the top of the element with the top of its parent's tallest letters. Some people prefer this way of aligning instead of using the value "super."
- **middle** – aligns the vertical midpoint of the element (typically an image) with the baseline plus half the x-height of its parent element, that is, the middle of the parent's lowercase letters. More precisely, the element is centered on a line 0.5 ex above the baseline.
- **text-bottom** – aligns the bottom of the element with the bottom of its parent's font.

Here are example rules using these values of the **vertical-align** property:

```
SUP { vertical-align: super; font-size: 7pt }
SUB { vertical-align: sub; font-size: 7pt }
SPAN.index { vertical-align: sub }
IMG.initial { vertical-align: middle }
```

Figure 8.10 shows examples of the various alignments that can be obtained using these six values of the **vertical-align** property.

(a) text & image

(d) text & image

(b) text & image

(e) text & image

(c) text & image

(f) text & image

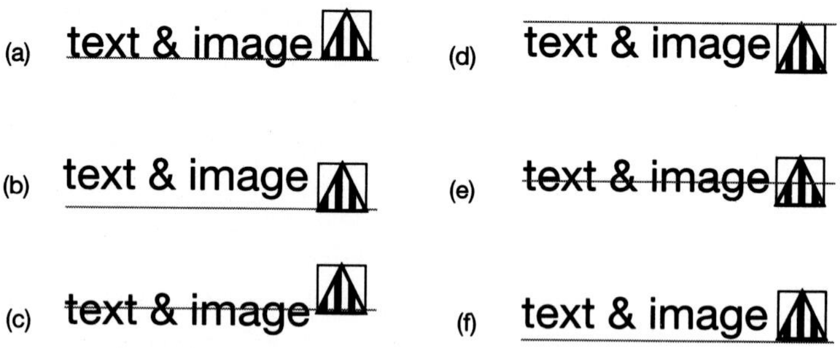

Figure 8.10 Different ways to vertically align the triangle: (a) baseline; (b) sub; (c) super; (d) text-top; (e) middle; (f) text-bottom.

The top and bottom keywords

The last two keywords, **top** and **bottom**, have definitions that look no more difficult than those of the six just described. The element with **vertical-align** set to **top** will have its top aligned with the top of the tallest thing on the line. The value **bottom** aligns the bottom of the element with the bottom of the lowest thing on the line. Sounds easy enough, doesn't it? Ah, but there's a snake in the grass.

The problem is, there may be two fairly tall elements on the line, one aligned to the top, the other to the bottom. If both elements are taller than the surrounding letters, the one aligned to the top will then also be the lowest thing on the line and the other one will be aligned to its bottom. But then that second element may be taller than the text and thereby cause the first element to move to align with the second element's top. But now the second element has to be aligned again... .

Sounds confusing? Not surprising. What you end up with is a loop. Implementations eventually will break out of this loop, but the vertical position that results cannot be determined clearly. Luckily, this situation is very rare.

Here's an example (Figure 8.11). Consider a line that has two images that are not the same height. Image 1 is set to **top** and image 2 to **bottom**:

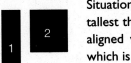

Situation 1: image 2 is aligned to the bottom of the lowest thing on the line, which is 1, but 1 is not aligned with the top of the tallest thing (other than itself), which is 2.

Situation 2: image 1 is aligned to the top of the tallest thing on the line, which is 2, but 2 is not aligned with the bottom of the lowest thing, which is 1.

For image 2 to align with the bottom of the lowest thing on the line, image 1, it must move down. It is now base-aligned with image 1. However, image 1, set to **top** must be top-aligned with the highest part of the line, now image 2, so it moves down. And we're right back where we started. We're in a loop.

You can handle this situation by ensuring at least one of the following exists:

1 Only one of the values is used, not both, at least not on the same line of text.
2 There is something else on the line that has a different vertical alignment than **top** or **bottom** and that is taller.
3 The item aligned at the top and the item aligned at the bottom are of equal height.

However, in the last case the result is not always the same either. In the example above there was no solution, but in this case there are many solutions, which may be just as bad (Figure 8.12).

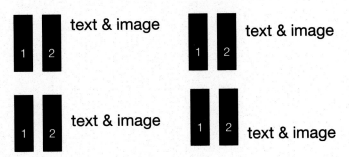

Figure 8.12 Too many possibilities for placing the two images.

In each of the four situations above, images 1 and 2 are now aligned to each other's top and bottom, but there is no way of knowing how high above the baseline they should be.

The value as a percentage or length

Apart from using the keywords, you may also specify a percentage or length as a value that indicates by how much the element is to be raised or lowered. A value of 50% means the element will be raised by half the element's line-height (all elements have a **line-height** property, even images). Negative values lower the element similarly. Here is an example:

```
He climbed higher,
<SPAN STYLE="vertical-align: 50%">
and higher,</SPAN>
<SPAN STYLE="vertical-align: 100%">
and higher still...</SPAN>
<SPAN STYLE="vertical-align: -100%">
until he fell</SPAN>
<SPAN STYLE="vertical-align: -200%">
down!</SPAN>
```

He climbed higher ^{and higher} ^{and higher still…}

until he fell

down!

Chapter 9

Space around boxes

In this chapter, we discuss properties that affect spacing around block-level elements. Recall from Chapter 7, "The fundamental objects," that we talked about the box model. In accordance with that model, a block-level element – such as a paragraph or heading – is drawn inside an imaginary rectangular bounding box that fits tightly around the text, as illustrated in Figure 9.1. (The dashed line is for illustration purposes only and does not show up on the screen.)

A block of text – such as a para-graph – forms a "box", as shown by the dashed line you see around it.

Figure 9.1 A paragraph within a bounding box.

Outside the bounding box are three "belts" that can be manipulated in a style sheet:

*   margin
*   padding
*   border

Figure 9.2 shows how these belts are layered around a paragraph.

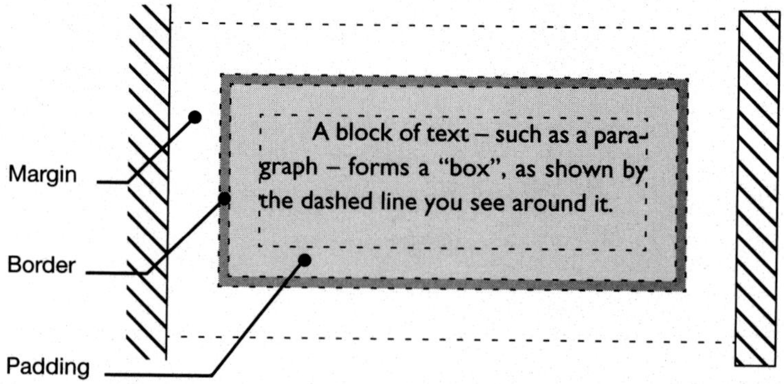

A block of text – such as a paragraph – forms a "box", as shown by the dashed line you see around it.

Margin

Border

Padding

Figure 9.2 Example block-level elements with bounding boxes shown by dashed lines (not shown on the screen) and with three belts around each.

In the next three sections, we discuss the properties that let you adjust the margins, padding, and borders of block elements. Then we discuss additional properties that let you fine-tune the spacing of elements:

- width
- height
- float
- clear

MARGINS AND THE MARGIN PROPERTIES

One of the most common ways to specify spacing in your document is to adjust the margins. The margin is the space between the element's bounding box and the bounding box of any adjacent element. There are five margin properties. Four let you set the margins for the left, right, top, and bottom margins individually or in any combination: **margin-left**, **margin-right**, **margin-top**, and **margin-bottom**.

The fifth one – **margin** – is a shortcut by which you can set all four margins in one step.

IE3	NS4	IE4	O3.5
⊙	⊙	⊙	⊙

Name:	**margin**
Value:	[*<length>* | *<percentage>* | auto] {1,4}
Initial:	0
Applies to:	all elements
Inherited:	no
Percentages:	refer to width of containing block

Name:	**margin-top, margin-right, margin-bottom, margin-left**
Value:	*<length>* | *<percentage>* | auto
Initial:	0
Applies to:	all elements
Inherited:	no
Percentages:	refer to width of containing block

Margin can have between one and four values, the other four can only have a single value. The properties have three possible types of values. The default is 0, and negative values are acceptable.

• a length – either an absolute or relative value
• a percentage – a percentage of the width of the block-level element that contains this element, usually the parent element; for example, 10% means leave a space as large as 10% of the width of the parent element
• "**auto**" – we discuss "**auto**" in more detail in "The whole story on width computation" later in this chapter

These properties affect all content of an element, for example, all the lines of a paragraph. (To set the margin for only the first line of a paragraph, see "The text-indent property" in Chapter 8.)

Figure 9.3 shows example rules for using the **margin-left**, **margin-right**, **margin-top**, and **margin-bottom** properties.

USING THE MARGIN PROPERTY

Using the **margin** property, you can set all four margins at once. Here's how it works:

• If only one value is set on this property, then that value applies to all four sides.
• If two values are set, the first is for top and bottom, the second for right and left. For example, suppose the value is "3em" "2em", then the top and bottom are set to 3em, and the right and left to 2em.
• If three values are set, the first is the top, the second the right and left, and the third the bottom margin.
• If four values are set on this property, the order they are applied is top/right/bottom/left.

Following are examples of rules for using the **margin** property in these various ways:

Figure 9.3 (a) Initial situation,
all margins zero.

(b) Setting the left margin:
`margin-left: 3em.`

(c) Setting the right margin:
`margin-right: 25%.`

(d) Setting the top margin:
`margin-top: 5pt.`

(e) Setting top and bottom:
`margin-top: 1.2em;`
`margin-bottom: 1.2em.`

(f) Setting left and right margins:
`margin-left: 5mm;`
`margin-right: 5mm.`

(g) Negative margins:
`margin-left: 1cm;`
`margin-right: -1cm.`

[a] The artist is the creator of beautiful things. To reveal art and conceal the artist is art's aim. The critic is he who can translate into another manner or a new material his impression of beautiful things.

[b] The highest as the lowest form of criticism is a mode of autobiography. Those who find ugly meanings in beautiful things are corrupt without being charming. This is a fault.

[c] There is no such thing as a moral or an immoral book. Books are well written, or badly written. That is all.

[d] The nineteenth century dislike of realism is the rage of Caliban seeing his own face in a glass.

[e] The nineteenth century dislike of romanticism is the rage of Caliban not seeing his own face in a glass. The moral life of man forms part of the subject-matter of the artist, but the morality of art consists in the perfect use of an imperfect medium.

[f] No artist desires to prove anything. Even things that are true can be proved. No artist has ethical sympathies. An ethical sympathy in an artist is an unpardonable mannerism of style. No artist is ever morbid. The artist can express everything.

[g] Thought and language are to the artist instruments of an art. Vice and virtue are to the artist materials for an art. From the point of view of form, the type of all the arts is the art of the musician. From the point of view of feeling, the actor's craft is the type. All art is at once surface and symbol. Those who go beneath the surface do so at their peril.

OSCAR WILDE

```
/* All margins will be 2 em */
BODY { margin: 2em }

/* The top and bottom margins will be 1 em, and the right
and left margins will be 2 em. */
BODY { margin: 1em 2em }

/* The top margin will be 1 em, the right and left will
be 2 em, and the bottom margin will be 3 em. */
BODY { margin: 1em 2em 3em }

/* All margins will be set, and values will be applied in
top/right/bottom/left order. */
BODY { margin: 1em 3em 5em 7em }
```

COMMON USAGES OF THE MARGIN PROPERTIES

One common usage of the margin properties is to indent a paragraph from the left and right margins to set it apart from the rest of the text. An example is a quotation. The following code example shows how you would do this:

```
BLOCKQUOTE { margin-left: 4em; margin-right: 4em }
```

This code would apply to all quotations in the entire document.

Another usage of the margin property is to provide space between paragraphs so as to visually distinguish them from each other. Here's the code for inserting space above and below paragraphs using the margin properties:

```
P { margin-top: 0.5em; margin-bottom: 0.5em }
```

A comparison of paragraphs before and after the extra space is added is shown in Figure 9.4.

Figure 9.4 Adding space above and below paragraphs to distinguish paragraphs from each other; (a) with zero margins; (b) with 0.5em top and bottom margins.

The first of three paragraphs without any spacing in between. Both the top and bottom margins are zero.
The second paragraph is directly below the first one.
The third paragraph follows the second, again without any space above it to separate it from the second one.

(a)

The first of three paragraphs with some space in between them. The top and bottom margins are now 0.5em.

The second paragraph is now much easier to read.

The third paragraph is again separated from the second one.

(b)

Note: another way to distinguish paragraphs visually is to indent the first line. We explained how to do this in Chapter 8 when we talked about the **text-indent** property. When **text-indent** is used, space above and below paragraphs is usually not necessary. Some people like to do it anyway, but it's a bit of an overkill.

You also can set negative margin values, although some browsers may not be able to handle them. You'll want to be careful when setting negative values, otherwise unexpected effects may result. Figure 9.5(a) shows an example of a negative margin that is too large – part of the text ends up outside the window. This resulted from input like this, where the text indent was set to −4em:

```
BODY { margin-left: 2em }
P { text-indent: -4em }
```

Figure 9.5(b) shows a potentially useful negative margin. In this case, we adjust the top margin by −50px:

```
<STYLE>
  H1.overlap { margin-top: -50px }
</STYLE>
<P><IMG SRC="flower.png">
<H1 CLASS="overlap">RARE FLOWERS</H1>
```

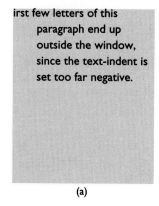

(a)   (b)

Figure 9.5 Using negative indents with the margin properties: (a) a too-large negative indent causes the text to move off the screen; (b) a negative top margin used to achieve a specific design effect.

While the five margin properties allow flexible spatial control, there is no way to control the appearance of margins. Margins are transparent. This means that whatever is underneath will show through. Figure 9.6 shows a child element with a 3em margin on all sides whose parent has a patterned background. Notice how the pattern shows through and seems to crowd the child element.

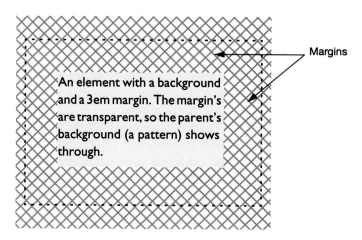

Figure 9.6 An element with a colored background and a 3em margin. The margins are transparent, so the parent's background (a pattern) shows through.

To control the appearance of the area immediately around an element, you use the padding and border properties, which we discuss in the next two sections.

THE PADDING PROPERTIES

The padding properties describe how much space to insert between an element and its margin, or if there is a border, between an element and its border. (We discuss borders next.) You set the length of the padding with one of the padding properties. There are five padding properties. Four let you set the amount of padding to insert on the left, right, top, and bottom individually: **padding-left**, **padding-right**, **padding-top**, and **padding-bottom**.

The fifth one – **padding** – is a shortcut by which you can set all four padding values in one step.

All of these properties can be described by the following definition, except that only padding can have up to four values, the others can have only one.

IE3	NS4	IE4	O3.5
○	⊙	⊙	⊙

Name:	**padding**
Value:	[<length> | <percentage>] {1,4}
Initial:	0
Applies to:	all elements
Inherited:	no
Percentages:	refer to width of containing block

IE3	NS4	IE4	O3.5
○	⊙	⊙	⊙

Name:	**padding-top, padding-right, padding-bottom, padding-left**
Value:	<length> | <percentage>
Initial:	0
Applies to:	all elements
Inherited:	no
Percentages:	refer to width of containing block

The properties can have one of two types of values. The default is 0, and the values cannot be negative.

- length – either an absolute or relative value
- percentage – a percentage of the width of the block-level element in which this element is contained; usually the parent element; for example, 10% adds padding that is as wide as 10% of the width of the parent element

With these properties, you can add some breathing room around the element. For example, although you can place a border right up against the bounding box of the element, we recommend that you always put some padding between the element and the border; otherwise they will look like they're crowding each other.

The padding automatically takes on the same appearance as the element's background. (You set the background using the **background** property, which we discuss in Chapter 11, "Colors.") That is, if the element has a yellow background, the padding will also be yellow.

Figure 9.7 shows an example of the use of padding to put space between an element and its margin.

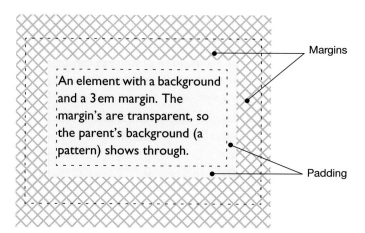

Margins

Padding

Figure 9.7 An element with padding around it: `padding: 1em`.

USING THE PADDING PROPERTY

Using the **padding** property, you can set all four padding lengths at once. Here's how it works:

- If only one value is set on this property, then that value applies to all four sides.
- If two or three values are set, the missing value(s) are taken from the opposite side(s). For example, suppose the top is set to 3ems and the right to 2ems and no values are assigned the bottom and left. The bottom is opposite the top, so it will take the value of the top: 3ems. The left padding is opposite the right padding, so it will take the value of the right side: 2ems.
- If four values are set on this property, the order they are applied is top, right, bottom, left.

Following are examples of code for using the **padding** property in these various ways:

```
/* All paddings will be 2em. */
BODY { padding: 2em }

/* The top and bottom margins will be 1em, and the right
and left margins will be 2em. */
BODY { padding: 1em 2em }

/* The top margin will be 1em, the right and left will be
2 em, and the bottom margin will be 3em. */
BODY { padding: 1em 2em 3em }

/* All paddings will be set, and values will be applied
in top/right/bottom/left order. */
BODY { padding: 1em 3em 5em 7em }
```

THE BORDER PROPERTIES GROUP

A border is a way of highlighting an element. It is placed between the element's padding and the element's margin. Figure 9.8 shows an example of the use of a border around an element.

Figure 9.8 An element with padding and a border.

There are 20 border properties that form the border properties group and with which you can set the width, color, and style of the border in various combinations. Five properties let you set the width, color, and style at the same time on one or more of the four borders of an element:

- **border-left**
- **border-right**
- **border-top**
- **border-bottom**
- **border**

We recommend that generally you use these five. The remaining fifteen are useful if you need to set only one aspect of a border; that is, only the width, only the color, or only the style. You can set these on one or more borders in any combination of borders:

- **border-left-color**
- **border-right-color**
- **border-top-color**
- **border-bottom-color**
- **border-color**
- **border-left-style**
- **border-right-style**
- **border-top-style**
- **border-bottom-style**
- **border-style**
- **border-left-width**
- **border-right-width**
- **border-top-width**
- **border-bottom-width**
- **border-width**

A border can be applied to any element. When applied to an inline element that contains text that spans more than line, the browser may render one border per line and possibly omit the edges. For example, this style sheet

```
EM { border: solid; padding: 1ex }
```

applied to this text:

```
... This line contains an <EM>long piece of emphasized
text, so long in fact that it is likely to be broken
across lines</EM> somewhere in the middle...
```

may produce this result:

...This line contains a *long piece of emphasized text, so long in fact that it is likely to be broken across lines* somewhere in the middle...

The border is not closed at the end of the first line to indicate that it continues on the next line. Note that this behavior is browser-specific; that is, the browser doesn't have to do this. With some borders, especially the 3D borders (groove, ridge, inset, and outset), closing the border may look better.

THE BORDER-COLOR PROPERTIES

The **border-color** property sets the color of the border. The color may be specified using any one of 16 predefined named colors or a numbered

RGB color. See Chapter 11, "Colors," for more information about specifying colors.

IE3	NS4	IE4	O3.5
○	⊙	●	⊙

Name:	**border-color**
Value:	*<color>* {1,4}
Initial:	taken from the **color** property of the element
Applies to:	all elements
Inherited:	no
Percentages:	N/A

IE3	NS4	IE4	O3.5
○	○	●	●

Name:	**border-top-color, border-right-color, border-bottom-color, border-left-color**
Value:	*<color>*
Initial:	taken from the **color** property of the element
Applies to:	all elements
Inherited:	no
Percentages:	N/A

With the **border-color** property, you set all colors on all four borders at once, as follows:

- One value is set: that value applies to all four sides.
- Two values are set: the top and bottom borders are set to the first value, and the right and left borders are set to the second.
- Three values are set: the top border is set to the first value, the right and left borders are set to the second, and the bottom border is set to the third.
- Four values are set: the values are applied in top/right/bottom/left order.

Following are examples of code for using the **border-color** property in these various ways:

```
BODY { border-color: red }
/* All borders will be red */

BODY { border-color: red black }
/* The top and bottom borders will be red, and the left
and right borders will be black */

BODY { border-color: red black yellow }
/* The top border will be red, the left and right borders
will be black, and the bottom border will be yellow */
```

```
BODY { border-color: red black yellow green }
/* All colors will be set, and values will be applied in
top/right/bottom/left order */
```

If no color is specified for the border, the border takes on the color of the
element itself. For example, in this case:

```
P {
    color: black;
    background: white;
    border: solid
}
```

the border does not have a color specified, so it will be black, the same as
the text of the P element.

THE BORDER-STYLE PROPERTIES

The **border-style** property sets the appearance of the border.

<table>
<tr><td>IE3
○</td><td>NS4
●</td><td>IE4
●</td><td>O3.5
●</td><td>

Name:	**border-style**
Value:	*<border-style>* {1,4}
Initial:	none
Applies to:	all elements
Inherited:	no
Percentages:	N/A

</td></tr>
</table>

<table>
<tr><td>IE3
○</td><td>NS4
○</td><td>IE4
○</td><td>O3.5
●</td><td>

Name:	**border-top-style, border-right-style, border-bottom-style, border-left-style**
Value:	*<border-style>*
Initial:	none
Applies to:	all elements
Inherited:	no
Percentages:	N/A

</td></tr>
</table>

These properties accept one of nine keywords:

- **none** – no border is drawn, regardless of any border width (see later in this section) that may be set. This is the default
- **hidden** – the border is transparent: it takes up space, but it has no color (just like the margin)
- **dotted** – a dotted line
- **dashed** – a dashed line

- **solid** – a solid line
- **double** – a double line. The sum of the two lines and the space between them will equal the **border-width** value
- **groove** – a 3D groove. The shadow effect is the result of using colors that are a bit darker and a bit lighter than those given by **border-color** or **color**
- **ridge** – a 3D ridge
- **inset** – a 3D inset
- **outset** – a 3D outset

Figure 9.9 shows examples of each type of border style.

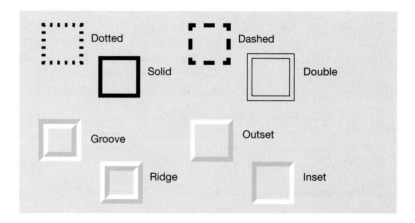

Figure 9.9 Border styles.

With the **border-style** property, you set the styles of all four borders at once, as follows:

- One value is set: that value applies to all four sides.
- Two values are set: the top and bottom borders are set to the first value, and the right and left borders are set to the second.
- Three values are set: the top border is set to the first value, the right and left borders are set to the second, and the bottom border is set to the third.
- Four values are set: the values are applied in top/right/bottom/left order.

Following are examples of code for using the **border-style** property in these various ways:

```
BODY { border-style: dotted }
/* All borders will be dotted. */

BODY { border-style: dashed solid }
/* The top and bottom borders will be dashed and the left
and right borders will be solid. */
```

```
BODY { border-style: inset solid double }
/* The top border will be a 3d inset, the left and right
solid, and the bottom border will be a double line. */

BODY { border-style: ridge groove dashed dotted }
/* Styles are applied in top/right/bottom/left order. */
```

THE BORDER-WIDTH PROPERTIES

The border-width properties set the widths of the border individually or
in any combination. There are five properties:

- Four let you set the border width for the left, right, top, and bottom
  of the element individually: **border-left-width**, **border-right-width**,
  border-top-width, and **border-bottom-width**.
- The fifth one – **border-width** – is a shortcut by which you can set all
  four border widths at once.

These properties can be described by the following definition. Four of the
five properties only accept a single value, while **border-width** accepts up
to four values.

IE3	NS4	IE4	O3.5		
○	☉	☉	●	*Name:*	**border-width**
				Value:	[thin | medium | thick | *<length>*] {1,4}
				Initial:	medium
				Applies to:	all elements
				Inherited:	no
				Percentages:	N/A

IE3	NS4	IE4	O3.5		
○	⇨☉	☉	●	*Name:*	**border-top-width, border-right-width, border-bottom-width, border-left-width**
				Value:	thin | medium | thick | *<length>*
				Initial:	medium
				Applies to:	all elements
				Inherited:	no
				Percentages:	N/A

These properties have six types of values:

- `thin`
- `medium` – this is the default
- `thick`
- a length value – either an absolute or relative unit

When the keywords **thin**, `medium` or **thick** are used, the actual width of the border depends on the browser. However, `medium` will be at least as thick as **thin** and **thick** will not be thinner than `medium`. The thickness remains constant throughout a document. For example, a thick border will be the same thickness throughout the document regardless of any other properties you set. In the following code sample:

```
H1 {
    border-width: thick;
    font-size: 18pt }
P {
    border-width: thick;
    font-size: 12pt }
```

the borders will be same width for both the H1 and the P elements even though the font sizes of the two differ.

Following are examples of various border width values (Figure 9.10).

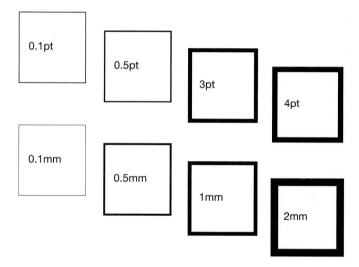

Figure 9.10 Examples of border-width values.

USING THE BORDER-WIDTH PROPERTY

Using the **border-width** property, you can set all four borders at once, as follows:

- One value is set: that value applies to all four sides.
- Two values are set: the top and bottom borders are set to the first value, and the right and left borders are set to the second.

- Three values are set: the top border is set to the first value, the right and left borders are set to the second, and the bottom border is set to the third.
- Four values are set: the values are applied in top/right/bottom/left order.

Following are examples of code for using the **border-width** property in these various ways:

```
BODY { border-width: 2em }
/* All borders are set the same, to 2em. */

BODY { border-width: 1em 2em }
/* Top and bottom = 1em; right and left = 2em. */

BODY { border-width: 1em 2em 3em }
/* Top = 1em, right = 2em, bottom = 3em, left = 2em. */

BODY { border-width: 1em 3em 5em 7em }
/* All borders are set and are applied in
top/right/bottom/left order. */
```

THE BORDER PROPERTIES

The border properties let you set the border width, color and style together on one or more borders. They build on the previously discussed properties and are the most commonly used properties to set border characteristics. Four of them let you set the border width, color, and style for each side of the element individually: **border-left**, **border-right**, **border-top**, and **border-bottom**. The fifth one – **border** – is a shortcut by which you can set all four border properties at once.

IE3	NS4	IE4	O3.5		
○	☉	☉	●		

Name:	**border-top, border-right, border-bottom, border-left, border**
Value:	*<border-width>* || *<border-style>* || *<border-color>*
Initial:	see the individual properties above
Applies to:	all elements
Inherited:	no
Percentages:	N/A

These properties accept all the legal values of **border-width**, **border-style** and **border-color**. Omitted values are set to their initial values. For example, this rule:

```
P { border: solid red }
```

sets all borders to be solid and red. Because "border-width" is not specified, its initial value – medium – is assumed. Also, the order in which you list the three values doesn't matter. All of the following will produce the same result:

```
border: thin solid red;
border: red thin solid;
border: solid red thin;
```

Following are example rules for using the **border-left**, **border-right**, **border-top**, and **border-bottom** properties. Figure 9.11 shows the results.

USING THE BORDER PROPERTY

Unlike the **margin** property and **padding** property, the **border** property cannot set different values on the four sides. With **border**, you can only set all four sides to the same style, color and width. To set different values on the four sides, you must use one or more of the other border properties.

```
DIV.warning {
    border: solid red thick;
    padding: 0.5em 1em; }
```

The style sheet above will put a thick red border around elements of type DIV with CLASS "warning." Between the text and the border there is half an em vertically and one em horizontally.

WORKING WITH THE BORDER PROPERTIES

The properties in the border properties group have overlapping functionality to some extent. Hence, the order in which the rules are specified is important. For example, in this example:

```
BLOCKQUOTE {
    border-color: red;
    border-left: double;
    color: black }
```

the border's color will be red, except for the left border ("border-left"), which will be black. This is because the **border-left** property sets the width, style, *and color* at one time on the left border. Because the color is not explicitly set in that property, the value of the **color** property is automatically picked up; in this case, black.

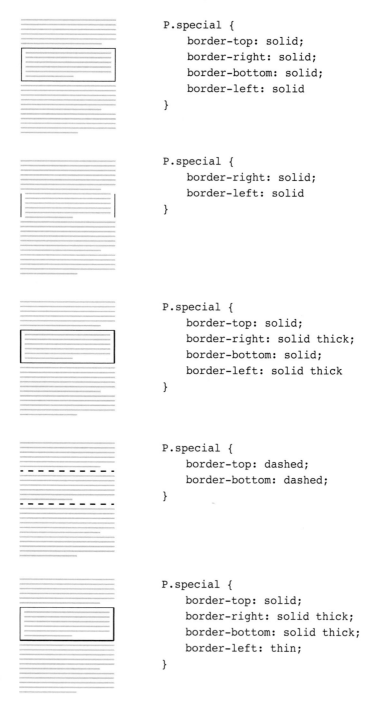

```
P.special {
    border-top: solid;
    border-right: solid;
    border-bottom: solid;
    border-left: solid
}
```

```
P.special {
    border-right: solid;
    border-left: solid
}
```

```
P.special {
    border-top: solid;
    border-right: solid thick;
    border-bottom: solid;
    border-left: solid thick
}
```

```
P.special {
    border-top: dashed;
    border-bottom: dashed;
}
```

```
P.special {
    border-top: solid;
    border-right: solid thick;
    border-bottom: solid thick;
    border-left: thin;
}
```

Figure 9.11 Example usages of the border properties.

OUTLINE BORDERS

IE3	NS4	IE4	O3.5		
○	○	○	○	*Name:*	**outline**
				Value:	<outline-width> || <outline-style> || <outline-color>
				Initial:	see the individual properties below
				Applies to:	all elements
				Inherited:	no
				Percentages:	N/A

IE3	NS4	IE4	O3.5		
○	○	○	○	*Name:*	**outline-color**
				Value:	<color> | invert
				Initial:	invert
				Applies to:	all elements
				Inherited:	no
				Percentages:	N/A

IE3	NS4	IE4	O3.5		
○	○	○	○	*Name:*	**outline-style**
				Value:	<border-style>
				Initial:	none
				Applies to:	all elements
				Inherited:	no
				Percentages:	N/A

IE3	NS4	IE4	O3.5		
○	○	○	○	*Name:*	**outline-width**
				Value:	<border-width>
				Initial:	medium
				Applies to:	all elements
				Inherited:	no
				Percentages:	N/A

CSS has another kind of border, called an "outline," which is like a normal border but doesn't take up any space. It is drawn around an element and may overlap the elements around it. Typically, this type of border is used for dynamic effects: borders that only appear for a short period of time; for example, while a new page is being fetched, or while the mouse hovers over an element. For situations like that it doesn't matter that the border overlaps something else, and you also don't want to reserve any space for it anyway, since most of the time there is no border.

Here is an example of an outline border added to a hyperlink while the mouse hovers over the link:

```
<STYLE TYPE="text/css">
  A:hover { outline: thick red }
</STYLE>
<BODY>
  <P>Here is a text with
    a <A HREF="other">link</A> in it.
</BODY>
```

You cannot set the four sides of the outline border to different styles, as with normal borders, but you can set the color, width, and style of the whole outline separately.

COLLAPSING MARGINS

The margins above and below elements are not simply added together to reach a total amount of space between the two elements. If they were, you'd often end up with quite a bit more space between elements than you want. Instead, the browser discards the smaller margin and uses the larger margin to space apart the two elements. This process is called *collapsing margins*. Collapsing margins affects only the top and bottom margins.

For example, suppose a P follows an H1 – a common situation – and that the P has less space above it than the H1 has below it – also common. To be more specific, assume the P has 1pc (1pica = 12pt) space above it and the H1 has 2pc space below it. The browser will discard the 1pc space and put only 2pc space between the two elements; it will not add the two and use the total, 3pc space.

Collapsing margins ensures that space is consistent between any pair of elements. In another example, a list (UL or OL) normally has more space above it than a P does, but when either follows an H1, designers usually want the same amount of space above both. By the browser's going with the larger H1 margin, this can be accomplished.

The browser reacts similarly when two elements begin or end at the same time. For example, at the end of a list there are usually three elements that end at the same time: the last list item, the last paragraph within that item, and the list itself. There is one element, P that begins at the same time as the other three are ending. Here is an example:

```
<UL>
  <LI><P>The first item in a list.
    <P>A paragraph below the first item of
    the list.
```

```
<UL>
  <LI><P>The second, and last, item in the list.
    <P>The last paragraph of the last item of
    the list.
</UL>
<P>Start of next paragraph. This paragraph is not part of
a list.
```

The space between the *last line of the list* and the *first line of the paragraph that follows it* will be the maximum of four margins:

1 The bottom margin of the last P in the LI
2 The bottom margin of the last LI
3 The bottom of the UL
4 The top margin of the P that follows the list

Normally, the UL is the largest, so that is the amount of margin that will be placed between the end of the list and the beginning of the next paragraph. Figure 9.12 illustrates this situation using these rules:

```
P { margin-bottom: 0em }
LI { margin-bottom: 0.6em }
UL { margin-bottom: 1.2em }
P { margin-top: 0em }
```

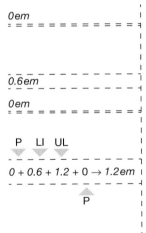

- The first item in a list.
  A paragraph below the first item of the list.

- The second item in the list.
  The last paragraph of the last item of the list.

Start of next paragraph. This paragraph is not part of a list.

Figure 9.12 A demonstration of collapsing margins.

However, there's a twist to this collapsing of margins: margins collapse only if they touch each other. In the previous example, we assumed there was no padding or border. Hence, the margins touch. However, if either or both of the UL or the LI has a nonzero padding or a border, the margins will no longer touch. Hence, they no longer collapse, since there is something — padding or border — that separates them.

For example, a style sheet like this:

```
P { padding-top: 5px; padding-bottom: 5px }
```

will keep any two paragraphs 10px apart (possibly more if there are other paddings and margins to consider).

THE WIDTH PROPERTY

The **width** property sets the width of the element. It is seldom used with block-level elements. In fact, its use with such elements may lead to some complications. This property is most useful with replaced elements (such as IMG) and floating text elements (see case study 5 on page 288).

IE3　NS4　IE4　O3.5
○　　⊙　　⊙　　●

Name:	**width**
Value:	*<length>* | *<percentage>* | auto
Initial:	auto
Applies to:	block-level and replaced elements
Inherited:	no
Percentages:	refer to parent element's width

This property has three types of values:

- length – an absolute or relative value
- percentage – a percentage of the width of the element in which this element is contained; for example, 80% means the element is 20% narrower than the containing block
- **auto** – this is the default

By default, **width** has the value "auto." Usually, you won't set the width of a block-level element explicitly; you'll set only the margins, padding, and border. Exceptions are possibly the HTML element and tables or table columns. The actual width of the element is what is left after subtracting the margin, padding, and border from the *available width*, also called the *inherited width*. We discuss in detail how to work with the **width** property in a later section, "The whole story on width computation."

THE HEIGHT PROPERTY

The **height** property sets the height of the element. As with the **width** property, the **height** property is seldom used with block-level elements and its use in those cases may lead to some complications. This property is used most often with images.

Name:	**height**
Value:	*<length>* | auto
Initial:	auto
Applies to:	block-level and replaced elements
Inherited:	no
Percentages:	N/A

This property has two values:

- a length – an absolute or relative value
- **auto** – this is the default

Usually, you won't set the height of a block element explicitly; you'll set only the margins and padding. By default, the height has the value **auto**. The height is determined simply by how much room is needed to display the number of lines in the element.

Explicitly setting the height is even rarer than specifying the width. If you do and the text needs more space to display than you have allotted, a scroll bar or similar device may be introduced into the element by the browser so that the user can get to the text that is out of sight. If the height is more than that needed by the text in the element, the extra space is treated as padding.

THE FLOAT PROPERTY

The **float** property allows you to place an element at the left or right edge of the parent element.

Name:	**float**
Value:	left | right | none
Initial:	none
Applies to:	all
Inherited:	no
Percentages:	N/A

A value of **left** causes the element to be moved (to "float") to the left edge of its parent until it encounters any margin, padding, or border of another block-level element. **Right** causes the same action on the opposite side. **None** causes the element to be displayed where it appears in the text.

The **left** and **right** values of the property, in effect, take the element out of the normal flow of elements. The element is then treated as a block-level element regardless of what **display** property setting it has. The text that followed the element either continues in the main flow or wraps around the floating element on the opposite side. If there is no room for the element to float at the specified edge, it will move down to the nearest spot in which it can fit.

This property is used most often for inline IMG elements, which are treated as a block-level element for purposes of this property. For example,

```
IMG.icon {
    float: left;
    margin-left: 0 }
```

will place each IMG elements of the class "icon" along the left side of the image's parent and flush against the parent's left edge (see Figure 9.13(a)).

With this rule:

```
IMG.icon {
    float: right;
    margin-right: 0 }
```

those same IMG elements will be placed along the right of the parent flush against the parent's right edge (see Figure 9.13(b)).

Figure 9.13 (a)   (b)

Typically, all of the floating element's margins, padding, and borders are honored; that is, margins are not collapsed with the margins of adjacent elements. There are cases in which a floating element can overlap with the margin, border, and padding of another element, e.g.:

1 When the floating element has a negative margin. Negative margins are honored as they are on other block-level elements (see Figure 9.14(a)).
2 When the floating element is wider or higher than its parent (see Figure 9.14(b)).

Figure 9.14 Two cases when a floating element can overlap another element's margin, border, and padding: (a) the floating element has a negative margin; (b) the floating element is wider than its parent.

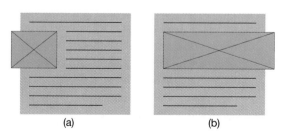

(a)   (b)

THE CLEAR PROPERTY

The **clear** property works with the **float** property. It specifies whether an element allows floating elements at its side, that is, more specifically, it lists the sides on which floating elements are *not* accepted.

Name:	clear
Value:	none | left | right | both
Initial:	none
Applies to:	all elements
Inherited:	no
Percentages:	N/A

This property has four values:

- **none** – this is the default
- **left**
- **right**
- **both**

None means the element allows floating elements on both of its sides. **Left** and **right** mean the element does not allow floating elements on its left side and right side, respectively. **Both** means the element will not have floating elements on either side.

This property enables you to control text wrapping as a result of setting the **float** property. Commonly, designers want text to wrap around a floating element. However, there are likely to be cases when you don't want this to happen. For example, if your document is starting a new section, you may want to ensure that the heading of that section doesn't occur next to an image that belongs in the previous section. You can set the **clear** property on the heading so that it doesn't allow floating elements at its sides (value "both"). Instead, the heading will move down until it is free of the floating element of the previous section. Figure 9.15(a) shows what would happen if you did not set **clear**, while Figure 9.15(b) shows the result when you do. Here is the code that you would write to achieve the latter effect:

```
/* Make all images float left: */
IMG { float: left }
/* H2 headings must not be next to images: */
H2 { clear: both }
```

The **clear** property can also be used on floating elements. For example, this style sheet:

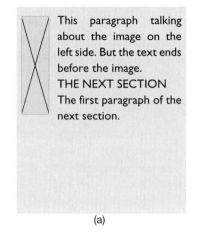
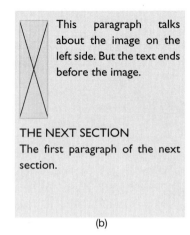

|(a)|(b)|

Figure 9.15 (a) With **clear** not set (the default **none** is assumed), the heading of one section is next to an image in the previous section; (b) with **clear** set to **both**, the heading moves down until it is free of the image.

```
IMG {
    float: right;
    clear: right }
```

will ensure that an image floats to the right edge of its parent *and* that it won't be placed next to another floating element that may already be on the right edge. It will instead move down until it finds a clear spot in which it can fit. Figure 9.16 shows how this works.

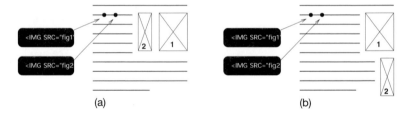

|(a)|(b)|

Figure 9.16 (a) Image 2, with **clear** not set (the default "none" is assumed), is placed next to image 1; (b) image 2, with **clear** set to "right," moves down to below image 1.

MINIMUM AND MAXIMUM WIDTHS AND HEIGHTS

In typical style sheets, block elements have margins, but their **width** property is not set (*i.e.*, it is **auto**). That allows the user to resize the window and the element with it. But you can protect the element from becoming too narrow or too wide, by setting the properties **min-width** and **max-width**, respectively.

IE3　NS4　IE4　O3.5
○　　○　　○　　○

Name:	**min-width**
Value:	*<length>* | *<percentage>* | inherit
Initial:	0
Applies to:	replaced elements and block-level elements
Inherited:	no
Percentages:	refer to width of containing block

IE3　NS4　IE4　O3.5
○　　○　　○　　○

Name:	**max-width**
Value:	*<length>* | *<percentage>* | inherit | none
Initial:	none
Applies to:	replaced elements and block-level elements
Inherited:	no
Percentages:	refer to width of containing block

More rare is the use of **min-height** and **max-height**, but they exist, in case you need them:

IE3　NS4　IE4　O3.5
○　　○　　○　　○

Name:	**min-height**
Value:	*<length>* | *<percentage>* | inherit
Initial:	0
Applies to:	replaced elements and block-level elements
Inherited:	no
Percentages:	refer to width of containing block

IE3　NS4　IE4　O3.5
○　　○　　○　　○

Name:	**max-height**
Value:	*<length>* | *<percentage>* | inherit | none
Initial:	none
Applies to:	replaced elements and block-level elements
Inherited:	no
Percentages:	refer to width of containing block

If the value is specified as a percentage, it is relative to the height of the block element in which this element is contained, but only if the height of that block is set explicitly, otherwise the percentage (and the property with it) is ignored.

THE WHOLE STORY ON WIDTH COMPUTATION

We explained the normal uses of the various margin, padding, and border properties earlier in this chapter as they relate to block-level elements. In this section, we summarize all this information. We also explain some of the unusual cases you may run into.

The horizontal position and width of a nonfloating, block-level element is determined by seven properties:

- **margin-left**
- **border-left**
- **padding-left**
- **width**
- **padding-right**
- **border-right**
- **margin-right**

For any element, the values of these seven properties must always total the width of the block element in which the element is contained – the *inherited width*. This width is always known and cannot be changed from within. An element's width is computed according to this formula:

Figure 9.17 The relation between margin, padding, border and width.

margin-left + border-left + padding-left + width + padding-right + border-right + margin-right = width of containing block

Figure 9.18 shows a diagram of how the width is computed.

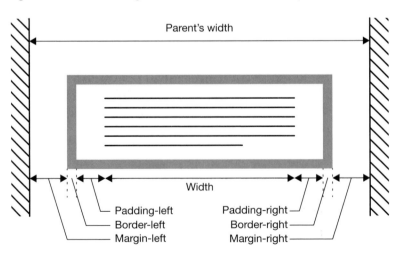

Figure 9.18 Diagram of the width computation.

When specific values are used, adjustments may need to be made to one or more values to ensure the total width does not exceed the inherited width. To simplify making these adjustments, CSS1 provides that the border and padding values are never adjusted. Only the **width**, **margin-left**, and **margin-right** values can be adjusted. That is, only they may be **auto**. However, the meaning of **auto** as it relates to these properties depends on the type of element.

For replaced elements (images, objects), the **width** is automatically set to the *intrinsic width*. An image is assumed to have a preferred or built-in size as determined by its artist or designer. Although the image may be scaled larger or smaller, it still has this preferred size. This is its "intrinsic size." Any other value means the element is scaled.

For normal (non-replaced) element, the meaning of **auto** depends on whether the element floats, and if not, on whether it is block or inline: for floating elements, a width of **auto** always means 0, so it is not very useful; for inline elements the **width** property is ignored altogether; for block (and list-item) elements, the width will be what is left after subtracting the element's padding, border and margin from the inherited width.

For inline elements and for floating elements, a value of **auto** on **margin-left** or **margin-right** means that margin is 0.

A margin with value **auto** in a block element, on the other hand, means that the margin should be as large as possible.

Table 9.1 below summarizes the meaning of **auto** for **width**, **margin-left** and **margin-right** (* = see explanation in text).

	inline elements		block elements		floating elements	
	replaced	non-replaced	replaced	non-replaced	replaced	non-replaced
width	intrinsic width	N/A	intrinsic width	maximize*	intrinsic width	0
margin-left, margin-right	0	0	maximize*	maximize*	0	0

Table 9.1 The meaning of auto on **width**, **margin-left** and **margin-right**.

What gets changed when depends on the interaction of **auto** and specified values. These are the possibilities:

1 None of the three values (**width**, **margin-left**, **margin-right**) is **auto**.
2 Exactly one of the three values has the value **auto**.
3 Two or three of the values have the value **auto**.

CASE 1: NO VALUE IS "AUTO"

When none of **width**, **margin-left** or **margin-right** is set to **auto**, the right margin is ignored and treated as if it had been set to **auto**, that is, it is the value calculated automatically, using the formula of Figure 9.17.

For example, if there is a P inside a BODY and the style sheet reads:

```
BODY {
    width: 30em }
P {
    width: 25em;
    margin-left: 3em;
    margin-right: 3em }
```

the P will be 25em wide and have a 3em margin on the left, but the right margin will be ignored and will be calculated as $30 - 25 - 3 = 2em$ (assuming there are no paddings and borders set elsewhere).

CASE 2: ONE VALUE IS "AUTO"

When only one value is set to **auto**, that value is the one calculated automatically, using the previous formula. That is, that value will be maximized – made as large as possible.

The previous example modified a little:

```
BODY {
    width: 30em }
P {
    width: 25em;
    margin-left: auto;
    margin-right: 3em }
```

Now the right margin will indeed be 3em and the left margin will be calculated (2em).

CASE 3: TWO OR THREE OF THE THREE VALUES ARE "AUTO"

There are two possible cases: one case is where **width** is auto, and one where width has some other value. First, if **width** is auto, the **width** value is the one that is calculated, using the formula of Figure 9.17. That is, the width will be maximized, after consideration of the size of the margins. Any margins set to **auto** will become 0.

If **width** is not **auto**, but both **margin-left** and **margin-right** are, the two margins will be of equal size and as large as possible.

Here is an example with **width** set to **auto**:

```
<STYLE>
  DIV {
    width: 12cm }
```

```
     P {
       width: auto;
       margin-left: 7cm;
       margin-right: auto}
     </STYLE>

     <DIV>
     <P>This paragraph is inside a DIV that is exactly 12cm
     wide. The paragraph itself has a 7cm margin on its left
     and an auto margin on its right. No padding or border has
     been specified, so we assume there aren't any.
     </DIV>
```

In this example, the parent of the P element, DIV, has a width of 12cm, so we use the formula as follows, filling in the blanks with the values of the various widths:

margin-left + border-left + padding-left + width + padding-right + border-right + margin-right = width of parent

7cm + 0cm + 0cm + **auto** + 0cm + 0cm + 0cm = 12cm

The right margin is 0, and since 12 − 7 = 5, the resulting width of the P element is 5cm.

The second example shows both **margin-left** and **margin-right auto**. In this case, the two margins will each get half of the available space, thereby causing the element to be centered in its parent:

```
     <STYLE>
       BODY { width: 10cm }
       P { width: 6cm; margin: auto }
     </STYLE>
     <BODY>
     <P>This paragraph is 6 cm wide and will be centered
     inside its parent (BODY, in this case).
     </BODY>
```

Completing the width formula:

margin-left + border-left + padding-left + width + padding-right + border-right + margin-right = width of parent

auto + 0cm + 0cm + 6cm + 0cm + 0cm + **auto** = 10cm

gives us 2cm of space each for the left and right margins; that is, 10 − 6 = 4cm total to be divided equally between the two margins.

OVERFLOW

What happens when an element has a certain width, but one of its children is wider? From the formula in Figure 9.17 it follows that one of the margins must be negative. Margins can indeed be negative, so formally speaking, this is a perfectly valid situation. The result is that the child will stick out of its parent, usually at the right hand side... .

But you may not want the child to stick out. If you don't want to change the width of the child either, a different solution has to be found. CSS offers two, in addition to the default behavior:

* The part that sticks out is simply cut off, and not displayed.
* A scroll bar (or something else with a similar function) is displayed, so the user can move the child element sideways.
* The initial situation: the child element is allowed to stick out.

The same may happen in the vertical direction, if the height of an element has been set to a fixed value. The property that determines the behavior is **overflow**.

IE3	NS4	IE4	O3.5
○	○	●	○

Name:	**overflow**
Value:	visible | hidden | scroll | auto
Initial:	visible
Applies to:	block level and replaced elements
Inherited:	no
Percentages:	N/A

Visible is the normal style: the children of this element may stick out. **Hidden** makes the parts that would stick out invisible. This is not very useful if the child elements can contain text, but if there is only an image inside, this may be the right thing to do. **Scroll** and **auto** both make a scroll bar or some such mechanism appear. The difference is that in the case of **scroll** the scroll bar is always there, even if none of the children is too large, while in the case of **auto**, the scroll bar only appears when there actually is something to scroll.

Chapter 10

Relative and absolute positioning

The normal way a document is laid out is that the boxes for all elements are put one after the other or below the other (depending on whether they are inline or block), with their distances and alignments specified by properties such as margin, padding and width. An occasional box is shifted to one side with the float property. In this way the boxes fill the canvas, or the pages, starting from the top and continuing until all boxes have been placed.

Relative positioning adds to this the ability to make corrections to the positions of individual boxes, without affecting other boxes. For example, a box may be moved up or down, to overlap some other box. It is seldom needed in a style sheet. The place where the properties for relative positioning usually appear is in scripts. For example, a dynamic effect that cannot be achieved with CSS2 (although maybe with a future level of CSS) is to move text into place on opening a document: the text moves in from the side and the headers fall into place from the top, slowly reducing their relative offsets to zero. Scripts aren't very good at creating smooth motion effects, but so far there is no other solution that works with HTML.

Absolute positioning is completely different. It takes an element out of the normal sequence (like `display: none` would do) but then it puts it somewhere else, without regard for what else might be there. Absolute

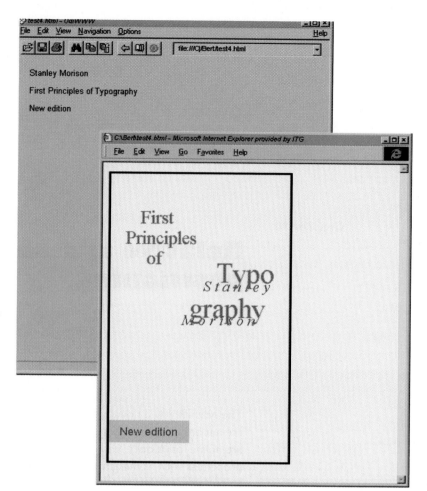

Figure 10.1 An example of absolute positioning: on the left in a non-CSS browser, on the right in a CSS2-capable browser. See Figure 10.8 (at the end of the chapter) for the document source. The example is an approximation in CSS of the cover of the 1996 edition (Academic Press, Leiden) of the essay, which first appeared in 1930.

positioning is good at creating displays with little pieces of text or images that are put seemingly independent of each other in fixed spots on the canvas. For an example, see Figure 10.1.

A variation of absolute positioning also allows elements to be put at fixed positions not on the canvas, but in the viewport: if you view a page with such fixed elements on a browser, the elements will appear to be glued to the glass of the monitor. While other elements scroll when you move the scroll bars, these fixed elements stay put. If you print such documents, you will see that the fixed elements are glued to the page box: they will appear in the same spot on every page that you print.

THE POSITION PROPERTY

The **position** property determines whether elements are "normal" elements, or whether they are subject to relative, absolute or fixed positioning.

IE3	NS4	IE4	O3.5
○	⊙	⊙	○

Name:	**position**
Value:	static | relative | absolute | fixed
Initial:	static
Applies to:	all elements
Inherited:	no
Percentages:	N/A

Elements that don't use any of the positioning methods are called "static." This is the normal case, and it is the only possible value for pseudo-elements (such as the "first-letter" and "before" pseudo-elements). The values **absolute** and **fixed** imply that the element must be a block. The value of the **display** property is ignored in this case.

Elements that are not **static** make use of the four positioning properties **top**, **right**, **bottom** and **left**:

IE3	NS4	IE4	O3.5
○	⊙	⊙	○

Name:	**top, right, bottom, left**
Value:	*<length>* | *<percentage>* | auto
Initial:	auto
Applies to:	elements with **position ≠ static**
Inherited:	no
Percentages:	width or height of "containing block"

These properties determine the position of a positioned element by setting the distance from the edge of a so-called "containing block," explained below. The meaning changes slightly with the type of positioning, and will be explained in following sections.

THE CONTAINING BLOCK

Normal (static) elements are placed relative to their parent and to elements that precede them, as explained in Chapter 7. Positioned elements are placed relative to so-called *containing blocks*, which may occasionally be their parents, but are usually some ancestor higher up in the document tree.

The containing block for fixed positioned element is always the viewport (in the case of scrolling media, such as most browsers) or the page box (in the case of paged media). The parent, or even any other positioned elements, have no influence on the position of an element with `position: fixed`.

Relatively positioned elements, like normal static elements, don't have a containing block. The positioning properties **top**, **right**, **bottom** and **left** move the element up, right, down or left from its normal position. However, relatively positioned elements can themselves be the containing block for absolutely positioned elements (see below).

The containing block for an absolutely positioned element is usually the root element, *i.e.*, the absolutely positioned element is placed somewhere inside the box of the root element with the help of the **top**, **right**, **bottom** and **left** properties. However, if the element is inside some other positioned element (either absolute, relative or fixed), then that element will be its containing block.

Here is an example. Consider the HTML fragment given below. The two DIVs are each absolutely positioned. The first one will therefore be put at a certain distance from the edges of the root element; the second, since it is inside the first, will be positioned relative to the first DIV:

```
<HTML>
  <STYLE>
    DIV.outer { position: absolute;
      top: 1cm; right: 2cm; width: 4cm }
    DIV.inner { position: absolute;
      top: 1cm; left: 1cm; width: 2cm }
  </STYLE>
  <BODY>
    <H1>Static header</H1>
    <P>Static paragraph.
    <DIV CLASS="outer">
      <P>Some text in outer...
      <DIV CLASS="inner">
        <P>Some text in inner...
      </DIV>
    </DIV>
    ...
```

The output may look like this (Figure 10.2):

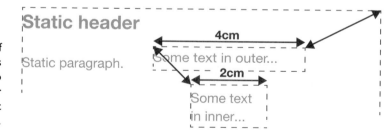

Figure 10.2 Example of absolute positioning: one box is positioned relative to the top and right of the root, the other to the top and left of the first box.

The edges that are used for positioning are the inside and outside of the border: the containing block is formed by the padding edges (*i.e.*, inside of the border) and the **top**, **right**, etc., are measured from there to the border edge (*i.e.*, outside of the border) of the absolutely positioned box.

When an absolutely positioned element is inside some other absolutely positioned element, or inside a fixed positioned element, it is easy to establish the edges of the containing block, but if the absolutely positioned element is inside a relatively positioned element, a complication may arise: if the relatively positioned element is inline, it may have been broken over several lines, and thus it has several boxes; which of them is the containing block for the absolutely positioned box inside?

What happens is that the top and left edges of the first of the inline boxes will become the top and left edges of the containing block, and the bottom and right edges of the last inline box are the bottom and right edges of the containing block. Figure 10.3 shows how this works. As the image also shows, the right edge may easily end up to the left of the left edge! It may be hard to predict where elements will be placed in such a case. So be careful when putting absolutely positioned elements inside relatively positioned ones.

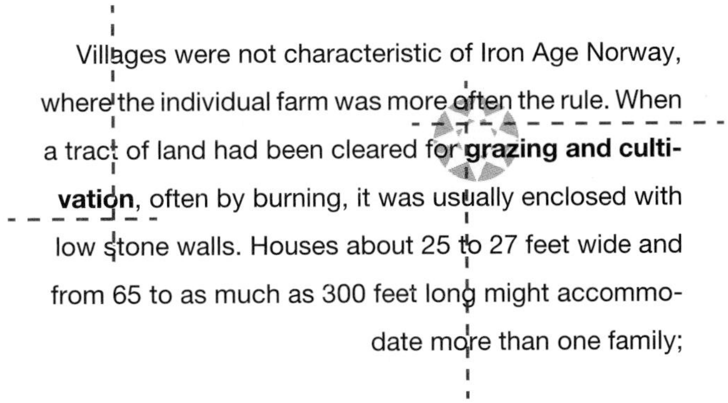

Figure 10.3 An image is placed near the upper left corner of an inline element. The inline element consists of two boxes; the first one determines the upper left corner of a containing block, the last one the bottom right (indicated by dotted lines).

Villages were not characteristic of Iron Age Norway, where the individual farm was more often the rule. When a tract of land had been cleared for **grazing and culti-vation**, often by burning, it was usually enclosed with low stone walls. Houses about 25 to 27 feet wide and from 65 to as much as 300 feet long might accommodate more than one family;

The code for this fragment is as follows. The SPAN element has been made relative, but without actually positioning it. It only serves as a containing block for the absolutely positioned image inside it.

```
<STYLE>
  SPAN.star { position: relative;
    font-weight: bold }
  IMG.star { position: absolute;
    top: -10px; left: -10px; z-index: -1 }
</STYLE>
```

```
... cleared for <SPAN CLASS="star"><IMG CLASS="star"
SRC="star.png" ALT="">grazing and cultivation</SPAN>,
often by burning,...
```

RELATIVE POSITIONING

As shown in the last example in the previous section, you can use relative positioning simply to create a containing block for some other absolutely positioned element. However, the typical use of relative positioning is to position elements away from their normal position, without influencing the position of other elements. There aren't many reasons for doing that in a style sheet, and the main reason relative positioning exists at all is to provide a way for scripts to animate the text: to make it "explode" when a page is unloaded, or make it slowly move into place when the page is loaded. These effects are well known in slide show presentations, and with relative positioning and a clever script you can do the same with HTML.

Unfortunately, scripting languages aren't very good at animation. The way they do it is to enter a loop in which the value of the positioning properties is slowly increased or decreased, until they reach some preset value. With every change, part of the screen is redrawn. However, even on the fastest computers the speed at which successive cycles of the loop are executed will vary slightly, causing jerky motion — enough for the human eye to notice. Real animation programs don't rely on such loops, but calculate the path of the element in advance, and even create blurry images on purpose, based on the measured speed of the computer, to fool the human eye into believing the object is moving more than it actually is.

For this reason, some of the most common animation effects may one day end up in CSS itself, to allow browsers to use the sophisticated animation algorithms, and to help designers, who don't have to write scripts anymore. But until that time, scripting and relative positioning will have to do.

By itself, relative positioning isn't hard to use or to understand. You can think of a relatively positioned element as a normal element, that is pushed away from its proper position after the page has been laid out. You use **top** to specify how far down the element goes from its normal top edge and **left** to give the distance to move it to the right of its left edge. Negative values move it up and left, respectively. (You can also use **right** or **bottom**, they work exactly the same, but with the direction reversed.)

Figure 10.4 shows an example. The word "high" has been moved up by 0.5 em (`top: -0.5em`). Note that this causes the word to overlap with the line above. The **vertical-align** property can also raise text, but it would have caused the lines to be pushed apart to avoid overlap.

Art is an individu
The **high** **point o**

Figure 10.4 The word "high" has been raised 0.5 em by means of the **top** property.

You can use percentages as the values of **left** or **right**, and they will be relative to the width of the element (if it is a block) or the width of the enclosing block-level element. Percentages on the **top** or **bottom** properties are only possible if the element (or the enclosing block, for inline elements) has a set **height**, *i.e.*, the **height** is not **auto**. Otherwise a percentage will be interpreted as **0**.

FIXED POSITIONING

Sometimes it is desirable to keep an element on screen at all times. For example, a short warning or a logo could be kept in the corner of the window at all times, no matter how the user scrolls the document. Similarly, when a document is printed, such an element may be printed in a fixed position on every page.

The containing block for a fixed element is thus always the viewport (*i.e.*, the browser's window) or the page box (see Chapter 12, "Printing and other media"). The positioning properties set the distance between the edges of the containing block and the element. If the element is not an image or other "replaced element," you will typically set the **width** property, and either the **left** or **right** property, and of course **top** or **bottom**. The height can usually be left unspecified (**auto**). For replaced elements you don't have to set the width, unless you want to scale the image. Setting both **left** and **right**, and leaving **width** as **auto** is also possible: the width will then be calculated as the width of the viewport minus the **left** and **right** values.

Here is a document that puts a small DIV along the left side of the window. Note that the left margin of the document has been made wide enough that the fixed element will not obscure any text.

```
<HTML>
  <STYLE>
    BODY { margin-left: 5em }
    DIV.status { position: fixed;
      top: 10%; left: 0; width: 4em }
  </STYLE>
    ...
    <DIV CLASS="status">
      <P><IMG SRC="logo" ALT="logo">
      <P>Draft!
    </DIV>
    ...
</HTML>
```

If this document is printed, the logo and the text "Draft!" will appear in the left margin, 10% from the top on every page. Of course, when you want it to appear somewhere else on paper than on screen, or you don't want it to repeat on paper, you can use the @media rules (see Chapter 12).

Another way in which fixed positioning can be used is to divide a document into a small number of parts, each of which is displayed in one area of the viewport. For example, the following document with four DIVs can be displayed in such a way that each DIV takes up one quarter of the screen. If the contents of the DIVs is too large, scroll bars will appear:

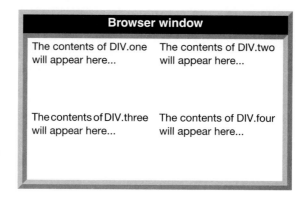

Figure 10.5 A window divided into four areas by means of fixed positioning.

```
<HTML>
  <STYLE>
    DIV.one, DIV.two, DIV.three, DIV.four {
      position: fixed; width: 50%; height: 50% }
    DIV.one { top: 0; left: 0 }
    DIV.two { top: 0; left: 50% }
    DIV.three { top: 50%; left: 0 }
    DIV.four { top: 50%; left: 50% }
  </STYLE>
  <BODY>
    <DIV CLASS=one>... </DIV>
    <DIV CLASS=two>... </DIV>
    <DIV CLASS=three>... </DIV>
    <DIV CLASS=four>... </DIV>
  </BODY>
</HTML>
```

This is very similar to what can be achieved with HTML frames, but the difference is that in this case the whole document is in one piece (which means quicker display, and avoids problems with the "Back" button) and the "frames" can be positioned much more freely. They can even overlap.

ABSOLUTE POSITIONING

The simplest form of absolute positioning is when the elements to position are positioned relative to the initial containing block, *i.e.*, the containing block of the root element. When absolutely positioned elements are descendants of other positioned elements, things become more complicated.

There are two major ways in which absolute positioning can be used. One is to have a few small absolutely positioned elements in an otherwise normal document; for example, to put a logo in a corner. The other way is to create "areas" for parts of the document, much like the last example for fixed positioning in the previous section. The difference is that the size of the window isn't taken into account. Although most browsers will use the width of the window for the width of the initial containing block, the height of the initial containing block is unspecified.

The method to position an absolutely positioned element is the same as for fixed elements: use either the **top** or **bottom** to determine the vertical position relative to the containing block, and either the **left** or **right** properties for the horizontal position. If the element is not a replaced element, you should normally also set the **width** property, although the value **auto** for **width** has a special meaning that may be useful in certain cases (see below). Instead of setting **width**, you can also set both the **left** and **right**. Here is an example:

```
IMG#stamp1 {
    position: absolute;
    top: 10px; right: 10px }
```

This puts the image with ID "stamp1" 10 pixels from the upper right corner. Since it is an image, it has an intrinsic width, and you don't need to specify it (unless you want to resize it).

Here is another example. This creates a containing block out of a DIV and puts all the words inside it at random places. (You might want to use dice, or their electronic equivalent, to generate the percentages… .) See Figure 10.6 for the result.

Figure 10.6 Six absolutely positioned words in a square.

```
<STYLE>
#container { position: relative; border: solid;
  width: 4cm; height: 4cm }
#w01 { position: absolute; top: 17%; left: 44% }
#w02 { position: absolute; top: 56%; left: 74% }
#w03 { position: absolute; top: 84%; left: 07% }
#w04 { position: absolute; top: 26%; left: 23% }
#w05 { position: absolute; top: 55%; left: 36% }
#w06 { position: absolute; top: 12%; left: 30% }
</STYLE>
```

```
...
<DIV ID=container>
  <P><SPAN ID=w01>This</SPAN>
    <SPAN ID=w02>line</SPAN>
    <SPAN ID=w03>has</SPAN>
    <SPAN ID=w04>exactly</SPAN>
    <SPAN ID=w05>six</SPAN>
    <SPAN ID=w06>words</SPAN>
</DIV>
```

Using auto values

The value **auto** has some special functions when set on the **top** or **left** properties of an absolutely positioned element. When both **top** *and* **bottom** are **auto**, the browser makes a guess as to where the element would have been if it had been a static element, and sets **top** to the value that puts the element there. Similarly for **left** and **right**: if both of them are **auto**, the browser will try to make the value **left** such that the element is put almost where it would have been as a static element.

The values are only approximations, because it is hard to compute the values precisely, without actually doing the layout. But computing the layout twice takes too much time. However, the approximations will usually be accurate within a few pixels, especially if the positioned element would have been a block element. If it would have been a static inline element, the chance that the values are more than a few pixels wrong is higher.

Using **auto** values on **top** and **left** allows us to write the example of Figure 10.2 (page 214) in a different way. The trick employed here is to use auto on top and left to put the image where it would have been (after the word "for"), and then use negative margins to move it up and left:

```
<STYLE>
  SPAN.star { font-weight: bold }
  IMG.star { position: absolute;
    top: auto; left: auto; z-index: -1;
    margin-top: -10px; margin-left: -10px }
</STYLE>

... cleared for <SPAN CLASS="star"><IMG CLASS="star"
SRC="star.png" ALT="">grazing and cultivation</SPAN>,
often by burning,...
```

Whether this solution is "better" is a matter of taste.

Note that setting **left** and **right** to **auto** thus doesn't center an absolutely positioned element, like setting **margin-left** and **margin-right** to

auto would do for a normal (static) block. But there are various other ways to center an absolutely positioned block in its containing block. For example, you can set calculate the correct value for **left** yourself, or you can set **left** and **right** to **0** and use the margins to center the element.

Let's also look at what happens when both **width** and **right** are **auto**. The situation is similar to what happens with static block elements when **width** and **margin-right** are **auto**: **right** is set to 0 and **width** takes the remaining space. This makes the absolutely positioned element extend from the position given by **left** all the way to the right edge of the containing block.

Everything said about left and right above applies only in languages that are written left to right. If the parent of the absolutely (or fixed) positioned element is written right to left (the **direction** property is **rtl**), then left and right switch roles: the magic **auto** value applies to **right** instead of **left**, and when both **left** and **width** are auto, **left** is set to 0.

THE Z-INDEX PROPERTY

Positioning elements frequently causes them to overlap, and in fact, the possibility of having elements overlap is an important reason for using positioning in the first place. The normal rule is that elements that come later in the source document are on top of earlier elements. But as we saw in the example with the star (Figure 10.2 on page 214), that is not always what we want. That example therefore used the **z-index** property to explicitly put the image behind its containing block. Here is an example:

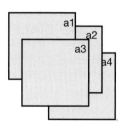

Figure 10.7 The effect of **z-index**: "a3" has the highest z-index, and is on top; "a4" has the lowest z-index, and is behind the others.

```
<STYLE>
  DIV {position: absolute; border: solid;
    width: 5em; height: 5em; background: silver;
    text-align: right}
  .a1 {top: 1em; left: 1em; z-index: 3}
  .a2 {top: 2em; left: 3em; z-index: 2}
  .a3 {top: 3em; left: 2em; z-index: 4}
  .a4 {top: 4em; left: 4em; z-index: 1}
</STYLE>
```

```
<DIV CLASS="a1"><P>a1</DIV>
<DIV CLASS="a2"><P>a2</DIV>
<DIV CLASS="a3"><P>a3</DIV>
<DIV CLASS="a4"><P>a4</DIV>
```

IE3	NS4	IE4	O3.5
○	●	●	○

Name:	**z-index**
Value:	auto | *<integer>*
Initial:	auto
Applies to:	positioned elements
Inherited:	no
Percentages:	N/A

A negative value means that the element will be behind its containing block, a value of zero or higher means it will be in front. **Auto** is the same as zero (but see below).

If two elements have the same containing block and the same **z-index**, then the element that comes later in the source will be in front of the earlier element.

The value **auto** has effect when containing blocks are nested. If an element that is a containing block for some other elements has a **z-index** of **auto**, it means that the z-index of the elements inside this block isn't relative to this containing block, but to the nearest enclosing containing block that doesn't have **auto** for its value. Thus, if you leave the z-index of all containing blocks as **auto**, all z-indexes will be relative to the root element, no matter how deeply nested the elements are.

MAKING ELEMENTS INVISIBLE

IE3	NS4	IE4	O3.5
○	○	●	○

Name:	**visibility**
Value:	visible | hidden
Initial:	visible
Applies to:	all elements
Inherited:	yes
Percentages:	N/A

With **display** you can remove elements from display (display: none), but there is another way to make elements invisible. The **visibility** property doesn't remove elements, but makes them completely transparent. In other words, if you set **visibility** to **hidden**, you will see an empty space where the element is supposed to be.

This is most useful if you have multiple alternative style sheets for the same page, or if you have a script that changes the style. You can use it to selectively show the answers to a quiz, for example, while keeping everything else on the page the same.

The value **visible** makes elements visible, **hidden** makes them transparent. The property actually has a third value, **collapse**, which can make table columns disappear, but we won't discuss it here (refer to the CSS2 specification for an explanation).

```
BODY {font: 30px/30px "Times New Roman", serif;
    background: #FEB; color: #874}
#co {position: relative; width: 10em; height: 16em;
    border: solid 0.1em black}
#fi, #pr, #of, #ed {position: absolute; text-align: left}
#ty, #gr, #st, #mo {position: absolute; text-align: right}
#fi {top: 12%; left: 10%}
#pr {top: 19%; left: 5%}
#of {top: 26%; left: 12%}
#ty, #gr {font-size: 150%}
#st, #mo {font: italic 80%/100% "Times New Roman", serif;
    letter-spacing: 0.2em; color: #C00}
#ty {top: 31%; right: 5%}
#gr {top: 43%; right: 8%}
#st {top: 36%; right: 5%}
#mo {top: 48%; right: 10%}
#ed {top: 88%; width: 45%; padding: 0.5em;
    background: #CCB; color: #C00; text-align: center;
    font: 60%/100% "Helvetica", sans-serif}
```
(a)

```
BODY {font: 30px/100% "Times New Roman", serif;
    background: #FEB; color: #874}
#co {width: 10em;
    border: solid 0.1em black}
#fi, #pr, #of, #ed {display: block; text-align: left}
#ty, #gr, #st, #mo {display: block; text-align: right}
#fi {margin: 1.9em 0 0 10%}
#pr {margin: 0.1em 0 0 5%}
#of {margin: 0.1em 0 -0.2em 12%}
#ty, #gr {font-size: 150%}
#st, #mo {font: italic 80%/100% "Times New Roman", serif;
    letter-spacing: 0.2em; color: #C00}
#ty {margin: 0 5% 0 0}
#gr {margin: 0.6em 8% 0 0}
#st {margin: 7.2em 5% -8.2em 0}
#mo {margin: 9.5em 10% -10.5em 0}
#ed {margin: 5em 0 1em 0; width: 45%; padding: 0.5em;
    background: #CCB; color: #C00; text-align: center;
    font: 60%/100% "Helvetica", sans-serif}
```
(c)

Figure 10.8 (a) The style sheet for Figure 10.1; (b) the HTML source. For comparison; (c) does the same without absolute positioning. (a) Expresses all positions as percentages of the size of the DIV element. (c) Makes use of margins. Note the negative bottom margins on "Stanley" and "Morison," to put what comes after it in the source, above it in the rendering.

```
<body>
<div id=co>
    <p>
    <span id=st>Stanley</span>
    <span id=mo>Morison</span>
    <p>
    <span id=fi>First</span>
    <span id=pr>Principles</span>
    <span id=of>of</span>
    <span id=ty>Typo</span><span id=gr>graphy</span>
    <p>
    <span id=ed>New edition</span>
</div>
</body>
```
(b)

Chapter 11

Colors

Printing color is expensive. Hence, in books color has always been used sparingly. On the Web, however, the use of color is virtually free. Most Web users have color monitors, so displaying color costs nothing, although printing it is still costly. So there is no reason for Web designers not to incorporate color into their designs.

Of course, color can be overdone. As with all aspects of print, and Web, design – whether fonts, space, or images – color should be used to achieve a purpose with the design. Color thrown in at random doesn't work well. Remember, too much variety obscures, rather than clarifies.

Some combinations of colors are very hard to read, such as red type on a blue background. A background that differs from the foreground text only in color and not in brightness also strains the eye. For some people, dark letters on a light background are easier to read, while for others, the opposite is true. People may also have associations with certain colors that may either help or hinder their understanding the text. For example, red seems to be almost universal in marking something that is important. But the interpretations of other colors often depend on culture and even on the user's personal experiences. Colors and how we perceive them are both very technical and complex subjects, far beyond the scope of this book. We encourage interested readers to further explore the subject of color, particularly to learn how to combine colors effectively to achieve the desired effects.

The range of colors that can be reproduced by a computer monitor is called its *gamut*. The gamut depends not only on the color and brightness that a computer monitor can produce but also on the brightness of the light that reflects off the screen. The effective gamut is reduced as the light in the room gets brighter; the largest gamut is available in a darkened room. Note that color printers work very differently from computers and their gamuts differ from that of computer monitors. Colors often appear one way on the monitor's screen and another when printed by a color printer or by a traditional printing process.

In this chapter, we show how to use CSS to specify the color of text and borders. This is done with the **color** property. Also, we describe how to set backgrounds – either to a certain color or to an image. This is done with the various **background** properties. Before we describe the properties, we have to look at the different ways color values can be set in CSS.

SPECIFYING COLORS

There are many ways in which color can be specified. The English language – and all other languages as well – has words for the most common colors; for example "red," "blue," and "brown." If you tell someone that your house is red, your listener will get a general idea about the color of your house, but there are many different shades of red which will all be described as "red."

Another way to describe a certain color is to use numbers. Paint manufacturers often provide sets of numbered color swatches so that you can ask for paint that is "blue number 216," for example. On computer screens, the most common way to specify a color is to give an RGB value which specifies the mixture of red, green and blue. However, this, too, is an imprecise way of selecting colors because the result depends on the type of screen you have and how much light is in the room in which the monitor is located.

A third way to specify a color is to refer to the color of something else. For example, you may want the color of your curtains to be the same as the color of your sofa. A more relevant example for a style sheet is to set the text color of a document to be the same as a system color, for example the foreground color of the user's window system.

CSS allows you to specify colors using all these methods. A small number of color names and system colors are defined, and other colors can be specified as RGB values.

Color names

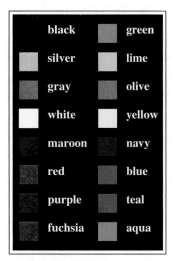

Figure 11.1 Samples of the 16 predefined colors in CSS.

CSS predefines 16 color names: aqua (a light greenish blue, sometimes called cyan), black, blue, fuchsia (light purple/pink), gray, green, lime (light green), maroon (dark red), navy (dark blue), olive, purple, red, silver (light gray), teal (blue-green), yellow, white.)

Figure 11.1 shows samples of all of the predefined colors. The exact same colors are also used in HTML. Note that colors on screen look different on paper and keep this in mind when selecting your colors. If you plan to print your page on paper, some of the colors you choose for screen display may surprise you once printed. If this book was specifically about color, we would have tried for a better match – and the book would have been much more expensive... .

Here is a simple example of a style sheet which sets the color and background using the color names:

```
BODY {
    color: black;
    background: yellow;
}
```

The predefined color names are easy to use for those who write style sheets in a simple text editor. More advanced tools allow designers to graphically select colors which are then turned into RGB colors.

RGB colors

Computer monitors commonly use the *RGB* – red, green, blue – *color model* to display color. In addition to RGB, there were are a few other color models which could have been used. One of them is the HSB (hue-saturation-brightness) model, which is often used by artists since it is similar to how artists mix colors. Another is CMYK (cyan-magenta-yellow-black), a color model commonly used by professional printers. We chose the RGB model because it represents how color is displayed on a color video monitor. Red, green, and blue light is mixed in specified proportions to represent colors on the monitor.

In the RGB color model, each of the three colors is represented by a value between 0 and 100%, where 100% represents the maximum brightness of a color. The values are arranged as a triplet, where the first number represents red, the second green, and the last blue. Black is represented as the triplet (0, 0, 0) – zero amounts of all three colors – and white by (100%, 100%, 100%) – 100% of all three colors. Every triplet with equal amounts of each color is a shade of gray. For example, (90%, 90%, 90%) is a light gray, while (40%, 40%, 40%) is a dark gray. When the values are not equal, it is often hard to predict what the color looks like. That (100%, 0, 0) is red is not too hard to see. But that a color with the values (65%, 16%, 16%) is a shade of brown is not so obvious.

As you know, computers work best with bytes. A byte can contain a number from 0 to 255, so when working on screen, it is usual to remap the RGB percentage values to values within the range of 0, inclusive, to 255, inclusive. Thus 100% remaps to 255. White, then, remaps as (255, 255, 255), red remaps to (255, 0, 0), and the brown we mentioned in the previous paragraph remaps as (165, 42, 42).

Because each color is represented by 3 bytes, each a value between 0 and 255, the number of potential available colors is 16,777,216, that is, 256 x 256 x 256. These are usually enough colors for most applications. Unfortunately, many monitors don't have enough memory to store 3 bytes for every pixel, particularly when it is not uncommon for a million pixels to be on a screen. So monitors play tricks (which we won't go into) in their efforts to display as many colors as possible. This usually means that although potentially you can use all 16,777,216 colors, you cannot use them all at the same time. Many monitors have a limit of 256 colors that can be displayed at any given time, although a 65,536-color limit is becoming more common.

This limit may not seem very important when you are working with a style sheet because usually you will specify only a handful of colors. However, a typical HTML document also contains images, which may use up colors quickly. There is actually very little you can do to ensure the desired color is available on the user's monitor. You can only hope that the browser will take care that if the exact color is not available (which it often isn't), then at least one that is close is available.

The RGB values of CSS1 are called "sRGB," for "standard-RGB." sRGB is a *color space* which ensures that all colors specified in CSS are exactly defined. This means that the computer which displays the document will know exactly what colors are specified in the style sheet and all Web devices should be able to display the exact color. As noted above, however, limitations in computer hardware make this a hard promise to fulfill. An article (see side note) describes the technical details of the sRGB system.

To specify an RGB color in CSS, three values – a triplet – must be provided. That can be done by using any of three methods. The first two we've already discussed. Which you use is a matter of taste, since they all produce the same result.

1 *Percentages:* for example, a color specification like rgb(100%, 35.5%, 10%) specifies a maximum amount (100%) of red light, 35.5% of green

See M. Anderson, R. Motta, S. Chandrasekar, M. Stokes: *Proposal for a Standard Color Space for the Internet – sRGB*, 1996. URL: http://www.w3.org/Graphics/Color/sRGB.html

Hexadecimal numbers

The relation between hexadecimal and the normal decimal numbers is as follows: the digits 0 to 9 stand for themselves, the letters A to F mean A=10, B=11, C=12, D=13, E=14 and F=15. In a group of two hexadecimal digits, the first one is multiplied by 16 and added to the second. For example: 11 (= 1 × 16 + 1) = 17. Some more examples:

- A7 = 10 × 16 + 7 = 167
- FF = 15 × 16 + 15 = 255
- 22 = 2 × 16 + 2 = 34
- 5B = 5 × 16 + 11 = 91
- 1A = 1 × 16 + 10 = 26

We can apply this to color values:

- #FF5B1A = rgb(255, 91, 26), since FF=255, 5B=91 and 1A=26
- #CEAA13 = rgb(206, 176, 19)

light, and 10% of the blue light. The result is a deep orange red.

2 *Numbers in the range of 0 to 255:* thus rgb(255, 91, 26) should be the same color as rgb(100%, 35.5%, 10%) in the percentage example.
3 *Hexadecimal numbers:* for example, #FF5B1A, which will produce the same shade of red as in (1) and (2).

In either of the first or second methods, if you enter a value that is outside the acceptable range, for example, 125% in method one or 300 in method two, the value will be "clipped." That is, the errant value will be reduced to the maximum value allowed by the Web device. Since different devices have different ranges (*e.g.,* a color printer is different from a computer screen) you should avoid values outside the acceptable range.

The third method for specifying a color needs a bit more explanation. You use the same numbers as with the second method, 0 to 255, but you write them as a single hexadecimal number preceded by a hash mark (#); for example, #FF5B1A, which produces the same color red as rgb(100%, 35.5%, 10%) and rgb(255, 91, 26). This notation is not very intuitive, but is included since it is also used in HTML. The hexadecimal notation can be written in two variations that use either three or six hexadecimal digits. The three-digit form defines the same color as the six-digit form does but with all digits doubled; that is, #A84 is the same color as #AA8844.

System colors

CSS2 introduces the concept of *system colors*. System colors aren't real colors, instead they are pointers to colors defined elsewhere in the computer which displays the document. For example, the system color **Background** refers to the background color of the user's desktop. Style sheets that use system colors can make documents blend into the user's environment. Figure 11.2 shows some of the most common system colors in use.

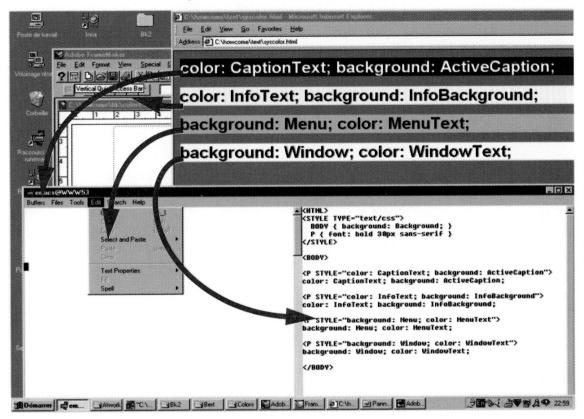

Figure 11.2 System colors can make documents blend into the user's environment. The figure shows some of the most common system colors and their respective sources.

A word of warning is in place for designers who are eager to use system colors: remember that the user's system is different from your own. So, even if the document is legible on your screen, this may not be the case on the user's screen. Here are two general rules to help preserve legibility:

- never mix system colors with other kinds of color specification; for example, colors specified in RGB
- always set both the foreground and the background color together, using matching pairs of system colors. For example, the system's default window text and background are likely to provide excellent contrast:

```
BODY { color: WindowText; background: Window }
```

System colors do not follow the common CSS naming scheme of hyphenating words. In the example above, the system color is not the expected **window-text**, but rather **WindowText**. As with all keywords in CSS, the system color names are case-insensitive but to maintain legibility we recommend using **WindowText** rather than **windowtext**.

The full list of system colors can be found in the "System colors" appendix.

THE PROPERTIES

We have already seen some examples of the **color** property and the background properties in use. The next section will define them more formally and give more examples.

The color property

The **color** property sets the color of the text of an element. It is the foreground color. It can also set the color of text decorations, discussed in Chapter 5, "Fonts" such as underline, as well as borders that have been created with the border properties discussed in Chapter 9, page 186 ("Using the padding property").

IE3 NS4 IE4 O3.5
●   ●   ●   ●

Name:	**color**
Value:	<color>
Initial:	UA specific
Applies to:	all elements
Inherited:	yes
Percentages:	N/A

The property takes one value – a color – which is specified by one of the methods discussed in the previous section. The following are examples of rules to specify a color for text or a text decoration:

```
EM { color: red }
P { color: rgb(255, 0, 0) }/* red */
H1 { color: #f00 }/* also red */
H1 { color: #ff000 }/* same as above */
```

A color is inherited by child elements. The default color is set in the user's default style sheet, if one exists. Otherwise, the default color depends on the browser.

SETTING THE COLOR OF A BORDER

Setting the color of a border can be done in two ways. One is to set it directly by including the color via the border properties, as done here:

```
P { border: medium double red }
```

The result is shown in Figure 11.3(a). We discussed this method in Chapter 9 ("The border properties").

Another way is to set the color of the text that is the content of the element, as done here:

```
P {
    border: thin dotted;
    color: blue;
}
```

In this case, no color has been set on the border, so it will assume the color of the text, which is blue. This is shown in Figure 11.3(b).

If we set a color on the border itself, as done here:

```
P {
    border: thin dotted red;
    color: blue;
}
```

we end up with the result shown in Figure 11.3(c). (Some padding has been added between the text and the border, as described in Chapter 9.)

Figure 11.3 Different ways to set the color of a border using the **color** property: (a) setting the border using the **border** properties; (b) setting the border to the text color; (c) setting the border color independent of the text.

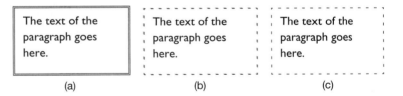

(a)   (b)   (c)

SETTING THE COLOR OF HYPERLINKS

Until CSS, the most common use of color in Web browsers (other than in images) was to draw attention to hyperlinks. Some browsers use two colors: one for links to documents that the user has traversed before and another for links that he hasn't tried yet. Others use a third color for the "active" link; that is, for the short duration while the user keeps the mouse button pressed over the text. In CSS, rules for these can be written through a pseudo-class on an A element, as follows:

```
A:link { color: blue }/* unvisited links */
A:visited { color: red }/* visited links */
A:active { color: yellow }/* active links */
```

See also "Pseudo-Classes" in Chapter 4, "CSS selectors," for more information.

THE BACKGROUND PROPERTIES

The **background** properties set aspects of the background of an element, that is, the surface onto which text is displayed. That background can be either transparent, a color, or an image. You can also set the position of an image, if and how often the image should be repeated on the screen, and whether it should be fixed or scrolled relative to the canvas. Five of the properties set specific aspects of the background, while the sixth, the background property, is a shorthand method that lets you set all of the first five properties at one time. The properties do not inherit. The following are the background properties:

- **background-color**
- **background-image**
- **background-repeat**
- **background-attachment**
- **background-position**
- **background**

We discuss each of these in the following sections.

THE BACKGROUND-COLOR PROPERTY

The **background-color** property sets the background color of an element.

IE3	NS4	IE4	O3.5
⊙	⊙	●	●

Name:	**background-color**
Value:	*<color>* | transparent
Initial:	transparent
Applies to:	all elements
Inherited:	no
Percentages:	N/A

This property has two values:

- a color
- the keyword **transparent** – this is the default

When a color value is provided, the specified color will be visible behind the text of the element. How much of the surface will actually get that color depends on the type of element and on the amount of padding. We discussed the effect of padding on color in "Using the padding property" (Chapter 9). It also depends on whether there is a background image in addition to the color, as specified with the **background-image** property below.

Background color in inline elements

For an inline element, the color will be visible only behind the text itself and behind the padding around the element. Hence, if the element is broken across lines, the background color will be visible behind the words and spaces at the end of the first line and also behind the words and spaces on the second line. For example, in Figure 11.4, the words in the middle of the sentence are displayed in white on black by putting them in an EM element with the color: white and background-color: black. Here is the code to produce this result:

```
<STYLE TYPE="text/css">
  EM {
    background-color: black;
    color: white
  }
</STYLE>
<BODY>
  <P>This paragraph has <EM>a few emphasized
     words</EM> in the middle.
</BODY>
```

Figure 11.4 Use of the **background-color** property with an inline element.

This paragraph has a few emphasized words in the middle.

Background color in block elements

For block-level elements, the color will occupy a rectangular region that includes the indent of the first line (if any) of the paragraph as well as any empty space at the end of each line. It will also occupy the padding around

This is the first paragraph, it has no CLASS attribute.

This is the second paragraph, it has CLASS="standout"

This is the third paragraph, it has no CLASS attribute.

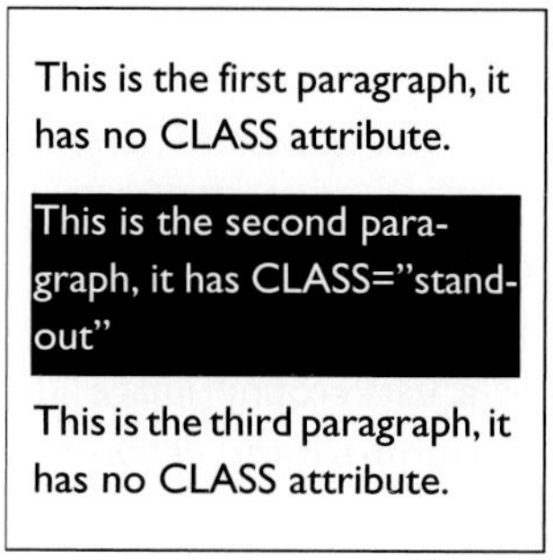

Figure 11.5 Use of the "color" value in a colored block-level element.

the block, if any. In such cases, it is a good idea to add a little padding to leave some room between the letters and the edge of the background, as has been done in the example shown in Figure 11.5. The figure was generated with the following style sheet set on the middle paragraph:

```
P.standout {
    background: black;
    color: white;
}
```

Background color in list items

For list item elements, the background is not applied to the label if the label is outside the text box. If the label is inside the text box, then the background will be behind the label as well.

The transparent value

If no color or image is specified, the background will be transparent. In this case, the background of the parent element is visible behind the text (or if that is transparent, the background of the parent's parent is visible, and so on). If all elements have a transparent background, the browser's default background is used; this is often white.

For example, the following code sets the background of certain paragraphs to red and the background of STRONG elements to yellow. Other elements keep their default transparent background. Figure 11.6 shows how a document with this style sheet may look.

```
P.special { background-color: red }
STRONG { background-color: yellow }
```

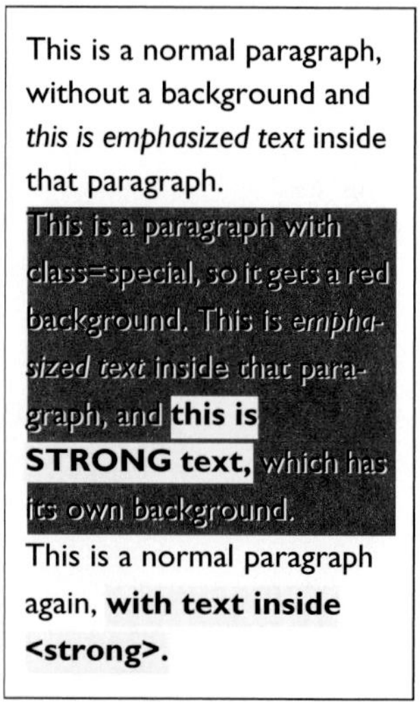

A background is not inherited; if it is not set explicitly, it will be transparent, so you often can omit this value. You'll only need to set it to **transparent** explicitly if you need to override an earlier rule – whether in your style sheet or another's – for the **background-color** or **background** properties.

This is a normal paragraph, without a background and *this is emphasized text* inside that paragraph.

This is a paragraph with class=special, so it gets a red background. This is emphasized text inside that paragraph, and **this is STRONG text,** which has its own background.

This is a normal paragraph again, **with text inside <strong>.**

Figure 11.6 Examples of transparent and colored backgrounds.

THE BACKGROUND-IMAGE PROPERTY

The **background-image** property lets you set an image as the background for an element.

IE3   NS4   IE4   O3.5
○   ●   ●   ●

Name:	**background-image**
Value:	[*<url>*	none]
Initial:	none
Applies to:	all elements
Inherited:	no
Percentages:	N/A

This property has two values:

* a URL
* the keyword **none** – this is the default

To specify an image as a background, you enter the URL of the image as the *<url>* value. When specifying an image as the background, you should also specify a color (using the **background-color** property). When the document is displayed, the image will overlay the color. You would do this for several reasons:

* The color can be used to fill transparent regions of the image; otherwise, these areas will remain transparent.
* It can be used to fill in the screen while the image is loading; for example, if loading takes too long.
* It can be used in place of the image if the image cannot be loaded; for example, if the browser cannot locate it.

The following rule specifies both an image and a color for the background. The result is shown in Figure 11.7.

```
P {
    background-image: url(dot.gif);
    background-color: #FFAA00;
}
```

Figure 11.7 Setting both an image and a color as the background of an element.

THE BACKGROUND-REPEAT PROPERTY

The **background-repeat** property determines whether and how an image is repeated in the element. By default, an image is initially placed in the upper-left corner of the element (or of the window if the image has the **background-attachment** value of `fixed`; we discuss this property shortly). Repetition of an element begins from either this default position or from a new position that you set with the **background-position** property, which we discuss shortly.

IE3	NS4	IE4	O3.5		
○	●	⊙	●		

Name:	**background-repeat**
Value:	repeat	repeat-x	repeat-y	no-repeat
Initial:	repeat
Applies to:	all elements
Inherited:	no
Percentages:	N/A

This property has four possible values:

- **repeat**: the image is repeated both horizontally and vertically as often as needed to fill the whole element. This process is called *tiling*. This is the default.
- **repeat-x**: the image is repeated horizontally (along the x-axis) across the element in a single row, both left and right from the initial position.
- **repeat-y**: the image is repeated vertically (along the y-axis) down the element in a single column, above and below the initial position.
- **no-repeat**: the image is not repeated. It appears only once, in the upper-left corner of the element, or wherever it is placed with the **background-position** property.

A repeated image is most often a picture of a repeat pattern, such as a dot or wave pattern. But you can repeat an image of anything you want. Note that repeating images may cause part of the images to be cut off at one or more edges of the screen, as Figures 11.8(a) and (c) show.

The following are examples of rules for each value of **background-repeat**. Figure 11.8(a)–(d) show the result of each.

```
background-image: url(wave);/* (a) */
background-repeat: repeat;

background-image: url(wave);/* (b) */
background-repeat: repeat-x;
background-position: center;
```

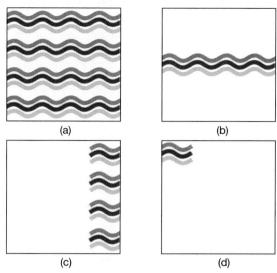

Figure 11.8 The four values of **background-repeat** in action: (a) repeat; (b) repeat-x; (c) repeat-y; (d) no-repeat.

```
background-image: url(wave);/* (c) */
background-repeat: repeat-y;
background-position: right;

background-image: url(wave);/* (d) */
background-repeat: no-repeat;
```

THE BACKGROUND-ATTACHMENT PROPERTY

The **background-attachment** property determines whether the image should be fixed or moveable on the canvas.

IE3	NS4	IE4	O3.5
○	○	●	○

Name:	**background-attachment**
Value:	scroll | fixed
Initial:	scroll
Applies to:	all elements
Inherited:	no
Percentages:	N/A

This property has two values:

- **scroll** – the image will scroll along with the content. This is the default.
- **fixed** – the image will be fixed with regard to the canvas.

A background image is visible only behind the element to which it belongs. When the element scrolls, you usually want its background to move along.

The "scroll" value causes the background to be attached to its element so that where the element goes, so goes its background. That is, as the user scrolls the document up or down or left or right, the background will stay behind its element. This is the default. The value **fixed**, however, means the background is not attached to the element. As the user scrolls the document, the element moves, but the background doesn't.

Unfortunately, we cannot show the effect in this book… .

The **fixed** value is most useful with BODY, where you would set BODY's background and you don't want it to move as the document is scrolled. Uses include the following.

You can use **fixed** to establish a "watermark" that will stay where you place it independent of the movement of any other element. A watermark is a translucent design that is impressed on paper during the (traditional) printing process and that can be seen faintly when the paper is held up to the light. They are often corporate logos or other designs and are often used for stationery. Obviously, we can't produce a true watermark on a Web page. But it is possible to create the general effect: an image (usually faint so that text and images can be placed over it and still be read) that remains fixed on the window. A good place for a watermark would be the HTML or BODY element. Here's an example rule that establishes a watermark:

```
HTML { background: white url(watermark)
    no-repeat center fixed }
```

(It uses the compound **background** property, explained further down.) You can also use **fixed** to keep a background aligned with another background, such as when a parent element has a certain pattern and a child has a slightly different pattern, but the two fit together. The only way to ensure they stay aligned is to fix both of them to the same point of origin; the only fixed point of origin in CSS is the window. Hence, **fixed** set on both elements will fix both backgrounds to the window (see Figure 11.9):

```
BODY { background: url(orangetile.png) fixed }
H1 { background: url(redtile.png) fixed }
```

You can use **fixed** further to form a horizontal or vertical band that will remain in place even as the document is scrolled over it. The following is an example code that shows how you could do this. It specifies a wave pattern image (back/waves.png) across the top of the BODY element that will repeat in a horizontal band (using the **repeat-x** value). Figure 11.9 shows the result.

```
BODY (background: url(backs/waves.png) repeat-x fixed }
```

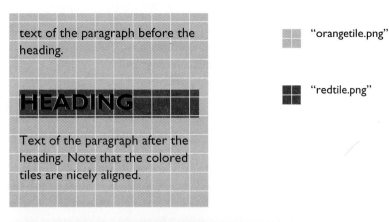

text of the paragraph before the heading.

HEADING

Text of the paragraph after the heading. Note that the colored tiles are nicely aligned.

"orangetile.png"

"redtile.png"

Figure 11.9 Using `fixed` to make sure the background pattern of the heading and the rest of the document are aligned.

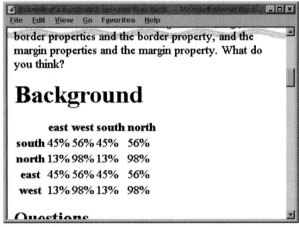

border properties and the border property, and the margin properties and the margin property. What do you think?

Background

	east	west	south	north
south	45%	56%	45%	56%
north	13%	98%	13%	98%
east	45%	56%	45%	56%
west	13%	98%	13%	98%

Questions

Figure 11.9 Using `fixed` to place a permanent horizontal band across the top of the BODY element: when the scrollbar is scrolled up or down, the pattern across the top will stay where it is.

THE BACKGROUND-POSITION PROPERTY

The **background-position** property lets you override the default position of an image and specify the image's *initial* position, whether a single image or an image that is repeated.

IE3	NS4	IE4	O3.5
○	○	●	●

Name:	**background-position**
Value:	<percentage>	<length>]{1,2}	[top	center	bottom] || [left	center	right]
Initial:	0 0
Applies to:	all elements
Inherited:	no
Percentages:	refer to the size of the element itself

Essentially, you can set the position of a background image in either of three ways:

- percentages
- absolute positions
- keywords

Placing images using percentages

When you place an image using percentages, you tell the browser where the background image is relative to the size of the element.

Here's an example of how this works. Suppose you have an element and you want to place an image in that element. Assume the element is BODY and your percentage values are **20%** and **60%**, written as a rule like this:

```
BODY {
    background-position: 20% 60%;
    background-image: url(tile.png)
}
```

First, you locate the upper-left corner of the element and the upper-left corner of the image. Then from there, find the point in BODY that is 20% across and 60% down. Next, find the point in the image that is 20% across the image and 60% down the image. Finally, you put the image in the element and match the points. This is where the image will appear in BODY. Figure 11.10 shows how this works.

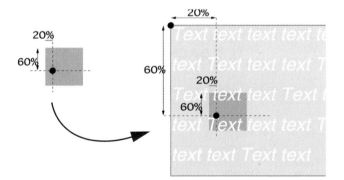

Figure 11.10 Using percentages to position images within an element.

You can enter either one or two percentage values:

- One value: that value will be used for the horizontal position, the image will be centered vertically. For example, if you enter a single value of **20%**, the image will be placed 20% across and 50% down the element. That is, **20%** equals **20% 50%**.

- Two values: the first one is the horizontal (*x*-axis) point and the second is the vertical (*y*-axis) point.

Positioning images using percentages makes it easy to specify some very common positions. For example, to center an image in an element you would write simply **50%** and to place an image against the right edge of the element requires simply **100%**. See also Figure 11.11.

If the background image is `fixed` (see the **background-attachment** property), the position is not calculated relative to the element, but relative to the window.

Placing images using absolute positions

When you give two length values instead of two percentages, the upper left corner of the image will be that far away from the upper left corner of the element. For example:

```
BLOCKQUOTE {
    background-image: url(shape.png);
    background-position: 1cm 5mm
}
```

will put the background image **shape.png** at **1cm** from the left and **5mm** from the top of the element.

As with percentages, if you only give one value, the image will be centered vertically. That is, a value of **1cm** is equivalent to **1cm 50%**.

Negative values are possible, if you want to put the image partially outside the element. Only the part that is inside the element will be visible, though.

Placing images using keywords

When placing an image using keywords, you use any combination of two keywords. One of three keywords – top, center, bottom – represents the horizontal (x-axis) dimension. And one of three keywords – left, center and right – represents the vertical (y-axis) dimension.

You cannot combine keywords with percentage values or absolute values.

Figure 11.11 shows the nine positions you can indicate with the keywords, and in parentheses the equivalent percentage values. The order in which you list the keywords in your code doesn't matter. For example, **top left** produces the same result as **left top**. This is not the case, however, when using percentages. The order in which you give the percentages makes a big difference in the result. For example, in the previous example in which we explained how to use percentages, we chose **20%** and **60%** as our values. Reversing the values – to **60%** and **20%** – in our code would produce a different effect than that shown in Figure 11.11.

If you specify only one dimension, say, **top**, then the unspecified dimension is assumed to be **center**. Hence, this rule:

```
BODY { background: url{banner.jpeg} top }
```

produces the same effect as:

```
BODY { background: url{banner.jpeg} top center }
```

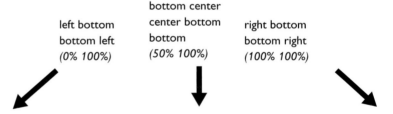

top left left top (0% 0%)	top center center top top (50% 0%)	top right right top (100% 0%)
left center center left left (0% 50%)	center center center (50% 50%)	right center center right right (100% 50%)
left bottom bottom left (0% 100%)	bottom center center bottom bottom (50% 100%)	right bottom bottom right (100% 100%)

Figure 11.11 The most common combinations of **background-position** keywords and their percentage equivalents and effects obtained.

THE BACKGROUND PROPERTY

The **background** property is a shortcut means of setting all of the first five properties at the same time. Its values are all of the possible values of those five properties. You may set from one to five of the properties, in any order. However, this property will always set all five of the properties, regardless of whether you explicitly set values for all five. If you don't explicitly set a value for a specific property, the **background** property uses that property's initial value as the property's value. For example, here:

```
BODY { background: red }
```

only the value of the **background-color** property has been set. The **background** property will assume the initial values for all of the other properties. In contrast:

```
P { background: url(chess.png) gray 50% repeat }
```

sets values for four of the properties, but not that for the **background-attachment** property; hence, that property's value will be the initial value (which is **scroll**). In other words, the rule above is exactly equivalent to:

```
P {
    background-image: url(chess.png);
    background-color: gray;
    background-position: 50%;/* = 50% 50% */
    background-repeat: repeat;
    background-attachment: scroll;/* implicit */
}
```

You can set separately the five aspects of a background – color, image, repeat, scrolling and position – but we don't recommend this as a rule. The different aspects of a background are so tightly linked in how they work to produce effects that you could end up with some unexpected, even weird, results. For example, setting a **background-repeat** value without setting the image at the same time may produce a very strange-looking background. The same is true with specifying an image without also setting the color behind it. In both cases, problems could arise when style sheets are cascaded. Cascading involves using more than one style sheet for your document; for example, yours (that is, the designer's), the browser's default style sheet, and possibly one attached by the user. If you were to specify an image without also setting a color behind it, the background might be composed of any combination of background from these three style sheets.

While the user might be able to adjust his style sheet to compensate for such an effect, you as the designer should be careful to set all pertinent aspects at the same time so that all aspects work together to produce pleasing results. The **background** property is the shortest way of setting all five aspects of the background and using it ensures that you don't forget one of them.

SETTING THE BACKGROUND OF THE CANVAS

Sometimes you need to specify the background color of the window; for example, if the document is so short that it doesn't fill the whole window.

The window (or *viewport*, as the CSS2 specification calls it, since it could also refer to paper if the document is printed) does not correspond to any element in the document. Hence, its color has to come from somewhere else. The background of the window will be the same as the background of the root element. In HTML, the HTML element is always the root element, but XML-based documents will have other root elements. Since it's common to set backgrounds on the BODY element in HTML, the BODY element will serve the role of the root element if the background of the HTML element is transparent.

It is as if the background of the root element is stretched to the edges of the window. Even if there is a margin set on the root element, the background will stretch into the margin as well. Some people have described this rule as the canvas "stealing" the background of the root element.

SHADOWS

Another use of color is as shadows or glow effects behind individual letters. We already referred to that in Chapter 5, "Fonts" when we described the text-decoration property. The **text-shadow** property works in a similar way as **text-decoration**: it adds a decoration to the text of an element and its children.

IE3	NS4	IE4	O3.5		
○	○	○	○	*Name:*	**text-shadow**
				Value:	none | <shadow> [, <shadow>]* | inherit
				Initial:	none
				Applies to:	all elements
				Inherited:	no
				Percentages:	N/A

A shadow is described by an offset, and optionally a color and a blur factor, to make the shadow less sharp:

- Two length values: the shadow is put to the right and down from the main text by the given distance (or left/up, if the length is negative). The shadow has the same color as the main text.
- Two length values and a color: as above, but the color of the shadow is explicitly specified.
- Three length values and a color: the third length is the blur radius. It determines over what distance, approximately, the shadow is smeared out.
- Several shadows separated by commas. When the shadows overlap, the last one is drawn behind the others.

In its simplest form, the property takes two length values. For example, the following rule:

```
H1 { text-shadow: 0.3em 0.3em }
```

creates a shadow of the text of an H1 element and puts it 0.3em to the right and 0.3em down from the normal text.

Figure 11.12

A little more interesting is a shadow of a different color than the main text. We can, e.g., make the shadow brown:

```
H1 { text-shadow: 0.3em 0.3em #CC7F00 }
```

Here is what it looks like:

Figure 11.13

Interesting effects are possible by applying more than one shadow. Here is an example with a white and a black shadow on opposite sides of the text:

```
H1 {
    background: #40FF40;
    color: #FF7F7F;
    text-shadow: 0.1em 0.1em white, -0.1em -0.1em black;
}
```

The above rules result in:

Figure 11.14

Shadows often look more realistic if they are a bit blurry. By adding a third length value (the blur radius), the shadow gets a fuzzy edge of approximately that thickness. Here is an example:

```
H1 { text-shadow: 0.3em 0.3em 0.1em #333 }
```

Which becomes:

Figure 11.15

A blurred shadow without any offset from the text will look like a halo around the text. You can make text "glow" with a style like this one:

```
H1 { text-shadow: 0 0 0.2em #F00 }
```

which becomes:

Figure 11.16

If the effect isn't strong enough, just add more halos, separated by commas.

Not recommended, unless you know what you are doing: but a very striking effect can be achieved by showing just the halo, and not the text itself. To achieve this, you set the text and the background to be the same color:

```
H1 {
    background: black;
    color: black;
    text-shadow: 0 0 0.2em #F00;
}
```

The result is:

Figure 11.17

The CSS Validator is a W3C service which will check your style sheets. You can find it from http://jigsaw.w3.org/css-validator

However, doing this is dangerous. When you send this style sheet to the CSS Validator, it will return a warning that the foreground and background are the same, because on browsers that don't support **text-shadow** (and at the time of writing, that means all browsers), the text will become invisible:

Figure 11.18

Chapter 12

Printing and other media

Most users see the Web through a looking glass, also known as a computer screen. One of the characteristics of the computer screen is that it's a highly dynamic device: it refreshes itself 60 times per second. This allows video clips, animations and other dynamic behavior to be incorporated into Web documents.

The printed page, on the other hand, is static: once printed a page never changes (except when the ink smears or the paper fades) and the hyperlinks on the page become inactive. Still, many people prefer to read from paper rather than from a computer screen: the paper provides higher resolution and higher legibility. You can make notes on paper and fold it into a plane and send it off. Try doing that with a computer screen!

Printouts from the Web are often of poor quality. CSS2 adds functionality to improve printing and this chapter describes the new features:

- page breaks: you can say where you want page breaks to occur, or where they should be avoided
- page margins and page orientation

Also, CSS2 introduces a way to say that a style sheet (or a section of a style sheet) only takes effect on certain output media, for example on a printer or a handheld Web device. This feature is known as media-specific style sheets and is described at the end of the chapter.

PAGE BREAKS

The term "page" has two meanings on the Web: it's an informal term for a document (a "Web page"), and it also refers to sheets of paper that come out of the printer when you choose to print a document. In this chapter, "page" always refers to the latter of the two.

One of the most common complaints people have when printing from the Web is that page breaks appear in the wrong places – and don't appear in the right places! For instance, a page break should not normally occur immediately after a heading. Instead, the page should be broken before the heading so that the heading occurs on the top of the next page. This way, the heading and the first paragraph, which logically belong together, will remain together visually as well.

Similarly, a single line of a paragraph should never be left alone at the bottom or top of a page. Typographers refer to these as "orphans" and "widows," respectively, and avoid them like the plague. The traditional remedy is to make sure that at least two lines always remain together on the same page. Figure 12.1 shows these common page-break mistakes

Printing

Most users see the Web through a looking glass, also known as a computer screen. One of the characteristics of the computer screen is that it's a highly dynamic device: it refreshes itself 60 times per second.

This allows dynamic be-

orphan

Figure 12.1 Some of the most common page break mistakes.

widow

havior in documents.

The printed page, on the other hand, is static: once printed a page never changes (except when the ink smears) and the hyperlinks on the page become inactive. Still, many people prefer paper.

Paper

heading on bottom of page

You can make notes on paper and fold it into a plane and send it off.

CSS2 introduces a way to say that a style sheet only take effect on certain output media, for example on a printer.

This chapter describes the new features:

list on top of page

- page breaks
- page margins
- page orientation

CSS2 has five properties for controlling page breaks: page-break-before, **page-break-after**, **page-break-inside**, **widows** and **orphans**.

IE3 NS4 IE4 O3.5
○   ○   ⊙   ○

Name:	**page-break-before**
Value:	auto | always | avoid | left | right | inherit
Initial:	auto
Applies to:	all elements
Inherited:	no
Percentages:	N/A

This property indicates if there should – or should not – be a page break before the element. For example, if each H1 element in a document is a chapter heading, you might like to force a page break before the element. This is easily done with the **page-break-before** property:

```
H1 { page-break-before: always }
```

The **left** and **right** values indicate that there should be a page break before the element, and that the element should end up on the left or right page, respectively. (A "left" page is a page that ends up on the left side of the fold when the pages are bound to a book; vice versa for "right" pages.) For example, it's common for all chapters to start on the right page, which can be achieved with this rule:

```
H1 { page-break-before: right }
```

Lists, on the other hand, should never start at the top of a page, and this can be avoided with this rule:

```
UL, OL, DL    { page-break-before: avoid }
```

Since there can be cases when the browser isn't able to fulfill this request, the keyword that was chosen is "avoid" rather than "never." This is true for all properties related to page breaks: they indicate preferences, but there is no guarantee that the wish can be granted. The reason is that the problem is "overconstrained" – the style sheet specifies too many wishes and not all of them can be granted. For example, consider this document which only contains lists with one list item each (unlikely, but possible):

```
<UL>
  <LI>item</LI>
</UL>
<UL>
  <LI>item</LI>
</UL>
<UL>
  <LI>item</LI>
```

```
</UL>
...
...
```

Given enough lists like the above, the browser will have to break the page at some point, and since the document contains only lists, one of them will end up on top of the page.

The **auto** value on **page-break-before** indicates that browsers should behave as they always have: breaking pages when they have to since there is no more space left on the page.

<table>
<tr><td>IE3</td><td>NS4</td><td>IE4</td><td>O3.5</td></tr>
<tr><td>○</td><td>○</td><td>☉</td><td>○</td></tr>
</table>

Name:	**page-break-after**
Value:	auto | always | avoid | left | right | inherit
Initial:	auto
Applies to:	block-level elements
Inherited:	no
Percentages:	N/A

This property takes the same values as **page-break-before**. In fact, the two properties are almost identical with the important exception that one of them indicates page breaks *before* an element and the other indicates page breaks *after* the element. So, a value of **left** means that the *next* element will end up as the first element on the next left page.

A typical use of this property is to declare that page breaks should not occur after heading elements:

```
H1, H2, H3, H4 { page-break-after: avoid }
```

The rule above is part of the default style sheet for HTML documents and authors should therefore not have to set it in their own style sheets.

<table>
<tr><td>IE3</td><td>NS4</td><td>IE4</td><td>O3.5</td></tr>
<tr><td>○</td><td>○</td><td>○</td><td>○</td></tr>
</table>

Name:	**page-break-inside**
Value:	avoid | auto | inherit
Initial:	auto
Applies to:	block-level elements
Inherited:	no
Percentages:	N/A

This property indicates if a page break can or can't occur within an element. For example, this rule tells all items of a list to remain on the same page:

```
UL, OL, DL { page-break-inside: avoid }
```

A problem arises when a list has too many items to fit on a single page. In these cases, the **avoid** value cannot be honored and the list will have to be broken when the page is filled up. Conceivably, the browser could honor the **avoid** value by reducing the font size. This would quickly make documents illegible, CSS therefore chooses to honor **font-size** instead of **page-break-inside** when there is a conflict.

<table>
<tr><td>IE3</td><td>NS4</td><td>IE4</td><td>O3.5</td></tr>
<tr><td>○</td><td>○</td><td>○</td><td>○</td></tr>
</table>

Name:	**widows**
Value:	<integer> | inherit
Initial:	2
Applies to:	block-level elements
Inherited:	yes
Percentages:	N/A

"Widows" is an old typographical term for isolated lines at the top of the page. For example, if a page break occurs within a paragraph, the lines which end up on top of the second page are called widow lines (see Figure 12.1). The value on this property specifies the minimum number of widow lines that can appear together. The value 2 is a very common value on this property – common enough to be the initial value.

<table>
<tr><td>IE3</td><td>NS4</td><td>IE4</td><td>O3.5</td></tr>
<tr><td>○</td><td>○</td><td>○</td><td>○</td></tr>
</table>

Name:	**orphans**
Value:	<integer> | inherit
Initial:	2
Applies to:	block-level elements
Inherited:	yes
Percentages:	N/A

"Orphans" is an old typographical term for isolated lines at the bottom of a page. When a page break occurs within a paragraph, the lines which end up on the bottom of the page (*i.e.*, the first lines of the paragraph) are called orphan lines (see Figure 12.1). The value on this property sets the minimum number of orphan lines which must appear together. As with **widows**, 2 is a common value, as well as the initial value, and authors seldom have to change it.

Usage of page break properties

As a designer, you will seldom have to set values on the properties described above. For **orphans** and **widows**, the initial value is 2 lines and this works well for most documents and they only rarely have to be changed. The other three properties (**page-break-before**, **page-break-after** and **page-break-inside**) don't have equally universal initial values, but the HTML default style sheet contains the most common settings. For example, this is what it says about headings:

```
H1, H2, H3, H4, H5, H6 {
    page-break-after: avoid;
    page-break-inside: avoid;
}
```

So, browsers will try to avoid page breaks after heading elements, thus eliminating some of the problems in Figure 12.1. To eliminate the page break before the list, this rule is also found in the default style sheet:

```
UL, OL, DL { page-break-before: avoid }
```

So, after eliminating page breaks after headings, page breaks before lists, widows and orphans, the sample page now looks like this (Figure 12.2):

Printing

Most users see the Web through a looking glass, also known as a computer screen. One of the characteristics of the computer screen is that it's a highly dynamic device: it refreshes itself 60 times per second.

This allows dynamic behavior in documents.

The printed page, on the other hand, is static: once printed a page never changes (except when the ink smears or the paper fades) and the hyperlinks on the page become inactive. Still, many people prefer paper.

Paper

You can make notes on paper and fold it into a plane and send it off.

CSS2 introduces a way to say that a style sheet only take effect on certain output media, for example on a printer.

This chapter describes the new features:
* page breaks
* page margins
* page orientation

Figure 12.2 The most common mistakes have been corrected. (Compare with Figure 12.1.)

PAGE AREAS

Before the browser can start putting content onto paper, it needs to know the dimensions of the area that can be printed on. This area depends on the size of the paper that is being used, and the width of the margins around the edges of the paper. Also, the browser will need to know if the page should be printed in "portrait" or "landscape" mode (see Figure 12.3). When all this has been established, the "page area" has been defined and printing can start.

Portrait page

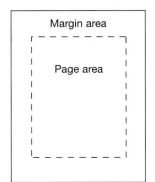

Margin area

Page area

Landscape page

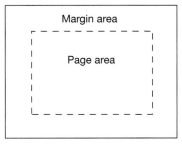

Margin area

Page area

Figure 12.3 Portrait and landscape pages.

Page selectors and margins

CSS provides designers with a special selector and a set of properties to define the page area. No element in HTML represents a page (since HTML has no concept of pages) and therefore we have no selector to attach the properties and values to. A special selector has therefore been introduced in CSS2:

```
@page { margin: 1in }
```

The "@page" selector selects pages. Declarations inside the curly braces apply to pages onto which the document is printed. The above example sets the margins on all four sides to be 1 inch.

Only a limited set of the CSS properties can be used in combination with the page selectors. The list includes all **margin** properties and the **size** property (which is described below). This means that, e.g., the **color** property is not valid so you can't make all text on a certain page have a certain color.

Margins that are set on the page will be in addition to margins specified on elements. Consider this example:

```
<HTML>
  <STYLE TYPE="text/css">
    @page { margin: 1cm }
    BODY { margin: 1cm }
    H1 { margin: 0 }
  </STYLE>
  <BODY>
    <H1>J'accuse</H1>
  </BODY>
</HTML>
```

First, the page has a 1cm margin on each side. Second, the BODY element also has a 1cm margin on each side. The result is a 2cm margin on the left and right side of the page, and a 1cm margin on the top:

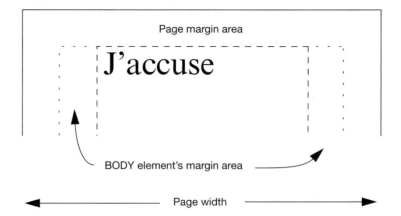

Page margin area

J'accuse

Figure 12.4 The figure shows how page margins and element margins add up on top of a page. The horizontal margins are simply added, while adjacent vertical margins are collapsed.

BODY element's margin area

Page width

The top margin is smaller than the left and right margins due to the collapsing of vertical margins which was discussed in Chapter 9. The fact that one of the margins is a page margin and not an element margin does not stop the margins from collapsing.

Left and right pages

When printing double-sided documents, it's common for "left" and "right" pages to have different margins. This can be expressed in CSS with left and right pseudo-classes:

```
@page { margin: 1in }
@page :left { margin-left: 2in }
@page :right { margin-right: 2in }
```

The style sheet above would result in left pages having a 2in. margin on the left side of the page, and a 1in. margin on the right side of the content. For right pages, the numbers are switched so that left and right pages are symmetrical (Figure 12.5).

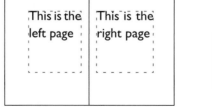

This is the left page

This is the right page

Figure 12.5 Left and right pages often use a symmetrical layout.

Just as there can be conflicts between normal selectors in CSS, there can be conflicts between @page selectors. In the previous example there is a conflict between the first rule, which sets all page margins on all pages, and the other two rules, which specifically set the margins for left and right pages. Just as with normal selectors, conflicts between page selectors are resolved through specificity: page selectors with pseudo-classes on them are more specific than page selectors without. Therefore, the last two rules will win over the first rule.

The :left and :right pseudo-classes will work even if the document is printed on a single-sided printer. There are two reasons for this. First, it is often impossible for the browser to know if a printer is single- or double-sided. Second, a set of sheets printed on a single-sided printer may later be transferred into a double-sided publication; for example, using a double-sided copying machine.

First pages

Often, the first page of a document uses a different page box from the rest of the pages. A third pseudo-class addresses only the first page:

```
@page :first { margin-top: 4in }
```

Just as the "@page :left" and "@page :right" pseudo-classes are more specific than the plain "@page" selector, the "@page :first" selector is more specific than :left and :right. Intuitively this makes sense: even if the first page of a document also is a "right" page (which is true in western books), the fact that it's the first page is more significant than it being a right page.

Units for page margins

The examples in the previous section used inches and centimeters to describe the width of the page margins. These are absolute length units that precisely describe how wide the margins should be. Absolute units work well when you know the exact dimensions of the sheets which are being printed. On the Web, this is generally not the case. If your documents are universally accessible, people from different parts of the globe will print the documents, and paper sizes vary depending on where you are.

In the United States the "letter" size (8.5in. by 11in.) is the most common, while "A4" (21.0cm by 29.7cm) is widely used in the rest of the world. One inch is equal to 2.54 centimeters, so the A4 page is slightly higher and narrower than its American cousin.

To make sure documents will print well on all paper sizes, we recommend using percentage units over absolute units when describing margins:

```
@page { margin: 10% }
```

Percentage value calculations are based on the size of the paper. So, if the document is printed "portrait mode" in Europe, the margins will be 21mm on each side horizontally and 29.7mm vertically. On US letter, the margins will be 0.85in. horizontally and 1.1in. vertically. Figure 12.6 shows the page boxes of A4 and US letter page sizes with 10% margins.

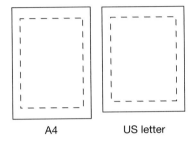

A4   US letter

Figure 12.6 A4 and US letter page sizes. The stippled boxes indicate the page box of a 10% margin.

The amazing "em" unit, which was given extensive coverage in Chapter 3, doesn't work when setting length values in the page box. The reason is that the page doesn't know anything about fonts – only elements do – and therefore has no font size to relate to.

Page box dimension and orientation

We've now seen how to set margins on the page, but we haven't seen how to set the size and orientation of pages. Normally, authors shouldn't specify the size and orientation of the pages but rather leave this to the user. Typically, the user will specify these preferences in the browser's print dialog box.

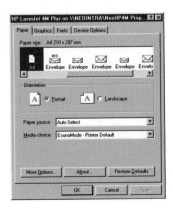

Figure 12.7 A typical print dialog box.

There are cases, however, when the author wants to indicate the preference for a certain size or orientation. This is done through the **size** property.

Name:	**size**
Value:	<length>{1,2} | auto | portrait | landscape
Initial:	auto
Applies to:	pages
Inherited:	no
Percentages:	N/A

This property specifies the size and orientation of the page. The property can be used in two different ways. First, we describe the keyword values that adapt to whatever page size the local printer has available. Thereafter, we describe how exact page sizes can be created by specifying one or two length values.

As a designer, you don't know what page sizes your documents will be printed on. Even if *you* always use one specific size of paper, the readers are in all parts of the world using all sorts of paper sizes. Therefore, we recommend using the keyword values (**auto**, **portrait** and **landscape**) on this property.

The **auto** value will make the page box as big as possible, but is neutral about the orientation of the page. Typically, when the auto value is specified (either through an explicit rule in a style sheet or by being the initial value) the browser will ask the user for guidance on what orientation should be used.

The **portrait** value will print the document on pages that are higher than they are wide:

```
@page { size: portrait }
```

The **landscape** value will do the opposite; pages are wider than they are high. In both cases, the browser may give the user the chance of overriding the choices set in the style sheets, for example through the print dialog box.

By giving this property one or two length values, a specific page size can be set. This is only useful when it's crucial that the document is printed on a page with an exact size. Here is an example:

```
@page { size: 4in 6in }
```

Most printers are not able to cut the paper sheets according to the length values above. Instead they will be try to use a page size which is bigger than the one specified and then add crop marks (described in the next section) to indicate where the page should be cut. If the available paper isn't big enough for the specified size, the browser should ask the user what to do; for example, scale or rotate the page.

Crop marks

In high-quality printing, certain marks are often added outside the page margins. For example, when the printed sheets of paper need to be cut before they are bound into a book, *crop marks* are added. When sheets of paper need to be aligned after printing, *cross marks* are used. For example, when the different colors are printed separately, the cross marks show whether the various colors were exactly superimposed on each other. Cross marks are also known as register marks.

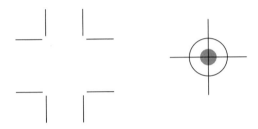

Figure 12.8 The figure shows 4 crop marks (the four corners) and a typical cross mark.

All marks are printed outside the page margins and are therefore only usable with absolute page sizes (since other pages always fill the whole sheet).

IE3	NS4	IE4	O3.5		
○	○	○	○		

Name:	**marks**
Value:	[crop || cross] | none
Initial:	none
Applies to:	pages
Inherited:	no
Percentages:	N/A

Named pages

Earlier in this chapter, we described three different kinds of pages: left, right and first. These are predefined classes of pages which exist in all documents, and they satisfy the needs of most authors. There are cases, however, when you want greater control over what page an element is printed on. For example, if you have a wide table in your document, you may want the table to be printed on a "landscape" page. To achieve this, you have to do two things. First, you need to define a page which will always be in landscape mode:

```
@page rotated { size: landscape }
```

In this example, the page has been given the name "rotated" but you are free to call it whatever you want, except "auto."

Second, you need to tell the table to insist on being printed on the "rotated" page. This is done with a simple rule:

```
TABLE { page: rotated }
```

IE3	NS4	IE4	O3.5
○	○	○	○

Name:	**page**
Value:	\<identifier> | auto
Initial:	auto
Applies to:	block-level elements
Inherited:	yes
Percentages:	N/A

The page property makes it possible for an element to request to be printed on a certain page. If the current page is of the kind requested, printing will continue as normal. Otherwise, the browser will perform a page break and create a new page of the kind requested.

The example above shows a common use of the **page** property: a wide element which wants to be printed in landscape mode. With the initial **auto** value, printing will continue on the current page.

MEDIA-SPECIFIC STYLE SHEETS

The bulk of this chapter is about writing style sheets for print. Besides computer screens, printers are the most common Web devices. However, there are many other types of Web devices as well and part of the motivation for creating style sheets is to ensure that content remains in a form that can be displayed on all devices. For example, by storing text as characters — and not as, say, images — speech synthesizers can read read documents out loud, and your cellphone screen can show Web pages.

CSS2 groups the different devices into *media types* and allows you to write different style sheets for each type. For example, here is a style sheet that will only have effect on computer screens:

```
@media screen {
    BODY { font-size: 12pt }
    H1 { font-size: 2em }
}
```

The "@media" keyword is followed by the name of a media type. (CSS2 defines nine different media types — see Table 12.1 below.) Inside the curly brackets that follow is a perfectly normal style sheet. Since it only applies to a certain media type, it is said to be a *media-specific* style sheet. You will note that media-specific style sheets come complete with selectors which have their own curly brackets. Always make sure that the left and right curly brackets are balanced – the left curly bracket should come after the media type name, and the right curly bracket should come after the style rules.

The **font-size** property is an example of a property that is useful for many different media types, but which requires different values depending on the media type. For example, since legibility is higher on paper, the same text can be read comfortably with a smaller font size:

```
@media print {
    BODY { font-size: 10pt } /* slightly smaller */
    H1 { font-size: 2em }
}
```

You can have many @media sections in a style sheet, so the two examples above can be combined:

```
@media screen {
    BODY { font-size: 12pt }
}
@media print {
    BODY { font-size: 10pt }
}
H1 { font-size: 2em }
```

Since the H1 rule is the same for both media types, it has been taken out of the media-specific parts and it now applies to all media types.

The **font-size** property used in the previous examples applies to several media types. Other properties are only defined for a certain media type. For instance, the **volume** property only makes sense in an aural style sheet:

```
@media aural {
    BODY { volume: soft }
}
```

Chapter 13 is dedicated to aural style sheets.

Media types

Screen, print, and aural are three of the media types defined by CSS2. Table 12.1 shows the complete list.

Media type	Intended use
screen	Scrollable color computer screens. See example in previous section.
print	Printers, when printing on paper (as opposed to transparencies). This media type should also be used when the browser does a "print preview." See example in previous section.
aural	Speech synthesizers which read out loud Web documents. See example in previous section and in Chapter 13.
braille	Electronic braille readers which "display" characters by making tactile patterns. ```@media braille {\n * { margin: 0 }\n}``` The above example will set all margins around all elements to 0 to economize the available display space.
embossed	Braille printers which emboss braille on paper. ```@media embossed {\n @page { margin: 0 }\n}``` The above example will set page margins to zero so all available space is used to display content
handheld	Handheld devices which typically have small screens and limited bandwidth. ```@media handheld {\n IMG { display: none }\n}``` The above example will not display images on handheld devices. If the style sheet is evaluated in a proxy server, this can save much bandwidth.
projection	Projected presentations, for example transparencies or a computer hooked up to a projector. Typically, these presentations have few lines per page and need large font sizes: ```@media projection {\n BODY { font-size:\n x-large }\n H1 { page-break-before:\n always }\n}``` The above style sheet will set the font size to be extra large and ensure a page break before every H1 element.

continued

Media type	Intended use
tty	Text-based terminals and other devices using a fixed-pitch character grid.

```
@media tty {
    H1 { margin-below: 1em }
}
```

Since these devices are based on characters and not pixels, they will not be able to display rich styles. Even the otherwise trusted "em" unit will have difficulties when used horizontally. The main benefit of style sheets for these devices is that text can be kept as text rather than images, and is viewable at all.

tv	Television-based presentations, typically on screens with colors, low resolution, long viewing distance, and limited capabilities for scrolling.

```
@media tv {
    BODY {
        color: white;
        background: black;
    }
}
```

The above example will set colors to be white on black (which is normal on TV) rather than the black on white (which is normal on computer screens).

all	This media type is suitable for all devices:

```
@media all {
    BODY {
        line-height: 1.4;
    }
}
```

Media types were not part of CSS1. Therefore, this media type can be used to hide style sheets from older browsers. For example, some early CSS browsers have problems handling declarations on the **line-height** property. In the example above, only newer browsers which are aware of media-specific style sheets will see the style sheet inside.

Table 12.1 The table lists the media types defined in CSS2 and describes their intended use.

Some people would like to have more detailed information about the device. For example, they would like to write one style sheet for computer screens with resolutions of 800 x 600, and another for 640 x 480 screens. While these distinctions make sense today, it was felt that they could soon be obsolete as new display technologies are introduced. Also, if detailed information about the resolution is available, one incentive to write scalable style sheets is lost.

Aural style sheets

This chapter is a reprint of Chapter 19 from the CSS2 Recommendation. Copyright © 1998 W3C (MIT, INRIA, Keio). All rights reserved. The property data sheets have been modified slightly to match the format used in the rest of the book.

INTRODUCTION TO AURAL STYLE SHEETS

The aural rendering of a document, already commonly used by the blind and print-impaired communities, combines speech synthesis and "auditory icons." Often such aural presentation occurs by converting the document to plain text and feeding this to a screen reader – software or hardware that simply reads all the characters on the screen. This results in less effective presentation than would be the case if the document structure were retained. Style sheet properties for aural presentation may be used together with visual properties (mixed media) or as an aural alternative to visual presentation.

Besides the obvious accessibility advantages, there are other large markets for listening to information, including in-car use, industrial and medical documentation systems (intranets), home entertainment, and to help users learning to read or who have difficulty reading.

When using aural properties, the canvas consists of a three-dimensional physical space (sound surrounds) and a temporal space (one may specify sounds before, during, and after other sounds). The CSS properties also allow authors to vary the quality of synthesized speech (voice type, frequency, inflection, etc.).

```
H1, H2, H3, H4, H5, H6 {
    voice-family: paul;
    stress: 20;
    richness: 90;
    cue-before: url("ping.au")
}
P.heidi { azimuth: center-left }
P.peter { azimuth: right }
P.goat  { volume: x-soft }
```

This will direct the speech synthesizer to speak headers in a voice (a kind of "audio font") called **paul**, on a flat tone, but in a very rich voice. Before speaking the headers, a sound sample will be played from the given URL. Paragraphs with class "heidi" will appear to come from front left (if the sound system is capable of spatial audio), and paragraphs of class "peter" from the right. Paragraphs with class "goat" will be very soft.

VOLUME PROPERTIES: VOLUME

Name:	**volume**
Value:	*<number>* | *<percentage>* | silent | x-soft | soft | medium | loud | x-loud
Initial:	medium
Applies to:	all elements
Inherited:	yes
Percentages:	refer to inherited value

Volume refers to the median volume of the waveform. In other words, a highly inflected voice at a volume of **50** might peak well above that. The overall values are likely to be human adjustable for comfort, for example with a physical volume control (which would increase both the **0** and **100** values proportionately); what this property does is adjust the dynamic range.

Values have the following meanings:

- <number>: Any number between **0** and **100**. **0** represents the minimum audible volume level and **100** corresponds to the maximum comfortable level.
- <percentage>: Percentage values are calculated relative to the inherited value, and are then clipped to the range **0** to **100**.
- `silent`: No sound at all. The value **0** does not mean the same as `silent`.
- `x-soft`: Same as **0**.
- `soft`: Same as **25**.
- `medium`: Same as **50**.
- `loud`: Same as **75**.
- `x-loud`: Same as **100**.

User agents should allow the values corresponding to **0** and **100** to be set by the listener. No one setting is universally applicable; suitable values depend on the equipment in use (speakers, headphones), the environment (in car, home theater, library) and personal preferences. Some examples:

A browser for in-car use has a setting for when there is lots of background noise. **0** would map to a fairly high level and **100** to a quite high level. The speech is easily audible over the road noise but the overall dynamic range is compressed. Cars with better insulation might allow a wider dynamic range.

Another speech browser is being used in an apartment, late at night, or in a shared study room. **0** is set to a very quiet level and **100** to a fairly quiet level, too. As with the first example, there is a low slope; the dynamic range is reduced. The actual volumes are low here, whereas they were high in the first example.

In a quiet and isolated house, an expensive hi-fi home theater setup. **0** is set fairly low and **100** to quite high; there is wide dynamic range.

The same author style sheet could be used in all cases, simply by mapping the **0** and **100** points suitably at the client side.

SPEAKING PROPERTIES: SPEAK

Name:	**'speak'**
Value:	normal | none | spell-out
Initial:	normal
Applies to:	all elements
Inherited:	yes
Percentages:	N/A

This property specifies whether text will be rendered aurally and if so, in what manner (somewhat analogous to the **display** property). The possible values are:

- **none**: Suppresses aural rendering so that the element requires no time to render. Note, however, that descendants may override this value and will be spoken. (To be sure to suppress rendering of an element and its descendants, use the **display** property.)
- **normal**: Uses language-dependent pronunciation rules for rendering an element and its children.
- **spell-out**: Spells the text one letter at a time (useful for acronyms and abbreviations).

Note the difference between an element whose **volume** property has a value of **silent** and an element whose **speak** property has the value **none**. The former takes up the same time as if it had been spoken, including any pause before and after the element, but no sound is generated. The latter requires no time and is not rendered (though its descendants may be).

PAUSE PROPERTIES: PAUSE-BEFORE, PAUSE-AFTER, AND PAUSE

Name:	**pause-before**
Value:	*<time>* | *<percentage>*
Initial:	depends on user agent
Applies to:	all elements
Inherited:	no
Percentages:	see prose

Name:	**pause-after**
Value:	*<time>* | *<percentage>*
Initial:	depends on user agent
Applies to:	all elements
Inherited:	no
Percentages:	see prose

These properties specify a pause to be observed before (or after) speaking an element's content. Values have the following meanings:

- *<time>*: Expresses the pause in absolute time units (seconds and milliseconds).

- *<percentage>*: Refers to the inverse of the value of the **speech-rate** property. For example, if the speech-rate is **120** words per minute (*i.e.*, a word takes half a second, or 500ms) then a **pause-before** of **100%** means a pause of 500ms and a **pause-before** of **20%** means 100ms.

The pause is inserted between the element's content and any **cue-before** or **cue-after** content.

Authors should use relative units to create more robust style sheets in the face of large changes in speech-rate.

Name:	**pause**
Value:	[*<time>* | *<percentage>*]{1,2}
Initial:	depends on user agent
Applies to:	all elements
Inherited:	no
Percentages:	see descriptions of "pause-before" and "pause-after"

The **pause** property is a shorthand for setting **pause-before** and **pause-after**. If two values are given, the first value is **pause-before** and the second is **pause-after**. If only one value is given, it applies to both properties.

```
H1 { pause: 20ms }
    /* pause-before: 20ms; pause-after: 20ms */
H2 { pause: 30ms 40ms }
    /* pause-before: 30ms; pause-after: 40ms */
H3 { pause-after: 10ms }
    /* pause-before: ?; pause-after: 10ms */
```

CUE PROPERTIES: CUE-BEFORE, CUE-AFTER, AND CUE

Name:	**cue-before**
Value:	*<uri>* | none
Initial:	none
Applies to:	all elements
Inherited:	no
Percentages:	N/A

Name:	**cue-after**
Value:	*<uri>* | none
Initial:	none
Applies to:	all elements
Inherited:	no
Percentages:	N/A

Auditory icons are another way to distinguish semantic elements. Sounds may be played before and/or after the element to delimit it. Values have the following meanings:

- *<uri>*: The URI must designate an auditory icon resource. If the URI resolves to something other than an audio file, such as an image, the resource should be ignored and the property treated as if it had the value **none.**
- **none**: No auditory icon is specified.

```
A {
    cue-before: url("bell.aiff");
    cue-after: url("dong.wav")
}
H1 {
    cue-before: url("pop.au");
    cue-after: url("pop.au")
}
```

Name:	**cue**
Example:	<'cue-before'> || <'cue-after'>
Initial:	not defined for shorthand properties
Applies to:	all elements
Inherited:	no
Percentages:	N/A

The **cue** property is a shorthand for setting **cue-before** and **cue-after**. If two values are given, the first value is **cue-before** and the second is **cue-after**. If only one value is given, it applies to both properties.

The following two rules are equivalent:

```
H1 { cue-before: url("pop.au"); cue-after: url("pop.au")}
H1 { cue: url("pop.au")}
```

If a user agent cannot render an auditory icon (e.g., the user's environment does not permit it), we recommend that it produce an alternative cue (e.g., popping up a warning, emitting a warning sound, etc.)

Please see the sections on the :before and :after pseudo-elements for information on other content generation techniques.

MIXING PROPERTIES: PLAY-DURING

Name:	**play-during**
Value:	*<uri>* mix? repeat? | auto | none
Initial:	auto
Applies to:	all elements
Inherited:	no
Percentages:	N/A

Similar to the **cue-before** and **cue-after** properties, this property specifies a sound to be played as a background while an element's content is spoken. Values have the following meanings:

- *<uri>*: The sound designated by this *<uri>* is played as a background while the element's content is spoken.
- **mix**: When present, this keyword means that the sound inherited from the parent element's **play-during** property continues to play and the sound designated by the *<uri>* is mixed with it. If **mix** is not specified, the element's background sound replaces the parent's.
- **repeat**: When present, this keyword means that the sound will repeat if it is too short to fill the entire duration of the element. Otherwise, the sound plays once and then stops. This is similar to the **background-repeat** property. If the sound is too long for the element, it is clipped once the element has been spoken.
- **auto**: The sound of the parent element continues to play (it is not restarted, which would have been the case if this property had been inherited).
- **none**: This keyword means that there is silence. The sound of the parent element (if any) is silent during the current element and continues after the current element.

```
BLOCKQUOTE.sad  { play-during: url("violins.aiff") }
BLOCKQUOTE Q    { play-during: url("harp.wav") mix }
SPAN.quiet      { play-during: none }
```

SPATIAL PROPERTIES: AZIMUTH AND ELEVATION

Spatial audio is an important stylistic property for aural presentation. It provides a natural way to tell several voices apart, as in real life (people rarely all stand in the same spot in a room). Stereo speakers produce a lateral sound stage. Binaural headphones or the increasingly popular 5-speaker home theater setups can generate full surround sound, and multi-speaker setups can create a true three-dimensional sound stage. VRML 2.0 also includes spatial audio, which implies that in time consumer-priced spatial audio hardware will become more widely available.

Name:	**azimuth**
Value:	*<angle>*	[[left-side	far-left	left	center-left	center	center-right	right	far-right	right-side] || behind]	leftwards	rightwards
Initial:	center
Applies to:	all elements
Inherited:	yes
Percentages:	N/A

Values have the following meanings:

- *<angle>*: Position is described in terms of an angle within the range **−360deg** to **360deg**. The value **0deg** means directly ahead in the center of the sound stage. **90deg** is to the right, **180deg** behind, and **270deg** (or, equivalently and more conveniently, **−90deg**) to the left.
- **left-side**: Same as **270deg**. With **behind**, **270deg**.
- **far-left**: Same as **300deg**. With **behind**, **240deg**.
- **left**: Same as **320deg**. With **behind**, **220deg**.
- **center-left**: Same as **340deg**. With **behind**, **200deg**.
- **center**: Same as **0deg**. With **behind**, **180deg**.
- **center-right**: Same as **20deg**. With **behind**, **160deg**.
- **right**: Same as **40deg**. With **behind**, **140deg**.
- **far-right**: Same as **60deg**. With **behind**, **120deg**.
- **right-side**: Same as **90deg**. With **behind**, **90deg**.
- **leftwards**: Moves the sound to the left, relative to the current angle. More precisely, subtracts 20 degrees. Arithmetic is carried out modulo 360 degrees. Note that **leftwards** is more accurately described as "turned counter-clockwise," since it always subtracts 20 degrees, even if the inherited azimuth is already behind the listener (in which case the sound actually appears to move to the right).
- **rightwards**: Moves the sound to the right, relative to the current angle. More precisely, adds 20 degrees. See **leftwards** for arithmetic.

This property is most likely to be implemented by mixing the same signal into different channels at differing volumes. It might also use phase shifting, digital delay, and other such techniques to provide the illusion of a sound stage. The precise means used to achieve this effect and the number of speakers used to do so are user agent-dependent; this property merely identifies the desired end result.

```
H1    { azimuth: 30deg }
TD.a { azimuth: far-right }              /*  60deg */
#12  { azimuth: behind far-right }       /* 120deg */
P.comment { azimuth: behind }            /* 180deg */
```

If spatial-azimuth is specified and the output device cannot produce sounds behind the listening position, user agents should convert values in the rearwards hemisphere to forwards hemisphere values. One method is as follows:

if 90 deg < x <= 180 deg then x := 180 deg − x
if 180 deg < x <= 270 deg then x := 540 deg − x

Name:	**elevation**
Value:	*<angle>* | below | level | above | higher | lower
Initial:	level
Applies to:	all elements
Inherited:	yes
Percentages:	N/A

Values of this property have the following meanings:

- *<angle>*: Specifies the elevation as an angle, between **–90deg** and **90deg**. **0deg** means on the forward horizon, which loosely means level with the listener. **90deg** means directly overhead and **–90deg** means directly below.
- **below**: Same as **–90deg**.
- **level**: Same as **0deg**.
- **above**: Same as **90deg**.
- **higher**: Adds 10 degrees to the current elevation.
- **lower**: Subtracts 10 degrees from the current elevation.

The precise means used to achieve this effect and the number of speakers used to do so are undefined. This property merely identifies the desired end result.

```
H1   { elevation: above }
TR.a { elevation: 60deg }
TR.b { elevation: 30deg }
TR.c { elevation: level }
```

VOICE CHARACTERISTIC PROPERTIES: SPEECH-RATE, VOICE-FAMILY, PITCH, PITCH-RANGE, STRESS, AND RICHNESS

Name:	**speech-rate**
Value:	*<number>* | x-slow | slow | medium | fast | x-fast | faster | slower
Initial:	medium
Applies to:	all elements
Inherited:	yes
Percentages:	N/A

This property specifies the speaking rate. Note that both absolute and relative keyword values are allowed (compare with **font-size**). Values have the following meanings:

- *<number>*: Specifies the speaking rate in words per minute, a quantity that varies somewhat by language but is nevertheless widely supported by speech synthesizers.
- `x-slow`: Same as 80 words per minute.
- `slow`: Same as 120 words per minute.
- `medium`: Same as 180–200 words per minute.
- `fast`: Same as 300 words per minute.
- `x-fast`: Same as 500 words per minute.
- `faster`: Adds 40 words per minute to the current speech rate.
- `slower`: Subtracts 40 words per minute from the current speech rate.

Name:	**voice-family**
Value:	[*<specific-voice>* | *<generic-voice>*],]* [*<specific-voice>* | *<generic-voice>*
Initial:	depends on user agent
Applies to:	all elements
Inherited:	yes
Percentages:	N/A

The value is a comma-separated, prioritized list of voice family names (compare with **font-family**). Values have the following meanings:

- *<generic-voice>*: Values are voice families. Possible values are **male**, **female**, and **child**.
- **<specific-voice>**: Values are specific instances (e.g., **comedian**, **trinoids**, **carlos**, **lani**).

```
H1 { voice-family: announcer, male }
P.part.romeo  { voice-family: romeo, male }
P.part.juliet { voice-family: juliet, female }
```

Names of specific voices may be quoted, and indeed must be quoted if any of the words that make up the name does not conform to the syntax rules for identifiers. It is also recommended to quote specific voices with a name consisting of more than one word. If quoting is omitted, any white-space characters before and after the font name are ignored and any sequence of white-space characters inside the font name is converted to a single space.

Name:	**pitch**
Value:	*<frequency>* | x-low | low | medium | high | x-high
Initial:	medium
Applies to:	all elements
Inherited:	yes
Percentages:	N/A

Specifies the average pitch (a frequency) of the speaking voice. The average pitch of a voice depends on the voice family. For example, the average pitch for a standard male voice is around 120 Hz, but for a female voice, it's around 210 Hz.

Values have the following meanings:

- *<frequency>*: Specifies the average pitch of the speaking voice in hertz (Hz).
- **x-low, low, medium, high, x-high**: These values do not map to absolute frequencies since these values depend on the voice family. User agents should map these values to appropriate frequencies based on the voice family and user environment. However, user agents must map these values in order (*i.e.*, **x-low** is a lower frequency than **low**, etc.).

Name:	**pitch-range**
Value:	*<number>*
Initial:	50
Applies to:	all elements
Inherited:	yes
Percentages:	N/A

Specifies variation in average pitch. The perceived pitch of a human voice is determined by the fundamental frequency and typically has a value of 120 Hz for a male voice and 210 Hz for a female voice. Human languages are spoken with varying inflection and pitch; these variations convey additional meaning and emphasis. Thus, a highly animated voice, *i.e.,* one that is heavily inflected, displays a high pitch range. This property specifies the range over which these variations occur, *i.e.,* how much the fundamental frequency may deviate from the average pitch.

Values have the following meanings:

- *<number>*: A value between **0** and **100**. A pitch range of **0** produces a flat, monotonic voice. A pitch range of **50** produces normal inflection. Pitch ranges greater than **50** produce animated voices.

Name:	**stress**
Value:	*<number>*
Initial:	50
Applies to:	all elements
Inherited:	yes
Percentages:	N/A

Specifies the height of "local peaks" in the intonation contour of a voice. For example, English is a stressed language, and different parts of a sentence are assigned primary, secondary, or tertiary stress. The value of **stress** controls the amount of inflection that results from these stress markers. This property is a companion to the **pitch-range** property and is provided to allow developers to exploit higher-end auditory displays.

Values have the following meanings:

- *<number>*: A value, between **0** and **100**. The meaning of values depends on the language being spoken. For example, a level of **50** for a standard, English-speaking male voice (average pitch = 122 Hz), speaking with normal intonation and emphasis would have a different meaning than **50** for an Italian voice.

Name:	**richness**
Value:	*<number>*
Initial:	50
Applies to:	all elements
Inherited:	yes
Percentages:	N/A

Specifies the richness, or brightness, of the speaking voice. A rich voice will "carry" in a large room, a smooth voice will not. (The term "smooth" refers to how the wave form looks when drawn.)

Values have the following meanings:

- *<number>*: A value between **0** and **100**. The higher the value, the more the voice will carry. A lower value will produce a soft, mellifluous voice.

SPEECH PROPERTIES: SPEAK-PUNCTUATION AND SPEAK-NUMERAL

An additional speech property, **speak-header**, is described in Chapter 19, "Tables."

Name:	**speak-punctuation**
Value:	code | none
Initial:	none
Applies to:	all elements
Inherited:	yes
Percentages:	N/A

This property specifies how punctuation is spoken. Values have the following meanings:

- **code**: Punctuation such as semicolons, braces, and so on are to be spoken literally.
- **none**: Punctuation is not to be spoken, but instead rendered naturally as various pauses.

Name:	**speak-numeral**
Value:	digits | continuous
Initial:	continuous
Applies to:	all elements
Inherited:	yes
Percentages:	N/A

This property controls how numerals are spoken. Values have the following meanings:

- **digits**: Speak the numeral as individual digits. Thus, "237" is spoken "Two Three Seven."
- **continuous**: Speak the numeral as a full number. Thus, "237" is spoken "Two hundred and thirty seven." Word representations are language-dependent.

Chapter 14

From HTML extensions to CSS

If you produce material for the Web, chances are you already use HTML extensions to achieve some of the stylistic effects that CSS offers. This chapter presents several case studies on how to convert current designs that use HTML extensions into a CSS-based design. Switching to CSS will result in a more compact document that will download faster and print better.

We have chosen the case studies because we like their design. We do not try to improve the end result, but rather describe ways to enhance the underlying code. Since good CSS implementations have not been available until now, the designers of these pages have had no other option than to use HTML extensions and images to convey their message.

The case studies in this chapter compare the CSS approach with that of HTML extensions. For more comparisons between CSS and alternative methods of conveying stylistic documents, see Chapter 17, "Other approaches."

CASE 1: MAGNET

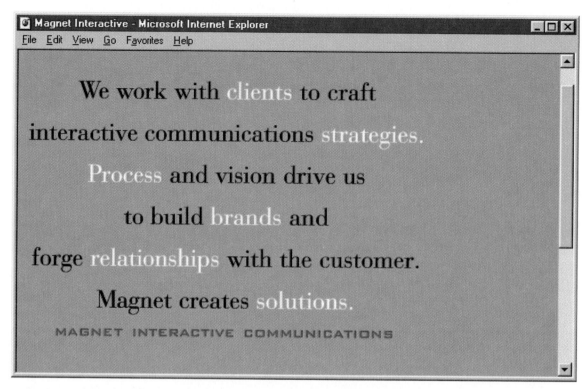

Figure 14.1 Original design: Magnet Interactive Communications (http://www.magnet.com/). The page is no longer available from their site.

The original page design (see Figure 14.1) is done as one single image that contains all the text. Also the background color of the document has been set (through an attribute on the BODY tag) to be the same as the background color of the image. While the page looks good on the screen, the image has the undesirable effects of being slow to download and hard to print (although few users would want to print short pages like this; printing is more important for longer documents).

When converting an existing design into CSS, you should start by collecting design features that are used throughout the page. These design features will be turned into declarations on the BODY element and thereby affect all elements through inheritance. Let's start with the colors. The background color throughout the page is brownish (with an RGB value of #c96 – see Chapter 11, "Colors," for a description) and the dominating text color is very dark (#424). This is easily expressed in CSS:

```
BODY {
    background: #c96;       /* brownish  */
    color: #424;            /* very dark */
}
```

Typespotting is the fine art of detecting font families when seeing them. Becoming a true connoisseur in the field requires years of training and an appreciation of details.

Giambattista Bodoni: Italian printer and type engraver, 1740–1813. The Bodoni fonts are much used in advertising and newspaper headlines.

Not all the text on the page is dark and we will later express the exceptions. For now, we are still collecting declarations on the BODY element.

The dominant font family in the original design is a *serif* (see Chapter 5, "Fonts," for a description), but unless you are a typespotter, it's not immediately clear which one is being used. Studies reveal that the font in use is "Bodoni."

Not all computers will have "Bodoni" installed and it's important to specify a generic font family as a fallback option:

```
BODY { font-family: Bodoni, serif }
```

The dominant font size should also be set on the BODY element and the two declarations can easily be combined with the font family on one line by using the **font** property:

```
BODY { font: 30px Bodoni, serif }
```

By using the **font** property you also set the other font properties to their initial values (see Chapter 5, "Fonts.")

The last declaration to be added to the BODY element is a value on **text-align** to center the text:

```
BODY { text-align: center }
```

In the original design, the lines are centered relative to each other, but are still on the left side of the window. With a **center** value on **text-align**, the lines will be centered in the window as well; arguably a better design.

The off-white text in the original design is clickable links, but since they are embedded in an image their appearance does not change when clicked. To set colors on links we use the anchor pseudo-classes described in Chapter 4, "CSS selectors." The following rules (there are three rules, although it may look like one since the selectors are grouped) express the same design in CSS by assigning the same color to all three pseudo-classes:

```
A:link, A:visited, A:active { color: white}
```

The only stylistic aspect that has not been described yet is the signature at the bottom of the window. It shows the name of the company that produced the page, and is embedded in the same image as the main text. When converting the image to HTML and CSS, it's natural to place this text inside an ADDRESS element. This gives us a selector for the element, and we can easily set the color:

```
ADDRESS { color: #c11 }          /* reddish */
```

Also, we need to set the font for the ADDRESS element. The font family is clearly *sans-serif*, but it's not the common "Helvetica" or "Arial." Rather, we're probably looking at a bold variant of "Eurostyle." The font size is roughly half that of the dominant text, and by using the **font** property we can set all the font values on one line:

```
ADDRESS { font: bold 50% Eurostyle, sans-serif }
```

Often, companies feel strongly about the presentation of their name and logo, and since "Eurostyle" isn't generally available, you may want to let the company name remain an image.

CASE 2: CYBERSPAZIO

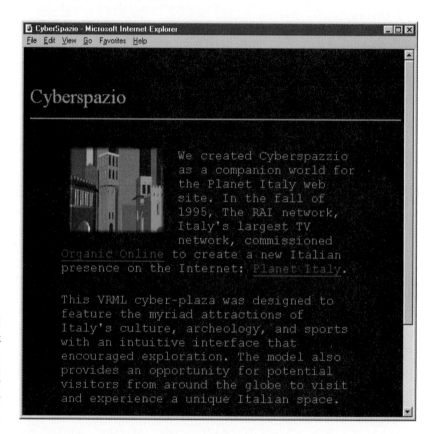

Figure 14.2 Original design: Construct Internet Design Co. (http://www.construct.com) http://www.construct.net/ projects/planetitaly/ index.htm

The original design uses some common HTML extensions to create this simple, balanced page. First, the background and text colors are set as attributes on the BODY tag. Second, the image (there is only one image on the page) has text wrapping around by way of an attribute on the IMG element. Third, to give the page more white space (actually, it's "black space" on this page), the whole page except the headline and horizontal rule has been put inside a table to set margins on the sides. Also, a chain of BR elements have been used to set more space around the headline. Fourth, TT elements have been used to set a monospace font.

Still, compared to most pages on the Web, this is a good page with a distinct design. No text has been put inside images, so the page will download quickly and print well. The main purpose of using CSS on a page like this is to simplify the HTML markup.

We follow the same strategy as in the first example: find design features that are used throughout the page and thereafter list the exceptions. Let's start with converting the attributes in the BODY element:

Colors

The BODY element of the Cyberspazio page looks like:

```
<BODY bgcolor="#000000" text="#999999" link="#006666"
vlink="#993300">
```

In Chapter 17, "Other approaches," you will find the full set of guidelines on how to convert these attributes into CSS rules. Here is the resulting style sheet:

```
BODY { background: #000000; color: #999999 }
A:link { color: #006666 }
A:visited { color: #993300 }
```

Since CSS allows color to be specified in only three digits, the above can be shortened into:

```
BODY { background: #000; color: #999 }
A:link { color: #066 }
A:visited { color: #930 }
```

Images

The only image on this page is found in the first paragraph. It has text floating around it due to the align attribute on the IMG element:

```
<IMG ALIGN=LEFT SRC="..">
```

It's easy to express the same in CSS:

```
IMG { float: left }
```

To set some space around the image, the original design uses the VSPACE and HSPACE attributes on IMG. In CSS, the **margin** property allows you to express the same:

```
IMG { margin: 5px 10px 10px 10px }
```

Fonts

The dominant font family on the page is monospace. In the original design this is expressed with a TT (see Chapter 1, "The Web and HTML," for a description) element, but since each element has a font family value in CSS there is no need for an extra element. By setting it on the BODY element, it will inherit to all other elements:

```
BODY { font-family: monospace }
```

The font size of the two paragraphs has been increased using the FONT element with a size attribute. Chapter 17, "Other approaches," describes the FONT element as defined in HTML 3.2 and gives examples of how it can be used. We would, however, recommend not using it at all and instead set CSS properties on existing elements. For example, to increase the document's default font size, you could say:

```
BODY { font-size: x-large }
```

If you hand-craft your style sheets (*i.e.*, write them in a text editor), you will appreciate the **font** property that allows you to combine the two declarations above into one:

```
BODY { font: x-large monospace }
```

The headline ("Cyberspazio") uses another font family. The original design does not specify a font family so the browser default will be used. This is fine, but most designers would probably set a font:

```
H1 { font: 20pt serif }
```

(The original design does not use the H1 element, but rather the presentational FONT element. Since the role of "Cyberspazio" is to be a headline, the use of H1 is recommended.)

White space

The original design uses empty columns in a table to create margins on the side of the text. In CSS, margins are more easily expressed:

```
BODY {
    margin-left: 10%;
    margin-right: 10%;
}
```

Since the margin properties are set on the BODY element, they will establish document-wide margins that also apply to the H1 element. In the original design, the headline (and the horizontal rule) only has a very small left margin. You can accomplish the same by setting a negative margin on the headline:

```
H1, HR {
    margin-left: -8%;
    margin-right: -8%;
}
```

Alternatively, we could have set only a small document-wide margin and then added extra margins on the P element:

```
BODY {
    margin-left: 2%;
    margin-right: 2%;
}

P {
    margin-left: 8%;
    margin-right: 8%;
}
```

This solution assumes that the paragraphs have been made-up using <P> tags.

To set some extra white space around the headline, the original design uses chains of BR elements to add blank lines. CSS offers a better solution by allowing you to declare exactly how much white space you want above and below the element. To replicate the effect shown in Cyberspazio, you could write:

```
H1 {
    margin-top: 3em;
    margin-below: 0.5em;
}
```

Recall from Chapter 5, "Fonts," that *em* units refer to the font size in use in the element itself. The above example will therefore give you three blank lines above the element and half a line below.

Similarly, you would want to set extra space below the horizontal rule:

```
HR { margin-below: 1em }
```

It may seem a little weird to use the em unit on the HR element. The em unit refers to the font size of the element, but the HR element has no text — it simply draws a horizontal line. For CSS, however, this is natural. All elements have a value for the **font-size** property even if the element never results in text being displayed.

CASE 3: "THE FORM OF THE BOOK"

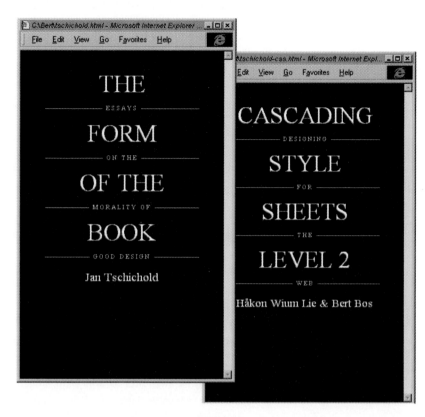

Figure 14.3 "The form of the book."

Jan Tschichold, *The Form of the Book,* Hartley & Marks Publishers Inc., Point Roberts, Wash, USA, 1991.

Figure 14.3 shows a recreation in CSS of the cover of a bundle of essays by one of the great typographers of this century, Jan Tschichold (1902–1974). He didn't design this particular cover, but in one of the essays he describes some very similar ones. Great reading! Just for fun, we have created an alternative cover for our own book in the same style.

Here is the HTML source we will be working with. Nearly every word will be positioned individually, so we needs lots of SPAN elements:

```
<html>
  <title>Jan Tschichold cover</title>
  <body>
  <p class=title>
    <span id=th>The</span>
    <span id=fo>form</span>
    <span id=of>of the</span>
    <span id=bo>book</span>
  <p class=subtitle>
    <span id=es><span id=es2>Essays</span></span>
    <span id=on><span id=on2>on the</span></span>
```

```
      <span id=mo><span id=mo2>morality of</span></span>
      <span id=go><span id=go2>good design</span></span>
    <p class=author>
      <span id=ja>Jan Tschichold</span>
    </body>
  </html>
```

Let's start with the basic fonts and colors. The background of the BODY will be black, and the text color white. We use a serif font, and center all text:

```
BODY {
    background: black;
    color: white;
    font-family: serif;
    text-align: center;
    line-height: 1.0;
    margin: 1em 4em
}
```

The reason the line height is set to **1** is to make the following computations easier. One line of text will be **1em** high.

Next we set the font size and text attributes of the three paragraphs: title, subtitle and author. The title's font is **4** times the size of the subtitle's font, and the author's font is twice the size. The title and subtitle are also converted to uppercase.

```
.title {
    font-size: 400%;
    text-transform: uppercase
}
.subtitle {
    text-transform: uppercase;
    letter-spacing: 0.2em
}
.author {
    font-size: 200%
}
```

Now we are ready to attack the vertical positioning. The trick is to make all the SPAN elements into blocks, give the four parts of the title plenty of padding (and a bottom border), and then use a negative margin to move back to the top of the page, before doing the same to the four parts of the subtitle.

```
#th, #fo, #of, #bo, #es, #on, #mo, #go, #ja {
    display: block
}
```

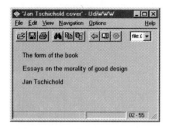

Figure 14.4 "The form of the book" in a non-CSS browser.

All SPANS are now blocks. (We use SPAN and not DIV, because in a non-CSS browser we want the words to be on one line, not below each other; see Figure 14.4.) Next add padding and border to the parts of the title:

```
#th, #fo, #of, #bo {
    padding: .6em 0 .4em 0;
    border-bottom: .025em solid white
}
```

A negative margin at the bottom of the last part of the title brings us back to the top of the page. The sum of the text, padding and border so far is 8.1 em (8.1 times the font size of the title).

```
#bo {margin-bottom: -8.1em}   /* back to top */
```

Between the four parts of the subtitle there is just a little over 7 times the font size. Remember that this is the base font size, or one quarter the size of the main title. We have backed up all the way to the top, so now there is nearly 8 em above the first part of the subtitle. The subtitle is printed right on top of the border of the title.

```
#es {margin-top: 7.9em}
#on, #mo, #go {margin-top: 7.1em}
#ja {margin: 0.8em 0}
```

Nearly done. If you were wondering why we needed two SPAN elements around the parts of the subtitle, here is the answer. The horizontal rules should not be visible behind the words of the subtitle, so we give them a black background:

```
#es2, #on2, #mo2, #go2 {
    background: black;
    padding: .3em
}
```

CASE 4: "THE NEW TYPOGRAPHY"

Jan Tschichold, *The New Typography,* University of California Press, Berkeley, Ca, USA, 1995.

Figure 14.5 shows the jacket of another famous book: Jan Tschichold's *Die neue Typographie* of 1928, in an English translation of 1995. The design is by Steve Renick, and, of course, the version shown is again only an interpretation. We haven't asked the designer how the layout should change if the window becomes wider, or the font larger.

This example is much simpler than the previous one. There is no need for negative margins. The interesting parts are the red rectangle behind the letters "typo" and the first line of the subtitle, which is in uppercase. For the red rectangle we'll need a SPAN around the four letters. The uppercase

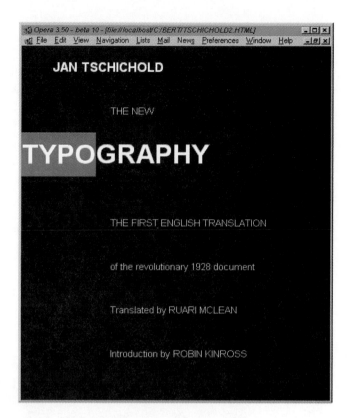

<figure>**Figure 14.5** "The new typography."</figure>

first line can be handled with a :first-line pseudo-element. For the rest, the design relies on a large line height and wide margins. Here is the complete document with its style sheet:

```
<style>
  BODY {background: black; color: white;
    font-family: "Helvetica", sans-serif;
    margin: 0; padding: 0; line-height: 4.5em}
  P {margin: 0 6em 0 9em}
  .author {font-weight: 800;
    font-size: 133%; margin-left: 2.5em;
    text-transform: uppercase}
  .title {margin: 0 0 2em 0;
    text-transform: uppercase}
  #th {display: block; margin-left: 9em}
  #ty, #gr {font-weight: 800; font-size: 280%}
  #ty {background: red; padding: 0.3em 0}
  .desc:first-line {text-transform: uppercase}
  .name {text-transform: uppercase}
</style>
<body>
```

```
<p class=author>
  Jan Tschichold
<p class=title>
  <span id=th>The new</span>
  <span id=ty>typo</span><span id=gr>graphy</span>
<p class=desc>
  The first English translation of the
  revolutionary 1928 document
<p>
  Translated by
  <span class=name>Ruari McLean</span>
<p>
  Introduction by
  <span class=name>Robin Kinross</span>
</body>
```

CASE 5: TSDESIGN

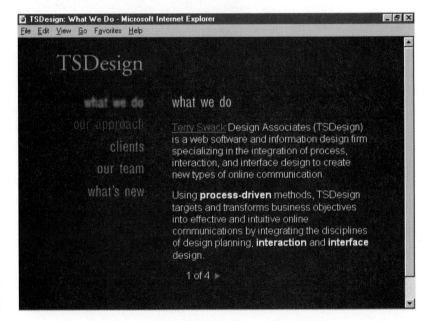

Figure 14.6 Original design:
TSDesign
(http://www.tsdesign.com)
URL: http://www.tsdesign.com/
tsdesign/html/whatwedo.html

This elegant and seemingly simple page is the first case study which uses HTML tables for layout. It also includes an interesting text effect (the "what we do" is blurred) and the spatial layout poses some extra challenges. Still, the design is within the scope of CSS, and the rewritten code, when converted into CSS, is considerably simpler and more compact than the original design.

This case study relies heavily on floating text elements and at the time this book went to press only two shipping browsers were able to display the example correctly: Opera 3.5 and Microsoft Internet Explorer 5. Previews of Netscape's Gecko indicate that the next Netscape browser will also support floating text elements correctly.

To follow the discussion in this case study, you will need an understanding of the concepts described in Chapter 8, "Space inside boxes" and "Using the padding property" in Chapter 9.

When converting a page like this into CSS, you should follow the same process as described in the previous case studies. In order not to repeat ourselves unnecessarily we skip the full description of that process and concentrate on the design features that make this page more difficult than the others.

First, you will notice that one of the lines on the left is blurred, as if it is out of focus. Manipulating focus is a common cinematographic technique that is also much used in contemporary graphic design. In CSS1 this effect was not supported, but CSS2 has a **text-shadow** property that can do this, among other things. In this case the type of shadow we need is a blurred shadow of the same color as the text in the same position as the text itself. A reasonable blur radius is 0.2em:

```
text-shadow: 0 0 0.2em
```

Second, the layout of the page is more complex than in the previous case studies. We can split the page into three distinct areas (see Figure 14.7):

1 the top-level headline ("TSDesign")
2 the vertical menu on the left side, below the headline
3 the right side which includes a second-level headline and some paragraphs

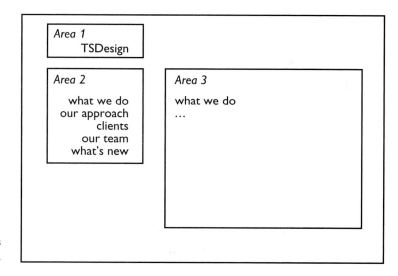

Figure 14.7 The three areas of the page.

In the original design, a table has been used to place the various elements on the page. CSS can work alongside tables, but offers layout features of its own that have several advantages: the markup is simpler and the pages will work in browsers that do not support tables.

Another design feature you will notice on this page is that the text in area 2 is right-aligned (see Chapter 8, "Space inside boxes," for a description of text alignment). Also, the headline in area 1 is right-aligned with area 2. Area 3 is more traditional; all text is left-aligned.

In order to express this layout in CSS, we start by finding one HTML element that will correspond to each area. Area 1 is the simplest since it only contains one element:

```
<H1>TSDesign</H1>
```

We need to set two properties to make the H1 element correspond to area 1. First, the width of the element must be limited; by default an element will stretch out as wide as possible. Second, the text within the element must be set to be right-aligned. The style sheet becomes:

```
H1 { width: 30%; text-align: right }
```

Area 2 is slightly more complex since it has multiple elements in it. The elements form a list, and it's therefore natural to put them inside a UL element, although the original design doesn't do this. The added benefit of using a UL is that we get an element that corresponds to area 2:

```
<UL CLASS=main-menu>
  <LI CLASS="what"> what we do
  <LI CLASS="approach"> our approach
  <LI CLASS="clients"> clients
  <LI CLASS="team"> our team
  <LI CLASS="new"> what's new
</UL>
```

Since there may be other UL elements in the document, we added a class attribute on UL. And since each of the list items has a different style we gave them a class as well.

Normally, LI elements within UL have a list marker. This is not the case in the original design, so we turn it off with:

```
UL.main-menu { list-style: none }
```

Also, we must set the width and the text alignment as we did for area 1:

```
UL.main-menu { width: 30%; text-align: right }
```

Area 3 is the last and the most complex among the three. It contains multiple elements of various types and the area has no natural enclosing element that corresponds to it. Thus we have to add one of our own, and the DIV element serves this purpose:

```
<DIV CLASS=main-text>
  <H2>what we do</H2>
  <P>...
</DIV>
```

Recall from Chapter 4, "CSS selectors," that DIV, in combination with a CLASS attribute, allows you to create your own elements. Now that we have an element we attach style sheet rules to it:

```
DIV.main-text {
    width: 60%;
    text-align: left
}
```

Setting the text alignment is probably not necessary since this is how western languages are normally presented. Setting the width, however, is very necessary unless you want the content of the area to use all the available space.

We have now found three elements that each represent an area as shown in Figure 14.7. Also, we have assigned values to the **width** and **text-align** properties so that they resemble the original design. What remains is to position the elements. The original design uses tables to accomplish the spatial layout, but we will – no surprise – use CSS.

The key property to achieving table-like behavior in CSS is the **float** property. Earlier in this chapter we used **float** to have text-wrap around an image, thus placing the image and the text next to each other horizontally. When using HTML extensions you can only make images float, but CSS has no such restriction: any element can float.

By making area 2 (or, more correctly, the UL element that represents area 2) float we will allow area 3 to be placed next to it:

```
UL.main-menu { float: left }
```

If you have trouble understanding why this will work, think of area 2 as an image for a moment: surely images can have text floating around them. The only difference is that area 2 is not an image, but a textual element (namely UL).

Actually, there is one more difference. The text in area 3 is to the side of area 2, but it doesn't wrap around it as text wraps around the image of Case 2. Instead it continues downwards along the same left margin. This is achieved by setting the left margin:

```
DIV.main-text { margin-left: 40% }
```

Recall from above that the width of the DIV element has been set to 60% of the available width. A left margin of 40% therefore makes sure the element moves over to the right.

Since not all aspects of recreating this example in CSS were discussed, the complete style sheet is included as a reference:

```
<HTML>
  <TITLE>TSDesign: What We do</TITLE>
  <STYLE TYPE="text/css">
    BODY {
      background: #003;
      color: #fff;
      font: 16px sans-serif;
      margin-left: 5%;
      margin-right: 5%;
    }
    A:link { color: #969 }
    A:visited { color: #666 }
    H1 {                              /* area 1 */
      font: 35px Garamond, serif;
      font-weight: 200;
      width: 30%;
      text-align: right;
      margin-top: 0.8em;
      margin-below: 0.8em;
    }
    UL.main-menu {                    /* area 2 */
      width: 30%;
      float: left;
      text-align: right;
      font-size: 20px;
      list-style: none;
    }
    LI.what { text-shadow: 0 0 0.2em }
    LI.what { color: #669 }
    LI.approach { color: #c33 }
    LI.clients { color: #996 }
    LI.team { color: #699 }
    LI.new { color: #f93 }
    DIV.main-text {                   /* area 3 */
      width: 60%;
      margin-left: 40%;
    }
    H2 { font: 20px sans-serif }
  </STYLE>
  <BODY>
```

```
      <H1 STYLE="color: #999">TSDesign</H1>
      <UL>
        <LI CLASS="what">what we do
        <LI CLASS="approach">our approach
        <LI CLASS="clients">clients
        <LI CLASS="team">our team
        <LI CLASS="new">what's new
      </UL>
      <DIV CLASS=main-text>
        <H2 STYLE="color: #ff9">what we do</H2>
        <P><A HREF="http://www.tsdesign.com">Terry
           Swack</A> Design Associates (TSDesign)
           is a web software... and information design
      </DIV>
    </BODY>
  </HTML>
```

Chapter 15

Cascading and inheritance

CSS is sometimes referred to as a style sheet *language* because the most visible part of CSS is the language in which one expresses style sheets. However, a major part of CSS is the mechanism that interprets style sheets and resolves conflicts between rules. All browsers that support CSS are required to use the same mechanism for this. The mechanism has two main parts: cascading and inheritance.

Inheritance was introduced in Chapter 2, "CSS," where we also briefly described cascading. However, we left out the technical details of how inheritance and cascading work. We present those in this chapter. You do not need to understand this chapter in detail to use CSS productively, but if you ever wonder why one rule wins over others, you will find the answer in this chapter.

"Cascading" refers to the cascade of style sheets from different sources that may influence the presentation of a document. Style sheets come from the browser and the designer, and may come from the user as well. The cascading *mechanism* is designed to resolve conflicts between these style sheets. Compared to other style sheet proposals, CSS is quite traditional in the stylistic properties it supports. However, as far as we know, cascading is unique to CSS.

The mechanism used now is not the first devised for CSS. The first published CSS proposal described a cascading mechanism that tried to combine conflicting rules to reach a median result in a process called *interpolation*. If the designer wanted, for example, headlines in sans-serif fonts while the user preferred serif fonts, the result would be something in between (fonts like this do exist). Interpolation didn't always work, however. For example, if the designer wanted fully justified text (`text-align:justify`) while the user wanted left-aligned text (`text-align:left`), there was no acceptable median alternative. So the interpolation of values was dropped at an early stage while the concept of cascading style sheets remained.

The current cascading mechanism always chooses only one value. That is, when there is more than one style sheet rule trying to set a certain property value on a certain element, the cascading mechanism will pick one of the rules. The selected rule will be given full control of the value in question. The challenge is to pick the right rule. This is not always easy, since conflicts can appear in several areas:

- *Designer style sheets versus user style sheets:* The most articulated conflict, and certainly the most political one, is the one between users and authors. Designers that come from a paper-based environment are used to having full control over the presentation of information. However, on the Web, users expect to have a say in how documents are presented. CSS supports the users' position by allowing user style sheets.
- *User style sheets versus browser style sheets:* Each browser has a built-in style sheet that is also part of the cascade. The default style sheet ensures that there is always a description of how documents are to be presented.
- *Conflicting rules set on the same element:* Different rules in the same style sheet may set conflicting values on the same element/property combination.
- *Added weight given to certain rules:* Designers and users can increase the weight of certain rules. These then escape the normal cascading order.

The inheritance mechanism is used only when no rules in any of the style sheets in the cascade try to set a certain property value. The property value will then be inherited from the parent element. If the property does not inherit, the initial value will be used instead. (Most properties do inherit. See the inside cover for a quick overview.)

The difference between cascading and inheritance can be illustrated graphically using a variation of the now-familiar tree structure. In the diagram below, inheritance works vertically. That is, values are inherited from parent elements to child elements as described in Chapter 2, "CSS". Cascading, in contrast, works horizontally. All rules that apply to an element, no matter what style sheet they come from, are collected and subsequently sorted. In the cascading order, rules coming from the browser default style sheet have the lowest priority, followed by user style sheets and designer style sheets, see Figure 15.1.

Figure 15.1 Cascading is horizontal; inheritance is vertical. Inheritance moves values from parent elements to child elements. Cascading collects rules that apply to the same elements. The "cascade" moves from left to right: the right-most style sheet has the highest weight.

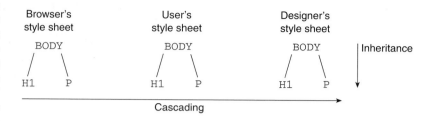

If you don't fully grasp the differences yet, don't worry. The following examples demonstrate how cascading and inheritance work.

EXAMPLE 1: THE BASICS

Here's a simple example of cascading and inheritance in action. We begin with a simple HTML document:

```
<HTML>
  <TITLE>A sample document</TITLE>
  <BODY>
    <H1>The headline</H1>
    <P>The text</P>
  </BODY>
</HTML>
```

Then, we add two style sheets:

Browser's style sheet

```
BODY {
    font-family: serif
}
```

Designer's style sheet

```
H1 {
    font-family: sans-serif
}
```

Graphically, the document structure with style sheets attached looks like this (Figure 15.2):

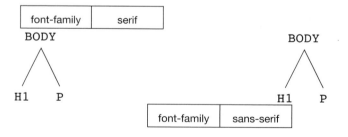

Figure 15.2 Style properties attached to elements.

CSS now must resolve differences between these style sheets. First, the cascading mechanism gets to work. For each element in the tree, rules are collected. In this example, no element has more than one rule for the same property, so there are no conflicts that need to be resolved. After cascading, the document structure looks like this (Figure 15.3):

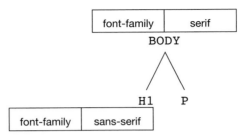

Figure 15.3

Next, the inheritance mechanism kicks in. The P element has no rule attached to it, so it inherits its parent's value. The document structure now looks like this (Figure 15.4):

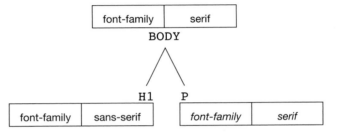

Figure 15.4

Since there were no conflicting rules in this example, combining the two style sheets only used the inheritance mechanism. In the next example, conflicts are introduced.

EXAMPLE 2: CONFLICTS APPEAR

The following example demonstrates how CSS resolves conflicts between designers and users:

```
<HTML>
  <TITLE>A sample document</TITLE>
  <BODY>
    <H1>The headline</H1>
    <P>The text</P>
  </BODY>
</HTML>
```

Two style sheets try to influence the presentation of the document:

User's style sheet	Designer's style sheet

```
BODY {                          BODY {
    color: black;                   color: white;
    background: white               background: black
}                               }
```

(Although the browser's default style sheet will always be there as well, we have omitted it to simplify the example.)

Graphically, the document structure with the style sheets attached looks like this (Figure 15.5):

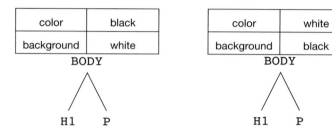

Figure 15.5

As you can see, both the user and the designer are trying to set the color and background for BODY, so the rules conflict. CSS first applies the cascading mechanism. The following principle resolves the conflict:

- Designer style rules override user style rules.

(Some people think this rule is unfair. Read on. We offer two alternatives in the next example.) Hence, after cascading the document structure looks like this (Figure 15.6):

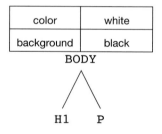

Figure 15.6

Next CSS applies the inheritance mechanism. The color property inherits, but the background property is among those that don't. So the background's initial value – "transparent" – will be used (Figure 15.7):

The background of the parent element will show through the transparent background, thereby producing, in effect, the same result as would

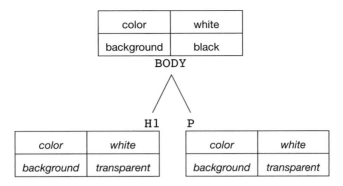

Figure 15.7

inheritance. In this example, both the H1 and P elements will appear to have black backgrounds.

EXAMPLE 3: ACCOMMODATING USER STYLES

In the previous example, we showed how the cascading mechanism gives designer style sheets more weight than user style sheets. Some people consider this unfair, so we include in CSS two alternatives for letting the user's rules prevail:

1 The user can turn off style sheets. The CSS specification recommends that browsers allow the user to selectively turn style sheets on and off. Typically, the opportunity to do this would be offered via a pull-down menu that displays all available style sheets, thereby allowing the user to pick the one desired.

2 Users can mark rules in their style sheets as "important," thus overriding the designer's rule for the same element.

In the previous example, the designer's style rules were given more weight than the user's. To do the opposite, we change the user's style sheet as follows:

User's style sheet

```
BODY {
    color: black !important;
    background: white !important
}
```

Designer's style sheet

```
BODY {
    color: white;
    background: black
}
```

Adding the keyword "!important" gives a rule added weight. That rule will thereafter override the designer's rule for the same property and element. After cascading, the document structure will be like this (Figure 15.8):

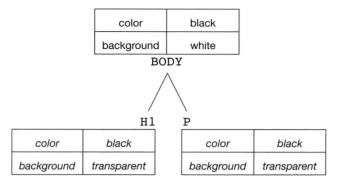

Figure 15.8

This is a change from CSS level 1. In CSS1, the designer's "!important" had more weight than the user's, but in CSS2, the weights of "!important" were reversed, to give users with special devices or with disabilities a better chance.

To keep CSS symmetric, we also allow the designer to mark rules as important. However, the designer's "!important" does not override the user's "!important."

A word of caution: overriding another style sheet will often be much harder than this example indicates. For example, if the designer's style sheet includes color and background rules for the H1 element, the user will have to override these rules as well. To fully override the effect of another style sheet, one must override each and every rule in it. This is hard to do if you don't know what the incoming style sheet contains.

Currently, it's hard to say how style sheets will develop on the Web. Will each and every document have its own style sheet, or will the whole Web converge around, say, 20 standard style sheets? The answer to these questions will to some extent determine the usefulness of the cascading mechanism.

EXAMPLE 4: A MORE COMPLEX EXAMPLE

In this example, we follow the steps a browser goes through to find the value of a certain property for a certain element. The numbered steps correspond to the definition of cascading in the CSS1 specification.

We will use a slightly more complicated sample HTML document:

```
<HTML>
  <TITLE>A sample document</TITLE>
  <BODY>
    <H1 CLASS=first ID=x45y>The headline</H1>
    <P>The text
  </BODY>
</HTML>
```

Also, the style sheets involved are more elaborate than earlier ones. They were written to demonstrate the specifics of the cascading and inheritance mechanisms.

- Designer's style sheet

  ```
  1   H1 { letter-spacing: 1em }
  2   H1.initial { letter-spacing: 2em }
  3   #x45y { letter-spacing: 3em }
  4   #x45y { letter-spacing: 4em }
  ```

- User's style sheet

  ```
  5   BODY H1 { letter-spacing: 3em }
  6   H1 { letter-spacing: 1em }
  7   BODY { letter-spacing: 1em }
  8   H1 { word-spacing: 1em }
  ```

The goal is to find the value of the **letter-spacing** property for the H1 element. This involves several steps. The search ends when the one specific rule is found that will set the value.

Step 1: Find all rules that apply

We begin by going through the rules in the style sheet examples and identifying the ones that apply:

- Rule 1 – A simple selector that matches all H1 elements. We are looking for the value of letter-spacing on an H1 element, so the rule applies.
- Rule 2 – The selector is more complex. It matches H1 elements, but only those that are of class "initial." The element in question is of class "first," so the selector does not match and the rule does not apply. Note that class matching is based on a comparison of the class names. That "first" and "initial" are synonyms isn't important.
- Rule 3 – The selector looks for an element with a certain id attribute. The element in question has an id attribute with a matching value, so the rule applies.
- Rule 4 – Same as rule 3: the id selector matches the element in question, so the rule applies.
- Rule 5 – The selector is contextual. It matches only if the element in question has a BODY element as an ancestor. This will always be the case in HTML, so the rule applies.
- Rule 6 – This rule is similar to rule 1 except it comes from the user's style sheet, not the designer's. The selector matches for the same reason rule 1's selector matches.
- Rule 7 – This rule tries to influence the property in question, but the selector is BODY, so the rule does not apply.

- Rule 8 – This rule has the same selector as rules 1 and 4, so it applies to the element in question. However, it sets a value for another property (**word-spacing**), so we ignore it.

Here's the situation after the first step. If a rule is marked ~~like this~~, it means it doesn't apply.

- Designer's style sheet

```
1   H1 { letter-spacing: 1em }
2   H1.initial { letter-spacing: 2em }
3   #x45y { letter-spacing: 3em }
4   #x45y { letter-spacing: 4em }
```

- User's style sheet

```
5   BODY H1 { letter-spacing: 3em }
6   H1 { letter-spacing: 1em }
7   BODY { letter-spacing: 1em }
8   H1 { word-spacing: 1em }
```

If no rules had applied, the inherited value would have been used. That is, the inheritance mechanism will only be used if there is no applicable rule. This demonstrates that the cascading mechanism is stronger than inheritance.

Step 2: Sort the rules by explicit weight

Rules can be given extra importance by labeling them "!important." None of the remaining sets of rules in the example are labeled, so this step has no effect on the cascading order. If a rule did have this label, it would have won the competition and the rule we seek would have been found.

Step 3: Sort by origin

Although CSS allows both designers and users to submit style sheets, users usually will be happy to accept the designer's style sheet. This assumption is reflected in this step: designer style sheets are given a greater weight than user style sheets. (As described in Example 3, however, users have ways to circumvent this.) Accordingly, the remaining user's rules can be dismissed. Here is the result:

- Designer's style sheet

```
1    H1 { letter-spacing: 1em }
2    H1.initial { letter-spacing: 2em }
3    #x45y { letter-spacing: 3em }
4    #x45y { letter-spacing: 4em }
```

- User's style sheet

```
5    BODY H1 { letter-spacing: 3em }
6    H1 { letter-spacing: 1em }
7    BODY { letter-spacing: 1em }
8    H1 { word-spacing: 1em }
```

Step 4: Sort by specificity

We now try to find the most *specific* rule among those remaining. The principle is that a very specific rule (for example, one that targets one specific element) should win over a more general rule that applies to a large number of elements.

CSS computes which is the specific rule based on the rules' selectors. A selector that addresses all elements of a certain type (for example, all H1 elements) is considered very general. This is the case with rule 1. Rules 3 and 4, however, apply only to one element (since the id attribute is guaranteed to be unique across the document), so their specificity is higher.

(The exact formula for computing the specificity of a selector is perhaps the most complex part of CSS, so we have elected not to explain it here. Instead, we point interested readers to the CSS1 specification for more information.)

We now have two rules left:

- Designer's style sheet

```
1    H1 { letter-spacing: 1em }
2    H1.initial { letter-spacing: 2em }
3    #x45y { letter-spacing: 3em }
4    #x45y { letter-spacing: 4em }
```

- User's style sheet

```
5    BODY H1 { letter-spacing: 3em }
6    H1 { letter-spacing: 1em }
7    BODY { letter-spacing: 1em }
8    H1 { word-spacing: 1em }
```

Step 5: Sort by order specified

Finally, we sort rules by the order in which they are specified. The later a rule is specified, the more weight it is given. Rule 4 will therefore have a higher weight than rule 3 and can be declared the winner: the H1 element will have a letter-spacing of 2em.

THE "INHERIT" KEYWORD

We've seen that inheritance only comes into play after cascading, when there are no rules that apply to an element directly. But just as the cascading order can be influenced with the "!important" flag, the importance of inheritance can also be increased. That is done with the keyword **inherit**.

Whenever you want to make sure that an element inherits a property value from its parent, you can make an explicit rule for that element, and specify **inherit** as the value of the property. For example:

```
H1 { font-family: inherit }
```

This is a rule that will take part in the cascade as described above, and if it wins, it will cause the **font-family** value of H1 elements to be inherited from the elements' parents.

To make absolutely sure that a value is inherited, you can even combine **inherit** with "!important." For example, a user could put in his style sheet that the shape of the mouse pointer should never change when the mouse moves into an A element, with this rule:

```
A { cursor: inherit !important }
```

The **inherit** keyword can be used on *all* properties, even those that normally don't inherit. It won't happen often that you want to make a non-inherited property into an inherited one, but if needed, it can be done. For example, to make sure that Ps have the same borders as their parents (and no borders if their parents have no borders), you can write:

```
P { border: inherit }
```

The **inherit** value was introduced in CSS2 and is, at the time of writing, not supported by any browsers.

Chapter 16

External style sheets

In order for a style sheet to influence the presentation of a document, the two have to be linked together. In the HTML examples we have seen so far, the style sheets have been inserted into the document using the STYLE element (Chapter 2) and the STYLE attribute (Chapter 4). The tutorial chapter on XML documents (Chapter 18) shows a way to *link* to an external style sheet from a document. This chapter describes in more detail how to use external style sheets, both from HTML and XML documents. The quickest way to start using external style sheets is to point to one which already exists on the Web. W3C has published a suite of Core Style sheets which are also described in this chapter.

WHY EXTERNAL STYLE SHEETS?

Before going into the technicalities, we should review the arguments which show that separating style and content is a good idea. There exist document formats which do not separate the two (for example PostScript and PDF) so it's fair to ask what the benefits of making the separation are. Here are the most important reasons:

- *Reusability* – by putting all the style information in one place, it can be pointed to by many documents and maintaining a consistent Web site become easier. For example, you can design an organization-wide style sheet that applies to all documents so that they are all given the same background color.

- *Performance* – once a style sheet has been downloaded it can be cached by the browser. This means that the next document which uses the same style sheet can be displayed faster since the style sheet doesn't have to be fetched from the Web.
- *User selection* – a document can link to several external style sheets from which the user can make a selection. Unfortunately, at the time of writing, browsers don't let users make the choice.

EXTERNAL HTML STYLE SHEETS

In HTML, there are four ways to "glue" style and content together:

1 The STYLE element
2 The STYLE attribute
3 The LINK element
4 The @import declaration

The first two of these are described in Chapter 2 and Chapter 4 respectively. The last two are described below.

LINKING TO STYLE SHEETS

The easiest way to apply a style sheet to multiple documents is via the LINK element. For LINK to work, the style sheet being linked to must exist as a separate file. Then the following line must be added at the head of each document that is to link to the style sheet:

```
<LINK REL="STYLESHEET" TYPE="text/css" HREF="mystyle">
```

"mystyle" is the URL of the requested style sheet. The attribute REL="STYLESHEET" tells the browser that the link is to a style sheet and not to something else. Without this attribute, the browser will not attempt to load the style sheet designated by the URL. Here is a more complete example:

```
<HTML>
  <TITLE>Bach's home page</TITLE>
  <LINK REL="STYLESHEET" TYPE="text/css"
    HREF="http://www.w3.org/StyleSheets/Core/Steely">
  <BODY>
    <H1>Bach's home page</H1>
```

```
<P>Johann Sebastian Bach was a prolific
   composer. Among his works are:
<UL>
  <LI>the Goldberg Variations
  <LI>the Brandenburg Concertos
  <LI>the Christmas Oratorio
</UL>
</BODY>
</HTML>
```

The above example links to the "Steely" style sheet which is one of several in the suite of W3C Core Styles (described below). Figure 16.1 shows the result of linking Steely to the sample document from Chapter 2. Feel free to put the same link into your own documents.

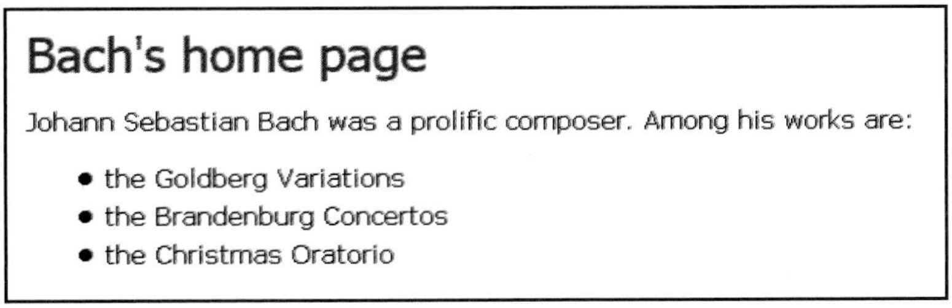

Bach's home page

Johann Sebastian Bach was a prolific composer. Among his works are:

- the Goldberg Variations
- the Brandenburg Concertos
- the Christmas Oratorio

Figure 16.1 The sample page from Chapter 2 styled with one of the W3C Core Styles.

In the example above, the external style sheet has replaced the STYLE element and Steely is fully in charge of the presentation. Often it's convenient to base the presentation on an extenal style sheet, but it's equally convenient to be able to make small adjustments specific to the document. This can easily be achieved by reintroducing the STYLE element:

```
<HTML>
  <TITLE>Bach's home page</TITLE>
  <LINK REL="STYLESHEET" TYPE="text/css"
    HREF="http://www.w3.org/StyleSheets/Core/Steely">
  <STYLE TYPE="text/css">
    H1, H2, H3 { font-family: serif }
  </STYLE>
  <BODY>
    <H1>Bach's home page</H1>
    <P>Johann Sebastian Bach was a prolific
       composer. Among his works are:
    <UL>
      <LI>the Goldberg Variations
      <LI>the Brandenburg Concertos
      <LI>the Christmas Oratorio
    </UL>
  </BODY>
</HTML>
```

The external style sheet and the rules in the STYLE element are now *cascaded* together – *i.e.* they are combined when displaying the document. The result is a page where headlines use *serif* fonts and all other stylistic settings come from Steely:

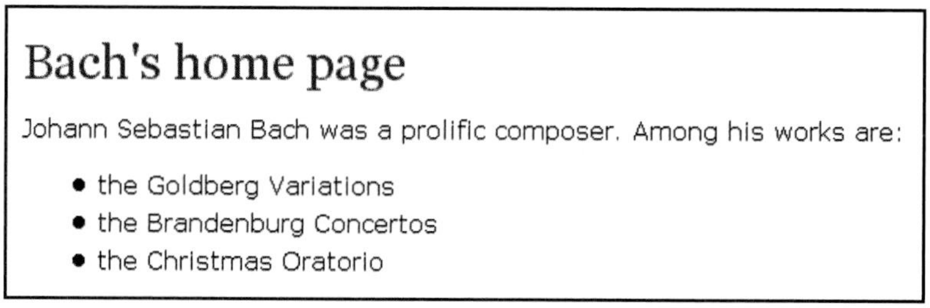

Bach's home page

Johann Sebastian Bach was a prolific composer. Among his works are:

- the Goldberg Variations
- the Brandenburg Concertos
- the Christmas Oratorio

Figure 16.2 A small document-specific style sheet cascades with an external style sheet.

Persistent, preferred and alternate author style sheets

This section is only of academic interest until browsers start supporting turning style sheets on/off as recommended by the HTML and CSS specifications.

As used in the previous example, both the external style sheet and the one inside the STYLE element are examples of what HTML calls *persistent style sheets*. Persistent style sheets are always applied to the document. That is, unless the user has turned off author style sheets in the browser setting, the persistent style sheets will always be applied to the document.

In addition to persistent style sheets, the HTML specification defines two other categories of author style sheets: *preferred* and *alternate*. *Preferred style sheets*, like persistent style sheets, are applied to the document by default. The difference between preferred and persistent style sheets is that preferred style can be turned on and off individually by the user. For this reason, preferred style sheets are given a name (through the title attribute) which can be used in a dialog box with the user.

Alternate style sheets are not applied by default. In order for them to have any effect, the user has to actively select the alternate style sheet. CSS doesn't describe *how* this user interaction should be performed, but having a pull-down menu which lists alternate style sheets seems like a natural way. Table 16.1 below summarizes the differences between the three categories.

Category	Applied by default?	Has a name?	Syntax
Persistent	Yes	No	`<STYLE TYPE="text/css">...</STYLE>` `<LINK REL="STYLESHEET" ...`
Preferred	Yes	Yes	`<LINK REL="STYLESHEET" TITLE=".." ...`
Alternate	No	Yes	`<LINK REL="ALTERNATE STYLESHEET" TITLE=".." ...`

Table 16.1 The difference and similarities between persistent, preferred and alternative style sheets.

Here is a document which uses all three types of author style sheets:

```
<HTML>
  <TITLE>Bach's home page</TITLE>
  <LINK REL="STYLESHEET" TITLE="Steely" TYPE="text/css"
    HREF="http://www.w3.org/StyleSheets/Core/Steely">
  <LINK REL="ALTERNATE STYLESHEET" TYPE="text/css"
    HREF="http://www.w3.org/StyleSheets/Core/Midnight">
  <LINK REL="ALTERNATE STYLESHEET" TYPE="text/css"
    HREF="http://www.w3.org/StyleSheets/Core/Swiss">
  <STYLE TYPE="text/css">
    H1, H2, H3 { font-family: serif }
  </STYLE>
  <BODY>
    <H1>Bach's home page</H1>
    <P>Johann Sebastian Bach was a prolific
        composer. Among his works are:
    <UL>
      <LI>the Goldberg Variations
      <LI>the Brandenburg Concertos
      <LI>the Christmas Oratorio
    </UL>
  </BODY>
</HTML>
```

The braces in the left margin label the `<LINK ... "Steely">` pair as **preferred**, the two `ALTERNATE STYLESHEET` links as **alternate**, and the `<STYLE>` block as **persistent**.

In the above document, the Steely style sheet and the rules inside the STYLE element will initially be applied to the document. User interaction might lead to Steely being turned off and Midnight or Swiss (two of the other W3C Core Styles) being turned on. The STYLE element is always persistent and will only be turned off if the browser provides a switch to turn all author style sheets off.

A word of warning is needed here. When providing a combination of persistent, preferred and alternate style sheets, it's important that you test all combinations to make sure that they work well together. For example, the Midnight style sheet (one of the alternate style sheets in the example above) displays light text on a dark background while Swiss and Steely do the opposite. The STYLE element, which is applied after the external style sheets, therefore shouldn't say anything about colors since it doesn't know if the text is light on dark, or dark on light.

The MEDIA attribute

CSS2 allows you to write different style sheets for different kinds of Web devices. These are known as media-specific style sheets and Chapter 12 showed how you could label a style sheet – or part of a style sheet – using an at-rule:

```
@media screen {
    BODY { font-size: 12pt }
    H1 { font-size: 2em }
}
```

The above method is good if only part of the style sheet is media-specific. In cases where the entire style sheet applies to one media type, there is a better way. By using the media attribute of the LINK element, browsers can find out what media types a style sheet applies to without downloading it. Here is an example:

```
<LINK REL="STYLESHEET" TITLE="Steely" TYPE="text/css"
    MEDIA="SCREEN"
    HREF="http://www.w3.org/StyleSheets/Core/Steely">
```

The value of the media attribute is one of the media type keywords described in Chapter 12: *screen, print, aural, braille, embossed, handheld, projection, tty, tv* and *all*. The above example makes the external style sheet (the by-now famous Steely) apply only to computer screens.

The media attribute can take a list of different media types to indicate that the external style sheet applies to more than one media type:

```
<LINK REL="STYLESHEET" TITLE="Steely" TYPE="text/css"
    MEDIA="SCREEN, PRINT"
    HREF="http://www.w3.org/StyleSheets/Core/Steely">
```

In the above example, Steely would be applied to both screen presentation and printouts.

@IMPORT

The LINK element described above is HTML's way of linking to external style sheets. CSS also has a way of importing external style sheets which offer some of the same functionality:

```
<STYLE TYPE="text/css">
@import url("http://www.w3.org/StyleSheets/Core/Steely");
</STYLE>
```

Since there always comes a URL after @import, you can safely drop the "url()" notation. The example below therefore has the same effect as the one above:

```
<STYLE TYPE="text/css">
@import "http://www.w3.org/StyleSheets/Core/Steely";
</STYLE>
```

As used in the above examples, @import doesn't offer any benefits over using the LINK element. One example from W3C will illustrate how using @import can make your life easier. Along the way you will learn a bit more about how W3C produces specifications for the Web.

Using @import: a case study

W3C publishes technical specifications. A specification normally starts out as a *Working Draft* in one of several *Working Groups* inside W3C. Working Drafts are available to W3C Members and most often also to the public. When the Working Group considers it ready, the specification becomes a *Proposed Recommendation*. If the W3C Members consider the specification worthwhile, it is thereafter turned into a *Recommendation*.

For W3C, it's important to convey at what stage a specification is in. A Working Draft is often immature and is mostly made available for discussion purposes. A Recommendation, on the other hand, is an industrial-strength specification which W3C actively promotes. Style sheets are a good way of visually communicating at what stage a specification is at. For example, by using an informal font for Working Drafts, the style sheet will communicate that the draft is subject to change:

```
@import "W3C-specifications.css";
BODY { font-family: cursive }
```

In the above example, most of the style settings will be found in the imported style sheet. However, the rule on the second line will override any **font-family** setting on the BODY element inside the external style sheet. Figure 16.3 illustrates how the above example is put into a file (WorkingDraft.css). The two other style sheets (ProposedRecommendation.css and Recommendation.css) also import the same base style sheet (W3C-specifications.css) and add a rule of their own. The benefit of organizing your style sheets into hierarchies like this one is that you can more easily make changes to large sets of documents. For example, by changing the base style sheet (W3C-specifications.css), you can change the color and background for all three types of specifications.

The examples in this case study are fictional – the style sheets in use by W3C are slightly more complex than those in Figure 16.3!

WorkingDraft.css:

```
@import "W3C-specifications.css";
BODY { font-family: cursive }
```

ProposedRecommendation.css:

```
@import "W3C-specifications.css";
BODY { font-family: sans-serif }
```

Recommendation.css

```
@import "W3C-specifications.css";
BODY { font-family: serif }
```

W3C-specifications.css:

```
BODY {
    font-family: monospace;
    color: black;
    background: white;
}
```

Sample HTML:

```
<HTML>
<TITLE>Cascading Style Sheets, level 3</TITLE>
<LINK HREF="WorkingDraft.css" TYPE="text/css">
<BODY>
    . . .
```

Figure 16.3 By importing one base style sheet (W3C-specifications.css), changes can easily be made to a wide range of documents.

@import: the details

You always write the @import declaration as the first declaration in the STYLE element. The local rules follow, as the following example shows, and will override any conflicting rules in the imported style sheet:

```
<STYLE TYPE="text/css">
  @import "mystyle";
  H1 { font-style: palatino, sans-serif }      ⎤ local
  P { color: blue; background: white }         ⎦ rules
</STYLE>
```

You can import any number of external style sheets using @import by inserting multiple @import declarations, each with the URL of a style sheet.

Importing multiple style sheets can result in a tier of style sheets. This is because an imported style can have its own @import declarations, which point to style sheets that may also have @imports, and so on. The order of the declarations is significant. Each additional level of @import has lower priority in case of conflicting rules, that is, style sheets that are imported later override those imported earlier. So you should place your primary style sheet(s) first and follow with supplementary style sheets included for specialized purposes.

You can use @import declarations in a modular fashion to customize your documents. For example, you may have as separate files style sheets that define different background images, default fonts, methods for handling tables, and special kinds of paragraphs and lists. Then in any particular document, you can use @import to pull in the appropriate style sheets to create the desired effect. For example:

```
<STYLE TYPE="text/css">
  @import "basics";
  @import "list-styles";
  @import "headings";
  @import "smaller-headings" print;
</STYLE>
```

Notice the word "print" after the last `@import` statement in the above example. Remember how the media attribute on the LINK element was used to declare media-specific style sheets? You can do the same on `@import` by adding the media types after the URL. If there is more than one media type, there should be commas between the keywords:

```
<STYLE TYPE="text/css">
  @import "bigger-headings" screen, projection;
  @import "smaller-headings" print, handheld;
</STYLE>
```

If no media types are specified, imported style sheets apply to all media types.

EXTERNAL XML STYLE SHEETS

The first part of this chapter shows how to link to style sheets from HTML documents. Most documents on the Web are HTML documents and we expect this to be the case also in the future. We also expect some new document formats to be developed for the Web. These are likely to be based on XML. Unlike HTML, XML-based documents will come with no conventions on how to display them and a style sheet will always be required. Therefore, work has been started to find a common way for all XML-based document formats to link to style sheets. So far, only the XML equivalent of HTML's LINK element has been defined. For example, in HTML you could use the LINK element like this:

```
<LINK HREF="/style/mystyle" REL="STYLESHEET"
TYPE="text/css">
```

The XML equivalent would be:

```
<?xml:stylesheet href="/styles/mystyle" type="text/css"?>
```

Note the question marks which appear inside the angle brackets – one at the beginning and one at the end. The question marks turn what would otherwise be a normal element into a *processing instruction*. Processing instructions are not used in HTML documents. In XML-based documents they are used to do various tasks and linking to style sheets is one of them.

In Chapter 18 we see that XML documents are case-sensitive. So, while you could write "`<LINK..>`" or "`<link .. >`" in HTML, you must always use the lowercase "`<?xml:stylesheet href... type...>`" in XML.

We expect that XML-based formats will also offer the equivalence of the STYLE element and the STYLE attribute as found in HTML, but this is only a proposal at this point.

W3C CORE STYLES

The quickest way to start using style sheets is to link to one that already exists. W3C has published a suite of style sheets called W3C Core Styles. Designed by Todd Fahrner of Studio Verso, these style sheets offer you professional designs without the need to learn how to write your own style sheets. And, if you decide to write your own style sheets – since you're reading this book, this has probably crossed your mind – you can combine the Core Styles with those of your own.

The W3C Core Styles are built up from a set of modules that can be combined in infinite ways, much as LEGO bricks can. Eight of the combinations have proved to be particularly pleasing and have been given names for easy reference. These names are: Chocolate, Midnight, Modernist, Oldstyle, Steely, Swiss, Traditional, and Ultramarine. You can see screen-shots of them over the following pages. To refer to one of them, put this in your HTML document:

```
<LINK REL="STYLESHEET" TYPE="text/css"
 HREF="http://www.w3.org/StyleSheets/Core/Steely">
```

Then exchange "Steely" with the name of your favorite style.

One important benefit of using the W3C Core Styles is that the W3C server will "sniff" what kind of browser you are using and withhold modules that are known to cause problems in your browsers. Unfortunately, not all CSS browsers handle all style sheets correctly. This is especially true for the first generation of browsers (see "Browsers and CSS" on page 35). The situation is improving rapidly and W3C expects to remove the need for "browser sniffing" in the future.

When using the W3C Core Styles, you should be aware that most HTML documents are not valid according to the HTML specification. Invalid

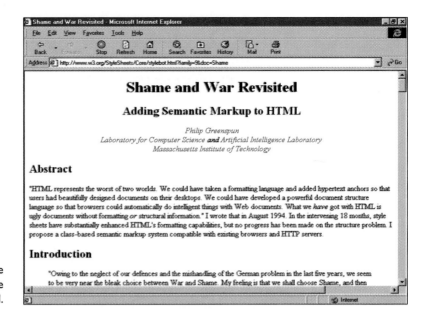

Figure 16.4 The sample document without any style applied.

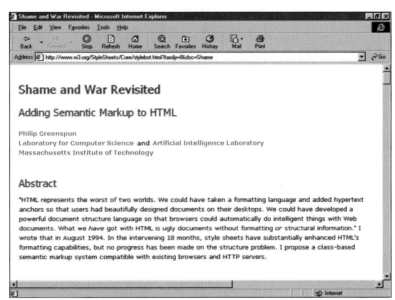

Figure 16.5 Steely.

documents, in combination with the Core Styles, may lead to unexpected results. W3C operates a validator service which will check your documents and help fix problems.

The W3C validator can be found from http://validator.w3.org/

Also, for best results, the HTML markup should be non-presentational (avoid, e.g., FONT tags, tables for layout, overuse of BR, etc.) and structural (e.g., use H1, H2 for headlines).

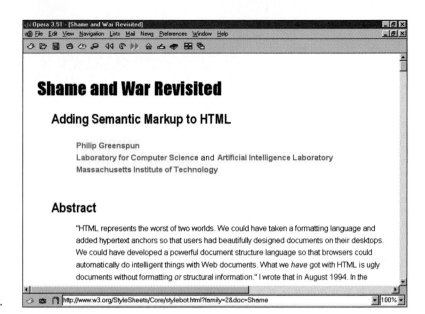

Figure 16.6 Modernist.

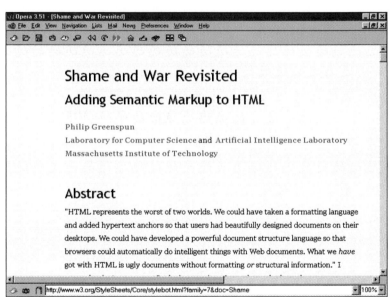

Figure 16.7 Traditional.

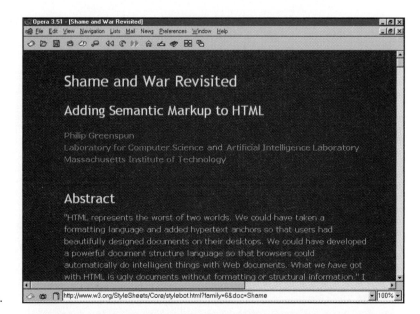

Figure 16.8 Chocolate.

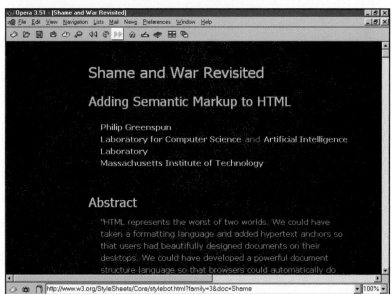

Figure 16.9 Midnight.

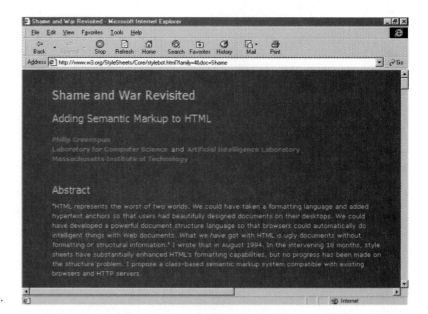

Figure 16.10 Ultramarine.

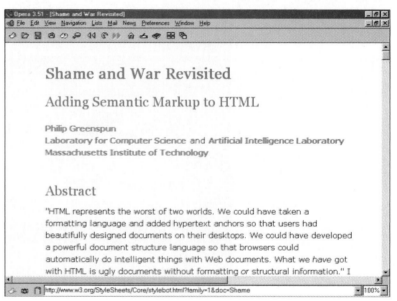

Figure 16.11 Oldstyle.

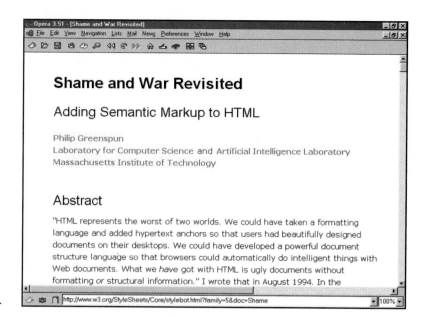

Figure 16.12 Swiss.

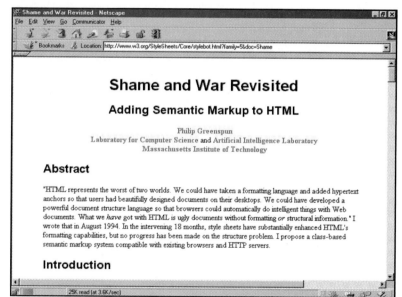

Figure 16.13 Swiss, shown in Netscape Navigator 4. Notice how the horizontal formatting module has been withheld due to bugs in the CSS implementation.

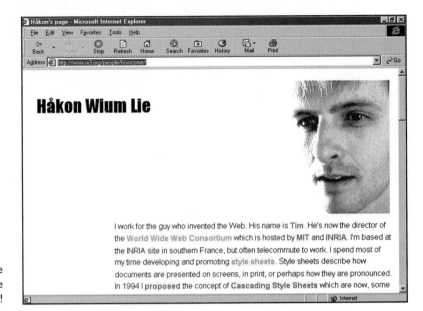

Figure 16.14 The W3C Core
Styles can even improve home
pages!

Chapter 17

Other approaches

We based this book on the premise that both the HTML text and the style sheet should be reusable as much as possible. The text must stay "clean" so that it can be shown with different style sheets or on different media, and the style sheet should be general enough to be applicable to other HTML documents.

In this chapter, we show what happens if we change some of those parameters, such as:

- using a different style language from CSS,
- creating a document without using a style sheet, or
- using a different format from HTML.

This chapter assumes a little more knowledge of Web-related technology than the preceding chapters. It is included for those who want to compare CSS to other systems. You can skip it, if you only want to know how to use CSS.

CREATING A DOCUMENT WITHOUT USING A STYLE SHEET

HTML 3.2 has some attributes and elements – commonly called "extensions" – that allow you to specify the layout to some degree. However, this is done at the cost of making the document less portable and harder to maintain. These extensions were added by various browser software vendors before it was clear that style sheets would provide a better alternative. Most of these stem from the Netscape browser.

In HTML 4.0, most of these extensions are no longer available, although there is a companion version of HTML 4.0, called "HTML 4.0 Transitional," in which they still exist. It is likely that in the next version of HTML many of them will disappear completely. When it is still necessary to use these elements and attributes (because the document is to be displayed on old, pre-HTML 4.0 browsers, for example), you will have to write your document in HTML 4.0 "Transitional" or in HTML 3.2.

Using elements for layout

There are some elements that have little or no meaning apart from indicating a certain style, while some others are structural elements that have often been misused for the effect they usually have on the layout. The first category contains the following elements. Note that many of these are not part of HTML, but are browser-specific extensions:

- B
- HR
- BASEFONT
- I
- BLINK (in Netscape Navigator)
- MARQUEE (in Microsoft Internet Explorer)
- BIG
- SMALL
- BR
- SPACER (in Netscape Navigator)
- CENTER
- SUB
- FONT
- SUP
- FRAME
- TT

Structural elements that are often abused for their visual effect include BLOCKQUOTE, DL (to indent paragraphs), and the heading elements H1 to H6 (to enlarge the text).

SUB and SUP are borderline cases: it is arguable whether they carry semantics or not. Their role is to indicate subscripts and superscripts, but they don't tell anything beyond that. They don't tell how the subscript or superscript is used (for example, as an index item, an exponent, an atom number, or other). However, inventing more meaningful names than SUB and SUP would be almost impossible because there are so many different functions. In mathematics, many of the roles subscripts and superscripts play don't even have agreed-upon names.

Also borderline is BR. Recall that it is an empty element that represents a hard line break; a line break will be placed where it is used no matter how the text of the paragraph around it is aligned or justified. Like SUB and SUP, BR doesn't tell *why* there is a line break at that point: is it because a line in a poem ended? does it separate lines of an address? It really should have been a character instead of an element, but the intended character is not part of the Latin-1 character set. This character set contains only about 200 characters and was the only one allowed in early versions of HTML. With the advent of support for the Unicode character set of more than 30,000 characters, BR could have been replaced by, for example, the line separator character. But people were used to BR, so it stuck.

Here is an example that uses the extension elements exclusively:

```
<font size="+2"><b>How to write HTML</b></font><br><br>
For headings, the FONT element is ideal, since it can
enlarge the font. The BR breaks lines, so two BR's in a
row make for a perfect paragraph separator. When a word
needs emphasis, the I tag will <i>italicize</i> it. For
even more emphasis, the B element puts the text in
<b>bold</b>...
```

Because extensions are inserted purely to force a particular style, their meanings can be expressed completely in CSS, as given in Figure 17.1.

MARQUEE is not translatable to CSS1. Its effect is to make the text scroll horizontally. It would be a text decoration, much like blink.

FRAME divides the window into a number of rectangles, each containing a different document. In CSS2, the same effect can be achieved with absolute positioning, in particular using **position: fixed**. That has the added benefit that the whole document is in a single file. See Chapter 10 for examples of fixed positioning.

Frames are often used to keep part of the user's screen the same while he navigates related pages. With fixed positioning that requires that the shared part of the screen is repeated in every page. If the shared part is large, that may result in slightly longer download time, but in view of the frustration that frames cause users (cannot bookmark, hard to get rid of unwanted frames, hard to navigate without a mouse) that is well worth it.

`<tt>`	`font-family: monospace`
`<i>`	`font-style: italic`
`<b>`	`font-weight: bold`
`<u>`	`text-decoration: underline`
`<big>`	`font-size: bigger`
`<small>`	`font-size: smaller`
`<sub>`	`vertical-align: sub`
`<sup>`	`vertical-align: sup`
`<hr>`	`border-top: solid` On some browsers, the border style is groove rather than solid.
`<center>`	`text-align: center`
`<font size=...>`	`font-size: ...` where the value depends on the value of the SIZE attribute: size=1 corresponds to `xx-small`, SIZE=7 to `xx-large`
`<font color=...>`	`color: ...`
`<basefont size=...>`	`BODY {font-size: ...}` where the value is determined as above
`<spacer>`	A shortcut for the "single-pixel GIF trick," see the next section
`<blink>`	`text-decoration: blink`

Figure 17.1 Meanings of elements used for layout.

Using attributes for layout

You also can use these extension attributes on a number of elements to set layout:

- ALIGN (various elements)
- LINK (on BODY)
- ALINK (on BODY)
- BACKGROUND (on BODY)
- TEXT (on BODY)
- VLINK (on BODY)
- BGCOLOR (on BODY)

- VSPACE (on IMG)
- HEIGHT (on IMG)
- WIDTH (on IMG, TABLE)
- HSPACE (on IMG)
- BORDER (on IMG)

ALIGN combines a number of functions, depending on the element to which it is attached and on the value. On headings and paragraphs, it sets the alignment of the text. For example, to center a title, you would write:

```
<H1 ALIGN=CENTER>Centered title</H1>
```

On IMG, it makes the image float to the left or right or align vertically with the text around it. For example, the following two lines have the same effect:

```
<IMG SRC="image" ALIGN=left>
<IMG SRC="image" STYLE="float: left">
```

as have these:

```
<IMG SRC="image" ALIGN=top>
<IMG SRC="image" STYLE="vertical-align: top">
```

WIDTH and HEIGHT on IMG allow an image to be scaled. HSPACE and VSPACE add padding around an image. BORDER sets the thickness of a border around an image, in case it is part of a hyperlink. All these attributes accept only numbers as values, which are interpreted as lengths in pixels.

WIDTH on table cells allow the cells to be rendered with a fixed size in pixels or as a percentage of the screen width. A fixed-size table is often misused to add fixed margins to a text or to align the text to a background image. On a browser that supports tables but not CSS this is the only way to get something that looks like margins or side heads, but it is also one of the worst offences against accessibility. We would like to urge authors not to do this, even if that means the text looks less attractive on certain browsers. Consider also that the number of such browsers will diminish, while the number of browsers that cannot show tables in this way is increasing: handheld devices, TV-based browsers, speech browsers. Some of those will even support CSS and @media (page 259).

ALINK, BACKGROUND, BGCOLOR, LINK, TEXT, and VLINK, set on BODY, to add a background image and color to the document and set colors for link anchors.

The single-pixel GIF trick for controlling space

One trick to control the spacing outside of a style sheet comes from David Siegel, author of *Creating Killer Web Sites*. He calls it the "single-pixel GIF

Siegel, D. (1996) *Creating Killer Web Sites*, 1st edition, Hayden Books.

trick." The trick is to create a transparent GIF image of 1×1 pixel. Although the image is essentially invisible, it still takes up space. Everywhere you need to add some space, you insert such an image. For example, here's how to indent paragraphs using this trick:

```
<P><IMG SRC="1pixel.gif" WIDTH=20 HEIGHT=1> text text
text...
```

Don't look at a document like this with image loading turned off!

You can even use this trick to affect line spacing. Here's how you would insert a few extra pixels between lines:

```
... some text<IMG SRC="1pixel.gif" WIDTH=1 HEIGHT=20
ALIGN=MIDDLE> with a narrow, tall<IMG SRC="1pixel.gif"
WIDTH=1 HEIGHT=20 ALIGN=MIDDLE> image every four
words<IMG SRC="1pixel.gif" WIDTH=1 HEIGHT=20
ALIGN=MIDDLE> or so...
```

Doing this is a bit of a gamble, since you don't know the size of the user's font. Assuming that in many cases the font will be around 14 pixels high, creating a 20-pixel image should therefore ensure about 6 pixels between lines.

The single-pixel GIF trick also can do word spacing and letter spacing. The nice part of doing this is that it doesn't add much to the download time. The downside is that pages containing these images are a nightmare to maintain: you have to make sure that there is an image between every two words or every two letters, and that they are all the same. If you change one, you'll have to change all of them. Also, robots will have a hard time finding the keywords among the images.

USING A DIFFERENT FORMAT FROM HTML

You can avoid using HTML altogether by using a different format from HTML, such as the Portable Document Format, or an image.

The Portable Document Format (PDF)

The Portable Document Format (PDF), often called the "Acrobat" format after the program most commonly used to display it, is a format for storing formatted documents in a device-independent manner. Created by Adobe Systems, it inherits much from PostScript, another page description language, also by Adobe.

PDF is like "digital paper." It can store one or more pages of text and images, ready to be printed or viewed on screen. Compared to image formats such as PNG, GIF, and JPEG, it has a number of advantages. First, it can contain actual text, not just images of text (bitmaps). As a result, it can scale the pages and print at any resolution: the text looks as good as the printer allows. Second, it can replace fonts by generated approximations ("Multiple Master fonts") in case the document uses uncommon fonts and the document's creator didn't embed the font, either for copyright reasons or just to save space. Third, since the text in the document is stored as text and not as bitmaps, you can search the document for keywords. Fourth, PDF can even contain hyperlinks, not only within the document but also as URLs that point to documents on the Web.

The disadvantage is that the text is already formatted as you get it. Resizing the window won't change the number of words per line, as it normally does in HTML. The structure of the text is also lost: you cannot save the document and edit it. Even if you manage to save the text and load it into some other program, there are no tags anymore that tell you that a certain piece of text is a heading or a list item. Since spaces are often not stored explicitly, and letters don't necessarily appear in the file in the order they appear on the screen, the PDF software has to use heuristics to even recognize words.

PDF is a good solution for old documents that cannot be converted to HTML, or would need a lot of work to allow conversion. Usually, when you can print a document, you can also convert it to PDF. Many documents created with old word processors were never meant for use on the Web and printing them is pretty much the only thing you can do with them.

Images

You can also use images that are stored in PNG, GIF or JPEG format. We briefly discussed using images in place of text in Chapter 1, "The Web and HTML." A Web page consisting of just an image gives the page's designer control over every pixel, especially when the PNG format is used. PNG is the most accurate when it comes to defining the color of pixels. But that level of control comes at a price.

First, robots cannot read the page. Second, the page is much larger in terms of bytes than a page that consists of text with a style sheet and thus takes longer to download.

Third, the page has a fixed size. As a result, users may have trouble reading the image, for several reasons. On large screens, the image may be too small. On small screens, the image may be too large. On monochrome screens, too many colors may be shown as almost the same shade of gray. And on text-only browsers, users won't see anything.

Fourth, printing the page will also give less than satisfactory results. Not many printers can print in color, so the result in black and white may either be very small or look grainy (see Figure 17.2).

Figure 17.2 (a) Shows normal text, (b) shows an image. On the screen, the two looked the same, but on paper, the text was printed with all the quality the printer could offer, while the image was just copied pixel for pixel.

Fifth, as with any format that doesn't rely on style sheets for the layout, it will not be readable by somebody who is blind (images can be converted neither to speech nor to Braille) and will be hard to read for somebody with limited eyesight (although the images can be enlarged, it is hard to change the colors, as you can with text).

And finally, when you want to modify the document, it is harder to change an image than a text or a style sheet.

For the above reasons, it is advisable to use images only for effects that cannot be achieved with a style sheet. And then only if the look is so important that it outweighs the disadvantages. Of course, you should also include the text in the ALT attribute of the IMG element, for people that cannot see the image.

USING XSL

XSL, the "eXtensible Style sheet Language," is so called because it is designed specifically for XML, the "eXtensible Markup Language." At the time of writing (autumn 1998), XSL is still under development by the World Wide Web Consortium, as a complementary system to CSS. The full syntax hasn't been decided yet, but a few of the principal characteristics of XSL can already be discerned.

The XSL language will itself be based on XML, which means it will look very different from CSS. Ease of reading and writing isn't as important for XSL as it is for CSS. Writing XSL requires more training than writing CSS.

XSL has two parts: transformation and formatting. The transformation can be used on its own, to translate XML documents to other XML documents, or other types of text-based formats. It can also be combined with formatting, to transform an XML document to a document with "formatting objects," which is just another XML document, but one in which all elements have a full set of CSS properties. You can think of the formatting process performed by XSL as a transformation of an XML document to an HTML document in which all elements have a STYLE attribute with the properties that apply to that element.

An XSL script contains a series of template rules, each of which contains a pattern similar to a CSS selector and a piece of text, representing how to rewrite a matching piece of the input document. An XSL interpreter tries to match all patterns and thereby replaces parts of the XML document with new text, until there are no more templates that match.

XSL is meant to be used for tasks like sorting parts of a document, generating a table of content, generating a report for an XML-based database, and other tasks related to formatting documents. The focus is on printed output. Much of XSL processing is expected to be invisible to users: a server might use an XSL script to create an HTML document dynamically from a large database of XML documents.

But XSL could also be used in browsers, as an alternative to CSS, for documents that need to be re-ordered before they can be displayed to a reader.

At this moment it is not yet clear what the best architecture for XSL will be: integrated into Web servers, into browsers, or as a separate program. In many cases, XSL will be used to condense a large document or set of documents into one or more small Web pages. In that case the logical place is near the server, since it would be wasteful (and time-consuming) to send the large document plus XSL script to a browser, when the user will eventually only see a small part of it. But if XSL is used to expand a compact piece of machine-data into a human readable description of the data, then sending the compact document and the XSL script to a browser for processing makes sense.

Although XSL will certainly look very different from CSS – no semi-colons (;), no curly braces ({ }), no colons (:), etc. – when XSL is used for formatting, it won't be hard to recognize the CSS properties. Nearly all CSS properties will be available, with the same names and the same values as in CSS.

Chapter 18

XML documents

The W3C XML recommendation can be found from http://www.w3.org/TR/REC-xml

Apart from HTML documents, there will also be documents on the Web in other formats, many based on XML. XML is a toolkit for creating data formats, defined in a W3C Recommendation of 1998. This chapter shows how CSS applies to XML-based documents. There aren't many such documents yet, so the examples in this chapter are hypothetical, but they should still give the general idea. And besides, there isn't that much difference between XML and HTML anyway.

Even though there are no widespread XML-based document formats yet, some browsers already support them. This is so that people can experiment with new formats, some of which may eventually become standardized.

XML is already used for certain other forms of data on the Web, but those formats are typically not meant to be displayed and read. They contain instructions to a program, such as how to subscribe to a "Web channel," a financial transaction between two personal finance applications, or the timing and positioning information for a multi-media presentation (SMIL, another W3C Recommendation). Applying CSS to these kinds of data is not very useful, as there is little or no text in them.

A mixed form is MathML (also a W3C Recommendation), a format for storing mathematical formulas. It contains some text, but the text consists of mathematical symbols. CSS can be used with it to a limited extent, but CSS has no specific support for mathematics, so we will consider MathML

XML "XML" stands for *eXtensible Markup Language*, a name that evokes its descent, rather than its actual use. XML was developed as a simpler and more flexible version of SGML, using insights gained with HTML. XML development started in 1996, and version 1.0 became a W3C Recommendation in May 1998.

In fact, neither of the three parts of the name tell you much about its purpose. Although in a mathematical sense, XML is indeed a *language*, it is not a language in the same sense as HTML. You cannot express anything in XML, but you can use XML to create other languages, such as SMIL and MathML. It is expected that the next version of HTML after 4.0 will be written in XML and titled XHTML.

A *markup* language is a set of marks that editors place in a text, either to mark corrections, or, if it is an electronic document, to instruct a program or a device, such as a printer. HTML is a markup language in that sense, since it consists of marks inserted in a text, that instruct various programs what to do with the text. However, few of the currently existing formats based on XML are markup languages. They are used to represent database records, spreadsheets, money deposits, or multi-media timing data, but they contain little or no human readable text.

The word *extensible* also doesn't apply to XML itself, but to the formats derived from it. XML has a fixed set of rules, and they can't be changed. But those rules ensure that when an XML-based format is combined with another XML-based format, the result is again an XML-based format. Not many XML-based formats make use of that feature, but those that do are called extensible. The 1999 version of HTML will probably be one of them. That should allow, *e.g.*, to put MathML formulas and HTML text together in one file.

a "non-displayed" format for now. Maybe a future level of CSS will support mathematical typography.

A document format is said to be based on XML, or written in XML, if it conforms to certain rules. Those rules cause XML-based documents to have a very recognizable form. If you look at the source of such a document, you will see something that vaguely resembles HTML, since it has elements and attributes inside "<" and ">" and the elements form a tree. The difference is mainly that the names of the elements and attributes will be different from those in HTML.

For example, this might be an XML document, written in a (hypothetical) format for aircraft maintenance manuals:

```
<manual>
    <aircraft>
        <brand>Boeing</brand>
```

```
            <type>747</type>
        </aircraft>
        <date>8 June 1998</date>
        <chapter type="main">
            <par>Wipe the aircraft regularly
            with a soft cloth.</par>
        </chapter>
    </manual>
```

It has none of the familiar HTML elements, but other than that it doesn't look too strange. A simple style sheet for this document may be as follows:

```
manual {display: block; margin-left: 10%}
aircraft {display: block: margin: 2em;
    font-size: xx-large}
chapter {display: block; margin-top: 1em}
date, par {display: block}
```

Inheritance works like in HTML. So, in the example, the **brand** element will be **xx-large**, since it inherits the font size from the **aircraft** element.

In most of the examples in this book, we have written the selectors of style rules in capitals, since in HTML lowercase and uppercase letters are interchangeable. XML is different in that respect. A style sheet for an XML-based document must use selectors with exactly the same letters as the elements in the document. Spelling "manual" as "MANUAL" will not work.

EXPERIMENTING WITH XML

If you have a browser that supports XML, such as Internet Explorer 5 or Netscape 5, you can create XML documents and style sheets for them and test them out. The basic rules are as follows:

1   If you use an element **<abc>**, you must end it with **</abc>**. Unlike HTML, no tags may be omitted.
2   If the element is empty (has no end tag), you must end it with a slash: **<xyz/>**
3   If you use an attribute **att="value"**, make sure you put quotes around the value. Unlike in HTML, all attributes, even simple ones, must be quoted.
4   Style sheets cannot be in the same file as the XML document. Instead, put a line like this at the top of the XML document (note the two question marks):

```
<?xml-stylesheet href="my-style.css"?>
```

This works the same as **`<link rel="stylesheet" href="my-style.css">`** in HTML. In fact, as in HTML, you can add "title" and "type" attributes, and you can have multiple alternative styles. But unlike in HTML, you cannot use capitals, e.g., "HREF" is not correct.

5 The browser doesn't have a built-in style for any XML-based documents, so all elements will be displayed inline. You'll have to use the **display** property.

But most of all, don't forget that these experiments are not documents that you can share with the world, like HTML. It may seem that you have a meaningful format, with names like "manual," "aircraft," "date" or "chapter," but without proper documentation, nobody can be sure what you mean by them. "Manual" could mean "by hand," and "chapter" might be a sub-group of a club or society. The larger the group of people you want to share this format with, the better the documentation must be.

SOME EXAMPLES

Here are some examples of (hypothetical) XML-based formats, and their possible style sheets.

The first example could be an electronic program guide. The structure is simple. The guide consists of number of "day" elements, each containing "program" elements, which in turn contain start and end times, the program's name, a short description, a code for programming a video recorder, and some elements that indicate whether the program is in stereo and in wide screen.

Figure 18.1 A screendump of the "guide" document, with the first style sheet.

```
<?xml-stylesheet href="guide.css"?>
<guide>
    <day>
        <date>1 Jan 2000</date>
        <program>
            <start>06.00</start><end>09.30</end>
            <name>Good morning, world!</name>
            <description>News, weather, and interviews</description>
```

```
        <code>tv://channel2000/20000101T0600-0930</code>
        <stereo/>
    </program>
    <program>
        <start>23.40</start><end>01.15</end>
        <name>Late(st) news</name>
        <description></description>
        <code>tv://channel2000/20000101T2340-0115</code>
        <stereo/>
        <wide/>
    </program>
  </day>
</guide>
```

The XML starts with a link to a style sheet "guide.css." A simple style sheet to make this readable could be as follows (see Figure 18.1):

```
day {display: block}
program {display: block}
description {display: block}
code {display: none /* Don't show the code */}

guide {background: black; color: white; padding: 1em}
day {font-size: large; margin: 1em 0}
program {margin: 1em 2em; text-indent: -2em}
start, end {font-weight: bolder}
end:before {content: "-"}
end:after {content: ". "}
name {color: red}
stereo:before {content: "stereo "}
wide:before {content: "16:9 "}
stereo, wide {font-size: small}
```

The information could also be displayed in tabular format: every program is one row, and each field is a column (see Figure 18.2).

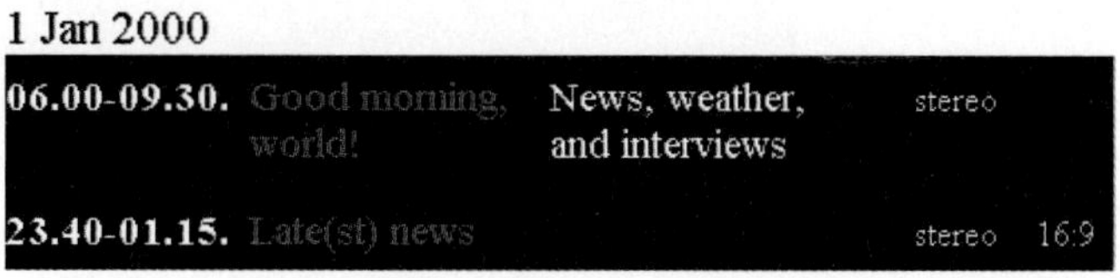

1 Jan 2000

Figure 18.2 A screendump of the "guide" document, with the second style sheet.

```
guide {display: table}
day {display: table-body}
date {display: caption}
program {display: table-row}
start, end, name, description, stereo, wide {
```

```
              display: table-cell}
    code {display: none} /* Don't show the code */
    date {font-size: larger; text-align: left}
    guide {background: black; color: white}
    program {vertical-align: baseline}
    name, description, stereo, wide {padding: 0.5em}
    start, end {font-weight: bolder}
    start:after {content: "-"}
    end:after {content: ". "}
    name {color: red}
    stereo:before {content: "stereo "}
    wide:before {content: "16:9 "}
    stereo, .wide {font-size: smaller }
```

For more information on the style properties for tables, see Chapter 19.

The next example could be part of a dictionary. The document consists of gloss elements, containing head and sense elements, the latter in turn containing def and ex elements:

```
<?xml:stylesheet href="dict.css"?>
<dictionary>
    <gloss><head>pen</head>
        <sense type="n" num="1">
            <def>Goose feather used for writing.</def>
        </sense>
        <sense type="n" num="2">
            <def>Fenced area for keeping sheep.</def>
            <ex>At night, the sheep are in the pen.</ex>
        </sense>
    </gloss>
    <gloss><head>pen-knife</head>
        <sense type="n">
            <def>Knife for sharpening pens (1).</def>
        </sense>
    </gloss>
</dictionary>
```

The style sheet is contained in a file called "dict.css." We want every gloss to be a block, with the head outdented. The head term will be bold, the definition will be italic. The type of the word ("n" for nouns) will be taken from the attribute and inserted before the definition. If there are multiple senses for a word, there will be a "num" attribute with a number and the style sheet will insert that number before the definition.

Figure 18.3 Possible rendering of a dictionary.

pen 1. n. *Goose feather used for writing.* 2. n. *Fenced area for keeping sheep.* At night, the sheep are in the pen.
pen-knife n. *Knife for sharpening pens (1).*

```
gloss {
    display: block;
    margin-left: 1em;
    text-indent: -1em
}
head {
    font-weight: bold
}
sense:before {
    content: attr(type) ". ";
}
sense[num]:before {
    content: attr(num) ". " attr(type) ". ";
}
def {
    font-style: italic
}
```

Figure 18.3 shows how this might be rendered. See Chapter 7 for information about the ":before" *pseudo-element,* and the use of the **content** property to display the value of an attribute.

There are two set of rules for the "sense" element. The second one will only be used if there is a "num" attribute and in that case the value of the **content** property will be taken from this rule, instead of the earlier one. The effect is to display both the "num" and "type" attributes. See Chapter 4 for more information on constructing selectors and on how they determine the precedence of rules.

Chapter 19

Tables

Tables are a way to visually show relations between pieces of data. Lists do the same, but tables allow you to show multiple relations at the same time. Each cell in a table holds a number or some short text that has some relation to other data in the same column or the same row.

To make it easier to see the structure of the table, rules (*i.e.*, lines) are often added between the rows or columns (or both), sometimes only between certain groups of rows or columns. Colors and changes in font can of course also be used. Cells don't have margins (although there is a **cell-spacing** property that works in a somewhat similar way), but padding is available.

CSS2 offers two ways of setting borders on cells. In one model, called "collapsing borders," there is only one border between two cells; in the other, called "separate borders," there are two. Depending on what "look" you are trying to achieve, and on personal preference, you may find one or the other easier to use.

THE PARTS OF A TABLE

Tables are made up of rows and columns, which in turn contain cells. That is the general idea, but in practice tables can be a bit more complex. For example, some cells can be in two or more columns at the same time. Here

Figure 19.1 A simple table with borders around all cells.

is an HTML table with a style sheet that makes the boundaries of the cells visible by means of a simple border (see Figure 19.1):

```
<TABLE>
  <TR><TD>1   <TD>2   <TD>3
  <TR><TD SPAN=2>4   <TD>5
</TABLE>
```

with style:

```
TD {border: solid}
```

The HTML table model, which is the basis for CSS's table model, is actually quite complex, if all parts are considered. But luckily most tables are simple, and only need a small part of the full model.

The essential parts of any table, the parts that cannot be omitted in HTML, are the table itself (the box that contains all the rows and cells), the rows, and the cells. The rows are boxes inside the table, and the cells are boxes inside the rows. The complication that cells can span several rows, is handled by saying that a cell box can actually extend outside the row box.

Here is a table in which the row boxes are made visible, by giving them each a different background. The cells are shown the same way as before, with a border (Figure 19.2):

```
<TABLE>
  <TR CLASS=r1><TD> 1 <TD> 2 <TD ROWSPAN=2> 3
  <TR CLASS=r2><TD COLSPAN=2> 4
  <TR CLASS=r3><TD> 5 <TD> 6 <TD> 7
</TABLE>
```

Figure 19.2 A table with three differently colored rows and a cell that spans two rows.

and the style:

```
TD {border: solid}
TR.r1 {background: #F99}
TR.r2 {background: #9F9}
TR.r3 {background: #99F}
```

There are a number of optional parts in a table, that are needed for more complex tables. The caption is one. It is typically one or a few lines of text above or on the side of the table.

Rows can also be grouped into row-groups, which puts all of them into a box and allows them to be visually distinguished as a group. There are three kinds of row groups: the ordinary group, of which there can be as many as desired; the table head, of which there can be at most one, and the table foot, which can also only be used once per table. The latter two behave in a special way: a table head group, if present, will always be shown above any other rows, and a foot will always be shown after any other rows.

Furthermore, if a table is so large that it is broken among several pages, the head and foot will be repeated on each page.

Here is an example of a table with three row groups, visually delimited by a thick line between them. The style sheet was:

```
TBODY {border-bottom: thick; border-top: thick}
```

and the HTML source:

```
<TABLE>
  <TBODY CLASS=nov>
    <TR><TH>1-10 <TD> 45 <TD> 67 <TD> 34
    <TR><TH>11-20 <TD> 54 <TD> 76 <TD> 43
    <TR><TH>21-30 <TD> 57 <TD> 78 <TD> 23
  <TBODY CLASS=dec>
    <TR><TH>1-10 <TD> 57 <TD> 67 <TD>84
    <TR><TH>11-20 <TD> 75 <TD> 56 <TD>85
    <TR><TH>21-31 <TD> 75 <TD> 91 <TD>48
  <TBODY CLASS=jan>
    <TR><TH>1-10 <TD> 72 <TD> 64 <TD>85
    <TR><TH>11-20 <TD> 35 <TD> 63 <TD>87
    <TR><TH>21-31 <TD> 71 <TD> 19 <TD>38
<TABLE>
```

1-10	45	67	34
11-20	54	76	43
21-30	57	78	23
1-10	57	67	84
11-20	75	56	85
21-31	75	91	48
1-10	72	64	85
11-20	35	63	87
21-31	71	19	38

Figure 19.3 A table with three table bodies with thick rules above and below.

Tables can also have column and column group elements, which can be used by the style sheet to visually distinguish columns. The next section shows an example of a table with all the optional parts. We'll use it to explain the "collapsing borders" model.

THE COLLAPSING BORDERS MODEL

The first of the two methods for setting borders on tables allows you to set borders on all parts of a table: the outer edge of the table itself, each of the rows, columns, groups of rows and columns, and of course the cells themselves. However, no matter how many style rules you write, there will in the end only be one border between every pair of cells or on the outside of the table.

For example, if you specify a border style for the rows, for the cells and for the row groups, then there will be places in the table where all three of these declarations apply. The border that is drawn there is the one that is the "strongest," in the sense of the most visible. For example, if these are the style rules:

```
TBODY { border: thick double }
TR { border: medium solid }
TD { border: medium dotted }
```

then the strongest is the **`thick double`**, next is the **`medium solid`**, and the weakest is the **`medium dotted`**. The result is that there will be a dotted line between all cells, and a solid line between all rows, except at the edge of a row group (TBODY), where the border will be a thick double line.

Thicker lines are stronger than thinner lines, and double lines are stronger than single ones, which are in turn stronger than dashed lines, and dotted lines. The "3D" styles (ridge, outset, groove, and inset) are the weakest of all, but that is because they are more commonly used with the separated borders model, explained further down. If the specified styles for the cells, rows, columns, etc., differ *only* in color, then a different rule is applied: the cell's border style wins over the row, row over row group, and so on in the following order: cell, row, row group, column, column group, and table.

Here is an example of a complex table. We will use it in several examples in the following sections. First the HTML code:

```
<TABLE SUMMARY="The count of things each person saw,
  organized by thing, time of day and person">
<CAPTION>What we saw on our trip
  to the beach</CAPTION>
<COLGROUP>
  <COL CLASS=when><COL CLASS=who>
<COLGROUP>
  <COL CLASS=dog><COL CLASS=cat><COL CLASS=croco>
<COLGROUP>
  <COL CLASS=bak><COL CLASS=ant><COL CLASS=book>
<COLGROUP>
  <COL CLASS=yel><COL CLASS=pur><COL CLASS=blk>
<THEAD>
  <TH> <TH> <TH COLSPAN=3>Animals
    <TH COLSPAN=3>Shops <TH COLSPAN=3>Cars
  <TR><TH>When? <TH>Who?
    <TH>Dogs <TH>Cats <TH>Crocodiles
    <TH>Bakeries <TH>Antiques <TH>Book
    <TH>Yellow <TH>Purple <TH>Black
</THEAD>
<TBODY>
  <TR><TH ROWSPAN=3>Morning
    <TH>Judy
    <TD>4 <TD>0 <TD>0
    <TD>4 <TD>6 <TD>2
    <TD>0 <TD>0 <TD>5
  <TR><TH>Alan
    <TD>3 <TD>1 <TD>0
    <TD>3 <TD>2 <TD>1
```

```
             <TD>1 <TD>0 <TD>2
        <TR><TH>Tim
          <TD>2 <TD>0 <TD>2
          <TD>2 <TD>1 <TD>7
          <TD>0 <TD>0 <TD>1
      </TBODY>
      <TBODY>
        <TR><TH ROWSPAN=3>Afternoon
          <TH>Judy
          <TD>2 <TD>1 <TD>0
          <TD>4 <TD>2 <TD>2
          <TD>0 <TD>1 <TD>1
        <TR><TH>Alan
          <TD>2 <TD>1 <TD>0
          <TD>1 <TD>2 <TD>3
          <TD>0 <TD>0 <TD>1
        <TR><TH>Tim
          <TD>4 <TD>4 <TD>1
          <TD>3 <TD>3 <TD>6
          <TD>1 <TD>1 <TD>5
      </TBODY>
    </TABLE>
```

We'll first show a style that uses only borders to indicate the way the information is grouped: a thick double border below the headings, a thick border underneath the groups of rows, and a thin border between the groups of columns (Table 19.1):

| When? | Who? | Animals | | | Shops | | | Cars | | |
		Dogs	Cats	Crocodiles	Bakeries	Antiques	Books	Yellow	Purple	Black
Morning	Judy	4	0	0	4	6	2	0	0	4
	Alan	3	1	0	3	2	1	1	0	2
	Tim	2	0	2	2	1	7	0	0	1
Afternoon	Judy	2	1	0	4	2	2	0	1	1
	Alan	2	1	0	1	2	3	0	0	1
	Tim	4	4	1	3	3	6	1	1	5

Table 19.1 What we saw on our trip to the beach.

The style sheet that draws these borders is rather simple:

```
COLGROUP { border-left: thin solid }
THEAD { border-bottom: thick double }
TBODY { border-bottom: thick solid }
TABLE { border: hidden }
TH { text-align: left }
```

We've thrown in a `text-align: left`, because it looks better than the default style for HTML, which centers all TH elements. But the real trick is in the 4th line. The border style **hidden** is a "style" that is peculiar to tables, and in fact to the "collapsing borders" method of creating borders.

If you look at the first line, you'll see that there is a thin rule specified for the left side of all column groups. But we don't want a rule on the left side of the first column group. The **hidden** style gets rid of that extra border. Because this border is shared with the table itself, we can set a style on the table that overrides the border. The same happens with the third rule: setting a thick rule below the row groups will produce one rule too many, but the **hidden** style on the table will take it away.

Setting the style to **none** wouldn't have helped, because **none** is the weakest style of all. In fact, all cells implicitly have a `border: none`, but any other border style will override that.

THE SEPARATED BORDERS MODEL

In the separated borders model, you can only set borders on cells, and on the table itself, not on rows, columns, or groups of rows or columns. Every cell has its own borders, so there are never any conflicts. This method is not so easy if you want to visually delimit row or column groups with borders, but it works well for the "3D" border styles, especially **inset** and **outset**. Here is an example (Figure 19.4):

```
TABLE { border-collapse: separate;
    border: 2mm outset; cell-spacing: 2mm }
TD, TH { border: 1mm inset }
```

Figure 19.4 A table with "3D" borders and cell spacing.

This makes use of the **cell-spacing** property, which only works for the separated borders model. Note also that the **border-collapse** property must be set on the TABLE element.

Name:	**border-collapse**
Value:	collapse | separate
Initial:	collapse
Applies to:	tables and inline tables
Inherited:	yes
Percentages:	N/A

The **border-collapse** property determines what border model a table uses. If all tables in a document use the same model (which they usually do), then you can set the property most easily on the BODY element, and all tables will inherit it.

Name:	**border-spacing**
Value:	*<length> <length>?*
Initial:	0
Applies to:	tables and inline tables
Inherited:	yes
Percentages:	N/A

border-spacing is only used by tables with the separated borders model. It determines the space between every pair of borders. You cannot set it on individual cells. Whatever the value of **border-spacing** is for the table element, it is used throughout the table. You can, however, set different values for the space between vertical borders and between horizontal borders. If the property has only one value, it will be used for both horizontal and vertical spacing. If it has two, the first gives the horizontal space (between columns) and the second the vertical space (between rows).

Borders for empty cells

Name:	**empty-cells**
Value:	show | hide
Initial:	show
Applies to:	table cells
Inherited:	yes
Percentages:	N/A

The separated borders model distinguishes between empty cells and non-empty cells. Normally borders are drawn around all cells, but the **empty-cells** property makes it possible to suppress borders if the cell has no content. This property can be set for each cell individually, but usually you would set it on the table, or even on the BODY element, to apply to the whole document. Figure 19.5 shows the effect.

Figure 19.5 The effect of the **empty-cells** property.

`empty-cells: show`   `empty-cells: hide`

ALIGNMENT

In normal paragraphs, text can be aligned on the left, right, or center, or can be justified, by setting the **text-align** property. Text in table cells can be aligned in the same way, but in tables another type of alignment is possible: all cells in a column aligned on their decimal point. In fact, CSS allows you to align on any character (or even words), not just on the decimal point.

The content of cells can also be aligned vertically across rows, since the contents of cells are not necessarily the same height, but the cells are. The **vertical-align** property, which otherwise determines the vertical position of words in a line, can also be applied to table cells, to align the contents of cells in a row.

See page 162 for the full definition of **text-align**; here we only explain how to align columns on a decimal point or other shared character.

If the **text-align** property for a certain cell is set to a string, for example the decimal point, then the contents of the cell are aligned as follows: in all cells in the column that have a string as value of the **text-align** property, the string is found in the text of the cell, and an imaginary vertical line is drawn just in front of that string. Then the contents of those cells are moved left or right until the vertical lines are exactly below each other. If the string is not found in the text, then the vertical line is drawn after the text.

This alignment only works if the content of the cell fits on one line. If the contents have to be broken over several lines, then the cell will not be aligned on the given character or string, but will simply be left-aligned (or right-aligned, in a right-to-left language).

Let's look at an example (Figure 19.6). Here is a fictional train schedule, where the times need to align on the colon (:):

Nice	6:50 A	7:20	9:50	10:20	10:50 B,C
Villeneuve	6:59	|	9:59	|	10:59
Biot	7:10	|	10:10	|	11:10
Antibes	7:16	7:48*	10:16	10:48*	11:16 A
Cannes	7:31	8:03	10:31	11:03	11:31
St. Rafael	7:52	8:26	10:52	11:26	11:52

Figure 19.6 A table showing cells that are aligned on a text string, in this case the string ":".

The style sheet for this table aligned the header cells to the left, and the data cells on their colons:

```
TH { text-align: left }
TD { text-align: ":" }
```

Note that the four cells that don't have a colon are aligned as if they had a colon after the vertical bar.

Of the **vertical-align** property, only the values **`baseline`**, **`top`**, **`bottom`** and **`middle`** apply to table cells. The initial value, **`baseline`**, ensures that the baseline of the first text line in a cell lines up with the first baseline of all other cells in the row that have their **vertical-align** property set to **`baseline`**. Figure 19.7 shows the four different alignments.

Some text over two lines	Some text over three lines	Large text	small text	Baseline
Some text over two lines	Some text over three lines	Large text	small text	Top
Some text over two lines	Some text over three lines	Large text	small text	Middle
Some text over two lines	Some text over three lines	Large text	small text	Bottom

Figure 19.7 A table showing the four vertical alignments applicable to table cells: from top to bottom: **`baseline`**, **`top`**, **`middle`**, and **`bottom`**.

SIZES

Browsers normally determine the width and height of each cell automatically, finding a balance between the available width for the whole table and the widths of the individual columns. Most browsers follow a recipe similar to the following:

1 Try to format each cell without introducing line breaks. If the resulting table fits between the margins of the table's parent, then this will be the final layout.
2 If the table won't fit without adding line breaks in the cells' content, try first to make the table exactly as wide as the parent's margins allow. If the cells' content can be broken into lines so that the table fits, then this will be the chosen layout.
3 If there is no possibility to make the table narrow enough to fit in the parent, then make each column as narrow as possible, and let the table stick out on the right.

This will usually result in a reasonable table, but seldom a beautiful one. If you want a certain column to take more space, at the cost of another, or if you want several columns to be the same width, you'll have to set the **width** property of some cells or columns.

Setting the **width** property on a cell or column has a slightly different effect than on other elements. On normal elements, it sets the exact width, on table cells and columns it sets the minimum width. If the content of a normal element is too wide for the specified value of **width**, the content will stick out and overlap the border (see the **overflow** property, page 210). But if the content of a table cell is too wide for the given **width**, the width itself will be increased, and that of all other cells in the column as well.

If different cells in the same column have different **width**s, the maximum width will be used. The width of a cell that spans several columns will impose a minimum on the sum of the widths of the columns it spans.

If you set the **width** property on the TABLE element itself, that, also, will act as a minimum width: if the columns together require more than the specified width of the table, the table's width will be increased. On the other hand, if the specified width is larger than what the columns require, the columns are made wider. This is often used to make a table as wide as its parent (or wider):

```
<STYLE>
  TABLE {width: 100%}
  TD {border: thin solid}
</STYLE>
  ...
```

```
<TABLE>
  <TR><TD>This <TD>table <TD>needs
  <TR><TD>only <TD>little <TD>space
</TABLE>
```

which is rendered as a full-width table:

This	table	needs
only	little	space

You can use percentages for the widths of cells or columns, and the browser will try to make that column as wide as specified. But since it is possible to create circular dependencies (the width of the columns is a percentage of the table's width, but the table's width depends on the columns), browsers may choose to handle only the most simple cases, e.g., when the table's width is given explicitly and is larger than the minimum required width.

Be careful when using percentages, since it is easy to forget the borders and padding. Setting the column widths of a 4-column table to 25% only makes sense if the borders and padding are 0, otherwise the sum of the widths will be more than 100%, which is obviously impossible. Here is an example with percentages:

```
TABLE {border-collapse: separate; cell-spacing: 4%}
TD {width: 20%}
```

This will work for a 4-column table. The four columns and the five spacing areas together add up to 100%. However, if you want your columns to be all the same width, the easier way is to use the fast size algorithm below.

Fast size

IE3	NS4	IE4	O3.5		
○	○	○	○	*Name:*	**table-layout**
				Value:	auto | fixed
				Initial:	auto
				Applies to:	tables and inline tables
				Inherited:	no
				Percentages:	N/A

If the table is simple and sufficiently regular that you can set the size of each column explicitly and be sure that the sizes are wide enough, then you can tell the browser to use your sizes directly, without checking each cell's minimum requirements. The advantage is that the browser gains time. It can start formatting and displaying the first row, using the column widths that you gave in the style sheet, without waiting for the rest of the table.

Of course, any failures are the designer's responsibility. If a cell can't be made narrow enough to fit the preset width, results are undefined. Usually some text will end up overlapping the text in the next cell.

The property that controls whether the browser uses the fast mode is **table-layout**. Not all browsers will look at this property; some will use the normal mode anyway, deeming it fast enough. Here is an example of a style sheet using the fast table algorithm. It creates a table with a preset width and all columns the same width:

```
TABLE {table-layout: fixed: width: 100%}
```

Two conditions must be met before the fast algorithm can be used: **table-layout** must be **fixed**, and **width** must *not* be **auto**, both on the table element. If these two properties are set as required on the table element, the widths of the columns are computed after the first row, without waiting for the other rows. First all the column elements are inspected (elements COL in HTML). If there are any with a **width** property other than **auto**, their columns will have the indicated width. For the other columns, the **width** property of the cells in the first row is checked. If there are any **width** properties that are not **auto**, their value will be used for the columns. If there aren't any columns left without a width, then the **width** of the table element is not used, and the width of the table is instead computed from the column widths, plus any paddings and borders. Otherwise, the columns that don't have a width yet will divide the remaining space.

That leads to three possible situations:

1 All columns have an explicit width, e.g.:

```
TABLE {table-layout: fixed; width: 100%}
COL {width: 4.5em}
```

If we apply this to our large "trip to the beach" table (page 340–341), which has 11 columns, we get a table of 49.5 em plus any borders and paddings. The **width** property of the TABLE is ignored (although it has to be set to something; if you set it to **auto**, the fast algorithm will not be used).

2 Only some columns have an explicit width, e.g.:

```
TABLE {table-layout: fixed; width: 50em}
COL.when, COL.who {width: 4em}
```

Applied to the same table, this will make the first two columns 4em wide, and the remaining columns will equally divide the remaining space. Assuming three borders of 0.1 em and padding for all cells of

0.3em, that will leave 42em − 3 × 0.1 em − 22 × 0.3em = 35.1em for the remaining nine columns, or 3.9em for each column.

3 No columns have an explicit width, e.g.:

```
TABLE {table-layout: fixed; width: 55em}
```

This will make all columns equally wide. You may not be interested in the exact width of the columns, but if you wish, it can be computed: using the same example as above, the columns will be (55em − 3 × 0.1 em − 22 × 0.3em)/11 = 48.1 em/11 ≈ 4.4em.

SETTING BACKGROUND COLORS

All parts of a table have a background. The initial value of **background** is `transparent`, but all elements, cells, rows, row groups, columns, column groups, and of course the table itself, can be given a color and a background image. Here is an example in which a row, a column, and a cell have been given a background color:

```
<TABLE>
  <COL CLASS="a"><COL CLASS="b">
    <COL CLASS="c"><COL CLASS="d">
  <TR CLASS="a"><TD>aa <TD>ab <TD>ac <TD>ad
  <TR CLASS="b"><TD ID="c1">ba <TD>bb <TD>bc <TD>bd
  <TR CLASS="c"><TD>ca <TD>cb <TD>cc <TD>cd
  <TR CLASS="d"><TD>da <TD>db <TD>dc <TD>dd
</TABLE>
```

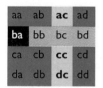

Figure 19.8

with the style sheet:

```
TABLE {background: green}
COL.c {background: rgb(191,191,191)}
TR.b {background: rgb(255,170,0)}
#c1 {background: black; color: white}
TD {padding: 0.25em}
```

As Figure 19.8 shows, the background of the table is hidden by the column background, which in turn is hidden by the row. The cell is on top of everything.

Column groups (COLGROUP) and row groups (THEAD, TFOOT, TBODY) can also be given backgrounds. Column groups are in front of the table background, but behind the columns, row groups are in front of columns and behind rows.

"COLLAPSING" COLUMNS AND ROWS

The **visibility** property has a special value, **collapse**, that only applies to columns. It is primarily meant to be used by scripts that dynamically expand and collapse columns. Browsers that don't support a scripting language are not likely to support it.

When the **visibility** property of a column is set to **collapse**, the width of all the columns is computed including this column, but then the column is not displayed, and the width of the table is reduced by the width of this column. The other columns are shifted sideways to fill the gap. The idea is that inserting and removing columns is much quicker if the browser only has to move the other columns and not recompute their width every time.

When a column has **visibility** set to **collapse**, the column is hidden without regard for what is in it. If there are cells that span several columns, the part of their content that is in the collapsed column is simply clipped. Borders may also be cut in half.

The **collapse** value doesn't apply to rows. To hide rows, use the **display** property with value **none**.

INLINE TABLES

By default, tables in HTML are displayed as blocks: they end the previous paragraph, and any text after it will be in a new paragraph. However, CSS also supports inline tables, that will not break the line, but are displayed in the sentence in which they occur. Here is how that looks:

> Magic squares are formed by placing the numbers 1, 2, 3, etc. in a square grid, in such a way that the sum of the numbers in all rows and all columns is the same. A magic square with 9 cells, such as
>
> this:
>
> | 3 | 5 | 7 |
> |---|---|---|
> | 4 | 9 | 2 |
> | 8 | 1 | 6 |
>
> has a sum of 15 for every row and every column.
> Try it with squares of 16 or 25 cells!

Tables are put inline with the **display** property:

```
TABLE { display: inline-table }
```

XML AND TABLES

At the start of this chapter, we showed the various parts of a table in HTML. The same parts can occur in an XML-based format, but in that case the browser probably has no built-in knowledge about which XML element corresponds to which part of the table. To help with that, the **display** property has keywords for each of the parts. The keywords are:

- **table** (corresponding to TABLE in HTML). Specifies that an element defines a block-level table.
- **inline-table** (doesn't exist in HTML). Like **table**, but the table doesn't start on a new line. Instead, it is placed inline.
- **table-row** (In HTML: TR). Specifies that an element is a row of cells.
- **table-row-group** (In HTML: TBODY). Specifies that an element groups one or more rows.
- **table-header-group** (In HTML: THEAD). Like **table-row-group**, but wherever it occurs in the table, it is always displayed before all other rows and rowgroups (but after any captions). On printed pages, the header group is often repeated on each page, in case the table is too long for one page.
- **table-footer-group** (In HTML: TFOOT). Like **table-row-group**, but it is always displayed after all other rows and rowgroups (but before captions). Like **table-header-group**, this element is often repeated at the bottom of all pages, if a long table is printed.
- **table-column** (In HTML: COL). Specifies that an element describes a column of cells. Column elements cannot have content, but they may be useful for setting column widths, borders and backgrounds.
- **table-column-group** (In HTML: COLGROUP). Specifies that an element groups one or more columns.
- **table-cell** (In HTML: TD, TH). Specifies that an element represents a table cell.
- **table-caption** (In HTML: CAPTION). Specifies a caption for the table.

For example, if some document contained markup similar to this:

```
<timetable>
    <title>
        Airport bus time table
        <from>Black Lake Hotel</from>
        <to>Pine International Airport</to>
    </title>
    <fields>
        <bus>Bus no.</bus>
        <dep>Departure time</dep>
```

```
        <tim>Journey time</tim>
        <ar2>Arrival terminal 2</ar2>
        <ar1>Arrival terminal 1</ar1>
    </fields>
    <rec>
        <bus>501</bus>
        <dep>06:25</dep>
        <tim>85 min.</tim>
        <ar2>07:50</ar2>
        <ar1>08:00</ar1>
    </rec>
    <rec>
        <bus>301</bus>
        <dep>06:50</dep>
        <tim>140 min.</tim>
        <ar2>09:10</ar2>
        <ar1>09:20</ar1>
    </rec>
...
    <rec>
        <bus>515</bus>
        <dep>17:55</dep>
        <tim>115 min.</tim>
        <ar2>19:50</ar2>
        <ar1>20:00</ar1>
    </rec>
</timetable>
```

a good way to present this information is in tabular form. The <timetable> element will become a table, <field> is a heading row, and <rec> is a normal row, etc. A skeleton of a style sheet could be as follows:

```
timetable {display: table}
fields {display: table-header-group}
rec {display: table-row}
bus, dep, tim, ar2, ar1 {display: table-cell}
title {display: table-caption}
```

This is enough to display the data in tabular form. We will flesh out the skeleton below with some padding and other style properties, to make it look better, but let's first take a look at why this works. If you look closely, you will see that not all of the parts of a table are present. For example, <fields> has been made a **table-header-group** (corresponding to the THEAD in HTML), and its children are **table-cell** (like TH/TD in HTML), but there is no row element to contain those cells.

The table model of CSS allows many elements to be omitted. Where necessary, they will be automatically inserted. In the above style sheet, the `table-row` that must enclose the children of <fields> is automatically inserted between the <fields> element and its children. It is created as a so-called "anonymous box," which means it has no corresponding element in the source document, and no name, and hence, that you cannot set properties on it. You can tell its presence indirectly, because the cells are correctly lined up in a row, but you cannot make the row box itself visible.

Let's add a few more properties, to make the table easier to read: some horizontal rules, padding, etc. The result is shown in Table 19.2.

```
title {font-style: italic}
fields {font-weight: bold;
    border-bottom: medium solid}
rec {border-bottom: thin solid black}
bus, dep, tim, ar2, ar1 {padding: 0.5em}
to:before {content: " - "}
```

Airport bus timetable Black Lake Hotel – Pine International Airport

Bus no.	Departure time	Journey time	Arrival terminal 2	Arrival terminal 1
501	06:25	85 min.	07:50	08:00
301	06:50	140 min.	09:10	09:20
…				
515	17:55	115 min.	19:50	20:00

Table 19.2 XML table example.

Because CSS automatically inserts missing elements in a table, it is sometimes possible to use the table layout for something that, at first sight, doesn't look like a table at all. For example, the following (hypothetical) mark-up could be rendered as a table:

```
<scene-list>
    <scene><name>Opening scene</name>
        <item>Camera 1 left</item>
        <item>Camera 2 on rails</item>
        <item>Camera 3 close-up</item>
    </scene>
    <scene><name>Balcony scene</name>
        <item>Camera 1 left</item>
        <item>Camera 2 close-up</item>
    </scene>
</scene-list>
```

We can align the cameras in columns:

```
scene-list {display: table}
scene {display: table-row}
name, item {display: table-cell;
    border: thin solid; padding: 0.5em}
name {font-weight: bolder}
```

Opening scene	Camera 1 left	Camera 2 on rails	Camera 3 close up
Balcony scene	Camera 1 left	Camera 2 close-up	

Figure 19.9 A table created from a list.

Chapter 20

The CSS saga

The saga of CSS starts in 1994. One of the authors of this book works at CERN – the cradle of the Web – and the Web is starting to be used as a platform for electronic publishing. One crucial part of a publishing platform is missing, however: there is no way to style documents. For example, there is no way to describe a newspaper-like layout in a Web page. Having worked on personalized newspaper presentations at the MIT Media Laboratory, Håkon saw the need for a style sheet language for the Web.

Style sheets in browsers were not an entirely new idea. The separation of document structure from the document's layout had been a goal of HTML from its inception in 1990. Tim Berners-Lee wrote his NeXT browser/editor in such a way that he could determine the style with a simple style sheet. However, he didn't publish the syntax for the style sheets, considering it a matter for each browser to decide how to best display pages to its users. Other browsers, including Pei Wei's Viola (1992) and the Harmony browser (1993), for the Hyper-G system had comparable style languages.

The Hyper-G system was one of the Web's early competitors). See, e.g., http://www.igd.fhg.de/www/www95/proceedings/papers/105/hgw3.html

But instead of more advanced style sheets, the browsers that followed offered their users fewer and fewer options to influence the style. In 1993, NCSA Mosaic, the browser which made the Web popular, came out. Style-wise, however, it was a backwards step as it only allowed its users to change certain colors and fonts.

The message is available from the www-talk archive at http://ksi.cpsc.ucalgary.ca/ archives/WWW-TALK/ www-talk-1994q1.messages/ 643.html

Meanwhile, writers of Web pages were complaining that they didn't have enough influence over how their pages looked. One of the first questions from an author new to the Web was how to change fonts and colors of elements. HTML at that time did not provide this functionality – and rightfully so. This excerpt from a message sent to the *www-talk* mailing list early in 1994, gives a sense of the tensions between authors and implementors:

```
In fact, it has been a constant source of delight
for me over the past year to get to continually
tell hordes (literally) of people who want to -
- strap yourselves in, here it comes -- control
what their documents look like in ways that would
be trivial in TeX, Microsoft Word, and every
other common text processing environment:
"Sorry, you're screwed."
```

The author of the message was Marc Andreessen, one of the programmers behind NCSA Mosaic. He later became a co-founder of Netscape and by then his views – if they ever were his views – on formatting had changed. On October 13, 1994 Marc Andreessen announced to *www-talk* that the first beta release of Mozilla (which later turned into Netscape Navigator) was available for testing. Among the new tags the new browser supported was CENTER and more tags were to follow shortly.

The original is online at http://www.w3.org/People/ howcome/p/cascade.html

The "Mosaic and the Web" conference was held on October 17–20, 1995. It was the second conference in what has later become the WWW Conference Series.

The Argo browser was part of a project to make the Internet accessible to scholars in the Humanities. It featured plug-ins (which it called "applets") before Netscape added them. See http://www.let.rug.nl/ %7Ebert/Stylesheets/ and http://www.let.rug.nl/~bert/ argo.html

Three days before Netscape announced the availability of its new browser, Håkon published the first draft of *Cascading HTML Style Sheets*. Behind the scenes, Dave Raggett (the main architect of HTML 3.0) had encouraged the release of the draft to go out before the upcoming "Mosaic and the Web" conference in Chicago. Dave had realized that HTML would and should never turn into a page description language and that a more purpose-built mechanism was needed to satisfy requirements from authors. Although the first version of the document was immature, it provided a useful basis for discussion.

Among the people who responded to the first draft of CSS was Bert Bos, the co-author of this book. At that time he was building Argo, a highly customizable browser with style sheets and he decided to join forces with Håkon. Both of the two proposals look different from present-day CSS, but it is not hard to recognize the original concepts.

One of the features of the Argo style language was that it was general enough to apply to other markup languages in addition to HTML. This also became a design goal in CSS and "HTML" was soon removed from the title of the specification. Argo also had other advanced features that didn't make it into CSS level 1, in particular attribute selectors and generated text. Both features had to wait for CSS2.

Robert Raisch's message to www-talk is at http://ksi.cpsc.ucalgary.ca/archives/WWW-TALK/www-talk-1993q2.messages/443.html

"Cascading Style Sheets" wasn't the only proposed style language at the time. There was Pei Wei's language from the Viola browser, and Robert Raisch of the publishing house O'Reilly had written another, as early as June 1993. And then there was DSSSL, a complex style and transformation language under development at ISO for printing SGML documents. DSSSL could conceivably be applied to HTML as well. But CSS had one feature that distinguished it from all the others: it took into account that on the Web the style of a document couldn't be designed by either the author or the reader on their own, but that their wishes had to be combined, or "cascaded," in some way; and, in fact, not just the reader's and the author's wishes, but also the capabilities of the display device and the browser.

As planned, the initial CSS proposal was presented at the Web conference in Chicago in November 1994. The presentation at Developer's Day caused a lot of discussion. First, the concept of a balance between author and user preferences was novel. A fictitious screen shot showed a slider with the label "user" on one side and "author" on the other. By adjusting the slider, the user could change the mix of his own preferences and those of the author. Second, CSS was perceived by some as being too simple for the task it was designed for. They argued that in order to style documents, the power of a full programming language was needed. CSS went in the exact opposite direction by making a point out of being a simple, declarative format.

WWW3, the third conference in the WWW series, was held on April 10–14, 1995 in Darmstadt, Germany.

At the next WWW conference in April 1995, CSS was again presented. Both Bert and Håkon were there (in fact, this was the first time we met in person) and this time we could also show implementations. Bert presented the support for style sheets in Argo and Håkon showed a version of the Arena browser which had been modified to support CSS. Arena had been written by Dave Raggett as a testbed for new ideas and one of them was style sheets. What started out as technical presentations ended up in political discussions about the author–reader balance. Representatives from the "author" side argued that the author ultimately had to be in charge of deciding how documents were presented. For example – it was argued – that there may be legal requirements on how warning labels has to be printed and the user should not be able to reduce the font size for such warnings. The other side, where the authors of this book belong, argued that the user, whose eyes and ears ultimately have to decode the presentation, should be given the last word when there are conflicts.

See http://www.w3.org/Mail/Lists#www-style

Outside of the political battles, the technical work continued. The *www-style* mailing list was created in May 1995, and the discussions there have often influenced the development of the CSS specifications. Three years later there were already more than 4,000 messages in the archives of the mailing list.

In 1995 the World Wide Web Consortium (W3C) also became operational. Companies were joining the Consortium at a high rate and the organization became established. Workshops on various topics were found to be a successful way for W3C Members and Staff to meet and discuss future technical development. It was therefore decided that another workshop should be organized, this time with Style Sheets as the topic. The W3C technical staff working on style sheets (namely the two authors of this book) were now located in Sophia-Antipolis in Southern France where W3C had set up its European site. Southern France is not the worst place to lure workshop participants to, but since many of the potential participants were in the US it was decided to hold the workshop in Paris, which is better served by international flights. The workshop was also an experiment to see if it was possible for W3C to organize events outside the US. Indeed, this turned out to be possible and the workshop was a milestone in ensuring style sheets their rightful place on the Web. Among the participants was Thomas Reardon of Microsoft who pledged support for CSS in upcoming versions of Internet Explorer.

At the end of 1995, W3C set up the HTML Editorial Review Board (HTML ERB) to ratify future HTML specifications. Since style sheets were within the sphere of interest of the members of the new group, the CSS specification was taken up as a work item with the goal of making it into a Recommendation. Among the members of the HTML ERB was Lou Montulli of Netscape. After Microsoft had signalled that it was adding CSS support in its browser, it was important also to get Netscape on board. Otherwise, we could see the Web diverge in different directions with browsers supporting different specifications. The battles within the HTML ERB were long and hard, but CSS level 1 finally emerged as a W3C Recommendation in December 1996.

In February 1997 CSS got its own working group inside W3C and the new group set out to work on the features which CSS1 didn't address. The group was chaired by Chris Lilley, a Scotsman recruited to W3C from the University of Manchester. CSS level 2 became a Recommendation in May 1998, and level 3 will probably follow towards the end of 1999. In the meantime, not only HTML relies on CSS for its presentation. Many XML-based formats also need CSS, and the browsers that come out in late 1998 show the first, still somewhat limited, steps towards presenting XML data.

The W3C working group, whose official name is "Cascading Style Sheets and Formatting Properties Working Group," since they do more than just CSS, has about 15 members, delegated by the companies and organizations that are members of W3C. They come from all over the world, so the "meetings" are usually over the phone, about an hour every week. About four times per year, they meet somewhere in the world. Recent venues have been Provo, Redmond, San Francisco and Paris. In Paris the meeting was held at the offices of EDF, the French electricity company. At that meeting, the group was offered a superb dinner: French cuisine overlooking Paris and the Seine – one of the few glamourous moments in the history of a hard-working technical working group.

BROWSERS

The CSS saga is not complete without a section on browsers. Had it not been for the browsers, CSS would have remained a lofty proposal of only academic interest. The first commercial browser to support CSS was Microsoft's Internet Explorer 3 which was released in August 1996. At that point, the CSS1 specification had not yet become a W3C Recommendation and discussions within the HTML ERB were to result in changes that Microsoft developers, led by Chris Wilson, could not foresee. IE3 reliably supports most of the color, background, font and text properties, but does not implement much of the box model.

The next browser to announce support was Netscape's Navigator, version 4.0. Since its inception Netscape had been sceptical towards style sheets, and the company's first implementation turned out to be a half-hearted attempt to stop Microsoft from claiming to be more standards-compliant than themselves. The Netscape implementation supports a broad range of features – for example, floating elements – but the Netscape developers did not have time to fully test all the features which are supposedly supported. The result is that many CSS properties cannot be used in Navigator 4.

Netscape implemented CSS internally by translating CSS rules into snippets of Javascript, which were then run along with other scripts. The company also decided to let developers write JSSS, thereby bypassing CSS entirely. If JSSS had been successful, the Web would have had one more style sheet than necessary. This, fortunately for CSS, turned out not to be the case.

Meanwhile Microsoft continued its efforts to replace Netscape from the throne of reigning browsers. In Internet Explorer 4 the browser display engine – which among other things is responsible for rendering CSS – was replaced by a module code-named "Trident." Trident removed many of the limitations in IE3, but also came with its own set of limitations and bugs. IE4 does not fully support CSS1 – something that the Web Standards Project (WaSP) highlighted in November 1998 when they published "IE's Top 10 CSS Problems" (Figure 20.1).

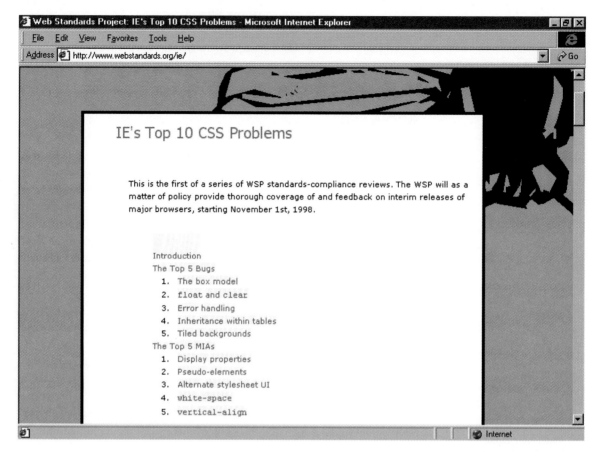

Figure 20.1 The WaSP project tracks browser conformance to W3C Recommendations. One of their first reviews was the CSS support in Microsoft Internet Explorer.

In addition to displaying static documents Trident is also capable of dynamically changing stylistic properties. For example, elements can be animated on the screen by continuously changing their top and left properties thus creating "Dynamic HTML" (DHTML). In principle, DHTML is very similar to JSSS (they both use scripting languages to set stylistic properties) but DHTML was never marketed as an alternative style sheet language. Indeed, CSS is an integral part of DHTML.

The third browser which ventured into CSS was Opera. The browser from the small Norwegian company made headlines in 1998 by being tiny (it fits on a floppy) and customizable while supporting most features found in the larger offerings from Microsoft and Netscape. Opera 3.5 was released in November 1998 and it supports most of CSS1. The Opera developers (namely Geir Ivarsøy) have also found the time to test their implementation before shipping it. The CSS1 test suite, developed by Eric Meyer with help from countless other volunteers, has made it significantly easier for implementors to test and improve their products.

As this text is being written, both Netscape and Microsoft are also working hard to get their next browsers out the door. Netscape has decided to replace the display engine in Navigator with "nglayout," which has been written from scratch with CSS as one of the foundations. Their new browser is code-named "Gecko" and you can download beta versions from http://www.mozilla.org. Microsoft has been releasing preview versions of Internet Explorer 5. Some CSS improvements are already in place, and it is expected that the WaSP initiative will remind the company that there is still some work to do before CSS1 is fully supported.

This book's Web site (http://www.awl.com/css) will have pointers to the latest CSS browsers.

HTML 4.0 quick reference

This appendix gives a brief overview of HTML 4.0. This version of HTML is the first to contain the elements and attributes necessary for effective use of style sheets, in particular style and class. There are, in fact, two versions of HTML 4.0, called HTML 4.0 and HTML 4.0 "Transitional." The latter contains a number of tags (the so-called "extensions") that existed in HTML 3.2, but are now deprecated in favor of style sheets. We will only describe HTML 4.0 below, which doesn't contain the "extensions."

The text below focusses on the elements that are most useful in combination with a style sheet. Other elements are also mentioned, but with less explanation. For the same reason, not all of the possible attributes are described. The rules for how elements can be nested have been stratified, by leaving out some cases that are allowed in HTML 4.0. The result is much simpler to explain than the full rules, but a little more restrictive.

The text is not a tutorial on HTML. It assumes you've read at least Chapter 1. The purpose of this appendix is merely to list most of the elements of HTML and the rules for combining them.

DOCUMENT STRUCTURE

An HTML 4.0 document consists of elements nested inside other elements. Each element starts with a *start-tag* <...> and ends with an *end-tag* </...>.

In some cases one or both of the tags may be omitted. In general, it is safest always to include both of them. When a document is created with the help of a dedicated HTML editor, the tags will be inserted automatically by the editor.

At the highest level, a document consists of one element, called HTML. Inside that are two elements, HEAD and BODY.

```
<HTML>
<HEAD>...</HEAD>
<BODY>...</BODY>
</HEAD>
```

Elements can have attributes, which have a name and a value, separated by an equals sign (=). The value is enclosed in quotes ("..." or '...'). Attributes are listed only in the start-tag, never in the end-tag:

```
<EM CLASS="surname">
<A REL='copyright' HREF='copy.html'>
```

Element names and attribute names can be spelled with capitals or small letters, and even mixtures of the two. The example above can also be written as:

```
<em class="surname">
<a rel='copyright' href='copy.html'>
```

THE HEAD ELEMENT

The head contains information about the document. It is normally not displayed. The elements that can occur in the HEAD are: BASE, ISINDEX, MAP, META, LINK, STYLE, and SCRIPT.

- TITLE
  There must be exactly one TITLE element. It can contain only text, no other elements. The title is often used in the title bar of a window.
- LINK
  LINK specifies a relationship between the document and some other document. The relationship is a keyword that is put in the REL attribute. The URL of the other document is put in the HREF attribute. There may be zero or more LINK elements. The element has no content and the end-tag must be omitted. The relation "stylesheet" is used to associate a style sheet with a document.

```
<LINK REL="stylesheet"
  HREF="http://place.com/sty/rf.css">
```

- STYLE

  The STYLE element can contain a style sheet, as described in Chapter 2. An attribute TYPE must be added that declares the type of style language, e.g., **`<STYLE TYPE = "text/css">`**.

- META

  The META element is used for attaching various kinds of meta-information about the document. The element has no content and the end-tag must be omitted.

- BASE

  BASE can contain the URL of the document itself or the URL that serves as the base for relative URLs in the document. The URL is included as the value of the HREF attribute. The element has no content and the end-tag must be omitted. Here is an example of a typical HEAD:

```
<HEAD>
<TITLE>The oak tree</TITLE>
<LINK REL="author" HREF="../people/Jones">
<STYLE>
  H1 {font-family: Helvetica, sans-serif}
  BODY {font-family: Bodoni, serif}
</STYLE>
</HEAD>
```

THE BODY ELEMENT

The BODY can contain three types of elements: container elements, bridge elements, and special elements. Container elements are elements that themselves can contain exactly the same elements as the BODY. These elements are used to create divisions, interactive forms, long quotations, and other high-level structures. Bridge elements contain text and text-level elements. Paragraphs and headings are examples of bridge elements. Special elements include lists, tables, and certain elements for interactive forms.

All the elements that can appear in the BODY can appear any number of times. All of them accept these five attributes: CLASS, STYLE, ID, LANG (to indicate the language in which the element is written), and DIR (to indicate the writing direction if it is not clear from the language: ltr is left-to-right, rtl is right-to-left).

Container elements

The container elements are: DIV, BLOCKQUOTE, ADDRESS, FORM, and FIELDSET.

DIV is a general division, such as a chapter, section, abstract or note. It is customary to indicate the type of division in the CLASS attribute, e.g., **<DIV CLASS="verse">**.

BLOCKQUOTE is a quotation consisting of one or more paragraphs.

ADDRESS is a name and/or address, usually after a heading or a block-quote, or at the end of the document, to indicate the author of something.

FORM is a container for an interactive form. The ACTION attribute contains the URL of the server that will process the form. The METHOD attribute contains the method used to send the form data to the server, either "get," "post" or "put."

The FIELDSET element is used to group a part of a form. In addition to all other elements that can occur in BODY, it can also have one LEGEND element in its content, which, if present, must be the first element in the FIELDSET. Browsers can use the FIELDSET to activate a set of form elements together. The LEGEND is a text-level element.

Bridge elements

The bridge elements are: P, H1, H2, H3, H4, H5, H6, and PRE. The P is a normal paragraph. H1 to H6 are headings of different levels. H1 is the most important. PRE means "preformatted." Typically the **white-space** property for this element is set to **pre** (page 156).

Special elements

The special elements are: OL, UL, DL, HR, and TABLE. OL and UL are simple lists. They contain only LI (list item) elements (one or more). The LI element itself acts like a container element: it accepts the same content as the BODY element. UL is typically shown with a bullet as a label, OL typically uses numbered labels. For example (see Figure A.1):

- First item
- Second item

1 First item
2 Second item

Figure A.1 Unordered and ordered lists.

```
<UL>
<LI><P>First item</P></LI>
<LI><P>Second item</P></LI>
</UL>
<OL>
<LI><P>First item</P></LI>
<LI><P>Second item</P></LI>
</OL>
```

DL is a "definition list." It contains one or more definitions, where each definition consists of one or more DT (term) elements, followed by one or more DD (definition) elements. The DT element is like a bridge element: it contains text and text-level elements. The DD is a container: it contains the same elements as BODY.

```
<DL>
  <DT>term A</DT>
  <DD><P>Definition for term A</P></DD>
  <DT>term B1</DT>
  <DT>term B2</DT>
  <DD><P>Definition for terms B1 and B2</P></DD>
</DL>
```

term A
        Definition for term A
term B1
term B2
        Definition for term B1
        and B2

Figure A.2 Definition list.

HR is an element without content and without an end-tag. Its purpose is to separate paragraphs, without grouping them. It is usually rendered as a horizontal rule (hence its name) or simply as white space.

The TABLE element creates a table. A table has a complex structure (see Chapter 19), but the main part consists of rows of cells. The content of the table starts with three optional parts: a CAPTION, a THEAD and a TFOOT (in that order), after that are one or more TBODYs, which contain the actual table.

The CAPTION is a bridge element: it may only contain text and text-level elements. It defines a caption that can be displayed above or below the table.

The THEAD contains the first few rows of the table, those that contain the headings of the columns. Putting those headings in the THEAD allows certain browsers to treat them specially, but they can also be put in the table's body. TFOOT also contains column headings, possibly the same, but meant to be put at the bottom of the columns. For small tables, it is OK to omit the TFOOT and put any headings directly in the table's body.

The table's body is contained in one or more TBODY elements. In large tables, rows can be grouped together into multiple TBODYs. For small tables a single TBODY suffices.

THEAD, TFOOT and TBODY all have the same structure: they contain one or more TR elements (Table Row). Each TR contains zero or more table cells.

There are two types of table cells: TH and TD. The former is for table headings, the latter for table data. TH and TD act like containers: they can contain the same elements as the BODY element. TH and TD can have two attributes: COLSPAN and ROWSPAN. They indicate, respectively, how many columns and how many rows the cell spans. Default is 1.

Here is an example of a simple table (to make it easier to read, all end-tags are omitted; this is allowed according to HTML 4.0):

	year 1996			
	Q1	Q2	Q3	Q4
cars	365	320	258	191
bicycles	165	208	358	391
trains	35	45	53	72

Figure A.3

```
<TABLE STYLE="border: solid">
  <TBODY>
    <TR>
      <TH ROWSPAN=2>
      <TH COLSPAN=4><P>year 1996
    <TR>
      <TH><P>Q1
      <TH><P>Q2
      <TH><P>Q3
      <TH><P>Q4
    <TR>
      <TH><P>cars
      <TD><P>365
      <TD><P>320
      <TD><P>258
      <TD><P>191
    <TR>
      <TH><P>bicycles
      <TD><P>165
      <TD><P>208
      <TD><P>358
      <TD><P>391
    <TR>
      <TH><P>trains
      <TD><P>35
      <TD><P>45
      <TD><P>53
      <TD><P>72
  </TBODY>
</TABLE>
```

TEXT-LEVEL ELEMENTS

Text-level elements are mixed with text inside the bridge elements and inside the element DT. Text-level elements indicate the function of a certain word or a phrase. Here is an example of a paragraph with text and several text-level elements. Note that text-level elements can be nested inside each other.

A **square** is a rectangle of which all sides are of equal length. *Squares should **not** be used for solving problem A.*

Figure A.4 DFN, EM and STRONG elements.

```
<P>A <DFN>square</DFN> is a rectangle
of which all sides are of equal
length. <EM CLASS="instruction">Squares
should <STRONG>not</STRONG> be used for
solving problem A.</EM></P>
```

All text-level elements accept the attributes CLASS, LANG, DIR and STYLE.

Most text-level elements can be nested inside each other arbitrarily, but a few have restrictions. The unrestricted ones are: ACRONYM, ABBREV, B, BDO, CITE, CODE, DFN, EM, I, KBD, LABEL, Q, SPAN, STRONG, SUB, SUP, VAR, LEGEND. The ones with restrictions are: A, BR, IMG, INPUT, SELECT, TEXTAREA.

Normal text-level elements

EM and STRONG mark words or phrases that need emphasis or strong emphasis. DFN contains a word or term that is being defined. The first occurrence of a new term in a technical document is often marked this way. CODE and KBD are mostly used when talking about computer-related topics. They indicate literal code (such as a word from a program or a command) and literal text to type on the keyboard. VAR indicates a variable, either in a computer program or in a formula. SUB and SUP are for subscripts (like the 2 in H_2O) and superscripts (like the 2 in $E=mc^2$). Although HTML doesn't have support for mathematical formulas, these elements can help create the most simple one.

ACRONYM and ABBREV are used to mark acronyms (abbreviations that are pronounced as a single word, like NATO, NASA, UNICEF, Benelux) and abbreviations (such as USA, viz., i.e., W3C, CSS). Marking them might allow a smart browser to expand them, but it is especially useful for a speech synthesizer.

B and I are used to indicate that words were bold or italic in the text from which the current words are derived. They are useful when the text is converted from a document format that doesn't allow the role of the words to be encoded. For text entered directly in HTML, EM and STRONG are usually better choices.

CITE encloses a bibliographic reference (a type of link that is not a *hyperlink*...), such as (Raggett 1996). Q encloses a short quotation or a word that is used metaphorically. The appropriate quote marks are inserted by the browser; e.g., the sentence: `He said: <Q>Hello!</Q>`.

A LABEL is used in conjunction with a form element (SELECT, TEXTAREA, INPUT, FIELDSET) or with an OBJECT element, to provide a description for it. Usually it occurs quite near that other element. It has an extra attribute, FOR, that is required and that contains the ID of the element that it is associated with. Typically, in a browser, clicking on a label will activate the element to which it is joined and put the cursor on it.

LEGEND can only occur inside a FIELDSET, and provides a caption for the group of form controls enclosed by the FIELDSET.

The BDO element is needed for certain rare cases that can occur in documents that contain both left-to-right text (such as English) and right-to-left text (such as Hebrew). It stands for Bi-Directional Override. It has a required attribute DIR that is either ltr or rtl. Depending on this attribute, it tells the HTML program that the content is left-to-right or right-to-left, even if the characters inside the element would normally be used in the opposite direction. (Note that this is different from the DIR *attribute* that all elements have, and that only indicates the default direction, for those characters that don't have a definite direction. For more information see the CSS2 specification.)

SPAN is a general purpose element, that can be used when none of the other text-level elements is suitable. It must have either a CLASS attribute to indicate the role of the element, or a STYLE attribute to set a style directly; e.g., to mark people's names, you could do:

```
<SPAN CLASS="person">Berners-Lee</SPAN>.
```

Restricted text-level elements

Restricted text-level elements differ from normal text-level elements in what can be nested inside them. Apart from A, they don't allow other text-level elements in their content.

A is perhaps the most important element of HTML: it is the source anchor of a hyperlink. Besides the normal attributes (CLASS, ID, STYLE, LANG, DIR) it has a required attribute HREF that contains the URL of the target anchor. It accepts all text-level elements in its content, except other A elements.

The BR indicates a forced line break, without starting a new paragraph. It has no content and no end-tag.

The IMG element inserts images and other simple objects. It has a required attribute SRC, that holds the URL of the image, and another required attribute ALT, that can hold a short text that is displayed when the image itself can't be displayed; e.g.: **<IMG SRC="w3c_48x48" ALT="W3C logo">**. The element has no content and no end-tag.

INPUT is an element that is used in interactive forms. It creates a button or a short text field, depending on the value of the (required) TYPE attribute: "text," "password," "checkbox," "radio," "submit," "reset," "file," "hidden," or "image." It has a required NAME attribute and a VALUE attribute that is required for some values of the TYPE attribute. INPUT has no content and no end-tag. Here are some examples of INPUT elements.

```
<FORM ACTION="xx">
<P><INPUT TYPE="text" NAME="fld9" VALUE="initial">
    Name
<P><INPUT TYPE="radio" NAME="r7" VALUE="a" CHECKED>
    Option 1
```

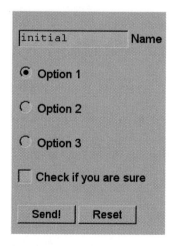

Figure A.5 Examples of INPUT elements.

```
<P><INPUT TYPE="radio" NAME="r7" VALUE="b">
  Option 2
<P><INPUT TYPE="radio" NAME="r7" VALUE="c">
  Option 3
<P><INPUT TYPE="checkbox" NAME="pu8">
  Check if you are sure
<P><INPUT TYPE="submit" VALUE="Send!" NAME="sub-a">
  <INPUT TYPE="reset" VALUE="Reset">
</FORM>
```

SELECT is a list or menu for use in an interactive form. It can only contain one or more OPTION elements. An OPTION element contains only text, no other elements. The SELECT element has a required NAME attribute, with an arbitrary text as its value. For other attributes, please refer to a full HTML specification.

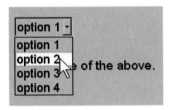

```
<FORM ACTION="xx">
  <P><SELECT NAME="hh44">
    <OPTION SELECTED>option 1</OPTION>
    <OPTION>option 2</OPTION>
    <OPTION>option 3</OPTION>
    <OPTION>option 4</OPTION>
  </SELECT>
  <P>Select one of the above.
</FORM>
```

Figure A.6 Example of a SELECT.

TEXTAREA is another element for interactive forms. It represents a fill-in field of more than one line. It can contain text, but no other elements. It has required attributes: NAME, which contains an arbitrary text, ROWS, which contains a number indicating the height of the field, and COLS, which contains the width of the field. Other attributes are optional.

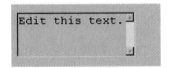

```
<FORM ACTION="xx">
<TEXTAREA NAME="kk12" ROWS=3 COLS=15>
Edit this text.
</TEXTAREA>
</FORM>
```

Figure A.7 Example of a TEXTAREA.

OBJECT is a very sophisticated element. It can be used to insert images into the text, to include applets (small programs that run inside a document), and in general to put arbitrary multimedia objects inside the text, including other HTML documents. In principle, it makes IMG obsolete, but IMG is retained for simple cases. The most important attribute of OBJECT is DATA, which contains a URL that points to an external object. It has several other attributes, that are used for some types of objects. This is only a quick reference, so we can't list all the different multi-media objects and their attributes here.

Although OBJECT is itself a text-level element, its content is the same as that of BODY. However, in the ideal case that content is not displayed. The intention is that the content is displayed only when the OBJECT itself could not be displayed, for whatever reason. The content constitutes an alternative, in the same way that the ALT attribute of IMG is an alternative. But the alternative of OBJECT is much richer, it can be almost a complete HTML document. Here is a simple example:

```
<P>Look at yourself:
  <OBJECT DATA="nonexistent.ngf">
    <P>Your browser failed to load the
    NGF image. If it had worked, you
    would have seen a gold edged
    mirror that reflected your face.</P>
  </OBJECT>
</P>
```

BUTTON: a text-level container element

A BUTTON element is a bit like a 1-cell inline table (see page 350). It can occur only in bridge elements and text-level elements, but it is itself a container. It is normally used as a submit- or reset-button in a form, with the difference that the label is not restricted to one line of text without mark-up, but can be any HTML text. Usually, it is rendered with an **outset** border, but different browsers may show it slightly differently. Here is an example (see Figure A.8):

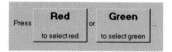

Figure A.8 Example of the BUTTON element.

```
<P>Press
  <BUTTON STYLE="width: 8em">
    <H2>Red</H2>
    <P>to select red</P>
  </BUTTON>
or
  <BUTTON STYLE="width: 8em">
    <H2>Green</H2>
    <P>to select green</P>
  </BUTTON>
...</P>
```

SPECIAL CHARACTERS

A few characters can be entered by name. This may be useful when the HTML file is to be sent over old mail systems, or when your keyboard doesn't allow you to enter those characters in an easier way. For example, instead of "é" you can enter "é" (including the & and the ;). Here is a complete list:

Letter	Code	Letter	Code	Letter	Code
á	á	é	é	í	í
Á	Á	É	É	Í	Í
â	â	ê	ê	î	î
Â	Â	Ê	ê	Î	Î
à	à	è	è	ì	ì
À	À	È	È	Ì	Ì
ä	ä	ë	ë	ï	ï
Ä	Ä	Ë	Ë	Ï	Ï
å	å	ó	ó	ú	ú
Å	Å	Ó	Ó	Ú	Ú
æ	æ	ô	ô	û	û
Æ	Æ	Ô	Ô	Û	Û
ç	ç	ò	ò	ù	ù
Ç	Ç	Ò	Ò	Ù	Ù
đ	ð	ö	ö	ü	ü
Đ	Ð	Ö	Ö	Ü	Ü
ñ	ñ	ø	ø	ý	ý
Ñ	Ñ	Ø	Ø	Ý	Ý
ß	ß	õ	õ	ÿ	ÿ
þ	þ	Õ	Õ	©	©
Þ	Þ	™	™	®	®
&	&	<	<	>	>
"	"		­		
—	—	–	–		
	‍		‌		

Table A.1 Special characters.

A non-breaking space ( ) is exactly like a normal space, except that it will never be broken at the end of a line. A soft hyphen (­) is an invisible mark in the text that indicates that a line may be broken at that point if needed, in which case it will expand to the appropriate type of hyphen to indicate that the word continues on the next line. A thin space ( ) is a space that is about half as wide as a normal space and that doesn't break between two lines (a common use is between a number and a percent sign).

An em space ( ) is a space that is as wide as the em of the current font and that doesn't break a line. An en space ( ) is half the width of an em space.

A zero-width non-joiner is an invisible mark between two letters to indicate that the two letters should not be combined visually. It can be used to avoid a ligature. In western languages it is almost never necessary. In some oriental languages it is more common. A zero-width joiner is the opposite. It combines two letters into a ligature that would otherwise not be combined.

Reading property value definitions

The box on page 91 describes how to read CSS property definitions. One of the fields, however, was left out since explaining it requires a few pages. The *Value* field is written in a formal syntax to ensure preciseness, but the end result isn't always very readable for humans. This appendix describes how to read the Value field.

Here is an example of a property defininition:

IE3	NS4	IE4	O3.5
○	⊙	●	●

Name:	**font-style**
Value:	normal | italic | oblique
Initial:	normal
Applies to:	all elements, except replaced elements
Inherited:	yes
Percentages:	N/A

The "button bar" on the left side indicates how major browsers support each property. The browser categories are: IE3 (Microsoft Internet Explorer 3), NS4 (Netscape Navigator 4), IE4 (Microsoft Internet Explorer 4), and O3.5 (Opera 3.5). The buttons have the following meaning:

○ the property is not supported by the browser
⊙ the property is partially supported by the browser
● the property is fully supported by the browser

For more detailed information about browser support, WebReview's CSS Charts (http://www.webreview.com/wr/pub/guides/style/mastergrid.html) is the best source. For example, it will tell you how the Mac version of IE4 differs from the Windows version. The buttons on the left indicates to what extent major browsers support the property. See the separate box on what the abbreviations and buttons mean.

The *Name* field is the first field in the formal definition. It simply lists the name of the property.

The *Value* field gives the possible values of the property. The example above says that this particular property accepts one of three keywords as value: **normal**, **italic** or **oblique**.

If a property offers many possible values or many possible complex combinations of values, you may find square brackets, vertical bars, and other symbols in this area. The syntax is defined in a shorthand notation using certain symbols:

- Angle brackets: < and >
- Vertical bars: | and ||
- Regular brackets: [ ]
- Question mark: ?
- Asterisk: *

Also used are *keywords*. A keyword is a word that appears in a value. Keywords must appear literally, without quotes, angle brackets, or other marks. Examples are **italic**, **oblique**, **thick**, **thin**, and **medium**. The slash and comma also must appear literally when used in a value.

When the above symbols are used in this shorthand, they have special meanings. All other characters that appear in a value stand for themselves. Note that spaces may be inserted between all values; they can also often be omitted, as long as the result is unambiguous. Below is an explanation of what each symbol means.

Angle brackets < >: The words between the angle brackets < and > specify a type of value. The most common types of values are "length" (*<length>*), "percentage," "color," "number," and "url." We discuss most of these in this chapter. We talked about "url" in Chapter 1, "The Web and HTML," and we dealt with "color" in Chapter 11, "Colors."

More specialized types include some you've already seen: "font-weight," "text-align," "font-style," "text-decoration," and "background." We describe these under the properties to which they apply in Chapters

4–8. For example, if the definition of a property (let's take the **color** property as an example) includes this line:

Value: `<color>`

---

this means that the property accepts values of type "color," for example "red." As a result, in the style sheet you might find:

```
H2 { color: red }
```

The "url" value is handled a little differently from others. Instead of simply typing in the URL, you type "url" followed by the actual URL in parentheses, with no space between the two: **`url(images/tree.png)`**, or **`url(http://www.w3.org/pub/WWW)`**. Example usage:

```
BODY { background: url(bg/marble.png) }
```

MULTIPLE VALUES

If multiple values must occur in a certain order, they are given as a list. The following example could be used in the definition of a property that always required a color and a number (there is no such property in CSS1, this is just an example):

Value:	`<color>` `<number>`
Example:	red 7.5
Example:	#CECECE 25

Vertical Bars | and ||: A single vertical bar | is used to separate alternative values. For example, in A|B, the | separates A and B; either A or B will be used. You may have any number of alternatives. *One and only one of the alternatives must occur.* In the following examples, exactly one of the listed values must occur:

Value:	normal | italic | oblique
Example:	normal
Example:	P { font-style: normal }
Example:	left | right | center | justify
Example:	right
Example usage:	H1 { text-align: right }

A double vertical bar || also separates alternative values; for example, A || B. However, the || means that *either A or B or both must occur.* Further, they may occur in any order. In the following example, there may be a color or a URL or both and their order is not important:

Value:	<url> || <color>
Example:	red url(logos/logo.png)
Example:	url(logos/logo.png) black
Example:	#00FF00
Example:	url(logos/logo.png)
Example:	DIV { background: url(wave.jpg) #11E }

(**#00FF00** and **#11E** are ways of writing colors; see Chapter 11, "Colors.") Another example, slightly more complicated, is taken from the definition of the border property, which has a value defined as follows. The types "border-width" and "border-style" are defined in Chapter 9, "Space around boxes."

Value:	<border-width> || <border-style> || <color>
Example:	1pt dotted blue
Example:	dotted
Example:	black 0.5pt
Example:	P.note { border: red double 2px }

Curly brackets { }: Curly brackets { } are used to indicate that the preceding value *may occur at least A and at most B times.* This is written as {*A, B*}. For example, in the following example, a "length" value may occur 1, 2, 3, or 4 times:

Value:	<length> {1,4}
Example:	2em
Example:	2em 3em
Example:	2em 3em 4em
Example:	2em 3em 4em 5em
Example usage:	P { margin: 2em 3em 4em 5em }

In this example, we used the **margin** property to set a different margin for each of the four sides of a P element. See Chapter 9, "Space around boxes" for a complete definition of **margin.**

Question marks ? asterisks * and plus +: Any type or keyword may be followed by one of the modifiers +, * or ?. A plus (+) indicates that the preceding item may be repeated. The item must occur *one or more times.*

Value:	*<percentage>+*
Example:	0% 50% 50% 11% 0.1%
Example:	37.5%

An asterisk (*) indicates that the preceding item may be repeated, but it may also be omitted. It may occur *zero or more times*.

Value:	*<length>**
Example:	12pt 12ex 3.5mm 12pt 12pc 3.6mm
Example:	1.1in.
Example:	

Note that the last example has no value at all.

A question mark (?) indicates that the preceding type or keyword is *optional*. For example:

Value:	*<url>? <color>*
Example:	url(http://www.w3.org/pub/WWW) black
Example:	white

In this example, the available values are a URL and a color. <url> is followed by a ?, while <color> is not. Hence, the URL may be omitted, but the color may not. The background property has a value similar to that and in that property the presence of both values means that the color is displayed with the image on top of it. If the image pointed to by the URL is unavailable, then just the color will be displayed.

Regular brackets [ ]: Regular ("square") brackets are used to group parts of the definition together. A question mark, asterisk or other special symbol that follows the closing bracket applies to the whole group. The example below shows a group with a vertical bar inside and curly braces on the outside, to indicate that the whole group may be repeated between one and four times:

Value:	[*<length>* | *<percentage>*]{1,4}
Example:	12pt 10pt 12pt 5pt
Example:	10%
Example:	10% 10% 1px
Example usage:	ADDRESS { padding: 5% 1em }

In each case, there are between one and four values, and each of the values is either a "length" or a "percentage."

Here is another, more complex example, it is a simplification of the definition of **font-family:**

Value:	[<family-name> ,]* <generic-family>
Example:	helvetica, arial, sans-serif
Example:	serif
Example usage:	EM { font-family: Helvetica, Arial, sans-serif }

The group has an asterisk, to indicate that it can occur zero or more times. The group itself consists of a "family-name" and a comma. In the first example, the group occurs twice – there are two families and two commas – while in the second example the group is completely absent; just the "generic-family" appears.

TYING IT ALL TOGETHER

The following are examples of how to read the syntax shorthand. The first example is of the **line-height** property:

Name:	**line-height**
Value:	normal | <number> | <length> | <percentage>

In this case, there is only one value, but it can be either the keyword "normal" or a number, a length or a percentage. Here are some example style rules that use the property:

```
P.intro { line-height: 14pt }
DIV.warning { line-height: normal }
H1, H2, H3 { line-height: 1.0 }
H4 { line-height: 120% }
```

The second example comes from the **text-decoration** property, which we discussed in Chapter 5. This example uses the single vertical bar, the double vertical bar, and the regular brackets:

Name:	**text-decoration**
Value:	none | [underline || overline || line-through || blink]

This is interpreted as follows:

1 The value is either the keyword, "none," or one or more of the keywords in the group within the regular brackets.
2 If you choose "none," you're done. If you choose the bracketed group, you have other choices. The group has four keywords. The double vertical bars indicate that one or more of these must occur. If you choose more than one, the order in which they are used doesn't matter.

There is thus a large number of possible values. Here are some of them:

- **`underline overline`**
- **`overline underline`**
- **`none`**
- **`underline blink line-through`**
- **`blink`**

Since the order of the keywords doesn't matter for the **text-decoration** property, there are really only 15 different decorations you can set with it, but you can write some of them in more than one way.

Appendix C

System colors

In addition to being able to assign predefined color values to text, backgrounds, etc., CSS2 allows authors to specify colors in a manner that integrates them into the user's graphic environment. Style rules that take into account user preferences thus offer the following advantages:

- They produce pages that fit the user's defined look and feel.
- They produce pages that may be more accessible as the current user settings may be related to a disability.

The set of values defined for system colors is intended to be exhaustive. For systems that do not have a corresponding value, the specified value should be mapped to the nearest system attribute, or to a default color.

The following lists additional values for color-related CSS attributes and their general meaning. Any color property (e.g., "color" or "background-color") can take one of the following names. Although these are case-insensitive, it is recommended that the mixed capitalization shown below be used, to make the names more legible.

ActiveBorder	Active window border.
ActiveCaption	Active window caption.
AppWorkspace	Background color of multiple document interface.
Background	Desktop background.

ButtonFace	Face color for three-dimensional display elements.
ButtonHighlight	Dark shadow for three-dimensional display elements (for edges facing away from the light source).
ButtonShadow	Shadow color for three-dimensional display elements.
ButtonText	Text on push buttons.
CaptionText	Text in caption, size box, and scrollbar arrow box.
GrayText	Grayed (disabled) text. This color is set to #000 if the current display driver does not support a solid gray color.
Highlight	Item(s) selected in a control.
HighlightText	Text of item(s) selected in a control.
InactiveBorder	Inactive window border.
InactiveCaption	Inactive window caption.
InactiveCaptionText	Color of text in an inactive caption.
InfoBackground	Background color for tooltip controls.
InfoText	Text color for tooltip controls.
Menu	Menu background.
MenuText	Text in menus.
Scrollbar	Scroll bar gray area.
ThreeDDarkShadow	Dark shadow for three-dimensional display elements.
ThreeDFace	Face color for three-dimensional display elements.
ThreeDHighlight	Highlight color for three-dimensional display elements.
ThreeDLightShadow	Light color for three-dimensional display elements (for edges facing the light source).
ThreeDShadow	Dark shadow for three-dimensional display elements.
Window	Window background.
WindowFrame	Window frame.
WindowText	Text in windows.

Index

INTRODUCTION

The index covers Chapters 1 to 20 and Appendices A to C. Index entries are to page numbers. Alphabetical arrangement is word-by-word, where a group of letters followed by a space is filed before the same group of letters followed by a letter, eg "em unit" will appear before "emphasis". Initial articles, conjunctions and prepositions are ignored in determining filing order.

left justification 162
left property 213, 214–15, 216, 217, 219, 220–1
:left pseudo-class 254–5
left-side value 270
left value 162, 201, 203, 249, 250, 270
leftwards value 270
LEGEND element 368
length units *see* fonts
length values
   borders 192
   fonts 100
   height property 201
   images 241
   margin properties 181
   padding 185
   shadows 244–5
   vertical alignment 178
   width 200
letter spacing 326
letter-spacing property 161, 172–4, 301
level value 271
LI element 17, 135, 137, 155, 365
Lie, Håkon Wium 320, 355–6, 357
Lilley, Chris 358
line break *see* BR element
line-height property 43, 99, 108, 109, 111, 161, 167–70, 178
line spacing 326
LINK attribute 324, 325
LINK element 306–10, 363
:link pseudo-class 68
linking
   external style sheets 306–10
links 68–9
   common tasks 47–8
list-item value 138–9, 142
list-style image property 144, 145
list-style-position property 145
list-style property 67, 136, 139, 141, 142, 145–6, 147, 151, 153
list-style-type property 143–4, 145
lists 44
   background color 234
   bullets 147
   HTML 16–18
   numbers 147
   page breaks 249
loud value 265
low value 273
lower value 271

lowercase value 117–19
Lycos 7
Lynx 6

Magnet case study, CSS conversion 278–80
male value 273
margin-bottom property 44, 45, 180–4
margin-left property 44, 45, 146, 180–4, 206, 207–9, 220–1
margin properties 253, 282–3
margin property 45, 46–7, 180–4, 195, 281–2
margin-right property 44, 45, 180–4, 206, 207–9, 220–1
margin-top property 44, 148, 180–4
margins 52, 180–4
   collapsing 198–200
   common tasks 43–7
   and float 201
   negative *see* negative margins
   printing 253–4, 255–6
   and width 200, 206–9
marker-offset property 155–6
markers 155–6
marks property 258
markup languages 4–5, 331
   see also HTML; XML
MARQUEE element 6, 322, 323
Massachusetts Institute of Technology Laboratory for Computer Science 3
matching descriptors 123, 129–31
mathline font descriptor 123, 133
MathML 330–1
max-height property 205
max-width property 204–5
maximum height 205
maximum width 204–5
@media 259–60, 310
MEDIA attribute 309–10
media-specific style sheets 259–60, 309–10
media types, printing 260–2
medium value 192–3, 195, 265, 272, 273
Menu value 382
MenuText value 382
META element 364
metrics, fonts 94–5
Meyer, Eric 360
Microsoft 6, 121, 358, 361

Microsoft Internet Explorer 7, 35, 36, 332, 359, 361
middle keyword 176
middle value 345
Midnight style sheet 309, 317
min-height property 205
min-width property 204–5
minimum height 205
minimum width 204–5
mix value 269
mixing properties 269
Modernist style sheet 316
monitors, colors 227
monospaced font families 87–8, 282
Montulli, Lou 358
Mosaic 24, 355, 356
Mozilla 356
Multiple Master fonts 327
multiple values 376–9

NAME attribute 369, 370
named pages 258–9
Navigator *see* Netscape Navigator
negative indents 165–6
negative margins 183–4, 202, 210, 286
nested elements 27–8
Netscape 6, 322, 332, 356, 358, 361
Netscape Navigator 7, 35, 36, 319, 356, 359
New Typography, The, case study, CSS conversion 286–8
NeXT browser/editor 355
no-repeat value 236
none value
  background-image property 235
  borders 190
  clear property 203
  cue-after property 268
  display property 139
  float property 201
  play-during property 269
  speak property 266
  speak-punctuation property 275
  text-transform property 117
normal font style 103
normal text-level elements, HTML 4.0 368–9
normal value 104, 266, 158
nowrap value 158
number values 168–70, 228
numbers, lists 147
OBJECT element 368, 370–1

oblique font style 103
OL element 16–17, 365
Oldstyle style sheet 319
OpenType 121
Opera 35, 360
OPTION element 370
ordered lists *see* OL element
orphans 248
orphans property 251
outline borders 197–8
outline-color property 197
outline property 197–8
outline-style property 197
outline-width property 197
outset value 191, 342, 371
overflow 210
overflow property 210, 346
overlining 113–17

P element 12–13, 135, 365
padding 51–2, 185–7
  collapsing margins 199–200
  color 233–4
  and float 201
  and width 200, 206
padding-bottom property 185
padding-left property 185, 206
padding property 46–7, 185–7, 195
padding-right property 185, 206
padding-top property 185
page areas *see* printing
page box 213
  dimensions and orientation 256–8
page-break-after property 250, 251–2
page-break-before property 249, 250, 251–2
page-break-inside property 250–2
page breaks 248–52
page property 259
@page selector 253, 255
page selectors 253
Palatino 85
panose-1 font descriptor 123, 129
paragraphs
  indenting using margins 183
  P element 12–13, 135, 365
  space between 183
pause-after property 266–7
pause-before property 266–7
pause property 267
PDF (Portable Document Format) 326–7

	Values	Initial value	Applies to[1]	Percentages	Page
	<absolute-size> | <relative-size> | <length> | <percentage> | inherit	medium		refer to parent font size	108
adjust[†]	<number> | none | inherit	none			121
ch[†]	normal | wider | narrower | ultra-condensed | extra-condensed | condensed | semi-condensed | semi-expanded | expanded | extra-expanded | ultra-expanded | inherit	normal			119
[†]	normal | italic | oblique | inherit	normal			111
ant[†]	normal | small-caps | inherit	normal			113
ight[†]	normal | bold | bolder | lighter | 100 | 200 | 300 | 400 | 500 | 600 | 700 | 800 | 900 | inherit	normal			114
	<length> | <percentage> | auto | inherit	auto	5)	see prose	213
	<length> | <percentage> | auto | inherit	auto	positioned elements	refer to width of containing block (CB)	227
letterspacing[†]	normal | <length> | inherit	normal			183
lineheight[†]	normal | <number> | <length> | <percentage> | inherit	normal		refer to font size of the element	178
list-style[†]	[<'list-style-type'> || <'list-style-position'> || <'list-style-image'>] | inherit	see individual properties	list-item elem.		155
list-style-image[†]	<uri> | none | inherit	none	list-item elem.		154
list-style-position[†]	inside | outside | inherit	outside	list-item elem.		155
list-style-type[†]	disc | circle | square | decimal | decimal-leading-zero | lower-roman | upper-roman | lower-greek | lower-alpha | lower-latin | upper-alpha | upper-latin | hebrew | armenian | georgian | cjk-ideographic | hiragana | katakana | hiragana-iroha | katakana-iroha | none | inherit	disc	list-item elem.		153
margin	<margin-width>{1,4} | inherit	0		refer to width of CB	192
margin-top margin-right margin-bottom margin-left	<margin-width> | inherit	0		refer to width of containing block	193
marker-offset	<length> | auto | inherit	auto	elements with 'display: marker'		165
marks	[crop || cross] | none | inherit	none	page context		274
max-height	<length> | <percentage> | none | inherit	none	3)	refer to height of CB	217
max-width	<length> | <percentage> | none | inherit	none	3)	refer to width of CB	217
min-height	<length> | <percentage> | inherit	0	3)	refer to height of CB	217
min-width	<length> | <percentage> | inherit	browser dependent	3)	refer to width of CB	217
orphans[†]	<integer> | inherit	2	block-level elem.		267
outline	[<'outline-color'> || <'outline-style'> || <'outline-width'>] | inherit	see individual properties			209
outline-color	<color> | invert | inherit	invert			209
outline-style	<border-style> | inherit	none			208
outline-width	<border-width> | inherit	medium			208
overflow	visible | hidden | scroll | auto | inherit	visible	block-level & replaced elem.		222
padding	<padding-width>{1,4} | inherit	0		refer to width of CB	197
padding-top padding-right padding-bottom padding-left	<padding-width> | inherit	0		refer to width of containing block	197
page[†]	<identifier> | auto	auto	block-level elem.		275
page-break-after	auto | always | avoid | left | right | inherit	auto	block-level elem.		266
page-break-before	auto | always | avoid | left | right | inherit	auto	block-level elem.		265
page-break-inside[†]	avoid | auto | inherit	auto	block-level elem.		266
position	static | relative | absolute | fixed | inherit	static			227
quotes[†]	[<string> <string>]+ | none | inherit	browser dependent			159

CSS QUICK REFERENCE (continued from inside front cover)

Name	Values	Initial value	Applies to [1]	Percentages	Page
font-size[4]	\<absolute-size\> | \<relative-size\> | \<length\> | \<percentage\> | inherit	medium		refer to parent font size	108
font-size-adjust[†]	\<number\> | none | inherit	none			121
font-stretch[†]	normal | wider | narrower | ultra-condensed | extra-condensed | condensed | semi-condensed | semi-expanded | expanded | extra-expanded | ultra-expanded | inherit	normal			119
font-style[†]	normal | italic | oblique | inherit	normal			111
font-variant[†]	normal | small-caps | inherit	normal			113
font-weight[†]	normal | bold | bolder | lighter | 100 | 200 | 300 | 400 | 500 | 600 | 700 | 800 | 900 | inherit	normal			114
height	\<length\> | \<percentage\> | auto | inherit	auto	5)	see prose	213
left	\<length\> | \<percentage\> | auto | inherit	auto	positioned elements	refer to width of containing block (CB)	227
letter-spacing[†]	normal | \<length\> | inherit	normal			183
line-height[†]	normal | \<number\> | \<length\> | \<percentage\> | inherit	normal		refer to font size of the element	178
list-style[†]	[\<'list-style-type'\> || \<'list-style-position'\> || \<'list-style-image'\>] | inherit	see individual properties	list-item elem.		155
list-style-image[†]	\<uri\> | none | inherit	none	list-item elem.		154
list-style-position[†]	inside | outside | inherit	outside	list-item elem.		155
list-style-type[†]	disc | circle | square | decimal | decimal-leading-zero | lower-roman | upper-roman | lower-greek | lower-alpha | lower-latin | upper-alpha | upper-latin | hebrew | armenian | georgian | cjk-ideographic | hiragana | katakana | hiragana-iroha | katakana-iroha | none | inherit	disc	list-item elem.		153
margin	\<margin-width\>{1,4} | inherit	0		refer to width of CB	192
margin-top margin-right margin-bottom margin-left	\<margin-width\> | inherit	0		refer to width of containing block	193
marker-offset	\<length\> | auto | inherit	auto	elements with 'display: marker'		165
marks	[crop || cross] | none | inherit	none	page context		274
max-height	\<length\> | \<percentage\> | none | inherit	none	3)	refer to height of CB	217
max-width	\<length\> | \<percentage\> | none | inherit	none	3)	refer to width of CB	217
min-height	\<length\> | \<percentage\> | inherit	0	3)	refer to height of CB	217
min-width	\<length\> | \<percentage\> | inherit	browser dependent	3)	refer to width of CB	217
orphans[†]	\<integer\> | inherit	2	block-level elem.		267
outline	[\<'outline-color'\> || \<'outline-style'\> || \<'outline-width'\>] | inherit	see individual properties			209
outline-color	\<color\> | invert | inherit	invert			209
outline-style	\<border-style\> | inherit	none			208
outline-width	\<border-width\> | inherit	medium			208
overflow	visible | hidden | scroll | auto | inherit	visible	block-level & replaced elem.		222
padding	\<padding-width\>{1,4} | inherit	0		refer to width of CB	197
padding-top padding-right padding-bottom padding-left	\<padding-width\> | inherit	0		refer to width of containing block	197
page[†]	\<identifier\> | auto	auto	block-level elem.		275
page-break-after	auto | always | avoid | left | right | inherit	auto	block-level elem.		266
page-break-before	auto | always | avoid | left | right | inherit	auto	block-level elem.		265
page-break-inside[†]	avoid | auto | inherit	auto	block-level elem.		266
position	static | relative | absolute | fixed | inherit	static			227
quotes[†]	[\<string\> \<string\>]+ | none | inherit	browser dependent			159